The publisher gratefully acknowledges the generous support of the African American Studies Endowment Fund of the University of California Press Foundation, which was established by a major gift from the George Gund Foundation.

Sept 8, 2018

For Jada

Letters from Langston

Listen to their voices;
    share their dreams
then imagine your
    own dreams!

Mary Louise

Letters from Langston

FROM THE HARLEM RENAISSANCE TO THE RED SCARE AND BEYOND

EDITED BY

Evelyn Louise Crawford and MaryLouise Patterson

With a foreword by Robin D. G. Kelley

UNIVERSITY OF CALIFORNIA PRESS

University of California Press, one of the most distinguished university presses in the United States, enriches lives around the world by advancing scholarship in the humanities, social sciences, and natural sciences. Its activities are supported by the UC Press Foundation and by philanthropic contributions from individuals and institutions. For more information, visit www.ucpress.edu.

University of California Press
Oakland, California

Library of Congress Cataloging-in-Publication Data

Hughes, Langston, 1902–1967, author.
 [Correspondence. Selections. (Crawford and Patterson)]
 Letters from Langston : from the Harlem Renaissance to the Red Scare and beyond / edited by Evelyn Louise Crawford and MaryLouise Patterson ; with a foreword by Robin D. G. Kelley.
    pages   cm
 Includes bibliographical references and index.
 ISBN 978-0-520-28533-0 (cloth : alk. paper)
 ISBN 978-0-520-28534-7 (pbk. : alk. paper)
 ISBN 978-0-520-96086-2 (ebook)
    1. Hughes, Langston, 1902-1967—Correspondence.   2. Authors, American—20th century—Correspondence.   3. African American authors—Correspondence.   I. Crawford, Evelyn Louise, editor.
II. Patterson, MaryLouise, 1943– editor.   III. Title.
 PS3515.U274Z48   2016
 818'.5209—dc23
 [B]

                                                              2015029780

Manufactured in the United States of America

24 23 22 21 20 19 18 17 16
10 9 8 7 6 5 4 3 2 1

In keeping with a commitment to support environmentally responsible and sustainable printing practices, UC Press has printed this book on Natures Natural, a fiber that contains 30% post-consumer waste and meets the minimum requirements of ANSI/NISO Z39.48-1992 (R 1997) (*Permanence of Paper*).

In loving memory of
Langston, Louise, Pat, Nebby, and Matt

AND

our dearly missed children,
Razak Bello and Sandra Camacho

CONTENTS

FOREWORD

Robin D. G. Kelley

Langston Hughes has become a household name. An icon of the Harlem Renaissance, the subject of numerous biographies, and one of the bona fide deans of African American letters, Hughes may be the best-known American poet after Robert Frost or Walt Whitman. But to characterize *Letters from Langston* as simply another epistolary window into the life and times of the Black Bard would be both a mistake and a grave injustice to the entire enterprise. *Letters from Langston* is a book of correspondence between five extraordinary people who sustained an extraordinary friendship during extraordinary times—lovingly and painstakingly reconstructed by Evelyn Louise Crawford and MaryLouise Patterson, who were, in more ways than one, the offspring of these relationships.

Careful readers of Hughes's biography will be familiar with Louise Thompson, the brilliant organizer, writer, and orator who became Langston's closest confidante. In her capacity as secretary of the Harlem chapter of the Friends of the Soviet Union, Louise led a large delegation of Black artists to the Soviet Union in 1932 to participate in a film about racial conditions in America. Though the film was aborted, she was thereafter dubbed "Madame Moscow." Many readers will also recognize the name of William L. Patterson, Louise's husband and one of the United States' highest-ranking Black Communists. "Pat," as he was called by his friends, is perhaps best known for authoring *We Charge Genocide,* a searing indictment of American racism, published in 1951. Matt and Evelyn "Nebby" Crawford are perhaps less known, but they are no less significant. Matt gave up a promising career as a doctor to become a full-time organizer as a labor leader, a Communist, and a fighter for racial justice. His wife, Nebby, never joined the party, but she did support struggles for racial and economic justice in the San Francisco Bay Area, where they lived, and she remained an avid, intelligent interlocutor within her circle of radical friends until her untimely death in 1972.

The Pattersons and the Crawfords were nothing like the working-class folk characters one finds in Hughes's poetry—except for their chronic financial struggles, and that was by choice. Each family had been poised to lead a comfortable, middle-class existence—bounded by Jim Crow laws, of course. They had everything: education, professional contacts and experience, and loads of opportunities. At some point in their respective lives, each stood in the eye of the cultural tornado we now call the Harlem Renaissance. Their circle of friends included W. E. B. Du Bois, Paul and Essie Robeson, Zora Neale Hurston, Aaron Douglas, and others. Louise, Pat, Matt, and Nebby were fine writers, excellent orators, and voracious readers, never bound by the limits of their community, race, or country. They could have become renowned scholars or mainstream Negro leaders. Instead, they independently chose to cast their fate with what would become the most despised movement in America: Communism.

Why? Because they believed that, through relentless global struggle, another world was possible—one that was free of class exploitation, racism, patriarchy, poverty, and injustice. They thought that an international socialist movement offered one of many possible paths to a liberated future. Through reading Marx and Engels and Lenin, they began to see the "wretched of the earth" with new eyes. As members of what Du Bois called "the talented tenth"—the educated elite presumably destined to lead the race—Louise, Pat, Matt, and Nebby were renegades from a class known for its contempt of the Black poor. The main task of the Black middle class during the first half of the twentieth century was to uplift their race, prove to white folks that their education, manners, and good behavior made them worthy of citizenship, and avoid the pale faces that populated the lynch mobs and enjoyed the rights and privileges associated with the color of their skin. But the four chose instead to empathize with the plight of *all* Americans, including new European immigrants, Jews, and working-class whites, from whose lips the word "nigger" flowed easily. They shared their vision of multiracial proletarian unity with Langston Hughes, whose 1935 poem "Let America Be America Again" expressed, in bold cadences, their common dream to rise "Out of the rack and ruin of our gangster death/The rape and rot of graft" and to "redeem/The land, the mines, the plants, the rivers./The mountains and the endless plain . . . And make America again!" The letters in this book constitute a powerful and indisputable reminder of that vision and Hughes's dedication to it, and of his Black radical comrades, who helped sustain that vision in spite of decades of police and FBI harassment, intimidation, violence, internal political dissension and intrigue, endless meetings, constant travel, and, in Pat's case, imprisonment. Their letters reveal a shared worldview and a passionate political dedication to humanity.

While none of the five correspondents had a conflict- or contradiction-free relationship with the Communist movement, their letters provide startlingly clear evidence that Hughes never broke his ties to the Left. But it wasn't just an ideological and political commitment that kept Hughes tethered to the Pattersons and the Crawfords; it was the depths of their friendship that mattered most. Matt, Nebby, Pat, Louise, and their precocious daughters, Nebby Lou and MaryLouise, loved Hughes like family. And, like family, they cajoled him, chastised him, celebrated him, thanked him, and never ever let him forget for whom he wrote. He endured their criticism if he strayed toward self-indulgence or sentimentality. They kept him abreast of the struggles of Black people, working people, and the oppressed. Thanks to their collective engagement, critique, and prodding, Hughes never lost that essential socialist impulse, the radicalism that so profoundly shaped his writing during the 1930s. The impulse changed and matured, but it did not disappear.

To be sure, the five friends changed and matured over time in response to conditions and crises that have come to define the "American Century." The beauty of *Letters from Langston* is that it provides a rich and fascinating alternative history of the American Left through Black eyes. The letters walk us through the era, from Harlem to Moscow, from Chicago to Paris, from the Great Depression to the Red Scare, from world war to civil rights. Beginning with the latter years of the Harlem Renaissance, the letters reveal the dynamic intersection of art and politics and allow for a fresh examination of how the interwar period saw America become home to a viable and dynamic Left, and they make visible the terrifying social, political, economic, and psychological effects McCarthyism had on families and friendships. Finally, these letters— the musings of Black intellectuals working through a radical critique of the United States and the world—reveal a deep concern for humanity and with securing a future for all people, without ever ignoring or belittling the very real crises confronting Black people.

Letters from Langston redeems not just Hughes's radical politics but our own. As we grapple with the consequences of neoliberal policies that promote the wealthy at the expense of the poor, privatize hard-won public institutions, and allow police to kill unarmed Black and Brown people with impunity, the letters and political lives of Matt, Nebby, Pat, Louise, and Langston are illuminating, to say the least.

This book of correspondence between Langston Hughes (1902–1967) and our two sets of parents began on a late spring afternoon in 2000. We traveled together to New Haven to spend the day in the reading room of Yale University's Beinecke Rare Book and Manuscript Library. We were anxious to read the letters that Langston had saved from his long correspondence with Louise Thompson Patterson (1901–1999), William L. Patterson (1891–1980), Matt N. Crawford (1903–1996), and Evelyn "Nebby" Graves Crawford (1899–1972)—who were our folks and his friends—letters that spanned almost forty years during the middle of the twentieth century.

Langston had been an important person in our lives since we were children, and as we grew into adulthood we read many of the letters he wrote to our parents. We, too, had been his occasional correspondents during our teen and young adult years. So, as we sat in the glass-walled reading room with white gloves on, silently reading our parents' letters to Langston, we were delightfully surprised to find out that our special friend and "uncle" had saved some of our letters to him. The discovery was overwhelming. We'd actually forgotten we'd written them. We barely recognized our own childlike handwriting as we held our own letters to him—and we were immediately reminded of the depth of his caring for us. Mary Lou was also a little embarrassed at her boldness in addressing him as "Dear Uncle Lang."

But on that day we had wanted to know more about his relationships with the Crawfords and Pattersons, and we'd found it. We left the library at closing and spoke little on the walk back to our hotel. When we entered the lounge, we needed to sit down to process our feelings and the experience of the day. As we relaxed in front of the glowing fireplace, we both came to the realization that we had to shine a light on the poet's relationships with our parents, who had been his comrades and confidants.

Their friendships started to come into focus in the 1970s, probably when author Faith Berry interviewed both Louise and Matt (who, by the early 1980s, were our two surviving parents) for a biography she was writing on Langston. Each also agreed to be interviewed by Langston's official biographer and editor, Arnold Rampersad, after some initial resistance, which yielded to persuasion from Evelyn Louise. Finally, they could trust two serious authors who were prepared to dig deep and write with integrity about their friend. Indeed, Louise and Matt seemed reenergized and buoyed by the sincere enthusiasm they detected in these two scholars. Opening up enabled them to share more of Langston with us. Subsequently we had many detailed conversations about their adventures with Langston and others who shared their interests and politics at critical moments in their lives.

Now, several decades later in New Haven, we were once again looking at old photographs and rereading letters and articles from Langston along with their responses to him. We were remembering our gregarious, cheerful, and affectionate "uncle," who sent us dolls, poems, and autographed copies of his children's books. We loved him, and he loved us. When Evelyn Louise (Nebby Lou) was born in 1938, he sent a card from Paris—a tender greeting to welcome her into the world. In 1943 he dedicated a special poem to MaryLouise (Mary Lou) in celebration of her birth.

We remembered Langston as a fitful family member, who darted in and out of our lives as children and young adults. In our early years, we spent time with him in our homes in New York or Berkeley; these gatherings always included delicious food, good cheer, much joking around, and laughter. Years later, Nebby Lou, with and without her parents, would meet Langston in New York and Paris. Mary Lou saw him occasionally in New York.

Langston remained one of our parents' most cherished friends, confidants, and comrades for over forty years. The five shared an intellectual and political curiosity, and they came of age during a period of radical ferment and conservative reaction. They had also lived through many similar experiences—family instability, loss, and upheavals as well as personal struggles with racism. All of this forged their friendships as they embraced a common vision of a just and peaceful world.

The letters that follow are the ones that survived the long years of their friendships. They are uniquely intimate and unguarded, capturing both the serious and not-so-serious aspects of their personalities through their humor and the deep mutual affection and respect they had for each other. We were born into the history this correspondence relates. We lived through much of it and carry all of its joys, triumphs, and disappointments. These letters have taken us on a profoundly personal journey. Through them, we now visualize our parents before they had us and in a way they couldn't have shown us. Our love and admiration for them has deepened, and we have gained a greater understanding of who we are and the sisterly love we share.

NEBBY LOU

"We know where your daughter goes to school." Those were the words of the FBI agent that trailed my father, Matt, on a cloudy Berkeley evening in the fall of 1951. He was on the sidewalk, walking home from his job at the Cooperative Food Store on University Avenue. The FBI agent was in a car, and he leaned out the window to offer a taunting invitation to "talk." "I have nothing to say to you" was the staccato reply of the trailed subject, Matt Nathaniel Crawford—Negro, forty-eight, married, father of one child—who was of interest to J. Edgar Hoover and his minions. By the time Matt reached home, he was shaking with rage.

He and my mother, Nebby, had built their white stucco house in 1937 on a corner lot in the working-class flatlands of West Berkeley. In fact, they had integrated the immediate neighborhood—they were the first "colored" family to stake a claim there. From an upstairs window, they had a postcard view of the San Francisco Bay. The completion of Matt and Nebby's new home was a subject of great interest to all the Crawford family and friends. Langston, who lived for long months in California during the late 1930s, kept track of news about the new house, which would become a familiar oasis for him in the following years. In June 1937, on his way to Denver by train, he wrote my parents, " I was delighted to hear about your new house being almost done, and certainly wish I could see it. But I will no doubt be out again, I hope next winter. I hate this Eastern cold. This morning there is snow along the tracks here in Colorado. . . . But drop me a line, if you have time, before I sail [for France], and a snap shot of the new house if it is done."

Years later, in the 1950s, the Crawford homestead was a kind of Grand Central Station for social and political activity of a particular kind. Matt had been active for nearly twenty years in Bay Area and California civil rights campaigns. But as a child, I was only vaguely aware of this until one summer day in 1948, when he asked me if I would like to go to "the City" with him to a campaign office. He had decided it was finally time to introduce me to a part of his life that had been a mystery up to that point.

In those days there was a train that ran to and from San Francisco, "the City," on the bottom deck of the San Francisco Bay Bridge. You caught the F train, which ran between Berkeley, Oakland, and San Francisco. I always loved making this trip—the sights were spectacular. Once you passed through the tunnel at Yerba Buena Island, you'd see the bright orange Golden Gate Bridge and fog misting in the distance, where the Bay meets the Pacific Ocean. After the train arrived at San Francisco's terminal building, we walked outside and hopped onto a streetcar, which rattled along First Street for a few blocks and then slowly snaked west up Market Street. After a few minutes, we arrived at our destination: an unremarkable office building that housed the presidential campaign headquarters of Henry A. Wallace, candidate of the Independent Progressive Party (IPP).[1] My father took my hand, and we entered the marble-floored lobby and took the elevator to the third floor. In a sprawling office that overlooked bustling Market Street, I was introduced to a large group of people who were making placards, talking on the phone, typing mailing lists, and shouting back and forth across the room. They all seemed to know my father, but I didn't know why. I wondered who they were and what all the activity was about. A few of their faces were vaguely familiar; had they visited our house in Berkeley?

When I was seven or eight years old, I began to be curious about where my father went after dinnertime on many evenings. My mother didn't seem to be at all concerned about this, but when I asked him where he was going, he would often reply: "Honey, I'm going to meet a man about a dog." This answer infuriated me, because I knew there was no dog involved in these disappearances. Langston had once promised to bring me a puppy from the

---

1. The Independent Progressive Party (IPP) was the California chapter of the left-wing Progressive Party of the United States. In 1948 the Progressive Party ran Henry A. Wallace, who was then vice president, for president. In 1952 it ran Vincent Hallinan for president, with Charlotta Bass for vice president. It was disbanded in 1955.

litter of his dog Greta, but that puppy never made it to Berkeley, so I didn't want to hear any talk about a dog. I had the feeling that my father was playing a game with me and that there was some explanation for why he didn't tell me where he went. It turned out that he was secretive for good reason—he and his political associates were on the radar of the local Red Squad[2] and the FBI. He was an active member of several Left organizations, including the National Negro Congress,[3] the Civil Rights Congress,[4] and the Communist Party. He had been radicalized in 1932 by a trip to the Soviet Union with Langston and twenty other young Black adventurers. He came back to California and immediately threw himself into the campaign to free the framed Scottsboro Nine of Alabama.[5]

At his office that afternoon in 1948, he explained to me that he and the campaign workers were members of the IPP, and that they were organizing for the election of Henry A. Wallace, a progressive white man and former vice president of the United States. They were mobilizing so that life would be better for Negroes and all working Americans. They were fighting for peace and an end to Jim Crow laws[6] in jobs, housing, health care, and

2. Red Squads were local police intelligence units developed at the end of the nineteenth century to target leftist groups of all stripes, including labor organizations and minority groups fighting racial and economic injustice. They specialized in infiltration, intelligence gathering, and subversion, and they were notorious for instigating and provoking unlawful activities. They were a significant presence throughout the entire twentieth century.

3. The National Negro Congress (NNC) was an organization formed in 1935 at Howard University in Washington, DC, with the goal of fighting for Black liberation. Its first meeting was held in Chicago in February 1936. Over eight hundred delegates attended and five thousand observed. Langston was one of the signers of "the Call," the official organizing document that argued for the creation of the National Negro Congress. The organization folded in 1947.

4. The Civil Rights Congress (CRC) was a US civil rights organization dedicated to the defense of victims of racist and political repression. It was founded in 1946 and headed by Pat in the 1950s, but the US government forced it out of existence in 1956.

5. The Scottsboro Nine, also known as the Scottsboro Boys, were nine Black youth, the youngest of whom was fourteen, who were falsely accused of raping two white women while on a train in 1931. They were dragged off the train, tried in Scottsboro, Alabama, found guilty by an all-white male jury, and sentenced to death. The International Labor Defense, a legal advocacy organization, led by Pat at the time, mounted a national and worldwide mass movement for their freedom and won, although the case dragged on for many years. The last man of the group was released from prison in 1950.

6. Jim Crow laws were anti-Black, segregationist laws enacted between 1876 and 1965 on state and local levels in the United States. These laws established the strict separation of Blacks and whites in all spheres of life. They followed the Black Codes established in the South in the 1800s. "Jim Crow" was a pejorative term for a Negro.

education. The 1948 election came and went, and, of course, Henry A. Wallace lost. But I am grateful to his campaign for giving me a new window into my parents' world.

My mother, Evelyn "Nebby" Graves, worked outside of the home from the time I was a small child, but she always managed to assure me that everything was all right. Before I was school-aged, I was cared for during the day by either a babysitter or my father's sister Gladys, who also lived in Berkeley with her husband and son. My parents had a set of close friends from growing up in Oakland and San Francisco, some of who had settled in the rural counties above Sacramento. There were the Watkins, the Browns, and the Wilsons, all young African American families whose parents had found their way to California from the South and the Midwest. In the summers we would travel to the towns of Woodland or Guinda for picnics and overnight stays. The adults would take hikes, play cards, and relax, and the children were free to explore as long as we didn't wander too far away. Sometimes there would be an exciting and scary encounter with a rattlesnake. On those occasions one of the men would show up with an axe, chop the snake's head off, and leave it writhing on the ground. We children could never get a satisfactory answer as to why the snake kept on moving.

Most summers our family would take a camping trip to a state park somewhere in California. Our trip in July 1951 was especially memorable. I helped my father pack up the car with his camping gear, and he, my mother, and I headed for D. L. Bliss State Park on the south shore of Lake Tahoe. My father had reserved the camping site in advance, and after a hot four-hour drive we arrived at the park and set up camp. The first order of business was to walk down to the beach for a swim in the crystal-clear, frigid lake. Every evening a park ranger gave a talk around a bonfire about some aspect of the park's history or the wildlife native to the area. I loved those starlit evenings. The smoke of the fire mixed with the sweet scent of the redwood and pine needles and the red-barked manzanita bushes. Sitting on a log bench with my parents one of those nights, I could not have imagined what the next day had in store for us.

The following morning we got in the car and drove out of the park to a small grocery store on Route 50 to buy some fresh eggs and milk. On the way back my father turned on the car radio to listen to the news. Reception was bad in the high mountain altitude, but through the static the announcer clearly said that there had been Communist raids in Oakland and San Francisco and named several people who had been arrested.

Suddenly I understood that my father was in danger. I didn't know exactly how or why, but it was clear that that morning newscast had changed everything. We rushed back to the park, packed up the campsite, and left. My parents explained that my father was going to leave us for a time and that my mother and I would drive back home alone. He told me that several friends of his had been arrested and that he had to be careful. I knew their names—they had come to our home for meetings with him from time to time.

We hugged my father and left him in a small town just outside of Sacramento; my mother drove us home. She was a good driver, but I knew she was frightened, and for the first time in my life I was overwhelmed with a sense of dread. After several hours, just as we approached the north end of the San Francisco Bay, my mother told me that we were not going home. She took the turnoff following the signs that read "San Rafael" and "San Francisco." We were headed toward the Golden Gate Bridge and the San Francisco home of her sister, my Aunt Alma.

My father stayed away from home for several days, and then, somehow convinced that he would not be picked up by the police, he came back to Berkeley. Life resumed more or less as normal, but the Lake Tahoe incident was a constant reminder that our family was being watched. Communists and other leftists were being harassed and arrested across the country, and the San Francisco Bay Area, with its long tradition of organized labor and civil rights activities, was in the crosshairs of many government agencies.

There were other signs that things had changed for our family and their friends. My father was involved in finding venues where the activist and singer Paul Robeson could perform in the Bay Area. The two men had met in the 1940s, and they kept in touch through a mutual friend, Revels Cayton, a leading Bay Area trade union organizer and the executive director of the National Negro Congress. Once I went with my father to meet Robeson at his hotel in San Francisco. I learned that Robeson had been banned from the major concert stages in the United States and that he was not welcome in San Francisco's major hotels either. He was forced to stay in a dingy hotel in a seedy area just north of Market Street. I don't remember what the two men discussed, but I do remember the feeling of the place—the lobby was dimly lit and smelled of old tobacco. We didn't stay long, and I didn't ask any questions on the ride back home. I just felt sad.

When the school year started in September, I took my usual morning walk down the street from our house, turning south to follow the Santa Fe railroad tracks to University Avenue and then over to Burbank Jr. High

School. Sometimes another girl or boy would catch up with me, and we'd walk together. That once carefree walk would never be the same after I heard my father say: "The man said, 'We know where your daughter goes to school.'"

In the 1950s, when I was in junior high school, my mother worked as an administrator at the Federal Civil Service Commission office on Sansome Street in San Francisco's financial district. Her tenure there soon came to an end, when she was forced out of her position because of my father's political activities. She put up a good fight to keep her job, but in the end she lost. She was not old enough to retire and as a result received only a small portion of her pension after almost thirty years of service.

Langston was often lecturing on the road during the early 1950s, so we saw less of him. Few letters were exchanged between him and my parents during this period. The three of them knew that they were constantly being watched by the local Red Squads and the FBI. Their mail was monitored, listening devises were planted in their homes, and their phone lines were tapped. In many ways, life seemed normal. I went to school, my parents went to their jobs, and we visited with our relatives in Berkeley, Oakland, and San Francisco. But there was a whiff of terror in the air.

In the spring of 1953, after testifying before Joseph McCarthy's committee in Washington, DC, Langston wrote my parents a short, bittersweet note, letting them know that he had not been forced to name any of his Red friends—except for Paul Robeson. Reading that missive years later brought me to tears.

Despite all the threats, harassment, and losses that my parents endured during the Red Scare[7] of the 1950s, they never wavered in their convictions and vision for a better world. They kept me safe against daunting odds, taught by example, and lived lives of great principle and dedication to justice.

MARY LOU

Spring in Chicago can be like winter in other places, and according to our family lore, it was a frigid and blustery March 15 when my mother, Louise,

7. "Red Scare" is the term used to define the periods in US history when the development and promotion of fear of a rise and potential takeover of the government by Communists and leftist radicals was pushed to the level of national hysteria, during which anti-Communist laws were passed. The first period lasted from 1919 to 1921 and the second from 1947 to 1954, although many progressives and civil rights activists believe the second period never really ended.

arrived at the Chicago hospital where I was shortly to be delivered. She was to have a scheduled Cesarean section. She got to the hospital before my father, Pat, and before her doctor. So she registered and was taken to a semi-private room. Another woman was already in it.

Then my father arrived. The staff at the front desk took one long look at the mahogany-colored man inquiring about his wife and started awkwardly scurrying about to find another room for her. They had made one of two embarrassing assumptions: that my mother was white and was having a Negro baby or that she herself was a Negro. Either way, she had to be moved! She wound up in a private room at the semiprivate rate. And so a small irony of American racism set the stage for my birth.

A week later, my mother received a congratulatory letter penned on March 23, 1943. It read, in part:

> I am truly happy that you have Mary Lou and I know that you will find in her a new kind of life. . . . For those of us who are preparing a better life in a new kind of world the rearing of a child has an added joy for we also prepare the child for a new world—but for you this will be quite simple for Mary Lou will more than likely have her first conscious experiences in the beginning of this new world. In the meantime the struggle for you becomes a "little" more personal. There is a special thrill when you think, during the coarse of your work "I'm doing this for Mary Lou too." All together Squeeza, you and Mary Lou are going to have a "mighty fine time" and I am glad.

This letter was written by Matt Crawford, one of my mother's cherished lifelong friends, who was married to her dearest friend, Nebby. He was truly happy for her and my father. He believed that motherhood would add a new dimension and meaning to "the struggle" for her, and strengthen her commitment to it, and that it would have the same effect on my father. He also believed that the life path I chose would add to and reflect theirs; I think that, in a few important ways, it did. He was convinced that I would grow up in the "new world" he and my parents had dedicated their lives to creating. Sadly, that was not to be, but they never ceased fighting for what they believed in, and they never ceased believing in it either. Pat had been rejected by some in his own family because of his beliefs, and since her early childhood, Louise had been distanced from her mother's family and denied by her father's. So my parents had made members of the Left—especially many of their African American Communist Party comrades—their family. The progressive American world and its culture were life sustaining for my parents and therefore for me as well.

Langston was a member of that cobbled-together family of ours. He and Louise became fast friends when they first met at Hampton in 1928. He and his mother, Carrie, became close friends with Louise's mother, Lula Mae, as well. During Lula Mae's terminal illness, Carrie visited her often. While I was growing up I didn't see Langston very often, but my parents often talked about him, and when we did see him it was like a favorite uncle had come: gifts, laughter, food, and stories abounded. I recall going to hear him read his poetry backed by jazz musicians and seeing his plays and listening to my parents discuss them afterward. I knew my father's correspondence with Langston meant a lot to him because Langston sought his opinions. Time has blurred my memories of Langston, but the impressions and the feelings his presence created in me have grown deeper and stronger since working on this book.

As Communists raising children during the 1950s, my parents wanted me to know why they'd chosen to believe in socialism while the mass media constantly railed and harangued against the "red peril" and the "red demons" that were hell-bent on destroying the American Way of Life. They lived what they believed, and that took a lot of courage during those times. They hoped that I would be not only accepting but also proud of them and how they were living their lives. Most of the time I was, but their choices weren't always easy or clear for me to grasp. Louise and Pat wanted me to understand that socialism meant a fairer distribution of wealth and a greater freedom for Black people and that was why he and my mother had chosen to believe in it and struggle for it, which meant they had to go to a lot of meetings. I remember my "Aunt" Mary (she was really my cousin, but I called her Aunt) once said disapprovingly to my father that he wasn't spending enough time with me, and he responded by telling her he was fighting for all the Mary Lous in the world.

My parents also embraced and championed the Black community's struggle for liberation. That is where their individual roads to the Left had begun. Racism had paved those roads, and my parents' had been led to them by their burgeoning passion for freedom and their growing consciousness of the constant daily injustices and indignities, large and small, that they themselves suffered and witnessed all around them.

They knew they needed to imbue in me a pride of being Black. They did this by living the way they did, by exposing me to the way their Black comrades lived, and by opening the worlds of African American history and literature to me. When I was a child they read to me from the many books on the shelves in our home, and later we would read those books together. The walls in our apartment were filled with artwork, much of it made by friends of theirs. I have that artwork and those books in my home now.

My mother would take me with her to Fourteenth Street in Manhattan, where she went to buy the fabric she used to make curtains and slipcovers. She knew how and where to shop. She knew quality. I loved the way she bargained to get the most out of every penny. She had an aesthetic eye and managed to make our home beautiful and comfortable with the small income she and my father had.

It was only as an adult that I realized how my parents' marriage also exemplified their politics. Whenever I would tell my friends that I never heard my parents argue or speak harshly or disrespectfully to one another, I was never sure they believed me. But it was true. My father once told me the battle outside his home was too fierce for him to have to battle inside as well. Maybe it also was because they were older than most other parents when they had me. When I was born, my father was almost sixty and my mother was in her early forties. They were mature and experienced—they weren't growing up alongside me.

There are so many questions I have for them now that I never got a chance to ask. My father's autobiography, *The Man Who Cried Genocide,*[8] has answered some of the questions I've wondered about, but reading the information is a distant second to sitting next to him or my mother, asking those questions and hearing their answers.

I was a latchkey kid through most of high school in Brooklyn. In the mornings my father would be the first up. He'd jump rope for what seemed like a long time, and then he would make breakfast for my mother and take it to her on a tray. He would call me in the afternoons when I got home from school and tell me to start dinner, reminding me that my mother had worked all day and was tired. On Friday nights we'd watch the Gillette-sponsored prizefights and *Dragnet* on our black-and-white TV. Years later we watched Julia Child on public television. We copied her famous recipe for leg of lamb, and when we made it we'd imitate her unique high-pitched voice and laugh. We also watched the "shoot 'em ups," as my father called the cowboy shows he loved, like *Gunsmoke.* For some strange reason he also really liked *Perry Mason;* I always found it too predictable and bland.

Our home was open to all; my father would even invite Jehovah's Witness canvassers in and debate with them, as he knew the bible better than most.

---

8. *The Man Who Cried Genocide* is William L. Patterson's autobiography, which was published in 1971 by International Publishers in New York.

This irked my mother to no end. I thought it was hilarious. A little-known concert singer named Ruth Reese lived with us for a time. She later moved to Europe and made a name for herself there. When the actress Beah Richards moved to New York, she lived with us for a number of years. Comrades and friends from out of town or abroad would always stay with us. It seemed we always had people about and that my mother or my father was always cooking and I was always doing the dishes. Although I remember these times fondly now, at the time I resented having to do these types of chores.

After dinner and on the weekends the three of us played Scrabble and card games. Sometimes my mother and Beah would take me to watch foreign films downtown in a theater, now long gone, that was on Seventh Avenue, between Thirty-Third and Thirty-Fourth Streets. It showed Russian movies like *The Cranes Are Flying* and films by Akira Kurosawa, Ingmar Bergman, and Satyajit Ray. Afterward we'd talk about them, and sometimes we'd go to the clam house on Thirty-Fourth Street, around the corner from the theater, as my mother loved clams and raw oysters. I learned to love them too. At the dinner table we discussed books and current events but *never* the content of my parents' meetings or who attended them.

My parents often took me to meetings and demonstrations, and sometimes we would march behind a Communist Party banner or a red flag. The red flag might be my invented memory, but I do vividly remember angry sneering faces and rotten eggs and tomatoes being thrown at us as we marched into New York's Union Square on May Day or Labor Day. The police never stopped the pelting—they sneered at us as well. It was scary, but it was also exciting. My parents would hold my hand tightly, which helped me to feel brave and like I was a part of something special, particularly when we would sing. It wasn't until I was an adult that I realized how much of an island the Left really was, surrounded by the shark-infested waters of conservative and racist mainstream American politics, and how easy it was to develop an island mentality, which occasionally led to paranoid behaviors. I heard about several Communist Party members who were wrongly charged as being FBI or police agents and know several who were expelled after being accused of being white chauvinists.

Growing up, I learned the lyrics to the workers' songs, protest songs, folk songs, and chain gang songs sung by Paul Robeson and Leadbelly, and later to those sung by Pete Seeger at summer camp or other gatherings with my friends, who were the white and Black children of other Leftists. The Communist Party was one of the few freely integrated spaces in America.

I used to love to go to party headquarters on Twenty-Sixth Street in New York City. It was an old, large, beautiful, and ornate townhouse that had belonged to a wealthy family whose renegade son had given it to the party. I recall the grandiose marble stairway with its highly polished wood banister that I loved to slide down, which sloped in a gentle curve from the second to the first floor. It was in that building that I learned how to make a leaflet, how to put out a mass mailing, how to run a mimeograph machine without getting ink all over my clothes, and how to fold eight-by-eleven-inch sheets of paper into thirds and stuff them into envelopes. I would practice sealing the envelopes in batches, staggering them with their flaps open, lining them up so that each one was just under the dry glue line near the edge of the flap of the one above, then taking a wet sponge to moisten the glue and finally serially folding the flaps down to seal them. When one got good at it, one could do up to twelve envelops at a time. It seemed like great fun and real important work. The fact that it was mostly my mother and other women doing it didn't raise any questions for me then. I knew my mother could do everything, from composing documents to typing stencils of them, mimeographing them, mailing them, doing follow-up phoning, putting event committees together, arranging speakers, and everything else that went into putting on an event, writing and then making a speech, and even doing the after-event party at our house! And she did it all superbly. She was an organizer par excellence, and she was beautiful and gregarious, with a warm laugh and open arms always ready to embrace someone.

Of course, like so many other children of Communists growing up during the 1950s, I was told not to talk to strangers, not so much because they might be potential child molesters but because they might be FBI agents. I also had to be careful when talking on the phone because it was probably tapped, not to open the door to strangers, and so forth. We all learned quite quickly how to recognize an open FBI agent. They wore dark suits and what must have been standard-issue plain black leather shoes, or at least the ones who sat in a car parked across the street from our house did. They were always in a dark-colored Ford sedan, or maybe it was a Chevy. They would sit in their car and stare at the house. They were always white. At that time, in the early and mid-1950s, we lived in a duplex on a tree-lined street in a mostly Black part of Brooklyn. Sometimes when I passed the car I'd stick my tongue out at them or place the tip of my thumb on my nose and fan my fingers at them, as if I smelled something foul. Sometimes my friends—who were other children of Communists— and I would snicker about how silly they looked and how *anybody* would know who they were. We had fun mocking them in our blind moments of child-hood naiveté. There was no way for us to know at that age that the agents wanted the neighbors to know who they were—all the better to intimidate them and alienate them from us by making it seem that we were dangerous and threatening, in need of overt monitoring to preempt a disaster. That way they could be more easily seduced into informing on us. The FBI agents were omnipresent, following us to school, telling school authorities who our parents were, and trying to inveigle us into false friendships so they could glean infor-mation from us. However, most of my Communist friends who experienced this kind of cruel hounding were white. Ironically, racism had generated a general distrust and dislike of "the Man"[9] in African American communities, and this protected me, sparing me much of the embarrassing and painful isola-tion and fear my other friends suffered. But I wasn't completely spared.

In 1951 my father was subpoenaed to testify before a congressional sub-committee about the organization he headed at the time, the Civil Rights Congress, which was a left-wing legal defense group he helped found in 1946. The organization gained notoriety for challenging police brutality, defending African Americans falsely accused of crimes and victims of the latest Red Scare, and for submitting a historic petition to the United Nations charging the United States government with submitting African Americans to geno-cidal policies. When Pat refused to answer questions, he was cited for con-tempt of Congress and sent to jail. He was first sent to the West Street Jail in New York City to await sentencing, after which he was sent to a new, modern prison in Danbury, Connecticut, which was dubbed the "country club" because it was surrounded by trees and grass and had glass brick windows instead of metal bars. I was eight or nine years old, and I thought it looked pretty as we drove up the manicured driveway to the entrance for visits. My mother would drive us there almost every weekend, taking along the family of Jack Stachel, who was in the same prison for the same "crime." We would be ushered into a large open room with groups of seats, where we would sit and wait for the prisoners to be brought in. When my father would appear, I'd run up to him and jump into his arms. I never noticed any tears in his eyes or in my mother's—but I'm sure they were there.

The task of making me feel safe and secure must have been challenging for my parents. Yet somehow they managed. One of the ways they found to

9. "The Man" is a popular term for "the white oppressor." It can be used to describe any-one from the local store owner or a policeman all the way to the people who run the country.

protect me was to send me to a wonderful summer camp in Vermont—
Higley Hill. The camp was a haven for those children whose parents were
jailed for being Communists, had been forced "underground" to hide from
the government, or were just having a rough time simply because they were
suspected of subversion. Higley Hill was where I first met and sang with Pete
Seeger. Many of us went every summer and forged long-term friendships
with other campers, some of which carried over into the rest of the year.
During the fall and winter we'd go to hootenannies together or to
Washington Square in Greenwich Village on the weekends to sing folk
songs. The camp's owners, Grace and Manny Granich, had been in China
around the time of the Long March[10] and had met Madame Sun Yat-Sen and
Mao Zedong.

Much later, when I was into having boyfriends, my father would always
corner them, or so it seemed to me, to ask them what they were thinking
about and then start a one-way discussion with them. I'd usually roll my eyes
and busy myself with some housework, but I would listen in. He would often
talk to them about the Soviet Union, China, and socialism or some current
event. He'd never miss an opportunity to discuss Black history with them or
with any young person who was visiting. He'd talk, with controlled outrage,
about the cruel lies and shameless sham of "emancipation," which simply
relegated the Negro people to second-class citizenship and continued their
oppression, all the while telling them they were free. He'd mention how he
believed racism dehumanized white people. And he would always urge my
boyfriends to read and to study. I can still hear his voice in my head saying,
"Young man, you must study!" He understood how ignorance made it easier
for "the Rulers" to keep their boots on our necks.

At some point in one's late childhood or early adolescence, as one is intellectually maturing and becoming socially and politically conscious, one is faced
with the need to accept or reject being or becoming like one's parents. One can
either accept or reject one's parents' legacy and place in history. I chose to
accept mine, and in so doing I was admitting a profound indebtedness for their
major contribution to who and what I became—to who I am today.

This is why I decided to undertake this book project with Nebby Lou—
the editing and annotating of the correspondence between my parents, the

10. During the Chinese Civil War, the Communists, surrounded by Nationalist armies
under the command of Chiang Kai-Shek, broke through enemy lines and, led by Mao
Zedong, began an epic, year-long trek known as the Long March, which lasted from 1934 to
1935 and covered about six thousand miles.

Crawfords, and Langston Hughes. This book is an open embrace of them and their contribution to the liberation of their people and the struggle to democratize this country. It's a book in their own words about themselves, their lives, their dreams, their friends and enemies, their daily trials and tribulations, their achievements and doubts and questions, and their unending search for knowledge and the road to victory.

Their letters, which they must have known were being monitored, were nonetheless candid, sensitive, inquiring, informative, supportive, imploring, explanatory, and often downright funny. This correspondence has allowed Nebby Lou and me to meet and know our parents as they were before becoming our parents: as young adults, buddies, and comrades, getting to know each other and maturing together.

Since what has survived of this correspondence is incomplete, we have assumed the task of creating a bridging narrative and a historical context where we thought this was necessary. We have also provided information on many of the unknown or little-known persons or events mentioned in the letters—the hunt for which often led us to archives and obscure nooks and crannies, with many detours and long phone calls and personal conversations with surviving elders and each other. It also sent us on separate personal journeys of introspection and soul-searching, which, as time went by, we learned to share with one another, bringing us closer together. As the years rolled by, the project was interrupted by other demands life conjured up, but we would always find a way to regroup and renew our commitment to finishing it.

We understand that our memories of people and events of many decades ago are subject to the usual inaccuracies and memory lapses that the passing of time brings about. But we have tried, to the best of our abilities, to recreate the past as accurately as anyone can, without intent to distort, exaggerate, clean up, or leave out anything important that actually happened, even when it casts our parents or Langston in a less positive light.

The book increased my commitment to what I believe in. It also confronted me with existential questions, such as: How was I living my life? What set of values was I using to make decisions? How did being a "red diaper baby"[11] influence my formation, and how could I tease it out from all the other influences on me? How are values, culture, and ideas transmitted in families and across generations? How did I do with my own children?

11. "Red diaper baby" is a term used to refer to children born to members of the Communist Party of the United States.

What is obvious to me now is that doing this book has helped me to reach out and strengthen my connections and relationships with family and friends, as it has heightened my understanding of how important those ties are. Reading their letters over and over again brought our parents and Langston alive to Nebby Lou and me in a way we could not have known them otherwise. We got to see them as they negotiated a difficult historical socio-political time and milieu.

I sent off for their Freedom of Information Act[12] papers, which neither of my parents, for various reasons, had wanted to do. Nebby Lou and I have read and reread them. They revealed how relentlessly and wastefully the two were surveilled, pursued, and reviled by the US government at all levels: federal, state, and city. Reading the papers deepened our respect and admiration for them—for their tenacity, for being able to sustain the courage of their convictions and face down their foes, for truly living those convictions, and for trying to pass them on to me and others. This book is our attempt to hold a candle high to them!

12. The Freedom of Information Act (FOIA) was a law passed by the federal government in 1966. It allows for partial or full disclosure of previously unreleased classified information and documents about people, organizations, and events gathered and controlled by the US government.

ACKNOWLEDGMENTS

Any book that journeys more than a decade before becoming published accumulates all kinds and measures of support along the way that result in an immense indebtedness. This book would still be just an idea if it weren't for Professor Robin D. G. Kelley. He has been with this project from its inception, and his generosity of spirit and commitment to a true and all-inclusive American history knows no bounds. He brainstormed concepts, organization, and research approaches and suggestions, read and reread manuscript versions, met with us whenever and wherever we requested, emailed, texted, and recommended publishers. He cooked fabulous meals for us and shared holidays and birthdays with us too. At no point did he doubt this book's validity, importance, or our ability to write it even when we wavered. His repayment will be in the knowing this book is read and used by generations to come.

There are many others to thank as well.

In the early years:

Patricia C. Willis, former curator of American Literature at Yale University's Beinecke Rare Book and Manuscript Library, helped us review our parents' letters, which are archived in the Langston Hughes Papers.

Dr. Mary Charlson and Renee Golden gave us free space to work in, away from home and daily worries and distractions, so we could focus on the task.

Roberto Patterson, MaryLouise's grandson, gave us the book title and always responded to our endless cries for computer help. He also cooked us some delicious meals.

We had a long walk down Riverside Drive in New York City with Howard Dodson, then the head of the Schomburg Center for Research in Black Culture in Harlem, New York. He told us, if we did nothing else, we *must* "let their voices sing." We have tried hard to do just that. Every time we'd see him after that, he'd ask about the project and encourage us onward.

Bettina Aptheker, Distinguished Professor at the University of California, Santa Cruz, and author Fred Jerome gave us suggestions for literary agents and other contacts.

Randall Burkett, curator of the African American Collections at Emory University's Manuscript, Archives, and Rare Book Library, together with the library's staff organized a symposium titled "Langston Hughes: Poet of the People" in April 2004, where we made our first public presentation about our two families and Langston Hughes. Randall also treated us to numerous events across the country, which always included delectable meals, good company, and witty repartee.

Francine Henderson, administrator at Auburn Avenue Research Library on African American Culture and History in Atlanta, hosted a reading of our material during our 2004 visit to Atlanta. The response at both the symposium and the reading was overwhelmingly positive, as we found ourselves surrounded by audience members demonstrating their excitement about the project and encouraging us to complete the book.

Arnold Rampersad, Emeritus Professor of English at Stanford University and author of the two-volume *Life of Langston Hughes,* encouraged and helped us for over ten years, from the book's birth to its completion. His critique of the penultimate draft showed us how we might revisit and deepen our understanding of some of the complex personal and political issues concerning Langston.

Lawrence Jackson, Professor of African American Studies and English at Emory University and author of *The Indignant Generation: A Narrative History of African American Writers and Critics, 1934–1960,* cheered us on from the earliest days, offering sage advice, critical dialogue, and kind words, even when we wondered if we would ever see the light at the end of the tunnel. He is also much appreciated for his Maryland crab cake recipe.

James E. Smethurst, Professor of African American Studies at the University of Massachusetts-Amherst, helped us obtain access to the Loren Miller papers, archived at the Huntington Library in Pasadena, California.

We also thank Loren Miller's family for granting permission to use two of his many letters to Langston.

In the middle years:

Professor Thulani Davis in the Department of Afro-American Studies at the University of Wisconsin-Madison met with us during the middle years and discussed some important considerations.

Professors Hakim Adi and Ani Mukherji also did invaluable research for us.

The James Weldon Johnson Institute at Emory University in Atlanta provided Evelyn with office space and doctoral student researchers. We are especially grateful to the late Rudolph P. Byrd, founder and director of the institute. He was an early supporter of our project and offered ideas and resources during the research phase. Former Institute staff, Calinda Lee and Dorcas Ford Jones offered generous administrative support and encouragement. Doctoral candidates Erica Bruchko and Yolande Tomlinson provided invaluable research assistance and expert knowledge of the Emory University libraries. Thanks also to Jessie Dunbar for her research help.

In the last few years:

Toward the end of this journey, in October 2011, we met with our friends Louis Massiah, Cheryll Greene, Richard Perry, Faith Childs, Robert Boyle, and Keith Gilyard at MaryLouise's New York apartment. They formed an informal one-day editorial committee and provided critical professional and scholarly perspectives on our book. Their comments were invaluable. Later, literary agent Faith Childs was most generous with her advice about the publishing process. For this, we thank her again.

At different points over the course of the decade we asked various people to read the developing manuscript and give us their candid feedback. They all did. Unfortunately a few of those people are no longer living. We thank the following dear and special friends who never doubted the completion of the book and will continue to be missed: Cheryll Greene, Jean Damu, Robert Chrisman, Rosa Guy, and St. Clair Bourne.

Throughout the journey we were supported, encouraged, fed, housed, entertained, enlightened, and given shoulders to cry on along with much laughter and music by the following: Daphne Muse, Margot Dashiell, Lisa Gay Hamilton, Kweli Tutashinda, MaryLouse's poker buddies and New York book club members, Evelyn's Atlanta "Literary Lunch Bunch," Carol Swainson, Sumi Takeda-Nakazaki, Nora North, Norma Harrell, Peter Harper, Marsha Walters, Reggie Woolfolk, Carlos Moore, Jean and Richard Presha, Garland Core, Jr., Jim Lacy, Jack Kurzweil, Bill Mitchell, Steven Mitchell, Anne Mitchell, Joyce King and Hassimi Maiga, Halimatou Maiga, Kate Amend and Johanna Demetrakis, Dave and Jeanie Dubnau, Diane Harriford, Dorothy Burnham, Claudia Burnham, Margaret Burnham and Max Stern, Carol and John Calhoun, Claudine Brown, Alita Anderson, Kathleen Cleaver, Roslyn Walker, Edward Spriggs and Margaret Counts-Spriggs, Malkia M'Buzi Moore, Peggy Dammond-Preacely, Shawna and Carlos Antonio Davis, Constancia "Dinky" Romilly and Terry Weber, Rodney Gillead, Adrienne Jensen, Mary Macauley, Jerome Pope, Gaidi Nkruma, Clarence "Razor" Nathan, Trimiko Melancon, Mab Segrest, Amelia Brito, Donis Cotin, Hattie Diop, Louise Meriwether, and Mildred Howard.

We thank our editors at University of California Press: Niels Hooper, Bradley Depew, and Dore Brown.

We thank the Langston Hughes estate and its representative, Harold Ober Associates, for their gracious permission to publish his letters to our families.

Very special thanks go to our families. MaryLouise is grateful to Joanna and Fred Jackson and their children, Jade and William; Evelyn Louise Camacho Patterson and Sven Gotdfredsen and their son, Andrea Femi; Roberto Patterson; and Olga Camacho. Evelyn thanks Afsa Lise Bello, Ganiou Bello, Kenya Bello, Holly Crawford, Lola Oketokoun, Kadir Oketokoun, Delores and George Napper, Bessie Winston, Samuel Winston, Chipp Napper, and Richard Parker.

If we have inadvertently missed anyone, it was not intentional; we trust you know you're deeply thanked.

A NOTE ON THE TEXT

The volume editors' wish was to reproduce these letters as faithfully as possible without sacrificing readability. However, these are candid letters among friends, and at times they include obviously unintentional typographical errors resulting from the familiar mode of writing. Typos that disrupt readability have been silently corrected. In other respects, the letters are presented as written, preserving the original spelling, grammar, and punctuation. Original underlining and strike-throughs are retained. Ellipses are reproduced as written. *Sic* is not used.

We have not attempted to replicate the spacing and alignment of text in the original letters. Dates, addresses, signatures, and salutations have been regularized and are aligned at the right margin. Salutations and signatures have also been standardized to appear on separate lines. Dashes have been regularized (i.e., "–––" is replaced with "—").

Letters are identified by writer and recipient, followed by the date of the letter. In the case of letters where the date or part of the date is not included in the original, the interpolated portion (in some cases the complete date) is enclosed in square brackets. In most instances, the subject matter contained in undated letters allowed the volume editors to date them with a measure of confidence. Letter writers and recipients are identified by their first names or nicknames: Langston, Louise, Pat, Matt, Nebby, Nebby Lou, and Mary Lou.

The letters vary from one another materially: a brief description of the object (letterhead, postcard, telegram), where provided, follows the header in square brackets. Letterhead is provided in full in the first instance and abbreviated thereafter. Some letters include drawings and marginal notes. Descriptions of drawings are given in square brackets (e.g., "So you see I am not missing many of the comforts of home [drawing of a smiling face]").

Marginal notes are placed at the end of each letter, preceded by "[Note in margin]" or, if the location of the note is known, "[Note above letterhead]."

Unless otherwise indicated, letters are typewritten. Handwritten letters are noted as such following the header. Postcards and letters that are entirely handwritten are reproduced in roman type. Authors' handwritten insertions and signatures in a typewritten letter are reproduced in italic. Insertions are indicated with a caret (e.g., "[^*got no dough*]").

Editorial insertions are enclosed in square brackets and set in roman type. Illegible words are indicated in square brackets. Missing first or last names are added the first time they appear in each letter (e.g., "[Herbert] Delaney").

INTRODUCTION

The Poet, the Crawfords, and the Pattersons

It is well known that Langston Hughes was a prolific correspondent, some-times writing a dozen or more letters a day. Four books of his correspondence have been published. The first volume, containing the letters sent between him and Arna Bontemps—his collaborator, coauthor, and friend—is rich with details of the intertwined lives of these two African American men of letters. The second book compiles the correspondence between Langston and the novelist and critic Carl Van Vechten, providing insights into the poet's relationship with his most influential white patron. The third book com-prises letters from his mother, Carolyn Clark.[1] Finally, the much-anticipated *Selected Letters of Langston Hughes,* published recently, highlights the many and varied relationships he had with several family members and a host of prominent American cultural figures—writers, musicians, wealthy patrons, literary agents, and publishers.

His correspondence with our parents is of particular significance, because the four of them were open African American leftists, activists, and thinkers, three of whom, at various times, were members of the US Communist Party. Our parents enjoyed a relationship with Langston that lasted over forty years, and they also had abiding friendships with one another that, in some instances, stretched for eight decades. The five shared many family experiences and a burgeoning intellectual and political curiosity, mostly focused on race and liberation. All of them came of age in a radical historical

---

1. *Arna Bontemps-Langston Hughes Letters, 1925–1967,* ed. Charles H. Nichols (New York: Dodd, Mead, 1980); *Remember Me to Harlem: The Letters of Langston Hughes and Carl Van Vechten, 1925–1964,* ed. Emily Bernard (New York: Knopf, 2001); and *My Dear Boy: Carrie Hughes's Letters to Langston Hughes, 1926–1938,* ed. Carmeletta M. Williams and John Edgar Tidwell (Athens: University of Georgia Press, 2013).

period marked by the Bolshevik Revolution of 1917, the execution of Sacco and Vanzetti, the labor upheavals of the Great Depression, and the rise and defeat of fascism. It was a time bubbling over with an intensity, energy, creativity, and promise that came in the wake of a new revolutionary movement. Langston, Louise, Pat, Matt, and Nebby shared a broad humanity, a deep human sympathy, an imagination for what was possible, and a genuine concern for the fate of humanity, especially that of their people. This led them all to embrace a common idealized vision of a new world, one without misery, hunger, war, racism, hypocrisy, class oppression, or elitism. They participated in many of the same organizations and movements dedicated to that vision. As their passions and involvements grew, Matt and Louise became avid readers and serious students of Marx, Lenin, and other socialist thinkers. With this new knowledge came a new confidence in their cause. Over the years, they both developed into compelling public speakers and respected organizational leaders. Pat, ten years their elder, was an important public figure in Harlem. For Langston, public speaking was often his profession, and at times he lived off of his spoken word.

Langston's leftist leanings and politics have come under intense scrutiny from scholars and have been subject to debate. Some writers have posited that he used his literary gift as a form of radical dissent only in his early career and later repudiated his ties with the Left. Indeed, there were instances when he pulled away from his earlier leftist writings, utterances, and affiliations, but only after intense right-wing harassment and attack. Those pressured compromises of his artistic integrity were torturous for him and usually left him physically ill. Yet, as his correspondence with our parents reveals, Langston's deep social commitment and expansive compassion never wavered or weakened. He was a revolutionary and a pragmatist, a dreamer and a realist, an artistic crusader against capitalist greed, racist oppression, hypocrisy, shams, cruelty, self-glorification, and everything that debased and oppressed people.

So we see the story as more nuanced and complicated. Even at the height of the anti-Communist zeitgeist of the 1950s, Langston openly remained a close friend and comrade of our parents while simultaneously trying to maintain his delicate balancing act as an independent writer and artist who was true to his ideals—challenging racism and racist oppression yet never forgetting that he was making a living in a commercial literary world that traded on and propagated stereotypes and distortions.

During the 1950s, as Senator Joseph McCarthy led his anti-Communist witch hunts,[2] thousands of Americans lost their jobs, their spouses, and their friends as a result of being labeled a Red, a pinko, or a sympathizer. Langston appeared before the McCarthy's committee in Washington in 1953. Louise was subpoenaed in New York on April 6, 1951, and Nebby was subpoenaed in San Francisco in the same year, to testify about their alleged leftist involvements. Yet Langston's fictional Harlem character "Simple,"[3] which appeared in the column he wrote for *The Chicago Defender* newspaper, regularly spoke out against or poked fun at the lack of democracy at home and abroad, racism, the House Un-American Activities Committee (HUAC), the bomb, the exploitation of workers, and the added exploitation if they happened to be Black. He would frequently send these articles to Matt and Nebby, because they lived in California and did not get the East Coast papers.

The correspondence between these four friends and Langston began in 1930 and ended shortly before the poet's death in 1967. The letters are a window into a unique, self-created world away from his life of celebrity and fame—a place where he lived comfortably, could safely "let his hair down" and be at ease, have in-depth political discussions, gossip, tell jokes and private stories, and play with us. These were friendships that bore no hidden agendas. They trusted and relied on one another, and that shared trust and camaraderie was unshakeable. Langston sent them early drafts of poems, articles, and newspaper columns, seeking their honest political critique or "the line" (the correct political slant or explanation). He also kept them up to date on his whereabouts and projects. And they, in turn, did the same, sometimes replying quite sharply to him, but always with deep respect and affectionate solidarity. They also had a lot of fun. They shared many lively times

2. For more information on the Senate Permanent Subcommittee on Investigations and the postwar Red Scare, see M.J. Heale, *McCarthy's Americans: Red Scare Politics in State and Nation, 1935–1965* (Athens: University of Georgia, 1998); David Oshinsky, *A Conspiracy So Immense: The World of Joe McCarthy* (New York: Oxford University Press, 2005); Michael Paul Rogin, *The Intellectuals and McCarthy: The Radical Specter* (Cambridge, MA: Massachusetts Institute of Technology, 1967); Ellen Schrecker, *Many Are the Crimes: McCarthyism in America* (Princeton: Princeton University, 1998); Victor S. Navasky, *Naming Names* (New York: Viking Press, 1980); and Gerald Horne, *Black Revolutionary: William Patterson and the Globalization of the African American Freedom Struggle* (Urbana: University of Illinois Press, 2013), 141–170 passim.

3. Simple, whose full name was Jesse B. Semple, was a fictional character that Langston began to develop in 1945 for his column in the *Chicago Defender* newspaper. Simple was an ordinary, blue-collar, working Harlemite who commented to friends on topical issues of the day. The column ran for twenty years and was turned into six books.

together, full of laughter, good food and music, shared favors, money (mostly from them to Langston), and stories and gossip (mostly from Langston to them).

There are also those letters that document the adventures they had together in their wide-eyed efforts to change the world. The first of these was a fateful trip to Moscow in 1932 that would forever change them, and it is well documented here. Louise (who was then Louise Thompson, not yet having married William L. Patterson), at the behest of the Black Communist leader James Ford, organized a group of twenty-two young African Americans, including herself, Langston, and Matt, to travel to Russia to make a film about race relations in the United States, which was to be entitled *Black and White*.[4] In the end, the film project was aborted. Needless to say, the young group of would-be actors was extremely disappointed by this turn of events, and they split into two political factions—each with its own set of explanations as to why the cancellation occurred. But immediately after the project's collapse, the Russians proposed that the group embark on a tour of the USSR. Langston, Matt, and Louise, along with most of the others, accepted the offer. They spent much of the fall of 1932 traveling across the country and down into Soviet Central Asia. The meetings and conversations they had with Russians, Georgians, Ukrainians, Uzbeks, and others, who were building a new society, sparked in them a burning new interest in socialism. Pat, who had studied in the Soviet Union from 1927 to 1930, returned to the country in late 1932 to campaign for international support for the release of the Scottsboro Boys—nine young Black men who had been falsely convicted of rape and sentenced to death in Alabama.

Although Langston was often accused of being a Communist, he never actually joined the Communist Party; yet he found in it a philosophical understanding and vision that informed his life and writings. Likewise, Nebby never joined the party either, but she sympathized with its idealized vision of a better world. The party's major attractions for the three of our parents who did join it and for other Black intellectuals and artists in the late 1920s and into the 1930s was its open membership policy and the campaigns it organized among workers and unemployed councils in many Black communities, including Harlem. White and Black Communists were in the

4. While conducting research for this book, the editors noted that the Moscow *Black and White* film project of 1932 continues to be of great interest to scholars. It is mentioned in scores of publications in the fields of African American history and the history of the American Left and of Blacks and the Soviet Union.

streets and neighborhoods fighting against evictions and racist violence—especially in its most heinous form, lynching—not just talking about it on the street corners or writing about it in their newspapers. By the early 1930s the case of the Scottsboro Boys of Alabama was the pivotal event that drew many Black Americans to the Communist Party and its affiliated organizations.

LANGSTON HUGHES

James Langston Hughes was the product of the turn of the early twentieth century Midwest. Born in 1902, he was raised in Missouri, Kansas, and Ohio by various family members, but mostly by his maternal grandmother, who regaled him with stories of his remarkable forebears, Lewis Sheridan Leary, who was fatally wounded while participating in John Brown's Raid on Harper's Ferry,[5] and John Mercer Langston, who was an attorney, abolitionist, and US Congressman. From time to time he was able to stay with his mother, but he had little contact with his father, who had abandoned the family to seek his fortune in Mexico. As the only "colored" boy in his school, he occasionally felt the sting of prejudice and received racist comments from some white classmates. But he also made genuine friendships. Many of the children he went to school with were the daughters and sons of first-generation European immigrants, who openly held socialist, communist, or anarchist views. Although he portrayed his childhood as lonely, unhappy, and poor, these hard times during his boyhood provided much of the early raw material for his literary genius.

In 1921 Langston arrived in New York City to attend Columbia University, and he witnessed a newly emerging and vibrant Harlem. More inspired by the city than by academic life, he abandoned his studies at the end of his first year and signed up as a "mess boy" on a freighter bound for Africa and Europe. In 1924, after several years of overseas adventures in Paris, Venice, and several seaports in France and Italy, he returned to the United States, first settling in Washington, DC, with his mother, where he eventually landed a job working

5. John Brown (1800–1859) was an American abolitionist who attempted an armed overthrow of the institution of slavery. He and twenty-two white and Black men, including three of his sons, seized the US Arsenal at Harper's Ferry, Virginia, on October 16, 1859. They were stopped by Colonel Robert E. Lee and a force of marines. Brown was hung. Lee later rose to the rank of general in the Confederate Army.

for Dr. Carter G. Woodson, founder of the Association for the Study of Negro Life and History. Wanting more time to write, he left Woodson in 1925 to take a job as a busboy at the Wardman Hotel, where he struck up a friendship with the poet Vachel Lindsay. Lindsay introduced Langston's poetry to a wider audience, consequently leading to the publication of his first collection, *The Weary Blues,* in 1926. That same year he published a seminal essay, "The Negro Artist and the Racial Mountain," in *The Nation* magazine, thus establishing his reputation as one of the most influential figures of the Negro cultural renaissance. In the essay, he brilliantly defined and proclaimed a bold sense of militant racial pride and unfettered creative independence for the Black artist—a new Black literary aesthetic.[6]

In 1927 he toured the South reading his poetry. During a stop at Hampton Institute in Virginia he met Louise, who was teaching there. By this time he had also met and been taken under the patronage of Mrs. Charlotte Osgood Mason, a Park Avenue matron who would support his literary efforts for the next three years. The author Zora Neale Hurston was already one of Mrs. Mason's "primitive protégés." During this period Zora and Langston became close and trusted pals, each recognizing the other's great talent, keen intellect, and sharp sense of humor. Langston and Louise's friendship deepened as well.

Meanwhile, Langston returned to school, enrolling in Lincoln University, a historically black college located in Chester, Pennsylvania. Upon graduation in 1929, he settled more or less permanently in New York City. By that time, Harlem had been deemed by some to be the capital of the Black world, where Black artists, intellectuals, and entrepreneurs thrived, Black police officers walked the beat, and Black dreams did not need to be deferred. For the generation of Langston and our parents, this "Negro Mecca" offered hope for a new beginning in an age of scientific racism barely sixty years removed from slavery. It promised the flowering of a Black intelligentsia and culture, a symbol of what sophisticated, urbane Black people could become if they held power and were left alone. As the poet and critic James Weldon Johnson explained, "[T]he Negro's situation in Harlem is without precedent in all his history in New York; never before has he been so securely anchored, never before has he owned the land, never before has he had so well-established a community life."[7] The Harlem Renaissance was in full swing.

6. See Arnold Rampersad, *The Life of Langston Hughes,* vol. 1, *1902–1941* (New York: Oxford University Press, 1986), 130–131.
7. James Weldon Johnson, *Black Manhattan* (New York: Arno Press, 1968), 158–159.

And yet, just three decades before, no one would have predicted that the choice block of land from 110th to 145th Streets would become a predominantly Black community, let alone the epicenter of the African diaspora in the United States. By the turn of the twentieth century, rising land values, boosted by the extension of the IRT subway line, lured Manhattan's bourgeoisie and real estate speculators to Harlem. They erected beautiful brownstones, luxury apartment buildings, and a few small mansions. Oscar Hammerstein I, who made quite a fortune buying and selling Harlem property, built the Harlem Opera House on 125th Street, between Seventh and Eighth Avenues, with the assumption that the elite was there to stay. William Waldorf Astor must have believed the same, for he sank a cool $500,000 into a luxury apartment building, Graham Court.[8] When the 1893 edition of the *Harlem Monthly Magazine* predicted that Harlem would become "the centre of fashion, wealth, culture, and intelligence," it didn't foresee Langston Hughes, W. E. B. Du Bois, Madame C. J. Walker, or the other black Renaissance figures that were to come. Indeed, most Harlem realty companies circa 1900 hung signs that read: "The agents promise their tenants that these houses will be rented only to WHITE people." But once the bottom fell out of the Harlem real estate market in 1904, due to over-speculation, these same realtors sold to anyone willing to buy.[9]

Harlem drew its share of Black middle-class "strivers," but it was largely a working-class enclave—and an increasingly radical one at that. After all, the Harlem Renaissance was also known as the "New Negro Movement," announced in part by the philosopher and critic Alain Locke in his 1925 anthology, *The New Negro*. Locke recognized that this incipient movement was not limited to Harlem, and he compared it to "those nascent movements of folk-expression and self-determination, which are playing a creative part in the world to-day. The galvanizing shocks and reactions of the last few years are making, by subtle processes of internal reorganization, a race out of its own disunited and apathetic elements. A race experience penetrated in this way invariably flowers. As in India, in China, in Egypt, Ireland, Russia,

8. Gilbert Osofsky, "The Making of a Ghetto," in *Harlem USA,* ed. John Henrik Clarke (New York: Collier Books, 1971), 9–10; see also Gilbert Osofsky, *Harlem: The Making of a Ghetto: Negro New York, 1890–1930* (New York: Harper and Row, 1963); Roi Ottley and William J. Weatherby, eds., *The Negro in New York: An Informal Social History, 1626–1940* (New York: Praeger, 1969); and David Levering Lewis, *When Harlem Was in Vogue* (New York: Random House, 1981).

9. Osofsky, "The Making of a Ghetto," 9–11.

Bohemia, Palestine and Mexico, we are witnessing the resurgence of a people."[10]

But as Langston quickly recognized, the New Negro also represented a *political* expression, or better yet, *expressions*. Some of the members of this new movement fought for fundamental rights and dignity within a constitutional framework. Others, like the Garveyites, sought to "escape" from the United States, or the West altogether, and find a new promised land. Still others chose a more radical third path. Rejecting both emigration and appeals for inclusion, they aimed to transform the nation's social, cultural, political, economic, and juridical institutions to the core. They sought to build a new society in which the notion of rights, privileges, commitments, and social relationships would be radically reformulated.

Langston sympathized with all three approaches, but he was especially drawn to the third, which found its clearest expression in the American Left. Like so many artists and intellectuals, he was drawn to the Left by the global economic collapse of the 1930s, the rise of fascism, and the Communist Party's militant campaign to defend the Scottsboro Boys. His poetry and prose took on a decidedly anti-capitalist, anti-imperialist tone, and he took public stances in support of a number of party-led campaigns. In 1934 he even became the titular head of the Communist-backed League of Struggle for Negro Rights.

For most of his literary career, Langston supported himself with his writing, which meant that he had to walk a thin, shaky high wire, balancing his values and beliefs against a literary industry stacked against him and, for the most part, against what he believed in and wrote so passionately about. That he succeeded for the most part is an achievement that has been largely ignored by the mainstream. When the literary industry's winds were cold and gale force, he found himself bending under them, but it always made him ill. We believe his friendship with our parents helped him back to even keel, as evidenced in this correspondence.

While the letters reveal a more personal, intimate side of Langston rarely seen, they also confirm impressions of him as a private and complex individual—someone who found it hard to reveal his innermost feelings about his intimate relationships, heartaches, loves, or losses. This, along with the fact that he never married, has led to much speculation about his sexuality. But to ask whether he was homosexual, bisexual, or even asexual seems to us

10. Alain Locke, *The New Negro* (New York: Arno Press, 1968), 4.

to be something of an anachronism, since these discrete sexual identities had not fully crystallized in the way we think about them today. Moreover, deviations from virtually compulsory heterosexuality were often policed with great intensity, as demonstrated by the fact that one component of the Red Scare was the "Lavender Scare," or the campaign to root out homosexuality in both public and private institutions.[11] For a celebrated writer like Langston, who was already doing his best to dodge accusations of being a Communist, he could ill-afford any hint of sexual deviancy.

The two of us discussed this issue as we read and reread the letters while working on this book. We noted how Langston would invariably ask our parents about one or the other's partner, yet in their letters to him there was never any mention of a partner or intimate relationship of his. Why was this? Perhaps Louise and Matt, who, out of our four parents, were the closest to Langston, were not privy to this facet of his life, or perhaps they knew not to ask if he wasn't forthcoming about it. Regardless, they chose not to offer opinions on that subject either publicly or privately—although they were often asked about it. They did not voluntarily share any of their thoughts on this with us either, and we never asked. Perhaps the apparent lack of a sustained intimate relationship in Langston's life led him to forge the very deep bonds he had with our families and the others he was so close to, for he was truly like a member of our families. After his death and up to theirs, Louise and Matt simply kept their thoughts about this to themselves, quietly respecting their friend's privacy.

LOUISE THOMPSON PATTERSON

Louise Alone Toles Thompson Patterson was born in Chicago in 1901. Her mother was Lula Mae Brown Toles Thompson, born in Ohio, and her father was William Toles of Chicago. In her infancy, Louise's parents separated, and by the time she was four years old she moved with her mother to the West Coast. Louise, like Langston, had an itinerant childhood, living with her mother (and sometimes her stepfather, Hadwick Thompson) in small

---

11. See, for example, David K. Johnson, *The Lavender Scare: The Cold War Persecution of Gays and Lesbians in the Federal Government* (Chicago: University of Chicago Press, 2004); and Robert J. Corber, *Homosexuality in Cold War America: Resistance and the Crisis of Masculinity* (Durham: Duke University Press, 1997).

towns in Nevada, Idaho, Washington, Oregon, and finally California. She seldom spent more than a year in the same school. Lula Thompson occasionally took live-in jobs as a housekeeper and cook, forcing her to leave Louise in the care of others—usually total strangers. As a rule, the Thompsons were the only Black family in these towns. In her later years, Louise recounted being called "nigger" as a child and being socially ostracized by her young schoolmates, often with the consent and encouragement of their teachers and other adults. The family finally settled in the San Francisco Bay Area, and Louise finished high school in West Oakland. Around 1915, on the playground of Cole School, she befriended young Matt Crawford and his brothers, Charles and Reginald.

In 1919, fresh out of high school, Louise was accepted at the University of California, Berkeley, where she graduated cum laude with a degree in Business Administration in 1923. She minored in Spanish. Possessing an insatiable intellectual curiosity, Louise was looking for a deeper understanding of the predicament facing Black people in the United States and around the world. During her time on the Berkeley campus, she attended a lecture on Negro history, given by the visiting W. E. B. Du Bois. She often recalled how she was transformed by his words. She left the lecture hall that day with a new sense of racial pride and a deeper appreciation of who she was and where she had come from. But after graduation she found all the doors to a career closed to her. Since she was relatively fair-complexioned and had some fluency in Spanish, she reluctantly decided to "pass" for Mexican in order to accept a secretarial position in San Francisco's business district.

Louise was increasingly disgusted with her deception. On her daily commute from Berkeley to San Francisco, she had to pretend not to know her Negro friends on the ferry. By 1925 she was feeling an acute need to see what the rest of the world looked like and what it might offer, so she moved back to Chicago with her mother. It was their first time "home" in twenty years. But Louise soon found herself alienated from the city's Black bourgeois life. She successfully applied for a teaching job in the South. Leaving her mother behind, she traveled to Pine Bluff, Arkansas, to teach for a year and then moved on to another teaching position at Hampton Institute in Virginia. Little did she suspect that this experience would be her first clash with "white philanthropy" and the perpetual gratitude and subservience it demanded from Black people. By the end of the 1927–1928 academic year, and after witnessing the courageous Hampton Student Strike,[12] Louise had had enough of the South. Bag and baggage in tow, she set off again—this time for New York City.

This time her mother came with her, and they settled in Harlem. She immediately began looking for work. Through the intervention of Dr. Alain Locke, whom she met through Langston, and her friendship with Langston, Louise was hired by Charlotte Osgood Mason. She was to work as a stenographer and typist to Mason's young protégées—Langston and Zora. At the time Langston and Zora were collaborating on a play that would be entitled *Mule Bone*,[13] based on one of Zora's folk tales. As work on the project progressed, a dispute over the authorship of the piece broke out between the two writers, with Louise and her role in their collaboration at the center. Varying accounts of the argument—attributing blame to different individuals—have been written. Regardless of who was at fault, the *Mule Bone* affair shattered Louise and Zora's new friendship and strained the old ties and collaboration between Langston and Zora. Unbeknownst to Louise, Locke was in the mix behind the scenes, siding with "Godmother" Mason and Zora. This resulted in Mason summarily dismissing both Louise and Langston. In her unpublished memoir, Louise would later recall: "The whole thing made Langston sick, but it made me mad!"

The friendship between Langston and Louise survived the maelstrom— both the explosive *Mule Bone* debacle and the firing. As a result of this perplexing and humiliating experience, and given their shared political and social outlooks, "Lou" and "Lang" drew closer together. Their personal

12. In 1929 the students of the Hampton Institute went on strike to protest one of the administration's many racist indignities: leaving the lights on in the campus theater during movies, claiming that they didn't know what the students might do in the dark. The strike began one day prior to a planned visit from General Jan Christiaan Smuts, who had been the prime minister of South Africa from 1919 to 1924. Smuts, who was a supporter of segregation, wanted to observe the system of education of American Blacks, upon which he planned to pattern Bantu education in his homeland. Louise wrote a letter to W. E. B. Du Bois, who edited the NAACP's monthly magazine, *The Crisis*, urging that the students be supported. Without her permission, he printed the letter. The strike lasted two weeks, after which the ringleaders were expelled.

13. *Mule Bone*, a play originally written by Langston and Zora Neale Hurston in 1930, was the ostensible reason for the breakup of the collaborative relationship between the two authors and of the dismissal of Louise and Langston from Mrs. Charlotte Mason's patronage. At Zora's insistence, Langston removed his name from the play, but it wasn't produced until 1991, on Broadway, by which time his name had been added back.

integrity and dignity had withstood a terrible test, resulting in their becoming even more trusting, loyal, and considerate toward one another.

For Louise, this was yet another painful and revelatory personal experience with white philanthropy—only this time in the person of Charlotte Osgood Mason, a woman of great social stature and prestige. It pushed Louise to look for more answers to her old questions about race and her new questions about the nature and nexus of social class and power. She began meeting with leftists she met during their political campaigns in Harlem. With great emphasis, she would later recall that these activists not only identified existing social problems, but more importantly, "they were committed to doing something about the situation, not just sit around and talk about it!" At some point in the 1920s Langston came into contact with Pat, who was also living, working, and visibly active in Harlem.

WILLIAM L. PATTERSON

William Lorenzo "Pat" Patterson was born in 1891 in San Francisco and raised there. His mother, Mary Galt Patterson, was an ex-slave, who had been born on a Virginia plantation. His father, James Edward Patterson, was a West Indian from the Caribbean island of St. Vincent, a British colony. In 1919, despite graduating at the top of his class at the University of California Hastings College of the Law, Pat found all law firm doors closed to him because of his skin color. Disillusioned by persistent racism and the complete denial of opportunity, he decided to leave the United States to seek out a career as a lawyer in Africa. Like Langston, he signed on to a freighter bound for Europe. From England he planned to continue on to Liberia. But during his stopover in London, a new British acquaintance convinced him that Liberians had no need for an American lawyer, Black or white, and that his own true struggle was back in the United States. The year was 1920, and he turned around and headed straight for Harlem.

Soon after arriving, Pat met Paul Robeson, and the two became close friends. Like Langston and Zora, Pat and Paul recognized each other's sharp minds and intellectual curiosity. Robeson had come to New York City to study law at Columbia University. They met at a Harlem rooming house, where Paul's future wife, Eslanda Cardoza Goode, and her best friend, Minnie Sumner, were roommates. Soon after, Sumner briefly became Pat's first wife.

Pat and Paul enjoyed each other's company and learned much from their intense discussions and debates about the problems and prospects for genuinely representative Black political leadership and the path to Black liberation. In their view, fearless Black leaders who could stand apart from the corrupt "machine" politics of the times were needed—leaders who would work with integrity and commitment for the good of the community. Paul introduced Pat to the vibrant and militant Harlem cultural scene, where he would soon meet Langston.

In 1924 Pat cofounded, with Thomas Benjamin Dyett and George Hall, the Harlem law firm of Dyett, Hall, and Patterson. The partners' offices soon became the regular meeting place for heated political debates and discussions among young Black lawyers and other professionals and intellectuals. The law practice prospered quickly, and the three attorneys became well-known members of Harlem's striving middle-class community. Pat, however, grew increasingly troubled and frustrated by his clients' cases and circumstances, and he would soon become dissatisfied with the entire system of so-called law and justice.

Pat often hosted after-hours political gatherings at his law office. One of the regular participants was Richard B. Moore, a Harlem intellectual and leftist political activist. Moore was a founding member of the radical African Blood Brotherhood[14] and had joined the Communist Party in the mid-1920s. He was the first to introduce Pat to Marxist ideology and leftist activism and activists. The two men soon began meeting away from the law office for more in-depth discussions. In his autobiography, *The Man Who Cried Genocide*, Pat recalls how Moore presented him with a series of legal cases that challenged him intellectually and caused him to question his decision to practice law. He soon began to seriously study Marxism, and through his contacts with Moore and others, he learned about the case of Italian anarchists Nicola Sacco, a fish peddler, and Bartolomeo Vanzetti, a shoemaker, who had been convicted of murder and were awaiting execution in a Boston prison.

The Sacco and Vanzetti[15] case became a political watershed for Pat, who describes in his autobiography how he began to connect the frame-up of the

14. The African Blood Brotherhood for African Liberation and Redemption was a quasi-secret militant organization founded in New York by Cyrill Briggs, a radical West Indian journalist, in the "Red Summer" of 1919.

15. Sacco and Vanzetti were accused of committing a murder during a botched robbery attempt. They were falsely convicted in Boston on July 14, 1921, and became an international cause célèbre due to the dynamic defense put forth by their labor attorney, the socialist Fred

pair with "justice routinely denied to Black Americans." He also came to understand the various strategies used to divide the poor and working classes, such as the manipulation of the economic system—especially unequal access to jobs and decent wages—and the emphasis of racial and social class differences among Americans. Pat became an active participant in the fight to save Sacco and Vanzetti and was arrested on several occasions during mass demonstrations in Boston. Shaken by the eventual execution of the pair but nonetheless undeterred, Pat emerged from the transformational experience a confirmed and dedicated radical. He had finally found the road to true liberation, and it led straight to Moscow. When he returned from Boston to New York, he resigned his partnership at the law practice and joined the Communist Party. The party sent him first to a New York "workers' school" for several months, after which he was selected to go to Soviet Russia for the formal study of Marxism, Leninism, communism, and revolution. He arrived in Moscow in 1928 and enrolled at the University of the Toiling People of the East. In his autobiography he wrote that he had no regrets about his decision.[16] He went on to head many progressive civil rights organizations, and he participated in progressive campaigns and activities his entire life.

MATT N. CRAWFORD

Matt Nathaniel Crawford Jr. was born in Anniston, Alabama, in 1903, the fourth of the five children of Matt N. Crawford Sr. and Emma Goodgame Crawford. In 1910 a fire destroyed the business where Matt Sr. worked as a carpet layer. The next year he moved his family to Oakland, California, following another Anniston family that had sent back word of new opportunities for Blacks in the West. Matt Jr., his sister, Gladys, and his three brothers, Charles, Reginald, and Artice, spent their formative years in the working-class neighborhoods of West and East Oakland, where they played with the children of other Black Southern families and of immigrant families from Italy, Germany, and England. The Crawfords, through active church mem-

---

H. Moore, and the mass international campaign to free them. But despite numerous appeals, conflicting evidence, a confession by one of the robbery participants, numerous demonstrations from Boston to Europe, and pleas from prominent writers, artists, academics, law professors, they were executed on August 23, 1927.

16. See also Gerald Horne, *Black Revolutionary: William Patterson and the Globalization of the African American Freedom Struggle* (Urbana: University of Illinois Press, 2013).

bership and involvement in civic groups, were well-known participants in the life of the small Black community that had begun to spring up in the San Francisco Bay Area.

After graduating from high school in Oakland, Matt went to work as an insurance clerk at the Board of Fire Underwriters in San Francisco's financial district. In 1921, it was one of the only companies in the city that hired "colored" office workers. Still in his twenties and always interested in the life of his community, Matt became an active member in the local chapter of the National Association for the Advancement of Colored People. He also joined a young men's group called the Acorn Club and a literary circle called the Phyllis Wheatley Club. In the mid-1920s Matt began to pursue a career in chiropractic medicine. He graduated from the San Francisco College of Chiropractic and Drugless Physicians in 1927 and soon became a licensed doctor. Along with two other young Black chiropractors, Dr. Clarence C. Rhodes and Dr. M. C. Austin, he founded a practice and opened offices in downtown Oakland. The three young men wrote a regular health column in the local Black newspaper and advocated the importance of preventive medicine and natural healing. During this period, Matt met his future wife, Evelyn Phyllis "Nebby" Graves, who was living in Berkeley at the time with Louise and Louise's mother, affectionately known as "Mother Thompson."

The year 1932 would be a transformational one in Matt's life. He and Nebby had married in September 1929 and were living in Berkeley. In the spring of 1932 Langston, who had been introduced to Matt in a letter by Louise, showed up at the couple's Acton Street apartment during a speaking tour of the West Coast. On May 14 he recited his poetry and lectured at Berkeley High School. The event was sponsored by Matt's men's club, the Acorns, and it was publicized as an evening with "Langston Hughes— Foremost Negro Poet."

Langston remained in the San Francisco area for several days and then proceeded with his tour up and down the Pacific Coast, reading his poetry and prose in several towns and cities. Matt resumed his routine of juggling the job in the insurance office in San Francisco—which he had kept—with his growing chiropractic practice in Oakland. Meanwhile, back in New York, Louise was busily organizing a group of young Black Americans for a trip to the Soviet Union to make a film about race relations in the United States.

Matt had no way of knowing that Louise's project would open up a new world to him. But it would do just that. Only ten days after appearing at

Berkeley High School, Langston wrote to Matt from the Northern California town of Eureka, asking if he could join the trip. The answer was an enthusiastic yes, and in early June, Matt, Langston, and one of their friends, the young Los Angeles journalist and attorney Loren Miller, set out by road from Los Angeles, bound for New York, where they would meet up with Louise and the eighteen other adventurers. Just past midnight on June 14, 1932, all twenty-two stood on the deck of the German liner *Europa* as it sailed out of New York harbor. They were off to Moscow to make a picture about Negro and white workers in America—the much anticipated but ultimately ill-fated *Black and White*.

Once in the USSR, Matt began to read and think more about the changing society that he was witnessing firsthand. He was greatly moved by what he saw so far away from home. The experience awoke in him a new social and political consciousness. He returned home in November 1932 and gave a series of lectures to Black congregations and civic groups in Oakland and San Francisco, recounting what he had seen in the Soviet Union.

He also became an active participant in the International Labor Defense (ILD),[17] the organization at the forefront of the national and international mass movement to free the Scottsboro Boys of Alabama. We don't know when or where Matt and Pat first met, but by 1933, the time of the Scottsboro case, they were working together. Matt worked on the case in close contact with Pat, who was the head of the ILD at the time and also one of the Scottsboro Boys' defense attorneys. Matt and Pat became close friends and collaborators, developing a heartfelt, brotherly friendship that endured throughout their lives. The fight to save the Scottsboro Boys marked the beginning of Matt's long involvement in civil rights struggles. Convinced that justice for Black Americans and others could only be won through the establishment of socialism, he joined the Communist Party in the early 1930s. Throughout the 1930s and '40s he was involved in many civil rights, labor rights, and social justice campaigns, including the 1934 General Strike in San Francisco.[18] He was a founder of the National Negro Labor Council,

17. International Labor Defense (ILD) was a legal advocacy organization established by the Communist Party USA in 1925 to counter groups like the Ku Klux Klan and to defend workers like Sacco and Vanzetti. In the 1930s it was headed by Pat, and it took on cases like the Scottsboro Nine and Angelo Herndon. In 1946 it merged with the National Federation for Constitutional Rights to form the Civil Rights Congress (CRC).

18. The International Longshoreman's Association (ILA) called a waterfront strike of all the ports on the West Coast in May 1934. On July 5 in San Francisco hundreds of policemen

the Communist Party affiliated labor organization that, from 1950 to 1955, fought to eliminate discrimination against Black workers who were barred from membership in trade unions.

EVELYN "NEBBY" GRAVES CRAWFORD

Evelyn "Nebby" Phyllis Graves Crawford was born in San Francisco in 1899 to Thomas Graves and Daisy Duprez Graves. Born in North Carolina around 1850 and raised in Virginia, Thomas probably spent his early years in slavery. He left the South sometime in the late 1880s and migrated to San Francisco with his brother Felix and his sister Sarah. He worked as a waiter at the elegant Palace Hotel, and he and his family lived in cramped quarters in a flat on narrow Minna Street, surrounded by newly arrived workers from Europe and the American South. When Thomas met Daisy in San Francisco, she too was a Southern transplant, originally from Louisiana. When Nebby was three years old, her mother died in childbirth, and Thomas found himself alone and unable to care for his four surviving children. He worked long hours at the hotel and had no choice but to leave Nebby and her siblings—her sisters, Julia and Alma, and her brother, Tom—in the care of a succession of relatives and church members in the city's small and tightly knit "colored" community. Nebby attended San Francisco public schools through high school. After graduation she completed a secretarial and stenography course and then took a job as a stenographer at the US Army base at Fort Mason, which was on the shore in clear sight of the Golden Gate Bridge, where San Francisco Bay meets the Pacific Ocean. Like Louise, her light complexion enabled her to obtain office work without revealing her racial identity.

She met Louise and Mother Thompson in her late teens, and by the early 1920s she was a member of the Thompson household, living with them at their home on Bancroft Way in Berkeley. The friendship between the two women would last over half a century. They were sisters through thick and thin, and these ties extended to a close friendship between their husbands, Matt and Pat, and between us, their daughters.

---

attempted to open the way for scabs to break the strike. A riot ensued, and two strikers were killed. The governor called in the National Guard, and the ILA called for a general strike, which would be the first ever held in the United States. The San Francisco General Strike began on July 15, 1934, and lasted four days. Federal arbitrators were brought in and most of the ILA demands were met.

In the summer of 1928 Nebby traveled by train from Oakland to New York for a vacation with the Thompsons, who had recently relocated there. Louise and Mother Thompson were settled in a large Harlem apartment, which would later become a center of much political and cultural activity. By this time Louise had been in Harlem for over a year and had gotten to know most of the young artists and intellectuals who were living there. She was quick to introduce Nebby to her new circle of friends, including Langston Hughes, writer Wallace Thurman (who was briefly married to Louise), and visual artist Aaron Douglas and his wife, Alta, plus their acquaintances. There were parties, excursions, political discussions, and a lot of joking around. Langston and Nebby hit it off immediately. After a grand time in Harlem, she returned to Oakland, and she would not meet Langston again until the spring of 1932, when he came west on a speaking tour. This was also the first time that Matt and Langston met in person, although they had exchanged letters about plans for poetry reading engagements in the San Francisco area.

For over thirty-five years the Crawfords and Langston would write, talk, and visit in California, New York, and places in between. In July 1966, in a little restaurant in the Latin Quarter of Paris, Langston and the Crawfords had a wonderful reunion. The couple was visiting their daughter, Evelyn (Nebby Lou), who was living in the French capital, and Langston was on his way back home from a trip to Africa. The old comrades and friends were in great spirits as they dined and laughed at a charming restaurant overlooking the river Seine. None of them could have imagined that this would be their last time together. The following February, Langston died after an operation in New York City.

PART I

The Tumultuous 1930s

What made the 1930s tumultuous was not the stock market crash or the global financial crisis, but the startling eruption of alternatives to unfettered capitalism, imperialism, and massive inequality. The early twentieth century marked a new age of revolution, beginning in Mexico and Russia. Both countries underwent a series of upheavals, swinging pendulum-like from constitutionalism and social democracy to radical social reforms and—in the case of Russia—Communism. Although the far left turn in Mexico's revolution didn't occur until the 1930s, its 1917 constitution promised to protect workers' rights and dramatically curb foreign investments—snubbing American corporate interests located just across the border. But the revolution that truly shook the world was that of Lenin and the Bolsheviks in 1917.

The Bolsheviks seized power in the midst of the Great War (1914–1918), a Western struggle over colonies, masquerading as a battle for democracy, where the dream of international working-class solidarity crumbled on the battlefield, and the proletarians of Europe and America made the fateful choice of nationalism over internationalism. The Russian Revolution ended the country's participation in the "war to end all wars" and replaced the Tsarist autocracy with the Union of Soviet Socialist Republics. The new Communist government immediately set out to restore that dream by forming the Third International, also known as Comintern, an international organization supporting worldwide Communism, to replace the collapsed Second International, which had advocated socialism.

The Russian Revolution and the Third International inspired socialist uprisings in many parts of the world, notably in Germany and Hungary. Even the United States appeared ripe for a revolution of its own, as postwar demobilization generated unemployment, the repeal of price controls, and huge strikes in the coal, steel, textile, and railroad industries. Workers succeeded in waging a general strike in Seattle, temporarily shutting down the city. But the wave of proletarian revolution came crashing down on the shoals of American racism. In the summer of 1917, just months before some four hundred thousand Black men would don US military uniforms and fight in the Great War, police and local militias joined white mobs in a horrific attack on the Black community of East St. Louis. Reportedly job competition, which was exacerbated by a swelling Southern Black migrant population, sparked the violence. Wartime industrialization, the temporary suspension of European immigration, the ravages of a boll weevil infestation on Southern agriculture, and the continued escalation of violence in the South had compelled over a million Black Southerners to seek new lives in Northern cities, such as St. Louis. "Make East St. Louis a Lily White Town," screamed one of the many incendiary headlines fueling what can only be described as a pogrom. When the smoke cleared, at least one hundred and fifty Black residents had been shot, burned, hanged, or maimed for life. Thirty-nine lay dead, and about six thousand were driven from their homes.[1]

During that same summer, "war" broke out in Houston, Texas. Just a year after the gruesome lynching of seventeen-year-old Jesse Washington in Waco, the US Department of War dispatched the all-Black Third Battalion of the 24th Infantry to guard Camp Logan, which was still under construction.[2] Tensions were already high, but when two Houston police officers beat and arrested a Black soldier for defending a Black woman they had been physically and verbally abusing, members of the Third Battalion revolted. "To hell with going to France," shouted one of the enlisted men. "Get to work right here." Approximately one hundred Black soldiers seized weapons and marched into town to take revenge. A shoot-out between the soldiers and police and armed civilians left sixteen whites (including four policemen) and four Black soldiers dead. A lynching was averted, but the US government acted swiftly to punish the men: nineteen were executed and fifty were sentenced to life imprisonment.[3]

1. Elliot Rudwick, *Race Riot at East St. Louis* (Urbana: University of Illinois Press, 1964); "Report on the Special Committee Authorized by Congress to Investigate the East St. Louis Riots," in *The Politics of Riot Commissions, 1917–1970*, ed. Anthony Platt (New York: Macmillan, 1971), 68; Herbert Shapiro, *White Violence and Black Response* (Amherst: University of Massachusetts Press, 1988), 115–117.

2. Shapiro, *White Violence and Black Response,* 107.

3. Ibid., 108; Robert V. Haynes, *A Night of Violence: The Houston Riot of 1917* (Baton Rouge: Louisiana State University, 1976).

Those Black soldiers who did get to Europe to fight to make the world safe for democracy returned home to segregation, lynching, and race riots. During the summer and early autumn of 1919, race riots erupted in at least thirty-five towns and cities, including Chicago, Illinois; Washington, DC; Elaine, Arkansas; Longview, Texas; Omaha, Nebraska; and Knoxville, Tennessee. It was known as the Red Summer. Lynching practically became a daily occurrence. In Georgia alone, twenty-two people were lynched that year, mostly returning veterans. The following decade, the so-called Jazz Age, was also the era of the Ku Klux Klan, whose membership swelled to between three and six million by the early 1920s. No longer limited to the South, the Klan developed strongholds in the West and Midwest, notably in the state of Indiana.[4]

The momentary crisis of Western civilization caused by the chaos of war, worker rebellions, anticolonial uprisings, postwar racial violence, and talk of self-determination for oppressed nations was the context for the rise of Marcus Garvey's Universal Negro Improvement Association and a generation of "New Negroes," who advocated a radical fusion of socialism and race politics. In 1917 socialists A. Philip Randolph and Chandler Owen launched *The Messenger,* a magazine dedicated to radical socialism and Black freedom. Its essays and poetry graphically portrayed racist violence and Black resistance. Randolph and Owen also published editorials supporting Irish nationalism, women's suffrage, and the Russian Revolution, which they initially called "the greatest achievement of the twentieth century."[5]

A year later a group of Black radicals formed the African Blood Brotherhood (ABB), a secret, underground organization founded by the Caribbean-born editor Cyril Briggs. Its leaders might be best described as Black nationalists sympathetic to Marxism and committed to universal suffrage, equal rights, and armed self-defense against lynching. As Briggs once wrote, they supported a "government of the Negro, by the Negro and for the

4. Shapiro, *White Violence and Black Response,* 145–157; Mary Frances Berry and John Blassingame, *Long Memory: The Black Experience in America* (New York and Oxford: Oxford University Press, 1982), 242.

5. Rod Bush, *We Are Not What We Seem: Black Nationalism and Class Struggle in the American Century* (New York: New York University Press, 1998), 83–112; Theodore Kornweibel, *No Crystal Stair: Black Life and the "Messenger," 1917–1928* (Westport, CT: Greenwood Press, 1975); Winston James, *Holding Aloft the Banner of Ethiopia: Caribbean Radicalism in Early Twentieth-Century America* (London: Verso, 1998); Philip Foner, *American Socialism and Black Americans: From the Age of Jackson to World War II* (Westport, CT: Greenwood Press, 1977); Jervis Anderson, *A. Philip Randolph: A Biographical Portrait* (New York: Harcourt Brace Jovanovich, 1973), 85–137.

Negro." The group published a monthly publication, *The Crusader,* which criticized President Woodrow Wilson for not applying the principle of self-determination to Africa. As a unique experiment in Black Marxist organization, ABB leaders had secretly joined the Workers (Communist) Party of America not long after the Brotherhood was founded.[6]

Part of what attracted the ABB and other black radicals to the new Communist Party was Lenin's elevation of the Black struggle to a place of importance. After half a century of being seen but not heard among white Marxists, Black radicals found a podium and an audience in the Comintern. One of the most important figures to take advantage of the Soviet bully pulpit was Claude McKay, the Jamaican-born writer of the Harlem Renaissance whose poem "If We Must Die" became the unofficial anthem of the New Negro Movement. On the heels of the end of World War I, McKay joined the editorial staff of *Liberator* magazine and became a close collaborator of the socialist journal's white founder, Max Eastman.

In 1922 McKay made his way to the Soviet Union, arriving in time to be an unofficial delegate to the Fourth World Congress of the Comintern. The Soviets were so fascinated with Negroes that he and the Communists' official

6. *Amsterdam News,* September 5, 1917; *Crusader* 1, no. 8 (April 1919), 8–9; *Crusader* 1, no. 12 (August 1919), 4; Robert A. Hill, "Cyril V. Briggs, *The Crusader* Magazine, and the African Blood Brotherhood, 1918–1922," in *The Crusader,* ed. Robert A. Hill (New York: Garland, 1987), v–lxvi; Mark Solomon, *The Cry was Unity: Communists and African Americans, 1917–1936* (Jackson: University Press of Mississippi, 1998), 3–21. Anselmo R. Jackson, associate editor of the *Crusader,* wrote that the publication was dedicated "to the doctrine of self-government for the Negro and Africa for the Africans" (*Crusader* 1, no. 3 [November 1918], 1). For more on the African Blood Brotherhood, see "Cyril Briggs and the African Blood Brotherhood," WPA Writers' Project, no. 1, Reporter: Carl Offord, Schomburg Collection; *Crusader* 2, no. 2 (October 1919), 27; "Program of the African Blood Brotherhood," *Communist Review* (April 1922) 449–454; Harry Haywood, *Black Bolshevik: Autobiography of An Afro-American Communist* (Chicago: Liberator Press, 1978), 122–130; Mark Naison, *Communists in Harlem during the Depression* (Urbana: University of Illinois Press, 1983), 3, 5–8, 17–18; Theodore G. Vincent, *Black Power and the Garvey Movement* (Berkeley, CA: Ramparts Press, 1971) 74–85 and passim; Tony Martin, *Race First: The Ideological and Organizational Struggles of Marcus Garvey and the Universal Negro Improvement Association* (Westport, CT: Greenwood Press 1976), 237–46; Draper, *American Communism and Soviet Russia, the Formative Period,* New York: Viking Press, 1960), 322–32; Cedric J. Robinson, *Black Marxism: The Making of the Black Radical Tradition* (London: Zed, 1983), 296–301; David Samuels, "Five Afro-Caribbean Voices in American Culture, 1917–1929: Hubert H. Harrison, Wilfred A. Domingo, Richard B. Moore, Cyril Briggs and Claude McKay" (PhD diss., University of Iowa, 1977); Theman Taylor, "Cyril Briggs and the African Blood Brotherhood: Effects of Communism on Black Nationalism, 1919–1935" (PhD diss., University of California, Santa Barbara, 1981).

Black delegate, Otto Huiswoud, were treated like celebrities. When McKay addressed the Congress, he put the question of race front and center, criticizing the American Communist Party and the labor movement for their racism and warning that, unless the Left challenged white supremacy, the ruling classes would continue to use disaffected Black workers as a foil against the revolutionary movement. For McKay, a commitment to Black freedom meant taking Black nationalist movements, such as Garveyism, more seriously. Racism, he argued, made it difficult for Black people to think like a "class." Instead they saw the world through colored glasses. He wryly observed, "The Negro in America is not permitted for one minute to forget his color, his skin, his race." In the end, his point was clear: there could be no successful working-class movement without Black workers at the center. Otto Huiswoud also addressed the Congress, emphasizing the incredible racism Black workers confronted back home in the South and the role that Garveyism played as a force against imperialism worldwide. The Comintern responded immediately, forming a Negro Commission and committing resources to recruiting Black cadres and supporting Black liberation on a global scale.[7] Comintern officials were so impressed with McKay's speech that they asked him to expand it into a small book, which was first published in Russian and eventually retranslated into English and published as *The Negroes in America*.[8]

McKay turned out to be much too critical for the American Communists, and they soon parted company. And although he later repudiated his Communist sympathies, the trip had a profound impact on him. The January 1924 issue of *The Crisis* magazine carried McKay's essay "Soviet Russia and the Negro," in which he described his experience in Russia as "the most memorable of [his] life. The intellectual Communists and the intelligentsia were interested to know that America had produced a formidable body of Negro intelligentsia and professionals, possessing a distinctive literature and cultural and business interests alien to the white man's. And they think naturally, that the militant leaders of the intelligentsia must feel and express the spirit of revolt that is slumbering in the inarticulate Negro masses."

7. Claude McKay, *A Long Way From Home* (New York: Rutgers University Press, [1937] 2007), 177–180; William J. Maxwell, *New Negro, Old Left: African American Writing and Communism Between the Wars* (New York: Columbia University Press, 1999), 74–77; Solomon, *The Cry Was Unity*, 40–42.

8. Claude McKay, *The Negroes in America*, trans. Robert J. Winter, ed. Alan L. McLeod (Port Washington, NY: Kennikat, 1979). The best discussion of McKay's book can be found in Maxwell, *New Negro*, 76–93.

However, despite the interest in Black movements, the Soviet recognition of the "spirit of revolt," and the many resolutions passed in Moscow in 1922, American Communist leaders were reluctant to go along with the program, and they generally distrusted Marcus Garvey and his appeals to race pride. They chose instead to launch their own Black organizations—first, they established the short-lived American Negro Labor Congress in 1925, and later, in 1930, they founded the League of Struggle for Negro Rights, which was at one point briefly headed by Langston Hughes.[9] In 1928, once again as a result of Black initiatives, the Comintern adopted its most extreme position on the "Negro Question" to date. Promoted by Harry Haywood, an American Communist Party member who had come through the ranks of the ABB, and South African Communist James LaGuma, the Comintern recognized Negroes in the "Black Belt" counties of the American South as an oppressed nation with an inherent right to self-determination. They could secede if they wanted, and perhaps even form a Negro Soviet Socialist Republic, but they were not encouraged to do so.[10]

Meanwhile, something like a nation within a nation was taking shape in Harlem. The early twenties had brought migration from the West Indies and Africa to America until the Immigration Act of 1924 was passed. Harlem's population had tripled from 1900 to 1930. The National Urban League[11] invited artists to come to Harlem. Aaron Douglas, an art teacher from Kansas; Zora Neale Hurston from Florida; Wallace Thurman from Utah via California; Claude McKay from Jamaica; Eric Walrond from British Guiana; Jean Toomer from Washington, DC; Dorothy West from Massachusetts; and Countee Cullen from Kentucky were among those who answered the

9. Haywood, *Black Bolshevik*, 139, 140–146; "Report of National Negro Committee, CPUSA" (tsc., 1925), box 12, folder "Negro-1924–25", Robert Minor Papers, Butler Memorial Library, Columbia University; James W. Ford, *The Negro and the Democratic Front* (New York: International Publishers, 1938), 82.

10. The best discussion of the history of the Black Belt thesis can be found in Solomon, *The Cry Was Unity*. For a copy of the original text of 1928 see CPUSA, *Communist Position on the Negro Question* (n.d., n.p.), 41–56. See also Roger E. Kanet, "The Comintern and the 'Negro Question': Communist Policy in the United States and Africa, 1921–1941," *Survey* 19, no. 4 (Autumn 1973), 101–104; Haywood, *Black Bolshevik*, 226; R.D.G. Kelley, "The Third International and the Struggle for National Liberation in South Africa, 1921–1928," *Ufahamu* 15, no. 1 (1986), 109–113; John W. VanZanten, "Communist Theory and the American Negro Question," *Review of Politics* 29 (1967): 435–456.

11. The National Urban League, established as the National League on Urban Conditions Among Negroes in 1910 in New York City, is currently a national civil rights organization that fights against racial discrimination.

call. Langston Hughes, who had arrived in 1920 to attend Columbia University but left after a year, returned to New York in 1925 to find that a "new" generation of Black artists had taken over Harlem. They and other artists had arrived and been immediately drawn into the rich political stew of socialists, nationalists, Communists, and the multitude of newly arrived Southern Black women and men. Harlem had become the center of radical Black thought. The so-called Harlem Renaissance was in full swing, and the neighborhood teemed with activity, creativity, and a sense of great promise. Prominent white patrons Carl Van Vechten and Charlotte Osgood Mason took several Black artists under their wings, helping them financially and offering them their influence with major New York publishers. Many of these literary artists and other Harlem intellectuals and cultural folk were connected to or influenced by the organized Left, especially by the Communist Left.

When the Wall Street stock market crashed in 1929, financial disaster and political ferment collided head on with the vibrant Black cultural movement. By 1930 the iron fist of the Great Depression was choking Harlem and thousands of minority and working-class communities across the country. Unemployment, hunger, homelessness, and dispossession reigned. The task of resisting starvation and homelessness rested with individuals. "Hoovervilles,"[12] itinerant hoboing, and pay-at-the-door rent parties became a way of life for millions of Blacks and whites alike. Simultaneously a horrific drought in many of the Great Plains states propelled thousands of Okies[13] and others to migrate west, where they had heard tales of sunshine, citrus groves, and an endless waterfront.

Everywhere, radical forces, including the Communist Party, organized millions of ordinary people to protest joblessness—to take back what was lost and prevent further losses. The leftist slogan "Black and White Unity" mobilized many to action, and Black and white comrades banded together to campaign across the United States for equal rights and an end to segregation and discrimination of all kinds. Even in the South, Communists, social-

12. Hoovervilles were shantytowns built by homeless people in and around American cities during the Great Depression. They were named after President Herbert Hoover, who was president at the onset of the Depression.

13. "Okie" is a disparaging term for poor white migrants who, in the 1930s, moved from the Oklahoma "dust bowl" to California's farmlands.

ists, and organizations like the Southern Negro Youth Congress organized sharecroppers, tenant farmers, and workers across the color line. Strikes, hunger marches, self-help efforts, Unemployed Councils meetings, street-corner speakers, organized defiance of dispossessions, political meetings, and open battles against the extreme intransigence and utter contempt and brutality of the authorities that shielded scabs and company thugs were daily happenings. The federal, state, and local governments' reactions via the FBI, military and defense intelligence agencies, and local police forces, especially their Red Squads, was amped up accordingly. Local vigilantes and ultra right-wing religious fundamentalists, often with the aid of the local press, were encouraged to thwart the organizing efforts of the millions of poor Black and white people. The celebrated frame-ups of radical labor leader Tom Mooney on the West Coast and the Scottsboro Nine and Angelo Herndon cases in the South were examples of all of this. These cases attracted tremendous attention and activity from all walks of society, from Hollywood stars to thousands of plain folk around the country, and also garnered international interest, primarily due to the involvement of the broad Left, the Communist Party, the International Labor Defense, and other activist groups. Langston and Matt, on the West Coast, were involved in the Scottsboro defense campaign, as were Louise and Pat in New York. Contentious political debates were happening everywhere, including in Harlem, where Black nationalists, NAACP members, socialists, Communists, liberals, artists and cultural workers, labor organizers, gangsters, bootleggers, and religious and social organization members abounded and so did their magazines.

American capitalism faced a serious challenge from the Democratic Party when the country resoundingly rejected Herbert Hoover in the presidential election of 1932. Franklin Delano Roosevelt triumphed on his promise of a "New Deal."[14] The mid-1930s saw a desperate nation dealing with continued social and political unrest. The rise of fascism abroad led to new political and cultural alliances at home. Popular Front organizations were formed to unite liberals and leftists to fight fascists and support labor and civil rights organizing. But the rise of religious fundamentalists, like Aimee McPherson, and aggressive internal surveillance by federal, state, and local governmental entities fanned the flames of anti-Communist hysteria and paranoia, which

14. The New Deal was a series of domestic programs President Franklin D. Roosevelt launched in response to the Great Depression after taking office in 1933. Some saw them as moves to save US capitalism, while other considered them to be merely an economic baby step.

would profoundly shape the sociopolitical climate of the country for decades to come.

In 1934 West Coast dockworkers went on strike, closing down all the ports on the Pacific Coast for eighty-three days. At one point there was a violent altercation between strikers and police, which left two workers dead. The wave of industrial unionism, sit-down strikes, and shop-floor resistance that was sweeping the nation gave rise to what would become the Congress of Industrial Organizations. In 1935 President Franklin D. Roosevelt established the Works Progress Administration (WPA),[15] which employed theater artists, writers, painters, sculptors, and photographers throughout the United States. Despite Langston's many financial challenges, he decided to live and write independently, without the help or possible hindrance of WPA rules and regulations.

The end of the 1930s saw a worldwide effort to stop the rise of fascism in Spain. The international community supported the young Spanish Republic[16] with concrete acts of solidarity—such as sending money, medical equipment, and relief supplies—in its fight against General Francisco Franco, who had military support from Germany and Italy. Louise and Langston went to Spain, Langston as a war correspondent for the *Baltimore Afro-American* newspaper and the Associated Negro Press news service, and Louise to promote US support for Loyalist civilian relief efforts. Matt, Pat, and Nebby were a part of the solidarity efforts at home. But ultimately, the effort was lost. Franco took power in Spain, and World War II led to the ebbing of the great militancy of the earlier part of the decade, as the war economy brought jobs with higher wages and unions agreed to no-strike pledges. Large numbers of women workers were employed in basic industry and factories. Yet the economic and political life for African Americans remained overwhelmingly

15. The Works Project Administration (WPA) was the largest and most ambitious New Deal program. It ran from 1935 to 1943 and provided jobs for millions of unemployed Americans—mostly men—during the Great Depression. It carried out public works projects, but it also employed musicians, artists, writers, actors, and directors.

16. In 1936 the Spanish Civil War broke out when the democratically elected Second Spanish Republic faced a coup d'état by a rebel group, called the Nationalists, inside the Spanish military. They were headed by generals Francisco Franco and Emilio Mola and aided by the rising fascist governments of Germany and Italy. The democratic government was defended by loyal Republicans, also called Loyalists, and an international brigade of mostly civilian volunteers from many countries, including the United States. The war lasted for four years, during which time other Western powers stood by and watched but did not intervene. Unfortunately, the Nationalists won, and General Franco ruled Spain as a ruthless dictator for thirty-five years, from 1939 to 1975. Had they been defeated, Europe might not have seen the rise of fascism that heralded World War II. Both Langston and Louise went to Spain while Franco was in power.

FIGURE 1. Pat (seated, second from left) and friends in Moscow, 1928.

hard and bleak. Jim Crow segregation, an entrenched way of life in most of America, was especially ugly in the South. But the social and civic life in most Black communities was still vibrant, and it was there that Black Communists generally found a base.

When the correspondence opens in October 1930:

Pat was in Moscow, having gone there in 1927 to study Marxism and Leninism at the University of the Toiling People of the East, although he was preparing his return to New York, where he would later head the Negro Commission of the Communist Party in Harlem. He was no longer the ambitious Harlem lawyer who during much of the 1920s was considered a member of the elite Black bourgeois that W. E. B. Du Bois referred to as the Talented Tenth.[17] By this point, Pat was an uncompromising revolutionary,

17. "The Talented Tenth" is a term used to describe a leadership class of African Americans in the early twentieth century. It originated in 1896 among Northern white liberals, specifically the American Baptist Home Mission Society and white philanthropists

who believed that socialism was the only road to freedom for black Americans.

Louise had just lost her job with her wealthy benefactor Mrs. Charlotte Osgood Mason. Simultaneously, Louise was reeling from the sting of insinuations leveled against her by Zora Neale Hurston about the play *Mule Bone,* which was coauthored by Hurston and Langston. A resilient Louise— putting "philanthropy" behind her—landed a job with the American Interracial Seminar,[18] a program of the Congregational Church. Her new position involved leading interracial citizen groups by train through the American South and to Mexico to promote better interracial and intercultural understanding. She was increasingly drawn to the socialist ideas of her radical friends in Harlem.

Langston had also suffered an anguishing break from Charlotte Osgood Mason, who had been his patron as well. As he recovered from the shock of the abrupt rupture, he was determined to make his living as a poet. Encouraged by Mrs. Mary McLeod Bethune, a board member of the American Interracial Seminar, and with funds from a Rosenwald Foundation grant, Langston toured the South, with Radcliffe Lucas as his driver and traveling companion.

Nebby was working as a clerk at the US Veterans Bureau regional office in San Francisco. Although she and Matt had gotten married in the fall of 1929, they were living apart for financial reasons—he at his parents' home in East Oakland and she at the nearby home of her adopted godparents, Mr. and Mrs. J. T. Allen. The following year the Crawfords moved into their own apartment on Acton Street in Berkeley, where Langston visited them in 1932. Nebby's social life at the time revolved around her sister and brother-in-law, Alma and Lloyd Powell, and their young daughters, Helene and Joy, who lived in San Jose, her aunts, uncle, and cousins on her father's side, living in San Francisco and San Mateo, and the larger Crawford clan in Oakland.

---

like John D. Rockefeller. It was picked up and publicized by W. E. B. Du Bois in an essay of the same name he published in 1903.

18. The American Interracial Seminars Project was a program founded by Hubert C. Herring in 1930 and sponsored by the Congregationalists to promote interracial and international understanding. National committee members included anthropologist Franz Boas; composer, writer, and diplomat James Weldon Johnson; theologian Reinhold Niebuhr; and educator and activist Mary McLeod Bethune. The Congregational Church is a branch of Protestant Christianity that allows each church and group within it to run its affairs independently.

Matt had opened a chiropractic practice—in partnership with two other Black chiropractors—on San Pablo Avenue, on the edge of downtown Oakland. However, he had kept his office job at the Board of Fire Underwriters, and so he was still commuting to work in San Francisco by ferry. Actively involved in the local chapter of the NAACP and the Acorn Club, a young men's fraternal group in Oakland, Matt had been committed to community service from an early age. He grew up in the historic Beth Eden Baptist Church in West Oakland, where his Alabama-born mother, Mrs. Emma Goodgame Crawford, was a prominent women's leader.

ONE

Thank You and God for
"The Weary Blues"

OCTOBER 1930–JANUARY 1932

Louise was in New York, and the letter she wrote to Langston, who was touring the South, on October 4, 1930, was largely her description of the ending of her relationship with her patron, Charlotte Osgood Mason, who had hired her a year earlier to serve as secretary to Langston and Zora Neale Hurston. Although both Langston and Hurston called Mason "Godmother," Louise insisted on using the more formal "Mrs. Mason."

Charlotte Mason, known for both her generosity and her tendency to patronize and manipulate beneficiaries of that generosity, had evidently decided that Louise was insufficiently appreciative of her patronage and summarily fired her. In an interview she gave years later for a documentary film on Langston,[1] Louise explained the contrast between her reaction and Langston's to losing the support of Charlotte Mason: "We . . . had the same patron, Mrs. Mason, and his reaction and my reaction were quite different. Langston was sick after that experience whereas I got mad."[2]

FROM LOUISE, OCTOBER 4, 1930

[Letterhead: The American Interracial Seminar]

October 4, 1930

My dear Langston:

I tried to get Zora [Neale Hurston] by telephone but the line is disconnected and I haven't had time to run by there to see if she is back. However,

---

1. The documentary film was *Langston Hughes: The Dream Keeper,* directed by St. Clair Bourne.

2. As quoted in St. Clair Bourne, "Louise Patterson on Langston Hughes," *Langston Hughes Review* (Winter 1997): 39–51.

31

this being Saturday and having the week end I shall try to get a lineup on her whereabouts.

Saw Mrs. Mason a week ago last Monday and it was short but excruciating. I said nothing and she said lots. I had failed utterly, all Negroes had failed utterly and she was through with us. It was all untrue and nothing I could say would make any difference. I offered to pay her for my desk and typewriter,[3] and she said that I didn't mean it. So I shut up and let her do all the talking, altho she would throw in such remarks as there was no use to argue and no need to implicate anyone. I didn't quite understand what she was talking about for I said nothing and called no names. But it is all a damn mess and I had quite a bad time. Miss [Cornelia] Chapin threw in her rather nasty amens to everything Mrs. Mason said. I must confess that I don't know what it is all about, and after a very unhappy evening thinking over the whole thing I have tried to forget it—that is the humiliation of it.

The job[4] is fine, but keeps me busy as hell. Don't you think you would like to come along on this trip of distinguished citizens.[5] I think that I shall get to go, but it depends on our budget. Pray for me as I would have a grand time getting down to all those places I have never been.

Mother[6] hasn't been so well. I am thinking of sending her to California if I can find the money somewhere. My cousin Mary [Savage] is here from Kentucky. She is a sweet kid and would make about two of me.

I am very much interested in your play[7] and hope that things materialize as you would like. Do come back, though, as we miss you lots.

Always,
Louise

3. The desk and typewriter were originally "gifts" to Louise from Mrs. Mason, who was initially generous and considerate to Louise because she knew that her mother was suffering from cancer. Years later Louise would describe Mrs. Mason as someone whose largesse came with heavy strings attached; gifts were never granted without some type of quid pro quo. Leaving Mason's employ was not easy, as it was the Depression. Louise needed the money to care for her sick mother, who was living with her and required constant care and large doses of medication to control her pain.

4. Louise had a new position at the American Interracial Seminars Project. Louise was hired to organize the trips, and she traveled to Mexico herself on at least one tour. There, she met Langston's father, James Hughes, and the three Patiño spinsters, with whom he lived.

5. The distinguished citizens included prominent figures such as Mary McLeod Bethune.

6. "Mother" is Lula Mae Brown Thompson, called "Mother Thompson" by Louise's friends. She worked as a domestic and a pastry cook her entire life. She had metastatic cancer, which she died of in 1933.

7. The play was *Mulatto: A Play of the Deep South,* which Langston wrote in 1930. It was his first full-length piece and was performed on Broadway in 1935.

[Marginal note above letterhead] *I'll see about the other things you mention over the week end.*

In October 1930 Louise was on the road in New England making public speeches about race relations on behalf of the American Interracial Seminar. In one of the speeches she gave before writing the following letter, she read from Langston's book of verse *The Weary Blues*.

FROM LOUISE, OCTOBER 24, 1930

[Letterhead: The American Interracial Seminar]

October 24, 1930

Lang dear:

I thank you and God for "The Weary Blues". What would poor speakers do when they have to talk on the RACE[8] if it wasn't for you? Since my return from Boston I am thoroughly convinced that you are not only the salvation of the race but of race speakers, too.

I had a grand time up in Boston and didn't get nervous a bit. Those people are so dead and drab and I had the time of my young life prancing up and down on the platform in front of them. I felt like a new-born babe alongside their deadness. Mr. [Hubert C.] Herring and reports from Boston say I did well—but I was satisfied anyway. My only grief is that in my last minute haste of making trains I left my copy of "The Weary Blues" on the ticket window—now what will I do?

I didn't know whether or not you would see the enclosed review from The New Freeman.[9] When are you coming home? I miss you a lot. Bruce [Nugent] gives me splendid reports of you down there. How about the play? I'll be glad to do all I can for you. What's the latest news of Zora [Neale Hurston]? No one in New York seems to have seen her.

Do hurry home—you have been away quite long enough.

Hasta luego,
Louise

---

8. "Talking on the race" refers to Black speakers addressing white audiences about Black people or matters concerning Black people. Louise had a long public-speaking career and was known to be an inspiring speaker.

9. *The New Freeman* was a short-lived magazine published by the libertarian feminist journalist Suzanne La Follette, a second cousin of US Senator Robert M. La Follette.

FIGURE 2. Louise speaking at a conference in New York, 1928. (Louise Thompson Patterson papers, Special Collections & Archives, Robert W. Woodruff Library, Emory University.)

On January 16, 1931, Louise wrote Nebby about her new life in New York. Nebby's Christmas present to Louise had been a pair of pajamas. In return Louise sent her friend an issue of the radical journal *New Masses*.[10] She had separated from her first husband, Harlem novelist and playwright Wallace Thurman, and was single in New York and deeply involved in Harlem's cultural and political life. Between the lines of news of family and friends, she confides that she is gradually finding a home in radical Left politics. She had joined the Friends of the Soviet Union[11] and wanted Nebby to keep up with left-wing thinking as well. Although Louise did not join the Communist Party until 1933, she was already studying Marxism and traveling in a new, interracial circle of leftist friends. She was also struggling with her own "bourgeois" tendencies and was convinced that true change could only take place through revolutionary measures. Although she mocked the social norms of the Black middle class, she acknowledged her own deep ties to highly educated Black professionals. She was on her way to becoming Red, describing herself as "Pink."

FROM LOUISE TO NEBBY, [JANUARY 16, 1931]

Nebby darling:

Your letter this morning brought home to me with a start how long it had been since I have written and that that letter bringing to you my happiness over the gorgeous pajamas you sent me [^ *hadn't been written*]. How are you going to turn me into a good proletariat when I get such a luxurious garment? On my side I salved my conscience by sending you The New Masses. Don't you love those things Langston is doing? I have hopes, high hopes, that he will become our real revolutionary artist. He is now in the South and I had an amusing letter from him telling of some of his experiences in Dixie.[12] I think that he is planning to come to Calif. in April, so you will have a chance to renew your acquaintanceship. Loren [Miller] is handling his

10. Louise probably sent Nebby the December 1930 issue of *New Masses* magazine. In a letter to the editor in that issue, Langston describes a recent message he sent to Russian readers on the publication of his novel *Not Without Laughter* in the Soviet Union: "Greetings to Soviet Workers." See *The Collected Works of Langston Hughes*, vol. 9, *Essays on Art, Race, Politics, and World Affairs*, ed. Christopher C. De Santis (Columbia: University of Missouri Press, 2002), 554.

11. The Friends of the Soviet Union was an organization established in the United States in 1921 to raise money for the new Soviet republic, which was battling a terrible famine as well as armed international intervention and internal armed resistance from Cossacks. The group also aimed to educate and inform people about the USSR.

12. Dixie is a colloquial name for the southern United States.

engagements. Did Matt's group[13] ever write him about coming to Oakland or Berkeley?

I share your sense of high speeding time. I don't know where the weeks go to—first it is Monday and then before I regain consciousness it is Saturday. And it is Saturday afternoon now. I came right home from work with the avowed intention of writing you first of all, and if I can hold out, dash off a few other notes. Mother and Sue [Bailey Thurman] are down town, so the house is quiet and I am taking advantage of it. It is hard to get time to one's self. In spite of good intentions you get caught with several engagements during the week, and when a free night comes I generally am glad to pile into bed early. And now that I am getting more and more drawn into revolutionary activities I find my weeks very crowded. I am trying to find a place for myself now, as long as I have to work with bourgeois forces, in which I can do something to help the worker's cause along. I have joined the Friends of the Soviet Union, which of course isn't a dangerous thing to do and yet, thru which I hope to interest others, first in Russia and then in the struggle in America. There are also some other plans afoot wherein I may be able to work sub rosa. I have to do it, Nebba. Having studied something of Marxian theory, and finding it a philosophy which I can accept, makes my position more contradictory and difficult. One gets impatient of halfway measures— the hypocrisy of social reform—the ever increasing misery of the mass of people. I can understand your disgust with the Hawaiian affair.[14] We have followed it closely here and have to acknowledge the spread of the old American custom. Even here the daily press has fallen into line and only such publications as The New Republic have recognized that a crime has been committed—and that that crime is MURDER, not rape. You might show the issue of January 20 to your fellow workers. Although I doubt that it will do any good. They have drunk too deeply of the poison of race chauvinism.

13. The group was the Acorn Club, a men's social club in Oakland that Matt belonged to.

14. The "Hawaiian affair" alludes to the infamous Massie criminal trials of 1931 in Honolulu, which were highly charged and infused with racism. In the first trial, Joe Kahahawai, a native Hawaiian man, was accused of raping Thalia Massie, the wife of a US naval officer. After a mistrial was declared, Kahahawai was kidnapped and shot to death at the behest of Massie's mother. She and her coconspirators were convicted of murder, but Lawrence M. Judd, who was the governor of Hawaii at the time, immediately commuted their sentences to only one hour, which they served in the custody of the sheriff.

And I agree with you about the new Alexander Dumas club.[15] I had read of it in the San Francisco SPOKESMAN.[16] It's just the same old philanthropy, and the same diverting of Negroes from the seat of their troubles. I have thrown the whole idea of "Negro art" over board, not that I think that art hasn't a place in life, but that this new fetish of "Negro art" is a lot of hooey. There ain't no sich.

I don't know why we all fell so hard for the thing. Of course I can understand some who have feathered their nests through it, but the rest of us just let ourselves be made asses of—that's all. Having suffered once under the cruel sting of white philanthropy, all I can say is "Never again!" It is so devitalizing—to bow down and worship before a god that is helping to keep us enslaved. And no matter how nice these people may be, it is always patronage, nothing more and nothing less.

It seems very strange to me sometimes, I find that many things I used to enjoy no longer appeal to me at all. I went to one dance during the holidays—a formal sorority affair—and found it particularly odious. The people looked so dull and stupid and artificial in their "dress-up" clothes— and the whole thing was unbearably dull to me. Seeking new revolutionary companions became a necessity, for aside from Marion [Smith] and Sue and a few others I found myself out of harmony with others. And I find these new friends particularly stimulating. They are studying all the time; they are aware of the world in which they live; and above all they have the guts to try to do something about it (which I cannot lay claim to as yet). And then I find the study of Marx, dialectic materialism and the like so fascinating. I know you have heard me rave before, but really this time, Nebby, I think it is real and I feel quite happy about it. I think that that is one of the things that drew me away from Joe[17] completely, and will make it impossible for me to be drawn to anyone except one who is traveling along the same path.

And the march of events is increasing its tempo so rapidly from day to day that I found myself wondering as the new year came in just what may

15. The Alexander Dumas Club was a "colored" social and cultural arts club in San Francisco that had close ties to prominent white socialites such as Noel Sullivan—who would later become a devoted patron and friend of Langston's. Louise was consciously trying to shed the pretentions of bourgeois society and her social ties to it—especially to Black bourgeois society.

16. The Spokesman (1931–1934) was a weekly African American newspaper founded in San Francisco by the radical Black journalist John Pittman. It was the primary source of local and national Black community news for residents of the San Francisco Bay Area and Northern California.

17. Joe was a young man Louise was dating.

happen before it runs its course. I know that my course won't be easy—I am saturated in bourgeois ideology and some of it is hard to get away from. I feel the necessity of maintaining a measure of economic security. But beside the march of world events my own seems very insignificant. With war a constant threat, with the poverty of the people on the constant increase, with the breakdown in our own government, municipal government particularly, a reality, and with revolution hovering in Germany, the Orient and elsewhere, one cannot possibly predict for the year. I don't imagine I will be going to Mexico this summer. First, the Committee[18] is particularly hard hit now—the Caribbean Seminar begins next Saturday with a fifth of last year's membership. The Mexican Seminar may share the same fate. Then with the new work I am doing I shall probably remain right here in New York. Aside from seeing you again, I would will it so, too, for I would not care to go to Mexico again with this good will crowd of Americans. In fact I think my days are numbered in this sort of thing but I don't see any other out as yet.

Sue came home full of plans for her coming nuptials and new life. She will marry probably the end of May at her conference in North Carolina. Howard [Thurman] is in California at this time and I told him to look you up, but I suspect he didn't find time to do it. He gave some lectures at the University of California as well as in other schools on the Coast. They plan to move to Washington during the summer, and he will be at Howard University beginning next fall. The engagement is no secret now, so you can tell anyone that Sue is going to marry Howard Thurman. Coincidence in name, isn't it?[19]

Marion is still in school and wondering what she will do for the next year. She is in somewhat the same position as I am—necessitating certain economic security. And as with me, she finds there is so little she can do to provide that economic security with which she is in sympathy. I don't believe she is as far gone in communism as I am, but she is extremely sympathetic and the result is the same. One of her friends who recently returned to New York said to me that she had heard that Marion was becoming more radical these days. I answered that I hoped so—what else was there for her to do. I wrote an article on race relations which has been accepted by <u>The Christian Century</u>[20] over the grave doubts of the editor

18. The "Committee" refers to the American Interracial Seminars Project.

19. Louise is referring to the fact that her ex-husband, Wallace Thurman, had the same last name as Sue's husband-to-be, Howard Thurman.

20. *The Christian Century* was a progressive Christian magazine affiliated with Louise's employer, the *American Interracial Seminar,* which was sponsored by the Congregational Church.

that this was the thing to do, although he agreed with what I said. It isn't radical, according to a real radical, but I suspect will rain down upon my head the invectives of many dear kind souls that are "giving their lives" for the good of the race. I'll send you a copy for criticism when it comes out. Mr. [Hubert C.] Herring is always after me to write—but it is so hard as you say to stay within the bounds of respectable circles, that often I prefer to keep still.

I shall watch for the Brothers Karamazov.[21] As I keep up so slightly with what is going on in the movie world I can't say whether it has been here or not. I do want to see Arrowsmith[22] as I have heard that it is very excellent. I saw The Five Year Plan[23] when it was here. The only play I have seen recently was "1931"[24]—a play on unemployment which was very good but lasted exactly nine days—it was too realistic for Broadway's taste. Right now Never No More[25] has claimed quite a bit of public applause—a story of a lynching with Rose McClendon. I was invited to go see it last week but refused as I felt that I just didn't want to sit through such a grueling ordeal. I want to see Mourning Becomes Electra and Of Thee I Sing[26] if I can ever find the money. I do wish it were going to be possible for us to be together this summer. I should like to go off to some isolated place for the summer with no diversions but sports and reading and studying. Sue is rooting for me to go to Russia in the fall, but it is scarcely a feasible idea. By no stretch of the imagination can I see how it could be done.

Mother will be writing you in her time—you know how she is about writing—but meanwhile she told me to thank you and Matt and convey her love to you for your constant thoughtfulness for her. We had a pleasant Christmas. Katherine [Jenkins], George [Sample], Marion and I gave Mother a radio for Christmas. We had a family dinner, Alta [Douglas] came over, and Mother seemed to enjoy herself very much. But as usual,

21. Louise is referring to *Der Mörder Dimitri Karamasoff*, a German film made in 1931.

22. *Arrowsmith* (1931) is an American film directed by John Ford. It was adapted from the novel of the same name by Sinclair Lewis.

23. *The Five Year Plan* (1931) is a Soviet documentary film that extols the virtues of a planned economy.

24. *1931* is a play by Claire and Paul Sifton. It tells the gritty tale of a young man in the Great Depression who loses his job and, along with millions of others, can't find another one. It was produced by the Theatre Group and featured Lee Strasberg, Clifford Odets, and Stella Adler, but it lasted only twelve performances.

25. *Never No More* is a tragic drama by James Knox Millen. It was produced on Broadway in January 1932.

26. *Mourning Becomes Electra,* a play written by Eugene O'Neill in 1931, is the retelling of an ancient Greek drama. *Of Thee I Sing,* by the Gershwin brothers, is a 1931 Broadway musical that parodies US presidential politics.

during these holidays, we wished for you. I have found the clippings you sent quite useful, as well as interesting. I don't always use everything I get in just for the News Service. I keep my material filed and classified and it is used as source material for articles and the like. Many thanks, dear, for doing this for me.

Well, if I am to write anyone else this afternoon I must stop. It is now nearly five o'clock and the folks will be home soon. I rather suspect they have gone to a show.

Love to you both—tell Matt I am so glad that things are getting better for him.

Always,
Your Squeeze

Langston wrote the following letter from his mother's home in Cleveland, where he had gone to recuperate. The whole conflict with Charlotte Mason had made Langston physically ill, and the continuing debacle with Zora Neale Hurston kept him ill. Louise had recently been in Cleveland on Interracial Seminar work and had seen Russell and Rowena Jelliffe, whom both she and Langston knew personally. Hurston was well known for her ability to be intentionally, flamboyantly, and unreasonably outrageous, as Langston's letter describes. In 1931 Langston copyrighted *Mule Bone*, under both of their names, but by 1934 he had signed over all of his rights to the play to Hurston.

TO LOUISE, [FEBRUARY 7, 1931]

Dear Lou,

As you probably know by now, Zora has been here. And how! There were two conferences, both with the Jelliffe's [Rowena Woodham and Russell W. Jelliffe], one on Monday, another on Tuesday. The Monday one was fairly agreeable, Zora and I went off alone in the front office, settled our private affairs (or so I thought) came out, and she admitted I had had a part in the play, that she would collaborate, and that she and I would both sign the contract for the production here (if the Gilpins[27] were going to do the comedy) as they had voted the night before Zora's

---

27. The Gilpin Players were a prominent Black amateur dramatic repertory troupe. They were the resident company at Karamu House in Cleveland, which was founded and run by the Jelliffes.

arrival to drop it as no one could get a sensible answer from her, or her new agent Elizabeth Marbury. However—overnight the change took place. In the early dawning Zora called up Mrs. Jelliffe and proceeded to attempt to bawl her out by phone for daring to put my name beside hers on the play, for taking your word for anything as you were this-that-and-the-other, etc. Mrs. Jelliffe said you were a friend of theirs that she wouldn't listen to any more over the phone, and that we could all meet again at five. I was in bed with tonsillitus, so every one came to my house. Zora brought a young man, Paul Banks, with her, one of the Gilpin Players who had been in New York and had made the trip back with her in her car. He, of course, was strongly on her side, and had previously written here that I had been stupidly untruthful since he knew I had had nothing to do with the play, and furthermore Zora said that my lawyer was so disillusioned with me that he wouldn't even represent me! . . . . . . Well, anyhow, this young man was with her, the Jelliffe's, my mother, and me. And such a scene you cannot possibly imagine. The young man, of course, said nothing. But Zora pushed her hat on the back of her head, bucked her eyes, ground her teeth, and proceeded to rear. She called Mrs. Jelliffe a dishonorable person, said she, Zora, had not come all the way to Cleveland to be made a fool of, implied that everybody was trying to pull sly tricks on her and she knew it, said who was you that anybody should take your word, (here again Mrs. Jelliffe said you were her friend). I said that you had nothing to do with the point under discussion anyway. Zora then shook [the] manuscript in my face and dared and defied me to put my finger on a line that was mine, and that what had been mine in there, she had changed in her new version, and furthermore, "the whole third act had been written by herself alone while you and I were off doing Spanish." Yes, I had helped some with the characterization—but what construction was there to it? And the story was hers, every line of dialog was hers except one line at the end of the first act, and she took that out. I was just trying to steal her work from her!!! And so on and on until Mr. Jelliffe asked his wife to no longer remain to be further insulted, whereupon they all left, Zora without even saying Goodbye to Mother or I. The whole scene on her part was most undignified and niggerish. Nobody else quarreled. And whenever she was asked to explain her wild statements she would say she hadn't come to be questioned or made a goat of . . . That was Tuesday . . . . I have not seen her since, but on Thursday who had the astounding nerve to attend a party given by the Omegas[28] for me, but to which I could not go on account of my throat. There Zora, I understand, told everyone that I was stealing her work, as well as saying some very

28. The Omegas are the members of Langston's fraternity, Omega Psi Phi.

unpleasant things about you. She has started a great swirl of malicious gossip here about all of us, the Jelliffes as well. The Gilpins have split up into groups some for the Jelliffes, some against, and the whole thing has developed into the most amazing mess I ever heard of. The Gilpins, of course, had to cancel their downtown date. Mrs. Jelliffe has been terribly upset about the matter, as she and I both had been as nice and as tactful as possible with both Zora and her agents, and with Zora herself when she arrived. Certainly none of us expected such a performance from the lady! It seems that now Zora chose to be not only contrary and untruthful, but malicious and hurtful as well. (I have received the most insulting note I have ever heard tell of from 399.[29] How she thinks of such ungodly things to say, I don't know.) . . . . Anyway, the Jelliffes feel that something should be done to stop Zora's irresponsible and malicious statements, even to the point of asking my lawyer to threaten a libel suit if she insists further on saying publicly that I have tried to steal her play. Personally, I think Zora must be a little off, as in all my letters to her, or talks here with her, I have been agreeable to further collaboration, and I have made no attempt, nor threatened to make one, to dispose of any part or parts of the play without her knowledge or consent. (She's the one. I kept quiet about it, now she's spreading the opposite tale.) So all that she is saying is crazy and without foundation in fact. She could not prove any of it—but how can people know that? So we all feel that you must be warned against her in New York. . . . . . . She contends that I wanted you to have a large interest in the profits of the play, therefore she withdrew. . . . Can you imagine it? . . . . . I think I had better tell every one of my friends in New York the story of the play now, because with both [Alain] Locke and Zora on the lying line, God knows what will get about. (I think I wrote you of Locke calling on [Arthur] Spingarn to back Zora up.) I wired him for an explanation and his answer was CONGRATULATIONS ON THE HARMON AWARD[30] BUT WHAT MORE DO YOU WANT? . . . . . . I think they all must be quite mad!

Anyhow, Louise, why Zora should be so ungodly sore at you for, is something I don't know. But you certainly have to know all this, at least in self-defense . . . Have you ever seen such amazing niggers or white folks either. I'm glad you have another job and that I have my new book well in

29. 399 Park Avenue in New York City was the address of Mrs. Mason.

30. The William E. Harmon Foundation Award for Distinguished Achievement among Negroes was a philanthropic and cultural award named after William E. Harmon, a real estate developer and philanthropist who was also an important patron of Harlem Renaissance artists. Langston won $400 and two medals, gold and bronze.

mind. They can all go to the nether regions as far as I am concerned . . . Best of luck to you, and love to Mother. I am going to write her . . . Take care of that cold you said you had, and find yourself a mule-bone because the free-for-all is on.

Sincerely,
Lang

By January 1932 Louise had become even "rosier" and was increasingly fascinated by her study of Marx and dialectical materialism. The following letter was written on a stationary notecard depicting a peaceful oriental garden. She references several current events in Japan, China, and Hawaii, and then goes on to talk about Langston's work and what was going on in New York. She had a lifelong passion for the theater and believed deeply in the power of dramatic art to deliver a social or political message. In this letter, she brings Langston up to date on the "Negro" plays that were recently in production on Broadway.

FROM LOUISE, [JANUARY 17, 1932]

[Handwritten]

Jan. 17

My darling Lang,

Greetings from the Orient![31] However, I must confess that the peaceful demeanor of this scene is a bit deceiving to say the least. And I may go further to say we are not really peaceful over here at all. In Honolulu[32] for instance, we are introducing a good old American custom and the back-fire still goes on. We tried to blow up our dear old emperor here in Japan[33]— but the old dear decided he would rather not die that way. We have done right well in Manchuria,[34] though, and are snuggled in all nice and comfy for the winter!

31. Louise is actually writing from New York.

32. She is referring to the Massie trials, which are described in note 14.

33. Emperor Hirohito of Japan narrowly escaped an assassination attempt by a Korean nationalist on January 9, 1932.

34. In September 1931 Japan used the pretext of a railway bombing to invade Manchuria. It set up a puppet government, which was denounced and refused recognition by the League of Nations. Japan was ordered out of Manchuria. Japan refused to withdraw its troops and resigned from the League. In January 1932 the United States refused to acknowledge the legitimacy of the new Manchurian government.

Your letter was happily received and contents digested. Knowing how busy you have been going from place to place, I realize you don't have much time to write, but I think you have done well by your family. Thanks so much Langston for "Dear Lovely Death".[35] It is handsomely done and means a great deal to me as I remember so well when some of the poems were written—back in the good old days (?) when we basked in sun light of white philanthropy.

My last point leads me to Zora's "Great Day"[36] performed last Sunday night. I enclose one review of it from today's Herald Trib.[37] Others I saw were quite commendatory. There was a note of acknowledgement to Mrs. R. O. Mason and an introduction by our mutual friend Dr. Locke.

"Never No More"[38] the new Millen play of a lynching with Rose McClendon starring has also been well received altho as something almost too realistic. There have been a number of other Negro plays of more or less mediocrity. "Sentinal"[39] in which Wayland Rudd was playing had a very short run.

I haven't seen any of them—haven't cared to. I am tired of the traditional Negro types in the theatre such as Sentinal or The [illegible] Honey of Comedy. The Never No More [I] am avoiding because of its defeatism. What's the use of seeing something that is going to sap one dry emotionally and show no [way] out. I think it is bad for Negroes for so many are involved with the idea of futility, impossibility of things being any better— the propaganda of submission like the weak and mild Gentle Jesus. But all Broadway wants from us is our primitive spontaneous nature expression or evidence of utter despair and emotional sublimation.

So I shall wait, Lang darling, until you write your revolutionary drama of the black masses, giving it all the rich coloring which our people have given to our common cultural life in this country. But leading the way to a new life, a new hope.

35. *Dear Lovely Death* is a small collection of Langston's poems, published by Troutbeck Press in New York in 1931.

36. *Great Day* is a theatrical musical written by Zora Neale Hurston. It was first performed on Broadway at the John Golden Theatre on January 10, 1932.

37. The *New York Herald Tribune* was a daily New York City newspaper.

38. *Never No More* was written by James Knox Millen and produced on Broadway in January 1932.

39. *Sentinels* is a Broadway drama written by Lula Vollmer, which had a short run in late December 1931 and early January 1932 featuring the African American actor Wayland Rudd. Rudd later became part of the group that Louise organized to travel to the USSR in 1932 to appear in the ill-fated film *Black and White*.

I am sorry you aren't coming back to NY soon, altho I think it will be swell for you to go to California. Gosh: I wish I could join you. Haven't forgotten about our plans and hope we can get together on them. I have just written an article on race relations which I want you to see as soon as it is published to see what you think of it. So let me know where to write to you after Jan. 18. I got the Contempo[40]—thanks a lot—and I distributed the extra ones around. I gave Henry [Moon][41] the devil about publishing your letter as Eddy's. I think he wrote you about it. Henry is a nice boy—but that's his trouble. He's too goddam nice!

Gee Lang, I am having a swell time. My pinkness is gaining a rosier hue from day to day—and maybe some day I will be a real red! I am beginning work with some of the organizations—ILD[42]—FSU[43]—sub-rosa of course, as I am not yet ready to give my all—that is, my bread and butter. But I feel so much better being a little bit useful. I am still going to school, too, and it's great stuff—Marxism dialectic materialism—and I feel as if I am learning something for the first time in my life. I wish you were [here] so we could be going together. But never mind—there's Russia beckoning to us!

Chapter II

Sue is home and has spoken of your expeditions together down thru the South. What a lot of fun you must have had. And then all of your experiences must be extremely valuable as well as entertaining. My good friend, Mary McLeod—how is she? And Mr. and Mrs. Sona? And our famous town of Scottsboro—did they meet you with the brass band. You know they even did that for the 9 boys—and they didn't call Christ a nigger. I think your experience at Chapel Hill was rare—and its repercussions more so.[44]

40. *Contempo* (1931–1934) was a radical magazine published in Chapel Hill, North Carolina. It was founded by Milton Abernathy and Anthony Buttitta, students at the University of North Carolina.

41. This is probably Henry Lee Moon, a writer and journalist at *New York Amsterdam News,* a weekly newspaper for the city's Black community.

42. The ILD (International Labor Defense) was a legal and civil rights organization founded in 1925 by the American section of the Communist International (Comintern). The ILD, under the national leadership of Pat, was instrumental in mobilizing national and international support in the Scottsboro case.

43. FSU (Friends of the Soviet Union) was founded in the United States in the 1920s as a relief organization to provide food, clothing, and material support for the Soviet people during a great famine. The FSU published the monthly magazine *Soviet Russia Today.* In 1927 the Comintern coordinated the activities of "friendship" societies in many countries, creating the International Association of Friends of the Soviet Union.

44. A famous incident occurred in November 1931, when Hughes was invited to speak on the campus of the all-white University of North Carolina, Chapel Hill. Prior to his visit, he was asked by the progressive editors of *Contempo* magazine to submit a poem for

There is a Scottsboro meeting today of the Nati'l Committee. Eric Waldrond is one of the speakers—to my great surprise I was going—but I don't feel a 100 per cent today. So in place of being in the meeting I am propped up in bed listening to the Philharmonic concert over the radio Mom got for X-mas and writing to you.

Well now—for any gossip I know little for I move about in gossip circles with greater rarity all the time. Alta [Douglas] is fine and planning on her trip to Paris this summer. Doug [Aaron Douglas] seems to be making it O.K. from those letters of his I have read. Poor Martelia [Mortelia Womack] wants to go along she says. Alta says it will be over her dead body. She is very fond (?) of her you know, and Doug—I am sure he would leave Paris if he heard Martelia was on her way there.

We now have a smaller family. Emily, Mildred and Helen[45] have moved into an apartment of their own. Was Doris [DuBissette] back here with us before you left? Katherine [Jenkins] and George [Sample] are still making it. Mother seems to be feeling better—she is under the care of a new doctor. She was very pleased with the box and its contents you sent her—"It's the [illegible]", says she.

Jesse Fauset's China Berry Tree[46] has blossomed with nice respectable people that [W. E. B.] DuBois loves to read about. Its write ups have been good although [Rudolph] Fisher in today's [New York Herald] Tribune Books takes columns to say nothing about it—maybe diplomacy. Henry Hansen praised it highly—but he has never shown any discrimination about things Negro any way. I shall never forget his review of Paul Robeson Negro.[47] Countee's book[48] comes out next month. I hear it is an amusing expose of Harlem's social and literary pretenders.

Our committee gave a dinner for Diego Rivera—I mean the Seminar in Mexico Committee. It was a terrible affair—stupid well fattened bourgeoisie. My dinner partner was an old man who insisted upon trying to pat me

---

publication. He chose "Christ in Alabama," an incendiary poem that echoes the plight of the nine Scottsboro Boys, who were imprisoned in Alabama at the time. There was a great uproar in Chapel Hill's white community. Langston escaped the wrath of the ensuing racist attacks and left to continue his tour through the South without speaking on campus.

45. Emily, Mildred, and Helen were friends of Louise's, who had boarded with her and Mother Thompson at their large Harlem apartment

46. *The Chinaberry Tree: A Novel of American Life* was the third novel of Jessie Fauset, published in 1931.

47. *Paul Robeson, Negro,* published in 1930, was a biography of Paul Robeson, written by his wife, Eslanda Goode Robeson.

48. The book is *One Way to Heaven,* a collection of poems by Countee Cullen, published in 1932.

on the knee. Jesus! Diego was more gross than ever in his dinner clothes—and his speech, trying to retain some proletarian phrases but set to the music of Hearts and Flowers. Did you hear about his debacle with the John Reed Club?[49] He was denounced openly.

I talked with Walt Carmen [Carmon] not so long ago and he said much about you, rejoicing in your new consciousness and expression of revolt. So I emphatically back up Loren [Miller]'s recommendation—keep up the good work. And when we are poor—we can eat beans together Lang—and have a swell time doing it, too. I don't know how much longer I shall hold out but certainly not so very long—I mean hold out in bourgeois circles. I should fairly love to kick over the traces right now.

I wrote Nebby you were probably coming to California. Did you ever hear from her husband Matt Crawford about an engagement?[50] He wrote me and I told him to write you in care of The Crisis. Noel Sullivan's address is 2323 Hyde St., San Francisco.

Let me know your plans and send me your itinerary. Mother sends her love. Everyone in the house sends greetings.

Best wishes for a continued successful tour—but don't stay away too long for I miss you.

Always your comrade,

Louise

49. The John Reed Club was a Marxist cultural organization named after the American Communist expatriate journalist John Reed. On New Year's Day, 1932, Rivera spoke before the club's New York chapter. He was subsequently denounced as a "renegade" and "counter-revolutionist" because he had painted murals for "imperialist" sponsors, such as the San Francisco Stock Exchange. The February 1932 issue of *New Masses* magazine carried a strong statement from the club, stating its regret at having invited Rivera to speak and its intention to return the $100 contribution he had made to the organization.

50. Louise is referring to Matt's interest in organizing a speaking date in Berkeley for Langston during the poet's planned tour of the Bay Area.

Moscow Bound in Black and White

MARCH 1932–FEBRUARY 1933

By spring of 1932 Louise was actively working with Communists and other leftists in Harlem. James W. Ford, the Communist Party's 1932 vice presidential candidate and the party's most prominent Black leader, had recognized Louise's talents as an organizer and recruited her to create a committee to support a film about Negro life in the United States that would be produced in Moscow. Its working title was *Black and White*.

Although Ford was the initial player promoting the idea of the film project, Louise was the catalytic force capable of organizing the project in the United States. In the months leading up to the spring of 1932, she had become convinced that the new Soviet Union had much to offer African Americans and others who were suffering the triple oppressions of racism, poverty, and economic exploitation. If she was somewhat idealistic about the promise of the new Russia, she had no illusions about the constant oppression of Blacks at home. She had become an ardent anti-capitalist and wholeheartedly believed in the power of a film depicting the lives of Black workers and their resistance to being continually treated as second-class citizens.

Louise's efforts were Herculean. She brought together a functioning interracial organizing committee of influential individuals charged with the task of turning the idea of the film into a reality. The Co-Operating Committee for Production of a Soviet Film on Negro Life was comprised of thirty-odd people and chaired by the socialist Jamaican journalist W. A. Domingo. Among the sponsors were Malcolm Crowley, the editor of *The New Republic* magazine; Rose McClendon, the famous actress and champion of Black arts; the novelist Waldo Frank; writer and labor historian Charles Rumford Walker; and educator Bessye Bearden, the mother of visual artist Romare Bearden. Officially, Louise served as corresponding secretary, but her role was far greater. Sometime in late March or early April 1932, both Langston and Loren Miller agreed to have their names added to the roster of the committee sponsors.

The challenge of recruiting the cast for the film rested largely on Louise's shoulders. Although most of the cast members were recruited from the East Coast, Louise also encouraged Langston, who was touring California and the Pacific Northwest, and Matt Crawford and Loren Miller, who both lived in California, to join the trip. Time was of the essence. In March 1932 Louise sent Langston an urgent telegram to his mother's home in Lawrence, Kansas, to ask him if he would join the project, and she immediately followed up with a letter explaining the plan. Hughes was about to embark on a spring speaking tour that would ultimately take him to the San Francisco Bay Area, where was he would be reunited with Nebby and meet her new husband, Matt Crawford, for the first time.

FROM LOUISE, MARCH 10, 1932

[Western Union telegram]

1932 MAR 10 AM 7 52

LANGSTON HUGHES =

813 LOUISIANA ST LAWRENCE KANS =

JAMES FORD HERE FROM MOSCOW AUTHORIZED SECURE NEGROS TO
MAKE RUSSIAN FILM ON NEGRO LIFE IN AMERICA NECESSARY RAISE
FUNDS HERE FOR FARES AS RUSSIA LACKS VALUTA[1] FOR SAME
SPONSORING COMMITTEE WITH CHARLES WALKER ROSE MCCLENDON
WALDO FRANK AND OTHERS BEING FORMED WILL YOU JOIN
COMMITTEE ALSO WILL YOU CONSIDER GOING WITH GROUP TO LEAVE
AROUND MAY FIRST WIRE COLLECT LETTER FOLLOWS =

LOUISE THOMPSON.

FROM LOUISE, MARCH 10, 1932

[Letterhead: 112 East 19th Street, New York City]

March 10, 1932

Lang dear:

I hope my telegram last night[2] did not shock you with its suddenness. In this brief note I shall try to tell you something more of the project. Also the enclosed clipping will give you some idea.

---

1. *Valuta* is the Russian word for foreign currency. The Russian ruble wasn't traded on the foreign exchange.
2. It appears that Louise drafted this telegram on the night of March 9, 1932, although it was time-stamped the next morning by Western Union.

[James W.] Ford has been authorized by Meschrabpom Film company[3] to secure these Negroes to come to the Soviet Union to make this film. It is to be called "Black and White" and the scenario is now in preparation, with Lovett Whiteman [Fort-Whiteman] as consultant to see that it is true to Negro life. At a conference held yesterday evening with Ford, Charles Rumford Walker, John Henry Hammond, Jr. and I, the question came up of some one going from here, a writer, and immediately your name was mentioned. Do you know Hammond? He is a young millionaire's son who has been won over from the NAACP it seems. Of course we had already talked of you and you were to be asked to cooperate with us any way. But it suddenly dawned upon me how really swell it would be for you to go along, as I know that you are interested in going over, and that this offers the opportunity, I have been hoping that you could shape up your plans in order to be free to go by May 1.

As I told you in the telegram the task of the committee here is to raise the funds to send the people over and back, between $2000 and $3000. The Meschrabpom Film lacks the valuta to send over for this purpose. But the players will be paid well in Russia (in roubles, of course) and will have the opportunity of travel and all the best of living facilities which the Soviet Union affords. There is a possibility of their remaining to make other films, etc., but this one will take five or six months to produce which will give them a nice little visit. Of course, for you I think there would be marvelous opportunities to write and it would be marvelous for them to have you. I am sure that the whole plan would gain a remarkable stimulus if it were known that you were to be a member of the group. Hammond also suggested Wm. Grant Still for music. His idea is that we should make it rather on the grand scale and that if we secure the right people to participate we may get substantial backing in this country. He is to see the Better Film Corporation about helping us.

I will be writing you more details of the plan from time to time so please let me have your schedule. Also have you any suggestions as to people whom we should ask for membership on the committee. The enclosed list gives the names that have been suggested so far. Also any people you think might be approached for financial aid.

I hope you consent to be a member of the committee—and most of all I do hope that you can find it possible to go. I got your valentine

3. The Meschrabpom Film Company was founded in Moscow in 1924. Its name is a contraction of the Russian name for the Workers International Relief organization. Meschrabpom's production facilities were in Moscow, but its headquarters were in Germany and its main staff was German.

and other greetings and am waiting for a letter telling me of your wanderings.

Regards to Raddy [Radcliffe Lucas].

Always your comrade,
Louise

Matt had written Langston in early March 1932 to inquire about hosting speaking engagements during Langston's time in the Bay Area. In his formally worded response, Langston addresses Matt as "Mr. Crawford," but, after meeting in early 1932, the two men would go on to have a close friendship that spanned thirty-five years.

TO MATT, [MARCH 19, 1932]

On Tour
Langston University
Langston, Oklahoma

Dear Mr. Crawford,

Thank you for your letter. I'd be happy to appear under the auspices you mention in Oakland or Berkeley. My California itinerary, however, is being arranged by Mr. Loren Miller, 847 Central Avenue, Los Angeles; so I would suggest that you get in touch with him at once...... I shall be in California in April. I hope we shall meet. Tell Nebby I'm anxious to see her.

Sincerely,
Langston Hughes

FROM LOREN MILLER, [APRIL 1932]

[Letterhead: 837 East 24th St., Los Angeles, Calif.]

Louise Thompson,
Langston Hughes,
435 Convent Ave.
New York City.

Dear Sir and Madam:

Your separate and individual letters have reached me at various times with[in] the past few weeks. I had an idea that I would write to each of you but seeing as how both of you will be at the same place at the same time and seeing further as how there is a scarcity of good cash in these parts at this particular time, I have decided to answer you both at once. What is unintelligible to one of you will probably be clear to the other of you and if some parts of the thing are Greek to both of you, never mind, it probably wasn't important anyhow. And don't you love this green paper? I use it to throw the Bitter Amerika Fakeration off the track. Who would ever guess that a Red would use anything but red or pink paper with red ink?— Clever, these newspaper men.

Add to the list of Great Americans: Langston Hughes. His play, Scottsboro Limited, was forbidden by the police here last Friday when the John Reed club attempted to give it as a part of the Paris Commune celebration. Great guys, these police of sunny California. Not long since they put the lid on a play called Lysistrata written by a guy named Aristophanes. When they raided the ritzy joint where the thing was staged one of the coppers says to another, sez he, "Let's arrest the guy who wrote this thing. Where is this gink, Aristopahnes?" But anyhow, we (meaning the John Reed) got the bright idea that we would produce this Scottsboro Limited thing. So we planked down our dough (don't mention it) for the hall. At the appointed time and place we started gathering ourselves together when up the steps the Red Squad and lets us know that the thing was off. Me, I was standing on the street corner trying to look like any other up and coming Babbit in burnt cork when one of the Protectors of Womanhood steps up to me and tells me to beat it. After the exchange of a number of uncomplimentary remarks on our various mugs me and the cop parted, decidedly unfriendly. But meanwhile one of the very bright young revolutionaries had written out the program on which a Communist speaker was scheduled to speak for the C.P. and me for the ILD. So the police grabbed him and confiscated him, program and all. That started a healthy rumor that they were seeking me to decorate the inside of the jail. After an exciting half hour or so of dodging around I went home to bed and nothing happened. Imagine my disgust. Just after I had conjured up pictures of the workers of the world demonstrating in Moscow, Hankow, Topeka, New York, and Birmingham parading with demands that Loren Miller be released. And me a guy who would give anything for a little publicity too. Anyhow what I started out to say was that Art got a boot in the rear again. Which is nothing when you stop to think that Lewis Browne was barred from our best Liberal Forum when he wanted to gab away about books by Emma Goldman. Incidentally, this same Liberal Forum was the place where you were going to speak. They would accept that April 18 date for you but they don't know whether or not they can get the hall after the row. You,

Langston, try to get out here as soon after the 15th as you can. Let me know what the date is and everything will be fixed up so you can blab away soon after arriving. We will have enough to pay for the gas and oil at any rate and probably more. Don't worry about me getting any commission. Glad to help you in any way I can and will take my pay out in making you listen to some rabid and reddical essays on the alleged art of Harlem, and on a multiplicity of other subjects too incendiary to mention.

Returning to you, Louise, for the moment. Guess you got my telegram saying to use my very valuable name. Am anxiously awaiting word from you as to what I can or can not do in relation to helping raise the dough. As you may or may not know, I have no money with which to go to the USSR but would be more than glad to go if I did have it. Do you suppose I could be the villain in the play. I wear a mustache, which is an invaluable part of every rascal's equipment and I can utter blood curdling oaths when the lines require. At any rate, I begin to have a hunch that I am washed up as far as this part of the nation goes and that I must make a change. You know how it is, I never like to stay in one place too long and two years and a half is too long for this Garden Spot of the World. You may tell the committee that I am willing to aid, assist, and abet the thing in any manner I can even to the point of quitting this land of prosperity to go to poor benighted Russia.

Although I do not drive a car well enough to mention, I will probably accompany Langston to Seattle and other points north of here. I need a vacation from this business of chronicling murder, rapes, and social teas anyhow. I already foresee that I am destined to be a very popular person in the next few months. Word is abroad that I know Langston and am in fact bringing him here and I notice an uncalled for note of cordiality in the voices, manners and activities of the fat headed—and fat bellied—petty bourgeois wimmen who lead the social set. For gawd's sake, Langston, require that each invitation to you be accompanied with an iron clad guarantee that dinner will be served and that ice cream and cake WILL NOT be served for desert because I don't like ice cream.

I do not know what arrangements you are making to stay when you arrive Langston. Would you like to bunk with a very intelligent chap, a common guy incidentally who is my idea of what the worker should be. Has read everything from poetry to anthropology and has a nice apartment where there is no phone and no women and which is used only by disgruntled gazaboos who gather there to cuss out Hoover and his aides. Or can find you some more ritzy place if you like. Don't know about some nice quiet place this summer but we should be able to find it. Arna knows something about the lay out. As for typists, that is easy. I suggest a nice ugly gal with no social ambitions and cheap (Oh, oh, doesn't that sound like a Communist).

I wish to warn you Langston that the loose talk floating around Topeka and Lawrence that I am either brilliant or radical (and I hate the word, too) is just the old home town baloney. I got the reputation for being brilliant because I could learn the patent idiocies of the text books in slightly less time than could the poor saps who believed it and hence were under some obligations to regard it and themselves seriously. As for the radical part, I earned that title by asserting back in 1926 and 1927 (you remember those hectic, stock market days) that capitalism was bound to end in a crisis, a theory that I copied bodily from the Communist International of 1926. Such literature was of course unknown to the rest of them and they still labor under the delusion that I figured it out by myself. But I made myself eternally famous and radical in those golden, by-gone days by perorating (after a certain number of drinks of corn likker) that the Harlem literary output and especially Nigger Heaven was tripe, trash and 100 per cent nogood. You remember Louise that the village was drinking in all the transparent literary hooey of sophistication then and they marveled that anybody could dare to dispute such estimable journals as Fire or such Outstanding Authorities as Haywood Broun.

There are a number of matters that should be taken up by our united minds but Louise, you tell Langston just what you think about anything, if any, and he will retail it to me. In turn I will get my soap box and red flag and deliver my shoutings to him and he can relay it to you when he sees you or better still, we will issue a joint statement setting out your errors and our own correct analysis of the situation. Gosh, wish that you could be here because this ought to be good.

I notice by the Amsterdam News that you are F.S.Uing around and that you held a tea not long since. I am active enough in the ILD and going great guns with the John Reed club where I am [a] functionary of some sort or other. The John Reed idea is quite a thing for this neck of the woods and is popular, too popular for any good but as soon as the cops raid the joint and clean up a little the hangers on will be eliminated and we can get in some good licks. Scott Nearing sent me his book which is only fair. Its craftsmanship is not of the best and the latter part does not do a good job of exposing race prejudice as an adjunct of class exploitation. Nor is the Negro petty bourgeois element adequately treated. Now, said Mr. Miller warming to his subject, can a book of this kind be called adequate which does not enter more thoroughly into the relationship between the white and colored workers in the revolutionary movement. The use of Negro dialect by class conscious or semi-educated Negroes is a mere concession to bourgeois prejudice, altogether unwarranted in view of the facts as I know them and the latter statement may not be so learned as it sounds.

Well, I started this thing yesterday and here it is late today and the thing still undone to say nothing of me having changed typewriters in the interim. In the same interim, I thought of a hell of a lot of bright things to say but I have forgotten them now. Oh yes, am lining up the churches at 60 per cent of the gross, that is to say I am getting organizations to sponsor you at churches which are the largest meeting places. Something tells me they are going to be profitable at that. While I am about it, the John Reed club asked me to ask you how about fetching us up a lecture apart from the regulation stuff at which we will charge admission and try to wheedle your commission down to the lowest possible point so we can make more dough and thus lift the burden off our working class pocket books. We could book it toward the last so that it would not interfere with your lucrative engagements at all. Don't make any concessions on my account. Just say what you really think about the matter and ask your little tin gods to guide you.

Write me your addresses and I will let you know early next week the exact date when you will appear. Will I never get through with this visit of yours? One more word and I will close. Norman McCleod and I are planning to go down to Las Vegas, the site of the Hoover Dam, and investigate the situation with a view to depicting conditions first hand for the radical press, and such others as will accept it. Would you like to go with us? Or will you have the time? If you would like to run down to the hell-hole we will wait for you. Otherwise we will probably go before you get here. I hear that it is a sink hole and I know that Negroes down there are barred from working on Herbie [Herbert Hoover]'s latest achievement. It should provide us with some good material.

Truth to tell, a cursory examination of Wallace [Thurman]'s Infants[4] left me unenthusiastic. Probably a good picture of those hectic days, if you say so, but tremendously unimportant. And have you sampled that insipid rot by Jessie Fauset, Chinaberry Tree? Somebody ought to tell her that her Negroes are about the most flaccid creatures that ever strutted through the printed pages. I shudder to think of them and their manners and politenesses. Did she ever see a nigger in overalls or does she really imagine the stuffed shirts she depicts are What We Ought To Be? Although I was convinced years ago that Countee Cullen had exhausted the subject of love—the only one that exists in his world—I am willing to let him return to it after reading One Way To Heaven. Which may be unkind. And has anybody seen Claude McKay's latest book? I haven't.

4. Wallace Thurman's 1932 satire, *Infants of the Spring*.

Incidentally, are you as appalled by the current scene as I am? I believe that I can appreciate how the souls in Purgatory must feel as they await word from the gods as to their ultimate destination. They know that a few words from the living will waft them to heaven but they must wait while the worldly decide and absence of just the few words will plunge them into hell. I have an idea that some up and coming Negro novelist ought to write a novel and call it Children of Chaos. We are the children. Here we are, brought up in a nice, safe bourgeois world, prepared for it. Just when we come of age the whole goddamned thing crumbles down on our heads. We have acquired a technique and all the encrusted prejudices that would have made us acceptable to that world. But we have had the light thrust into our eyes. We see what a rotten, rummy thing it is, that old order. So we turn to the new and revolutionary ideas. But we find ourselves unfitted in a dozen ways to this new thing. We would turn back to the safety of the old order if we could but we can't. There is no place for us there. The collapse of the old order is complete. On one hand is the confusion of birth, on the other hand the chaos of death. Children of Chaos, we face to the new but we are tied to the old. Take our racialism. We came to realization just when Racialism was at its height. Langston Hughes was the poet of the New Negro. Louise Thompson was one of them, Loren Miller was another. But racialism was a house-built-upon-the-sand, the shifting sands of capitalism, already poising for its swift plunge into chaos. If we saw beyond this temporary hysteria of Race it made little difference. We could not escape it. They bellowed it at us, pounded it into us, interwove our subconscious minds with it. It was warp and woof of our philosophy. Now we must un-learn it all. And what a job! Maybe you did, I know I regarded it cynically all the time but I have learned now that all of the ties that I had formed are bound to that old order. My friends, my associates, my career are tied to it. (Oh yeah, I hear you, what career?) My friends still strive to remain in the rotting shell of the old Racialism. But it avails them nothing. The black worker is learning fast that the paths of capitalism, whether it is black or white, lead but to starvation. But my friends can see no way out for the only working class paths they can tread lead to revolution. Starvation or Revolution—strong words! No wonder these friends of mine, softened by the petty bourgeois life they have led, softened mentally, morally, physically, shudder and try frantically to preserve something that is beyond their power. After all, they are not yet starving themselves and they have no stomach for revolution so they try to stay put. But they too are children of chaos since the decadence of the old is beyond their power to stop. Perhaps the only difference between them and me is the fact that I can see the storm rising and they have pulled the shutters and shades down and remain in the dark.

Not a good way to talk, certainly. I, we should have more courage, lash out more vigorously. But what the hell? Damn it all, I can't seem to break away and I don't want to remain. Even my pen, never very fluent is running dry, it balks at the necessity of writing the acceptable and it doesn't know the new ideology. There are countless others like that. The teachers, the lawyers, the doctors, condemned to wangle for a system that gnaws at them, wanting to turn away. Yep, children of chaos. No less than the black worker, who can't quite make up his mind to spit on the pretty baubles he was promised—and never got—and strike out for himself.

The question is how to resolve this muddled color ideology into a new working class ideology. How shall the new literature be written? How shall the worker be orientated? How best to face the situation. That however is the problem that my novelist will solve in his Children of Chaos for I insist that the novel shall strike a courageous note.

Willie, Damn-Them-Reds, Pickens will be here soon and forage around among us for a while. I don't know how he is going to meet the situation. Most of the old liberals on whom he used to depend to aid him are quite hot in the collar over his red baiting activities and tell me he can go to hell for all they care. Maybe the Red Squad will sponsor him in a series of anti-communist gabble fests. T. Arnold, he of the soft words and few brains, Hill has just left us. The man's monumental ignorance floored me completely. I had never met him before and thought he might privately know something but what a lemon he turned out to be. The star spangled jackass had the effrontery to tell the workers that they could help themselves by being more efficient and more appreciative of their jobs! Fawnsy that, now.

This letter must be finished some time, so here goes. This is the end. Hope that the Easter Rabbits bring you all of the things you would like them to bring, including a new 1932 model of The Revolution!

lorenmiller

P.S. Better come along Louise and let's get this thing settled once and for all time. And let me know Langston what I can do to arrange for your coming.

.,;:? I -.?:;—.?, (distribute ounctuation [punctuation] marks where needed)

FROM LOUISE TO LOREN MILLER, APRIL 12, 1932

[Letterhead: Co-Operating Committee for Production of a Soviet Film on Negro Life]

April 12, 1932

My dear Loren:

Langston will probably be with you by the time this note reaches you, so I will follow your example and double up on this letter. I have postponed writing until I could have something rather definite to tell you and Langston. And the Committee has been going through a series of ups and downs, until I got rather dizzy trying to keep up with it. We have gathered in no funds to speak of and in talking with [James W.] Ford yesterday he told me that he thought our major efforts should be on getting people who could pay their own way, or who could raise it.

Accordingly, he told me to write you to ask if you were seriously [^considering] going, and whether or not you might be able to raise the fare out there. If you would seriously consider it I thought you might drive back here with Langston ~~and at least save the expense of transcontinental fare.~~

Langston spoke of giving a benefit performance out there for the Committee. I presume he will take it up with you. Tell him, that counting him, there are four who will go so far, paying their own passage. You would make five. I wish you could go and would go, Max [Loren Miller].⁵ [^*got no dough*] I think it would be the best thing in the world for you to do now. I haven't time now to comment on your last epistle for it is late and I am so tired (I have been writing letters for the damn Committee all night) I scarcely know what I am writing. But I think that you need a clean break from the web of thoughts and life you now chafe under. You're still a damn bourgeois Max if you don't mind my saying it, and even if you do, and I here and now give you the opportunity of returning the compliment.

To come back to business. Please let us know what you think you can do about raising any money—any way you can. Are there some people to whom you would like to have the Committee send letters? Can you stage any benefits? If you thought of doing anything up North I know that Nebby and Dot [Dorothy Fisher-Spencer] would help out.

Do you know anything about the National Students Federation⁶ on the [West] Coast—or is it there? Are there any students whose names you could

---

5. Louise sometimes called Loren Miller by his nickname, "Max."

6. The National Student Federation of America (1925–1942) was a membership association of university student governments, created to represent issues of concern to American university students, including fostering understanding among students of the world to further world peace.

send me as possible contacts. [^<illegible> *no names yet.*] Since the Ky. trip the federation is getting away to a fast start around here. Also, how is Scottsboro going on the Coast? Is there much response—or any from the Negroes?

There is a bare possibility that some arrangement can be made with one of the steamship companies that does business with Amtorg[7] to take the people over for a little or nothing. But it is still a bare possibility and Ford scarcely thinks [it] will materialize. I will let you [^*know*] immediately, however, if it goes through. As then all our troubles would be over.

Write me promptly, will you please? And I will keep you and Langston informed as things develop. I know that it seems that we have laid down on the job, but if you knew the number [^*of people*] I have seen and the many tedious meetings we have sat through.

Gee, I wish I could drop in on you and Langston as I know that you will have a grand time driving up and down the Coast, running from Red Squads and Capt. [William F.] Hyneses, as well [as] high society teas and dinners (the latter I don't envy you). But being a wage slave I must stay by the job. Even if you don't go to Russia, why don't you pull up stakes and drive back with Langston any how?

Meanwhile, don't forget to write—remember the future of the race may be at stake.

Always,
Louise

P.S. I forgot to mention that I was relieved to find that you are still one of us.

FROM LOUISE, APRIL 24, 1932

[Letterhead: Committee for Production of a Soviet Film]

April 24, 1932

My dear Lang:

I am awaiting eagerly news of your various escapades in the land of sunshine, frameups and red terrorism. I look forward any day to seeing notice in the paper that Capt. Hynes and his brave boys have yanked you off the platform in the midst of a tirade on Scottsboro or Tom Mooney. Or are you doing the straight society act? Hope not.

But the purpose of this letter is to let you know how the Cooperating Committee is or is not cooperating. We have about given up the idea of raising

---

7. Amtorg was a Soviet government agency headquartered in New York City that dealt with trade and business transactions. The name is a contraction of Amerikanskaia Torgovlia (the American Trading Corporation).

any money to pay the passage of people who may wish to go but have not the wherewithal and are concentrating on those who want to go and can pay their own way. There are several interested in this way and Ford says that he will send along the number that can go and let them recruit others in Europe.

So he asked me to write you about your going. Will you go in case there are only a few and when will you be ready to go? The same conditions hold, of course, and your own plans can be worked out as you have planned them. Also, have you run across any one who wants to go and will pay his, or her, own way? What about Loren?

Write me as soon as you can, please, and let me know [y]our plans. I do wish that I was out there with you now. I had a letter from Nebby yesterday and she told me that they were looking forward to seeing you up north.

Remember me to all—friend or foe.

Always your pal,
Lou—ise

FROM LOUISE, MAY 9, 1932

[Western Union telegram]

1932 MAY 9 PM 10 33
LANGSTON HUGHES =
837 EAST 24 ST LOSA =

GUARANTEED EXPENSES AND SALARY ASSURED YOU AND LOREN IN RUSSIA ADVISABLE COME SOON AS POSSIBLE CONFIRM AND GIVE NEAREST DATE YOUR ARRIVAL NEWYORK STOP CARMAN AND FORD BEEN AWAY TRY SEND CABLE RE NOVEL TOMORROW STOP SCOTTS-BORO MEETING SUNDAY MCCLENDON OTHERS PARTICIPATING I AM SPEAKING WILL YOU SEND STATEMENT RE SCOTTSBORO=

LOUISE ..

FROM LOUISE, MAY 10, [1932]

[Letterhead: 112 East 19th Street, New York City]

May 10—Tuesday

Lang darling!

I sent the wire off to you today and hope that it will be intelligible. I am sorry that I had to wait, but Ford was away and did not return until Sunday night and I did not get to see him until yesterday. He was delighted to know that you and Loren would go. We heard from Moscow and they told us to send on those we had and then later to try to send others to include 15. So far I think that there are about 10 who will go. The first thing Ford told me to tell you was about your passport. He thought it advisable that you have it sent to New York to avoid any delay in its reaching you, thereby possibly holding up your departure from Calif. With all the delays of going from California to Washington, and the possibility of your having to get a birth certificate, etc., he thought it might take several weeks, especially if you had it sent there. So you could advise Washington to send it here to their office.

Next, he wished you to confirm your going and would like to know when you will reach New York and when you will be ready to sail. By the way, I think that you can figure on not spending more than $136 for round trip and possibly less. The Europa and Bremen third class are $136, and Ford says there is a possibility that even better rates may be obtained.

About my going. Gosh, Lang, you know I would love to, but I just don't see it. I had about made up [my] mind that such good fortune couldn't possibly come my way, but when I got your wire it made me want to go and how! You see, it is possible that I might be able to raise my fare, but how in the hell could things run here while I am away. But I am going to talk it over with a few people and if there is the slightest possibility, you know I will be along. What a grand time it would be. Maybe, you will meet some kindhearted philanthropist who will wish to help a poor girl attain her life's ambition.

Next, about the book,[8] I called the New Masses immediately and Frances Strauss told me that Walt Carman [Carmon] would not be in town until this week. I have tried to get him today, but I have not yet been able to reach him. I left a call. She said that he was the one that had handled the matter and would know most about how to find out about it. Ford's only suggestion was to cable Lovett Whiteman [Fort-Whiteman] who is in Moscow and could find out. But when I told him that Walt Carmen had sent it over he was inclined to wait until we could get in touch with him.

Again, about your hair tonic. Please forgive me and I will try to get it today and send it on to you. Thanks for thinking of all your little minor expenses—only you didn't enclose the check. However, my dear comrade, this has not kept me from getting that necessary to your sartorial splendor—lack of time and forgetfulness are my only alibis.

8. The book Langston refers to is *Not Without Laughter,* his first novel, which he wrote in 1930. It was translated and published in the Soviet Union in 1932, while he was living there.

Wish I could join you in San Francisco. However, I shall be eagerly looking for your return. I am tickled purple that you and Loren are going and that you have hit it off so well together.

Love to you,
Lou—ise

[Note in top margin] *About the Scottsboro meeting. The enclosed announcement will explain it. The National Committee thought it would be a swell idea if you would write a statement to be read there. Hence the request in the telegram. I'm rather scared over making my debut as a revolutionary speaker!*

FROM LOUISE, MAY 16, [1932]

May 16

Lang dear:

Your letter came this morning and I am writing you immediately to say THAT I THINK I CAN GO TO RUSSIA WITH YOU!?! I am so excited I don't know what to do and forgive me if I write very incoherently.

I have been thinking and trying to figure out some way of making the trip ever since I last wrote you and the more I thought about it, the more I wanted to go. Then too, everyone thinks that I should go. So first of all, Marion [Smith] said that she thought she could lend part of what I need. Then Mr. Herring came back to the office today and I told him about it all. He thought it just the thing for me to do and assured me of my extra month's vacation pay—so that brings it even closer. So close in fact that I am going to gamble and say that I am going!

The next thing—I think that it would be splendid if you could get here in time to sail on either the Bremen or the Europa on June 30. Alta [Douglas] is sailing then and it would be swell if we could all go together. I can't give you any details today, but I will write either tomorrow or the next day and tell you just how we should go, the exact fare, visas, etc. In case we sail on June 30 could you send money for deposits on your passage, or would you like me to go ahead and do it? It seems to me that it should be done before you get here since it will be so late in the month. But I will have more advice to give on this matter the next letter.

I am planning to send Mother to California for the year! And that thrills me as well. I will have but my bare fare for myself, but I don't care and I am sure that we won't have to worry after landing in Russia. The plans for the movie seem to be all right, the only thing the lateness of our departure. But I will try to see Ford tonight and get him to cable Moscow exactly when we will be coming. The others may go on ahead.

Lang, the meeting was a great success last night and your Comrade got through without any knee trembling.[9] In fact it was a lot of fun talking to such a large group and I wound up most dramatically by reading your telegram which everyone thought was swell. They had a marvelous program of entertainment and there were about one thousand out, we hoped for more, but this being the first large meeting in Harlem—you know how colored are. But a lot of "the" people were there. I saw Countee [Cullen] and Harold [Jackman], Alta and lots of others that I don't think had ever been to a red meeting before. Rose McClendon has been swell and has done all she can to make everything go over big.

I don't think you need to worry about how we will make it in Moscow. I talked with Walt Carman [Carmon] again and he told me that he was going over the correspondence and would try to find out, but that he thought that you wouldn't have to worry about anything. He thinks it swell that you are going and says you will receive a royal welcome. And that the John Reed Club in New York will have to throw a big party for you before we depart. (Notice how I use that "we", won't you—it makes my head swim at the thought of it—that I am going). But why don't you try to get some of Mr. Sullivan's millions—what are millions for if they aren't to help poor strugglers like us?

Love to you,
Lou—ise

[Note in top margin] *Your Waldorf Astoria goes off tonight [10]—I have been rushing about so, Lang, that you will have to forgive me for not sending it before. Thanks for the check—but why so much? Is Loren with you in San Francisco—tell him that I am very glad that he is going, too, and that if we starve we will all starve together. And by the way my boss assured me a job if I care to return in January. Maybe I will and maybe [I] won't. Whoopee!*

FROM LOUISE, MAY 23, 1932

LANGSTON HUGHES. CARE SULLIVAN=
2323 HYDE ST=

MOSCOW WIRES ALL PLAYERS MUST ARRIVE MOSCOW BY JULY FIRST
VERY NECESSARY YOU AND LOREN ARRIVE NEWYORK READY TO SAIL

9. By "your Comrade" Louise is referring to herself. She is recounting the speech she gave at a meeting in NYC the night before in support of the Scottsboro Boys defense campaign.

10. Louise had been assisting Langston with his typing and correspondence. Here she is referring to mailing him the typed manuscript of his long anticapitalist parody poem, *Advertisement for the Waldorf-Astoria*.

BY JUNE FIFTEENTH ADVISE CANCELLING ANY ENGAGEMENTS
NECESSARY EVEN IF MEANS LESS MONEY OR BORROWING MEANS LESS
EXPENSE OTHER END IF YOU COULD GO AT ALL PLEASE DO THIS HAVE
GOOD GROUP CONSULT MATT WIRE IMMEDIATELY GIVE MAIL
ADDRESS=

LOUISE..

In order to make the trip to Moscow, Langston needed to cancel some of his long-planned speaking engagements in the Midwest. Matt was unsure if he would be able to leave his job at the San Francisco Board of Fire Underwriters, and for a time it was unclear as to whether Loren Miller would join the group. But in the end Langston, Matt, and Loren set out by car from Los Angeles to make the cross-country trip to New York. The entire enterprise was a mad, last-minute scramble to obtain passports, scrape together fare for the trans-Atlantic passage, and reach their destination in time to board the SS *Europa* on the night of June 14, 1932. In anticipation of this adventure, Langston wrote to Matt from Eureka, California, about the possibility of leaving the state together.

TO MATT, MAY 24, 1932

Eureka, Cal.

May 24, 1932

Dear Matt—

Here is a copy of a wire from Louise:

Moscow wires all players must arrive Moscow by July first very necessary you and Loren arrive new york ready to sail by June 15th advise (personal)...... if you could go at all please do this have good group consult Matt wire immediately==============Louise

So which means I'd have to leave L.A. about June 5th. If you went, would you want to go with us via the Ford? Could you leave at that time? We'd have to express most of our baggage, I guess. If you're going, you'd have to get [a] passport at once. Louise says you could have it sent to New York. Air-mail Louise your decision. I'll phone you on Monday coming in S.F.

Langston

FROM LOUISE TO MATT, [MAY 25, 1932]

MATTHEW CRAWFORD

1940 ACTON ST BERKELEY CALIF =

DID LANGSTON COMMUNICATE WITH YOU NECESSITY SAILING JUNE
FIFTEENTH ABOUT ONE HUNDRED WILL COVER PASSAGE ONE WAY
RETURN ASSURED IF YOU ARE SHORT HOPE YOU WILL COME WIRE
IMMEDIATELY NECESSARY MAKE STEAMSHIP RESERVATIONS ALSO
SEND PASSPORT SOON AS POSSIBLE FOR VISAS ARE YOU COMING
WITH LANGSTON LOVE =

LOUISE

After Langston confirmed his plans to travel with the group, Louise wrote him an enthusiastic letter outlining some of the details and logistics of the trip.

FROM LOUISE, MAY 27, 1932

[Letterhead: Committee for Production of a Soviet Film]

May 27, 1932

Lang darling:

I was more than joyful when your telegram came yesterday that you could make the earlier sailing. My dear, our plans seem to be working out so perfectly that it seems almost (not quite) too good to be true. I am going to enumerate all the things I think you should know. (I have sent the same information to Loren today, too.)

1. We have to sail midnight of June 14, that is we have to be on board before midnight. Of course we sail later [^after midnite], hence the June 15 that I wired you. I hardly think that this will make a great difference to you though—I hope not. The boat is the Europa. We have been lucky through the World Tourist to get passage on it.

2. The route: From here to Bremen, thence to Berlin, thence to Helsingfors via the Baltic and over to Leningrad. Thence rail to Moscow. This is the cheapest way to go and the way most of the groups go, as all rail from Berlin to Moscow is expensive if taken with any degree of comfort, and higher than our route taken any way.

FIGURE 3. Matt's passport photo, age twenty-eight, 1932.

3. The fare: One way to Leningrad is $91. We are cabling Moscow to have our transportation from Leningrad to Moscow and to guarantee our way back. Of course, some of [us] may have the round trip, but if Meschrabpom will pay it, all the better. The round trip is $143.00. Although we have had communications from them assuring that they will guarantee our way back on their account I have cabled again today asking for a confirmation of all these points.

4. Passports and visas. Send me your passport as soon as possible so that the World Tourist, who are arranging our trip, may secure the necessary visas, with the exception of the Russian one. That I have cabled Moscow to have ready in Berlin.

5. Money. Deposits of $25 are necessary now to hold our reservations. I am putting up yours and Loren's until you can get the money to me. Also, it would be well to have the balance here by four days before date of sailing, that is June 10, so that your tickets can be prepared and ready for you when you arrive.

6. Costumes and Properties: We have to take over our outfits to be worn in the picture and as I have written Loren about this I shan't repeat. But I wanted to ask you about your books. They have asked us to bring along certain historical and sociological books on the Negro in America and Africa. Do you have the Buell Books on South Africa?[11] I was looking for it the other night and Mother said that she thought you had it. Then I know that you have other African books, some of them are at the house, I believe. But if you have your books here and won't get back in time to do anything about it, are they where I can get to them?

Another thing, I thought that I would get your portable vic. [Victrola] fixed to take along. They have asked us to bring several different kinds of phonograph records. I am sorry that I don't have one of those lists of stuff they want here at the office, but I will send one along to you and Loren later. I do not think that you need bother about most of the things (when you get the list) but if anything occurs to you or you know where to lay hands on some of the things, well and good. I know that you have loads of records at the house and I shall go over them to pick out what they might want.

I'll tell you some of those who are going that I think you know:

11. Louise is referring to the two volumes of *The Native Problem in South Africa*, written in 1928 by Raymond Leslie Buell.

Henry Moon

Dorothy West

Mollie Lewis

Mildred Jones

Wayland Rudd (not yet definite, but quite probable)

Alan Mackenzie [McKenzie] (you may remember him)

Oscar Hunter (from Cleveland) (I wrote Zell and he said he couldn't make it)

And of course, me and you and Loren and Matt Crawford. And enough others to make up the required fifteen and possibly twenty. The others whom I have met seem like good scouts, too.

I haven't time now to chat, Lang. I must go on home and interview another person who wants to go along. Really I shall need a six weeks' vacation after this is over—and I shall breathe a mighty sigh of relief when we board that Europa on June 14—isn't it grand though?

Let me know when you will be here and if there are any things you wish me to do.

Love to you,

Lou—ise

Please forgive me for delaying so long on the hair tonic. Hope you got it ok.

Langston almost missed the June 14, 1932, sailing of the *Europa*. He arrived in New York on the night of June 13 and then dashed to Harlem to gather up his record player and blues and jazz records. In a last-minute telegram to Louise (which has since been lost), he wrote: "YOU HOLD THAT BOAT CAUSE IT'S AN ARK TO ME."[12] The gangplank was pulling up as he ran up the pier, so they lowered it for him. He had a suitcase under one arm and the Victrola and records under the other.

Of the contemporaneous accounts of the trip to the Soviet Union, Louise's letters to her mother are among the most informative. Her initial enthusiasm, excitement, and later frustrations and disappointments are vividly depicted. She was torn about being away from her ailing mother but anxious to see and learn more about the evolving socialist society in the USSR. As the de facto leader of the eclectic group of young adventurers, she bore much of the responsibility for the trip's success, and therefore also the subsequent blame for the project's problems. At differ-

12. Arnold Rampersad, *The Life of Langston Hughes,* vol. 1, 1902–1941 (New York: Oxford University Press, 1986), 241.

FIGURE 4. Louise and Langston lounging on the deck of the SS *Europa* en route to Bremen, Germany, 1932. (Louise Thompson Patterson papers, Special Collections & Archives, Robert W. Woodruff Library, Emory University.)

ent points during the journey, she wrote to her mother, sharing her feelings and observations about the trip, her companions, and the complexities of the project itself.

FROM LOUISE TO LULA MAE BROWN, JULY 4, 1932

s/s ADRIADNE

Moscow

July 4, 1932

Mother darling:

It has seemed that I could never get time to write or do anything. Here it is July 4 and I have been in Moscow a week, and believe it or not this is the first time I have been alone long enough to do anything. I sent you a cable

FIGURE 5. *Black and White* film group on board the SS *Europa*, 1932. Front row from left: Mildred Jones, Louise Thompson, Constance White, Katherine Jenkins, Sylvia Garner, Dorothy West, Mollie Lewis. Middle row from left: Wayland Rudd, Frank Montero, Matt Crawford, George Sample, Laurence Alberga, Langston Hughes, Juanita Lewis, Alan McKenzie. Back row from left: Ted Poston, Henry Lee Moon, Thurston Lewis, Lloyd Patterson, Loren Miller. Absent: Homer Smith and Leonard Hill.

to let you know that everything is going along very nicely and after we get adjusted I shall be writing oftener.

Let me see—how to begin? I think that I left off last on the Europa. So I am going to start with Germany and travel through to Moscow. As I told you the trip across the Atlantic was ideal and we certainly had a good time. Upon arriving in Bremenhaven we were met by a representative of the North German Lloyd[13] and also a representative of Meschrabpom. We were taken immediately to Berlin by special train and I had my first experience of traveling in a European train which is divided into compartments. Upon arriving in Berlin we went to a hotel to spend the night and that night we spent in trying to see something of the city. We went to a place called the Vaderland which is a number of different cafes and bars decorated to

13. North German Lloyd (Norddeutscher Lloyd) was a shipping company based in Bremerhaven, Germany. It built the SS *Europa* in 1929 specifically for its transatlantic route between Bremen and New York.

represent different countries. In the American Bar we found a Haitian entertaining. From there we went to another night club and when we came out at three o'clock we found the dawn, our first acquaintance with the "white nights".

We were scheduled to leave Berlin at noon of the following day and so bright and early I went around and woke up all the sleepy heads to get up and see about our Russian visas. After going about all morning and going to the Russian consul I came back to the hotel about a half hour before train time to find that a message had come from the consul that we must pay $12.50 each before the visas would be issued to us. Then there was great confusion and I thought that the end had come, as you know that everyone did not have $12.50 and besides it did not seem that we should have to pay this. Most of the people had already gone to the station and we had to send some one after them and take them off the train, some scrambled off as the train pulled off. And there we were—seemingly stranded in Berlin and with not another boat leaving Stettin until Saturday—and this was Wednesday! Lang and Loren helped me pull myself together and we returned to the Russian consul—where in a very short time everything was straightened out—visas issued—they called Stettin to hold the boat two hours for us and we left Berlin on another train, two hours later, were hurried onto the boat—and thus ended a near tragedy.

The trip up the Baltic was the most beautiful of the whole journey. The sea was smooth and it was even warmer than on the Atlantic (there was really only one warm day on the Atlantic when we were in the Gulf Stream). And the nights were always light. At midnight I was standing on deck and could read by the natural light and the sun would rise about two. We traveled second class and ate the best food I have ever tasted in my whole life. I think that the Finns will have to be awarded for preparing the most varied and tasty menus. And on this boat, the Ariadne I had a good chance to relax from the arduous experience in Berlin. When we reached Helsinki on Friday, every one hated to get off the boat. But since I have been in Moscow I understand from Treadwell Smith[14] that we were very fortunate in our Baltic experience as his party which came about a week earlier ran into a terrible storm and everybody was sick for the whole trip.

We spent several hours in Helsinki—we drove about the city in droskis[15] (how do you spell it?) and drank tea in an open garden with the strains of dreamy music from the garden orchestra ringing in our ears. We took a

14. F. Treadwell Smith was a professor at the Columbia Teachers College and an acquaintance of Louise's. He was visiting Moscow in the summer of 1932.

15. *Droskis* are low, open horse-drawn carriages.

train at eleven that same night—on the last lap of our journey to the Promised Land. And I had my first experience of traveling in a European sleeper—third class. In one compartment are three berths, one above the other and I slept in the top one. They put a pad over the wooden seat and although it isn't the softest bed in the world I managed to sleep fairly well. Each compartment has a funny little washstand that you pull out and I should say that if all third class travel in Europe is as this it isn't nearly as bad as I thought for. In the morning we got off the train and had breakfast in the last Finnish station before reaching the border. And I bought the last orange I have seen. Then in a short time we reached the border and Lang jumped off the train and gave us a first handful of Russian soil.

We changed trains at the border and got into a funny little Russian coach and rode a few miles—then we changed trains again and rode to Belo Ostrov for customs inspection. I mention all these changes as I would like for you to get a picture of the situation. On each of these trains from Bremenhaven on, one travels in company with all his baggage—but it wasn't so complicated until we reached Helsinki as all our heavy baggage went directly from Bremenhaven to Stettin and was placed in the boat. But from Helsinki we had trunks, suitcases, phonographs and all in the same car and each time we had to change there was great bustle and furor and the boys in the party would begin to pitch in or out of the car windows, trunks, bags and all. And I think we had nearly a hundred pieces of luggage among us. At Belo Ostrov all this luggage had to be opened and inspected, although we were not given a very close inspection and nothing was taken from us (the word had already arrived that we were coming). After several hours at Belo Ostrov we went on to Leningrad and when we arrived at the station—such a reception we were given!! A brass band and a large delegation who greeted us with the International[16] and speeches in Russian. We were taken on to a hotel and given a sumptuous banquet—chicken, ice cream and everything one would not expect to find in Russia. Whiteman [Lovett Fort-Whiteman] was one of those who came from Moscow to greet us. We were taken on a tour around Leningrad under a very intelligent guide and then we left at ten Saturday night for Moscow.

We arrived in Moscow at ten o'clock Sunday morning and were brought immediately to the hotel where a special breakfast was prepared for us. And from then on there have been consultations and meetings and the general

16. "The Internationale" is a popular left-wing anthem. The title comes from the First International, a congress of left-wing and socialist political parties, formed by Karl Marx and Friedrich Engels. It was written in 1871 by a French transport worker after the Paris commune was crushed by the French government.

hubbub of 22 people in a hotel together which has not permitted any of us to do anything for ourselves. We participated in a Scottsboro demonstration at the Park of Culture and Rest—we have been taken to the kino[17] where I finally got to see the <u>Road to Life</u>[18] (I was so thrilled by it—you know that it was made by the same concern for which we are working.) We have also gone to one other theatre.

There are many other incidents which I might relate but I think you are most interested in knowing how we are living, about our work, and how we like the country.

At the present time we are all at the Grand Hotel. We live either two or three to the room—nice large rooms with every convenience. Most of the girls are two to a room. It might be any hotel with the exception that there is no toilet paper! I do not know how long we will remain here. One group has already agreed to go to a house Meschrabpom has purchased especially for us on the outskirts of Moscow. I went out to see it—there are three large rooms and a glassed in porch and a lovely garden. They will provide a cook and a maid and auto service and it is really quite nice. The only reason that some of us would not consider it is that ten have to live there and I for one would rather not live with ten people, even if the house were larger. But there are nine who have already agreed to go—Kat [Katherine Jenkins] and George [Sample] are among them. The rest of us will be housed otherwise, although my guess is that according to Russian time we may be at the hotel for some time. If it can be arranged, I shall live with Langston, Matt and Loren in a little apartment and we will get a servant to do all the cooking, etc. If such a place can not be found I shall probably room with one of the girls somewhere in the city—that is if we have to leave the hotel. My only objection to the hotel is that there is little privacy because of someone always visiting you. I am rooming with Mollie [Lewis] and we get along fine and so do not get in each other's way, but someone else is always dropping in. Today I announced that no one could come in for I wished to do some work and so here I am.

The greatest adjustment that we have had to make has been in regard to food. Of course in going from any country to another one faces this difficulty and here in Russia where they labor under special handicaps one would expect it. But it has been far better than I had expected. We have one regular dinner each day at one of the restaurants and it is up to us to look after our other meals. At first it was a little difficult for we did not know

17. *Kino* is the Russian word for a movie theater.
18. *Road to Life* was one of the first Russian sound films. The drama, written and directed by Nikolai Ekk, won an award at the 1932 Venice International Film Festival.

how to go about getting our breakfast and supper, but gradually we are learning certain little tricks of getting along.

For our main meal we get a soup, (or salad), meat course (or salad) and some sort of dessert. In the morning I go up to Lang, Loren and Matt's room and we breakfast together. We have tea, or sometimes we make coffee, bread or toast, and jam (Noel Sullivan gave Lang a big box of these things). Then in the evening we cook our own supper if we feel like it, or go out. We have not received our [food ration] books to trade in the special stores for foreign workers and to buy otherwise is very expensive. So Meschrabpom have sent supplies to us twice—butter, eggs, bread, sausage, fish in cans, cookies and the like—all things that even the Russian workers do not get. As soon as we get our books we can go to the store ourselves and buy these things. Last night we cooked ham and spinach (canned) and had other things and it was a nice supper. The greatest difficulty is in getting enough green things, although we have not really suffered from this. We get the most delicious strawberries. Then Langston, Loren and Matt went over to Torgsin[19] and bought for valuta canned peaches and other things difficult to buy for roubles.

A few people have been sick—Loren was one day, Thurston [McNairy Lewis], Henry [Moon] and Leonard Hill—but me—I am feeling fine and have been ever since we left New York. I eat everything, sleep like a log and have not a complaint to make. But their sickness has only been minor—A cold or stomach trouble and the like, all the things one expects in changing environments. But most of the people are well, thank goodness. The doctor comes at Meschrabpom's expense.

Now about our work. We have signed preliminary contracts and all the terms were as Ford stated. We have already been paid at the rate of 400 roubles per month until July 15 and we have roubles to burn. We pay for all our food and this can be very expensive if one eats out for each meal. For our dinner we pay 3 roubles, 75 kopeks daily and then we have to figure on the other two meals. But when we get our books and trade in the special store, these other meals will not be expensive. When we feel like treating ourselves we can go to any of the hotels and for enough roubles get anything we wish. Langston wasn't feeling so well today so we went to the Metropol[20] Hotel and had chicken for 9 roubles.

19. The name Torgsin is the Russian contraction of *torgovlia s inostransomi,* or "All-Union Association for Trade with Foreigners." Torgsin stores often carried products that were unavailable to ordinary Russians. Only foreign currency was accepted for purchases.
20. Hotel Metropol is in Moscow near Red Square.

We are not working on the picture yet. The scenario is not ready, that is being revised after seeing what people have come, and Langston is helping to revise it and to correct any misstatements of American Negro life. I think we may start on July 15. Meanwhile we are working up some songs for the picture and other entertainments we may be asked to participate in. We have been told that we will go to the Caucasus in August to make the African scenes and it should be a grand trip. The only fear I have is that it may take more than six months to make the picture at the rate it is pro-gressing and at the rate such things in Russia seem to take. But of course that is quite far off and cannot mean much to us now.

In my next letter I will tell you more about Moscow. It is a very interest-ing place and I really have only had a glimpse of it. Tell Doris [DuBissette] and Marion [Smith].

I find many beautiful things that I know they will want me to bring home.

Kat and George are fine and I don't think you need have any worries about him—at least while he is here. He looks very well. Matt is fine and is really enjoying himself. It is a really tremendous experience and these Russians are trying to do everything they can to make us happy. Of course there have been little petty frictions within the group, but considering everything, I think that we have managed marvelously.

I will write again within a few days.

Love to all,
Louise

[Note in margin] *This letter is for all. I will try to write separately soon. Have you been to see Helen [Ringe] and Lucy [Crain]?*

FROM LOUISE TO LULA MAE BROWN, JULY 14, 1932

Grand Hotel
Moscow

July 14

Mother dear and Everybody:

The days fly by faster in the USSR than I have ever seen before. Here it is, many days since I have written you, and since that time I have written no one else. We have not yet begun work, but each day is occupied fully with one thing or the other, and no one seems to get any writing done.

Well, my dear, we are just living like royalty used to be entertained in Tsarist Russia, I imagine. Everywhere we go we are treated as honored guests, given enthusiastic ovations and offered the best. It will really be difficult to scramble back into obscurity when we return to the old USA I suspect.

Now, to relate something more about Russia and our activities. We have not yet begun to work on the picture and I rather think it will be another week or two before we start. Russian time is worse than CPT[21] and tomorrow may mean next week or next month. Meanwhile various expeditions have been planned to acquaint us with Moscow. [Harry] Haywood is still here and Loren, Matt and I went with him and his wife to the revolutionary museum a few days ago. (He has a very nice wife). There in pictures and documents is the whole history of the revolutionary movement in Russia and also in other countries and it is an extremely interesting place. One visit of course cannot begin to do the thing justice and I hope to return several times and see it bit by bit. We also went to the anti-religious museum where the Bolsheviks[22] teach the people the role of the church in the lives of the people. There are many interesting places there collected from dismantled churches and other sources. The museums like everything else in the Soviet Union are organized with a social purpose, are mediums of propaganda, and I must say that the Russians are certainly masters of the art of propaganda. On every hand, in the parks, in the cinemas, along the streets—in fact everywhere—one sees pictures, posters, hears speakers, listens to group singing—all designed to educate the people for the socialist state.

Every sixth day is rest day. On the last rest day we went out to one of the workers' rest homes, the Kalinin home, and it was a most revealing trip. In this particular home, 1800 workers can be accommodated. It covers many acres in which are scattered the summer houses where the workers stay. The huge community dining rooms and kitchen were spotless and equipped with most modern cooking and cleaning facilities. There is a hospital, athletic fields, swimming and sun bathing, a large theatre and all sorts of educational features. The workers come here for a two weeks to a month's visit with no personal expense. We were greeted most enthusiastically and on every hand groups of workers would run to meet us. We joined them in

21. CPT stands for "colored people's time," an old and commonly used expression among African Americans that refers to arriving late.
22. The Bolsheviks, founded by Vladimir Lenin and Alexander Bogdanov, were the majority faction of the Marxist Russian Social Democratic Party. They broke away in 1903 and established the Communist Party. The name comes from the Russian "of the majority."

their group games and also sang for them at their evening's concert. And now we are invited back on July 21 for they wish to have a special day for us. I would love to go out there myself for a vacation for it is really a grand place.

On July 6 we were again in the Park of Culture and Rest for a demonstration. This time it was Constitutional Day (I think that I told you of the Scottsboro demonstration). We were again honored and sat in the presidium. It was a most interesting evening and the high point was when the wagons of vegetables from the collective farms paraded in front of us and one of them drove up on the platform, a real peasant woman descended and before the many thousand people began to relate how she had gone about raising these things on the collective farm. It was real drama. She was very bashful and would stop frequently and the applause of the people would force her to continue. Gee, it was a marvelous moment and also an excellent example of the way in which the soviets dramatize their social programs.

Something about our life—we continue to live in the hotel and will be here until we go south to Odessa in August. We are scheduled to go about the 15th, but of course that is to be seen. Eating is much better than I had expected. We do not have to eat black bread, or go without butter. I eat my meals with Lang, Loren and Matt and sometimes we prepare things right here in the hotel. Other times we go to the Metropol Hotel to eat where one can get the best meals in town and really as good in most respects as in New York. It is very expensive, a meal will cost about 20 roubles and we consider that we are indulging in a special treat when we eat there. We bought an electric pot and we are learning to do marvelous things with it. We trade at a special store for foreign workers and are able to get food that cannot be had by the majority of Russian people. It is a real complicated process buying at this store and you would be amused to see us. We have books and when we enter the store we get written into the book every article that we are to purchase and the amount. (You see we have a monthly quota.) Then we go around the store and see what there is to buy and note the price. Then we go to the cashier and get a check for each article and then we go back to the food counters, give the clerk the book, he marks off the article, and the check and gets the package. Of course, I haven't said anything about the complication of language and large crowds, etc., but you should know that it is very intricate business. We buy butter, bread, meat, cheese, sausage and the like. For fruit we can get strawberries (and such delicious ones) raspberries, apples, cherries and that's about all. And they are quite expensive, 4 roubles 50 kopecks for a kilo. Tomatoes are two roubles a piece. The other day we bought some string beans, some raw ham at our store and cooked them in our electric pot. And were they good! We all agreed on that being our best meal. There are many amusing things about buying and eating which I will tell you from time to time, but I think that this will give you some conception of how we live. Really on the fat of the land, as far as fat goes in Russia. An entirely new alphabet and new sounds and I fear that it will be some time before I have managed to learn anything. This makes getting about somewhat complex without a translator, that is, not knowing the language. I have become quite adept at the sign language, but this obviously has its very narrow limits. Russians are great people to enquire from any passerby the direction, about the number of the car or bus, and on the bus where to get off, and whenever I go on one by myself I feel like a dumb animal. Any one of my complexion is not taken for a Negro unless he is with darker people, so they assume that I should know what they are talking about and it is most amusing. About this matter of complexion—Russians, as do most Europeans I think, think Negro means literally black, and our group has been the subject of much discussion on this point. We have had to argue at great lengths to tell them that we are all Negroes, and to try to explain just what being Negro means in the United States. I think that before it is over we will be a liberal education for many people here.

Besides the Russian language, the most difficult thing for me is to try to catch a Russian tram car. They fairly bulge with people (the transportation system is very inadequate for the greatly increased population of Moscow—about 3,000,000). People stand on the steps and hang on anywhere, and they never wait for everyone to board without starting off. And you should see the way in which women here hop these cars on the run. Once inside, you may not be able to reach the conductor, so you pass your money from person to person until it finally reaches the conductor. Many of the conductors and motormen are women. In fact women do everything here. Work on building construction, on the streets, in factories of course, and everywhere.

As much as I have seen so far I am very much impressed by the socialism Russia is building. It is true that Russian people do not have all the luxuries that even we get in Russia, but they have enough to eat and along the streets you see no lean, hungry faces. Their clothes are shabby and they wear anything with no seeming self-consciousness, but although they may admire your things, they will tell you that in time they will have them too. Everyone seems proud of his work, too. At one of the demonstrations I sat next to an old worker who proudly took out his shock brigadier card and invited us to visit him in his home and in his factory. He said that he had lived in tsarist Russia and now in Soviet Russia and he wanted us to know of the remarkable changes that had taken place. Another worker stopped us on the street one day to talk, he wanted to know how were things in America and proudly proclaimed that he was the gardener in the public square. In the theatres and concerts there are crowds of workers,—peasants—whom you realize that before the revolution never saw such things. And they flock to these entertainments. And at this Park of Culture and Rest that I spoke of where the demonstrations were held there are all sorts of educational amusements for the workers—sports, even to table tennis, moving pictures, concerts, lectures, reading rooms, everything to enable the worker to enjoy himself, yet receive cultural development. One only need to compare this park with Coney Island to sense the difference. In the moving picture houses, there are reading rooms with an attendant where one may wait until time to see the picture. Here you do not go in except at the beginning of the picture, and if you come in between times, you sit in the reading room, or look at some of the exhibits scattered about, or partake of a light lunch until time.

These are of course first impressions and I want to see more and know more before saying much, but these are the things that greet you on every hand. Everyone is working at a tremendous speed and there is much to be done, and there are many sacrifices which the workers are called upon to make. But they believe in the thing they are building and would not want the few comforts we still are permitted to enjoy if they had to get them in the same way.

There was a young chap who came over with us and who has since started home and I asked him to see you when he comes through New York. His name is Morozoff and he lives in Chicago. Then Haywood will be returning soon and said that he will come out to see you and to tell you how we are getting along. We have seen quite a bit of him while he has been here. Then Comrade Ossipoff of the FSU whom you may remember, came in to see me today and will be returning August 10 and said that she will come to see you. So I hope that you will get at least some of this first hand information. I am sure that Haywood and Ossipoff will come to see you.

Everyone is well now. I have never been sick for a day. Leonard Hill had a harder time than any of the rest, but he is mending now and should soon be well. As a whole there have been little differences and Thurston Lewis has disappointed everybody and acts like a perfect fool, which I think he is. I get along fine, thanks to Lang, Loren and Matt. They room together and I stay with them most of the time.

I am anxiously awaiting another letter from you. I had the two that you wrote when I first left, but none since and I am eager for news. How is everything running? Please let me know how you are feeling and if you need anything and how the money is holding out.

Give my love to everybody and explain to all that they should consider some of this letter to them. I don't know why but no one gets any time to write and scarcely any letters have been written from the entire group. I make up my mind that I will do better and yet every day just when I get ready to write, some one will come in, or we have to go somewhere, or any one of a dozen things will interrupt me. But I feel a bit more adjusted now and will write some people at least within the next few days. Astra's aunt came and got the things. Also you might tell the woman who gave me the things to bring to her daughter, that I have seen both Mr. and Mrs. Huiswood [Otto and Hermina Huiswoud] and they are fine. I haven't seen Pat's wife,[23] but I sent her package to her.

How are Sue [Bailey], Marion [Smith], all the girls in the house, Helen Ringe, Lucy Crain and others? Give them all my love and tell them to write me care of the Grand Hotel. In all this time I have had but your two letters and I do feel far, far away. It takes a long time to get mail through.

Well, darling, I wish you were here to share what is the greatest experience of my life. There are so many things that happen and I cannot begin to tell them all. But I am so happy that I was able to have this trip. We will begin work soon, tomorrow we have our screen tests and it ought to be good!!! The making of a movie star!?!

With lots of love and all the hope that everything is going well with you.

Louise

[Note in margin] *I got my laundry done very nicely and very cheaply. I get a wave for two roubles, fifty kopeks. So you see I am not missing many of the comforts of home [drawing of a smiling face]. . . . . . me in the USSR.*

FROM LOUISE TO LULA MAE BROWN,
AUGUST 24, [1932]

Moscow

August 24

My dear Mother:

Here we are back in Moscow and I am taking the first opportunity to write and tell you all about things. I sent a cable last night as I learned that reports have appeared in the Herald Tribune which may worry you. I think

---

23. Pat had married a Russian woman, Vera Gorohovskaya, in Moscow in 1929. They had two daughters together, Lola and Anya, before divorcing in the mid-1930s.

that I shall discuss things in a chronological order that you may have a full understanding of the whole situation.

The last letter I wrote you was on board the Abhazia as we were returning to Odessa from the cruise. Upon arriving in Odessa a representative of Meschrabpom came and met us and informed us of the fact that the picture was postponed because of scenario difficulties. We all decided to return immediately to Moscow to inquire into the whole affair—and so we came, arriving three days ago. Since that time we have had meetings upon meetings until I am worn out. A few of the group, headed by Ted [Poston], Thurston [Lewis] and Henry [Moon] have sworn that we have been betrayed and that all the Negro people in the world have been betrayed and just scads of nonsense that isn't nonsense either when you consider that it will be, and has already been, used in the bourgeois press to further counter revolutionary propaganda. So Lang, Loren, Matt and I have had to fight desperately hard to keep the rest of the group from falling into the trap laid by these three. Their limited political understanding made it still more difficult and the three mentioned above piled upon our heads all manner of personal abuse and accusations.

But I am getting a bit ahead of my story. When we returned to Moscow we met with Meschrabpom and then drew up a list of what we considered the inefficiencies in the handling of the whole matter. It is our belief that Meschrabpom is telling the truth in saying that the picture has to be postponed until next summer, but not all of the truth. There was a great deal of internal wrangling in the Meschrabpom organization because some of them favored using the scenario as first prepared by a Russian, [G. E.] Grebner and some the use of the scenario as revised by our director [Karl] Junghans. At one of the meetings, which Langston attended, they argued all night without getting any place. It was finally decided that the scenario was to be revised, but later found impossible to do. Then other scenario experts were called in and the final decision was that nothing could be done until four or five months. Meanwhile, Junghans had stated that August 15 was the latest date to begin work on the picture, and on August 15 there was no scenario on which to begin work. Therefore there was nothing to do but to call off the making of the picture.

To explain the position of Ted and Thurston it is necessary to say something more about them and their actions. I have told you something about Thurston, but I think I have only hinted at what has been disgraceful conduct on both his and Ted's part. They have been thoroughly irresponsible and Thurston really incorrigible. Their actions have shamed us all for they have acted like two puppies, chained for a while and then let loose. Their attitude toward the Russian women was so obvious as to seem absolute proof of all the things white Americans say about Negro men and white women. They have steadily refused to cooperate with the group and do things in a group manner and have gone their own way. They have been loud mouthed and every other word Thurston utters is a curse word. And on the trip to Odessa and down the Black Sea they were perfectly awful. Thurston cussed our political leader, a responsible man from the Profintern,[24] and our interpreter, a very fine Russian girl. Ted's main role from the very beginning has been that of malicious troublemaker. He has done everything he can all along the way to demoralize the group. I take all this time right here to explain the actions of these two that you may know how to judge their actions in the present situation.

Henry it is a little more difficult to understand. I think that he is perhaps laboring under a mistaken line of reasoning, yet even he has not developed as I thought he would over here. From things that came out in the meeting yesterday I see, too, that he perhaps has felt that some of us, Lang and I especially, have rather cliqued with Loren and Matt and left him out. He did not say this, but from what he said I gathered as much. He has not acted in the disgraceful manner that Ted and Thurston have, but he has rather backed them up and has not been cooperative either. In his case it is hard to put one's finger on just what is wrong, but I have felt a rather resentful attitude on his part for some time.

With these remarks I shall continue on with the main thread of this story. From the time Henry came to Odessa to meet us (he did not go on the southern trip with us, but remained in Moscow and only met us on our return to Odessa) he has insisted that Meschrabpom has sold us and that the reason the picture was cancelled is because the Soviet Union wants American recognition and does not want [to] offend American opinion. Realizing the seriousness of such charges, Loren, Lang and I tried to reason with them and to ask that we investigate farther than hearsay before we even consider bringing such charges. When we arrived back in Moscow the two factions became sharply defined and every meeting became more and more bitter. We would fight for five or six hours and upon about the third day we finally won the group to the position of criticizing Meschrabpom for the inefficiencies in the handling of certain details of the group and for bringing this group over here before all preparations had definitely been made for their coming. We pointed out to them how this postponement would be used by the bourgeois press and all counter revolutionary organi-

24. Profintern was the international entity of the Comintern, or the Third Communist International, and was responsible for coordinating trade union activities. Its name is a contraction of the Russian title of the Red International of Labor Unions.

zations to poison the minds of Negroes against the Soviet Union and the revolutionary movement. With this as our position we met with Meschrabpom again and after we had presented our case (Loren presented it for the group), Ted rose and presented charges that the rest of us had never seen before, accusing Meschrabpom Film, and all revolutionary organizations of betraying the Negro workers of America. Their charges really sounded ridiculous and showed colossal ignorance of the real state of affairs, the relationship of Meschrabpom to the Soviet Union, and the basic principles of revolutionary theory.

Later we took the case to the Communist International, the highest governing body of the revolutionary movement in the world. Langston and Loren presented the position of the group, and again Henry and Thurston presented what by this time had become the minority report. Lang and Loren said it was a shameful experience and the bravado of Henry and Thurston in making such far fetched charges in the heart of communism was that of fools. Thurston, particularly posing as a communist, shows unbelievable ignorance of anything to do with communism.

We were given the following answer from the Comintern—that Meschrabpom had been very inefficient and that an investigation would be made and the assurance that the picture would be made next year. For all admit that it is too late in the year to do anything about it now.

And with the decision of the Comintern we have rested our case—that is the majority have. Our position was this[,] that we wanted Meschrabpom and the Comintern to know that we took the making of this picture seriously and that we did not take its postponement lightly and wanted to know definitely about it. We do not believe that the picture was cancelled because of political reasons and it is easy to trace how these reports got out that you have read in the Herald Tribune. There are many Americans here who have been against the picture, and among them newspaper men. Of course they are anxious that Negroes think not too well of the Soviet Union and they have made suggestions to various members of the group. Henry and Ted have been particularly friendly with the newspaper men and it is not very difficult to piece the thing together and see how these reports got out.

The minority are still trying to make trouble, and their latest move seems to be to send a letter to Stalin accompanied by their ridiculous charges. And here it is with regret that I must say that I fear that Kathryn [Katherine Jenkins] and George [Sample] are following them in this move. As the time progresses Kathryn seems to have come under George's influence more and more. And although George has behaved himself on this trip, I have had an excellent opportunity of seeing how empty brained he is.

Really his mind must be a vacuum. Anyway, although a week ago Kathryn was very bitter against Thurston and Ted and was all for throwing them out of the Soviet Union, yet she turned around yesterday and sided with them in this matter—and all [on] account of George. All the rest have stuck by the other side and have repudiated in writing the charges made by this minority. I think that it is good enough for Ted and Thurston, it is just what they deserve and shows clearly their trouble-making position all the way along. With Henry, I am sorry, and with Kathryn I am so sorry that I don't know what to do. But I don't think there is anything that I can say or do with her. She seems thoroughly unreasonable and only what George says means anything. So I suppose there is nothing to do but let them go ahead and hang themselves.

As to what is to happen next. Far from being left adrift Meschrabpom is carrying out their contract to the letter with the group and is giving them many choices of what to do. Those who wish to go home now may do so and they will be paid up to the end of October, the termination of the four months' contract we signed. Those who wish to remain until the expiration of the contract will be given a tour to interesting points in the Soviet Union. Those who wish to stay permanently, or for a longer period of time will be found jobs. And there will be a reimbursement of the fares (in valuta or dollars—not roubles) of the money we spent in coming here, as well as our return fare being paid. So aside from any disappointment at not making the picture there is nothing that any of us have to complain of, besides having a trip that we could not have had for a thousand dollars had we come here as tourists. We have had first class accommodations every where we have gone and these people have lived and dined in places they would not even dare to stick their heads into in America.

I think some of the group will go home immediately—others will go on the tour and some will remain. Homer Smith already has a very excellent position in the post office. Lang and Loren are going to stay—Mil [Mildred Jones] and Dorothy [West], Lloyd Patterson, Laurence Alberga, Juanita Lewis also. Thurston will probably be kicked out—and Ted too. Matt and I want to stay until the end of the contract and take in the tour and the remainder of the others fall in this category. Kathryn and George are not sure of what they will do—they are in rather an embarrassing position now, having lined up with the trouble makers but I think that they will see the light, or at least, I hope so. If they don't they probably will come home now.

So I have given you the entire situation in a brief sketch. Much has happened, that is in the group. You can see from what I have said that all has not been pleasant. Ted and Thurston have been more venomous than I could imagine any two people could be—I haven't minded this half as much as their actions which reflected on the group. You can see that if Thurston wrote back any stuff he was lying unless he talked about himself. On the whole the group has acted very well and I am sure that they would have a much better understanding of everything if Meschrabpom had given us more leadership. We were given very excellent living accommodations— food and hotel—but their neglect came in not providing sufficient guidance. [Lovett Fort-]Whiteman turns out to be an awful person and such a person that one can only have contempt for. Instead of helping us, he encouraged Ted and Thurston in their escapades. Not having any work to do the people had to find ways of amusing themselves and many of them became acquainted with Americans who did not provide the best of guidance. And there are many other negligences which it would take too much time to explain. But on the whole, as I have said before, everyone has acted very well and had it not been for the continuous evil machinations of the two troublemakers we would not have had any difficulties. As it was they kept those of us who attempted to offer guidance to the group continually on the alert for their deliberate acts of disruption. But I think that they are stilled now and that all see the part they have played. Yesterday in the meeting they, that is Ted led off and Henry and Thurston chimed in, with reasons as to why Langston, Loren, Matt, Alan McKenzie and I were betraying the rest of the group. The reasons were so ridiculous that I felt ashamed for them. They said that Langston was trying to make himself popular in Russia because there was too much competition in America for him. That Loren and I were trying to make ourselves popular with the Soviet Union to enhance our revolutionary positions in America, that I had a lot of pull with the Central Committee of the Russian Communist Party and that since Huiswood [Otto Huiswoud] was an important Negro in the Communist Party I wanted to be able to return to America and say that I know him—and such other ridiculous things that it was pathetic. My only answer was that I was sorry for such people who could not think of anyone working for a cause because he believed in it, but only for small personal motives, and that it seemed queer that people who had done everything they can to disgrace the Negro race since they have been in Russia, should suddenly become their staunchest champion. And I think that what they said really killed their influence in the group. It was really the most sordid thing I have ever been party too. Oh yes, not knowing anything about Matt, they said that he was only following his friends. It was ridiculous!

I haven't worried you with any of the details of the actions of my people, aside from mentioning Thurston, because I felt that it wasn't important enough to consider. As long as Ted's darts were against persons, and chiefly myself, it didn't matter. But in order that you may understand this present affair, which is important that you should have clear, it is necessary to know these relationships. You really couldn't imagine how anyone could change as Thurston has—it is beyond all of us.

I am going to leave Russia now and get to affairs in America—that is as they concern you. I am worried about what is to be done about the house for it is a tremendous thing for you to have to face alone. Will you write me immediately exactly how you stand financially? And about what to do. If you should move and take a smaller place, would Doris remain with you if you took an apartment. I don't think you should consider the idea about the room or going to work. Remember I told you before leaving, Mother, that if you should get short of money and not have enough to do until my return you were to tell me. I do agree that we cannot continue to keep this large apartment which is a terrible drain on our finances and with the deepening crisis[25] making it all the more difficult to maintain, as well as a tremendous responsibility. But suppose if Sue [Bailey] can only get $80 a month for it, can you not ask that she let it remain with you until my return. Then you have Doris, and is Marion Smith planning to return to us on her return. If necessary you could let her have the room cheaper. I understand that it is also a terrific responsibility for you as far as work is concerned. With only two or three of you there, can you not get out more—at least until I return. Then we can make definite arrangements. I say all this because I think that it is too much for you to try to move alone. Please let me know as soon as you can about all this as I am very much worried. And as far as you talking about going to work it is ridiculous from all angles.

Now about myself—I am writing to Mr. [Hubert C.] Herring today as to when I can return to work. As I say I shall be free to return the end of October, but when I left the office it was under the agreement that I would not return to work until January. If they do not wish me to return until that time it would be cheaper for me to remain here in Russia until it's time to come back to work, as I can live on roubles here—but not in New York. I think that I shall have some valuta as they promise to return the fare we paid in coming over, or at least a portion of it. I should like to stay here anyway until the November 7 celebration[26] and even until later if I cannot return to work until January.

25. Louise is referring to the economic depression gripping New York, and Harlem in particular. Without Louise's income, Mother Thompson was in precarious financial circumstances.

26. On November 7, 1917, Vladimir Lenin led the Russian Bolshevik Revolution, overthrowing the provisional government of Alexander Kerensky. The anniversary of this date became the most important patriotic celebration in Russia, and later the Soviet Union.

In spite of all the disagreeable things that happened within the group and the unfortunate publicity that has attended the postponement of the picture, this has really been a great experience. And the rest of it should be even better for it will be devoid of all this unpleasantness. And my only hope is that you have not been inconvenienced and worried too much in being left with the house in New York.

I had a lovely letter from Helen Ringe and she told me of your and Mary's visit. Also a letter from Marion Smith. And by the way, in replying to this letter, Mother, please send your letter air mail. I have received now I think all the letters you mentioned, because it takes about 20 days for one to reach me. If you send it air mail I receive it in much quicker time. Continue to send mail in care of Meschrabpom-Film, Moscow. If we are on tour they will arrange to get it to us.

Much of this letter is very confidential—particularly about the postponement of the picture. From what I have told you, you will know better what to tell people that will be asking you many questions. In brief the picture was cancelled because the scenario proved unacceptable after revisions in which Langston helped (although his assistance included only the English dialogue). It is not true that it was cancelled because of political reasons. The group is being taken care of and no one will be stranded. The only people that may be given scant consideration are those who tried to make trouble and have insisted in making counter revolutionary and unfounded accusations. There will be two different kinds of publicity issued—Loren will be writing for the Negro press giving the true state of affairs. Henry and Ted will be writing and trying their best to make it appear that they and all the black people in the world have been betrayed They will enlarge on all the petty defects and forget the cordial welcome and the splendid treatment they have received at the hands of the Russian people. Thurston will probably tell all sorts of lies and will try to blacken the reputation of all the people in the group, particularly those who cornered him in his dirty work. So it is necessary that you have a rather complete picture of the whole situation in order that you may be able to correctly interpret for yourself and others all the things you will read.

I must close now for I want to write to others, particularly Herring, [W. A.] Domingo and Ford. I hope that this will not be used against the latter, although I fear that it will. I sent you a cable and I hope that you were able to relay it to Ford. I shall send my letter to him in your care also.

I hope that you won't have any further worries about us, for we are being cared for excellently. I will write you tomorrow or the next day, telling you of the plans for our trip. We may have a trip down the Volga, I don't know yet, we will however, visit all the big points of socialist construction here.

Really, sometimes when I think of all the places I have visited and of those that I am still to see it doesn't seem that it is possible.

We are not in the Grand Hotel now, but in one directly across from the Kremlin. Enclosed is a photograph, showing the tomb of Lenin and the Kremlin walls. Thousands of people visit this tomb every day. We went some time ago. Lenin is lying in a glass case and looks like he is merely sleeping. The bells of the Kremlin ring all during the day and at midnight play the International.

Well, my dear, please write me all your worries and don't have any yourself. I will be writing within a day or two. Love to all.

Lovingly,
Louise

Try to have a talk with Domingo. Show him any of this letter you choose. He will receive a letter from me too, but I may tell you some points I will forget in writing him.

L.

[Note in margin] *I rec'd the package of letters for all of us*

As Louise recounted in the letter above, she believed the postponement of the film was due to problems with the scenario and not caused by political reasons. In reality it was probably a little of both. Back in Moscow the group became even more sharply divided, and the following two contradictory "majority" and "minority" statements were issued by the two sides about the status of *Black and White*.

THE MINORITY

Moscow, USSR, 8/22/32

Rejecting as unsound, insufficient, and insulting to our intelligence the reasons offered by Meschrabpom-Film Corporation for the cancellation of the "Black and White" film project, for the production of which 22 Negro men and women were invited to the USSR, we, the undersigned members of this group wish to state that:

WE BELIEVE that the production of the film, "Black and White", has been cancelled primarily because of political reasons.

WE BELIEVE that this cancellation is a compromise with the racial prejudice of American Capitalism and World Imperialism, sacrificing the furtherance of the permanent revolution among the 12,000,000 Negroes of America and all the darker exploited peoples of the world.

WE FURTHER BELIEVE that this act is one of Right Opportunism on the part of Meschrabpom-Film Corporation, a Soviet organization—an act of political expediency, comparable with those ignoble concessions to race prejudices made by the Christian Church, the Socialist Party, and countless other social fascist organizations. Such surrenders have been constantly exposed and relentlessly flayed by the Communist Party and its auxiliaries. Therefore, because of our aforestated convictions,

WE HEREBY CHARGE Meschrabpom Film Corporation and any other organization which may support it in this stand, with sabotage against the Revolution.

[Thurston] McNairy Lewis; Theodore R. Poston;
Henry Lee Moon; Laurence Alberga.

THE MAJORITY

We, the undersigned members of the Negro group invited to the Soviet Union by Meschrabpom Film to participate in a realistic picture of Negro life in America "Black and White," issue the following statement:

We greatly deplore and emphatically deny all slanderous charges and rumors concerning the postponement of the film "Black and White" and the subsequent welfare of our group. Because of scenario and technical difficulties, Meschrabpom Film has found it necessary to postpone work on the film for one year. This has in no way jeopardized the well being of our group. Throughout our stay in the Soviet Union we have been housed in the best hotels, given food privileges and accorded all courtesies that the Soviet Union affords. The terms of our contract are being entirely fulfilled by Meschrabpom Film and postponement of the film has in no way affected this relationship. In addition we have received many privileges not contained in our contract. We have been given a tour in southern Russia and along the Black Sea. At the present time an extended tour is being arranged for us to Turkestan, the Caucasus and Armenia. Those who return to America are not only given their return passage, but will be reimbursed in American dollars for the money spent in paying their fare to the Soviet Union. Work has been secured for those who wish to remain here. In short, everything is being done for our welfare and accommodation.

The statement that the picture has been cancelled for political reasons issued by four members of our group, McNairy Lewis, Henry Moon,

Theodore Poston and Lawrence Alberga, is without foundation in fact and unwarranted in the light of the general policy of the Soviet Union[.] These false allegations are ridiculous and have already been repudiated by the press in its consistent attempts to arouse the distrust of white and black workers in the success of socialist construction in the Soviet Union where exploitation and oppression of racial minorities have been eliminated.

We deeply regret these malicious and unfounded attacks upon the people whose guests we have been all summer and who are doing everything possible for our comfort and entertainment during our stay in the U.S.S.R.

Louise Thompson; Langston Hughes; Matt N. Crawford; Juanita C. Lewis; Mildred Jones; Loren Miller; Dorothy West; Alan McKenzie; Constance W. White; Homer Smith; Sylvia Garner; Wayland Rudd; Lloyd Patterson; Mollie V. Lewis; F. [Frank] Curle Montero

Behind the scenes, an international political drama was unfolding. Colonel Hugh Cooper, an American hydraulic engineer and long-time power broker between American business interests, the US Congress, and top Soviet officials, was pressuring the Soviets, who were seeking diplomatic recognition from Washington. Beginning in 1926, Cooper was chief consulting engineer on the Dnieprostroi Hydroelectric Station and Dam, a centerpiece of Stalin's First Five-Year Plan. Two members of the film group, Henry Lee Moon and Leonard Hill, had stayed behind in Moscow while the other members had gone to the city of Odessa on the Black Sea. Soon after, Moon and Hill showed up in Odessa bearing bad news. Moon bluntly and famously announced: "Comrades, we've been screwed!" He backed up his claim by showing the others a copy of the European edition of the *New York Herald Tribune*. The front-page story was titled "Soviet Calls Off Film on U.S. Negroes; Fear of American Reaction is Cause."

What they did not know was that Cooper, through the intermediary of V.M. Molotov, chairman of the Council of People's Commissars, had reached Stalin with the demand that if *Black and White* were not canceled, he would halt all work on the soon-to-be-completed Dneiprostroi Dam.[27]

Suddenly, the project clashed head-on with Russian political pragmatism. Work on *Black and White* was abruptly halted. The cancellation of the film removed one potentially thorny diplomatic issue for the Russians, and the United States would finally recognize the USSR on November 16, 1933.

27. See Faith Berry, *Langston Hughes: Before and Beyond Harlem* (New York: Citadel, 1983), 164–168.

In September, Matt expressed his idealistic enthusiasm in a letter to Nebby from Moscow, in which he suggests that the couple might want to move to the Soviet Union. However, it is unlikely that he would have pursued the idea with her, as she was extremely close to her sister, nieces, and the extended Graves family, who lived in San Francisco.

During the fall of 1932 there were few letters between Louise, Langston, and Matt, as they were together in the Soviet Union most of that time. Most members of the group went on a tour of Central Asia in September and October. Louise jotted a jolly postcard off to Nebby from the road. Matt wrote Nebby from a stop at the newly constructed Dnieperstroi Dam. His letter gives no hint as to whether he was thinking about the irony of the situation—that the demise of *Black and White* was, in large measure, due to the racist fears of the white American engineer supervising the building of the dam. It was only on their return to Moscow in October that the group became fully aware of the political machinations that ultimately led to the indefinite postponement of the film. Neither Meschrabpom nor the Comintern officials were willing to admit that the film had been canceled. In the fall of 1932 they were still pretending that the project would be reprised at a later date, although the decision to cancel it had already been made.

Langston stayed on in Central Asia after the tour, experiencing the sights and sounds of the area and befriending some of its denizens.

MATT TO NEBBY, SEPTEMBER 21, 1932

Moscow USSR

Sept. 21, 1932

Dearest Honey,

As usual we are about a week late leaving Moscow for the tour. As I told you in the cablegram we were to leave definitely on the 17th. Each day leaving was postponed until "Zavtra"[28] in typical Russian fashion. We had a meeting of the group that is going—twelve—with Meschrabpom's representative so it looks as though we shall really leave tomorrow 22nd.

Although I should be quite accustomed to delays and postponements, waiting and the uncertainty of the whole thing has been very irritating to me this time. Probably it is because the time is growing short and I want to get as much as possible done. I have done very little since we returned to Moscow. After the [illegible] about the picture was settled they began working on the trip and it was impossible to plan anything else.

28. *Zavtra* means "tomorrow" in Russian.

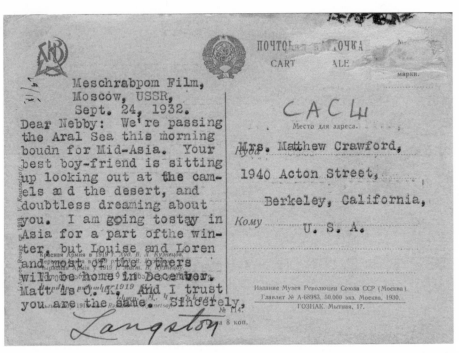

FIGURE 6. Postcard from Langston to Nebby, 1932. Langston reports on how her "best boy-friend," Matt, is doing in the USSR. (Evelyn Graves Crawford papers, Special Collections & Archives, Robert W. Woodruff Library, Emory University.)

There has been considerable rain here too, which prevented me from getting about very much. I have spent much time in the hotel reading, and for the first time since being here I have had time to reflect on the things I have seen and my experiences.

I realize now how much being in Russia has affected me. Unconsciously I have lost that depressing sub consciousness of being a Negro. The ever-present thought that my dark skin must circumscribe my activities at all times. I was a bit surprised how absolutely normal my moving about among the Russian people has become. All of the antagonism which I have always felt among ofeys[29] at home has left me. I can understand why the masses of Russian people are willing to endure any sort of hardship during this transitional period from capitalism and slavery to socialism and freedom. The knowledge that one is working under a system that will allow every opportunity to develop one's ability without regard to class position or racial differences is certainly worth a great price.

29. "Ofey" was a slang term for white people.

The thought of going home and plunging into the hopeless task of trying to squeeze a living out of conditions there is none too pleasing. Then added to the actual struggle to live is the necessity to readjust myself to a Negro's position in "White America." I have thought of the added pleasure of our lives together if it were possible for us to live under a system such as Russia is building.

My struggle to do something with the office[30] seems more futile now than ever before. I know that it is going to be difficult for me to continue there hoping against hope that things will improve. Then too the class consciousness that I have developed here has given me something of a different attitude toward Negro professional and business life that will influence me much more than it did before I left home.

Do not be alarmed sweetheart because regardless of what my attitude will be we shall plan together what will be the best thing for us to do. Who knows maybe we shall return to the Soviet Union!

I told you that life here is difficult which is true, but if proper arrangements are made one can live fairly well. One large consideration is finding a place to live. It is actually more difficult to find a room than it is to get a job. Then of course food can be a great problem here. This can be overcome to some degree by cooking one's own meals. Often or more exact always, food is spoiled by being poorly prepared in restaurants.

But in the face of all these difficulties Babe being free compensates a hell of a lot.

Langston has done quite a bit of work since being here. He has written several very good poems, one particularly good—"Good Morning Revolution." His book "Not Without Laughter" has been translated into Russian. He is going to stay in the Soviet Union until Spring to write a book about the national minority question in Soviet Asia. He is to go with us as far as Ashkabad where he will stay for a time and then travel throughout all of Central Asia. He has a contract with a publishing house here in Moscow for all of the work he can do.

Five of the fellows left for Paris several days ago. The three "Black White Guards,"[31] and Leonard Hill and Frank Montario [Montero]. Loren is returning with me in Nov. I think Louise will return at the same time but I am not sure. She wants to do some work here in Moscow after we return

30. Matt and two colleagues had opened a chiropractic medical office in West Oakland shortly before Matt left for Russia. By 1932 the economic depression was affecting the Bay Area's Black community especially hard, and the office was having a hard time staying afloat.

31. The three "Black White Guards" were Henry Moon, Ted Posten, and Thurston McNairy Lewis.

from the trip and if she decides to do so she will remain until the latter part of December.

Oh Yes—Meschrabpom is going to refund the entire passage over. The fellows who left got theirs along with their fare back to the States. Hill and Montario got their train fare from Washington to New York and I think Loren, Lang and I shall get ours from Calif. to New York. 'Aint that some'im? It is barely possible that Loren and I shall get our train fare from New York to California included in our passage back. I am not figuring on that too strongly however, for it is a hell of a lot to expect.

I think we shall get our reserve seat tickets in the Red Square for the Nov. 7 celebration before we leave tomorrow. For a time it looked as though we would not be able to get seats because there will be delegations from all over the world here and they have been issuing seats since the first of May. Our interpreter came to our rescue again. Through the secretary of the Central Committee of the party we were promised our seats. Weeze, Loren, the interpreter and I shall go. I have not received a letter from you since you left for your vacation and I certainly hope one comes today or tomorrow before we leave. There is no way of getting mail to me on the trip and if I don't hear from you by to-morrow it will be over a month before I shall get a letter. That really ain't no hell! Louise had a letter from Mother Thompson in which she said the man by whom I sent your blouse had not been to see her. The letter was written on the twenty sixth so I hope he has delivered it and that you have it by now.

We have received all sorts of damn reports about the postponement of the picture and the status of the group. Some of the worst lies I have ever read; there has not been one word of truth printed by the Negro or white press. The rumor about being stranded is the most ridiculous thing I can think of. The fact of the case is that these Negroes have never lived as well in all their lives. Just imagine being here for almost four months without doing a bit of actual work; being paid regularly—some of them drawing more than their salaries. Living in Moscow's best hotels and traveling all over the Soviet Union with all expenses paid. If that isn't a freebee I want to see one. Added to all of this of course, their fare is being paid over here and back.

Well honey babe time continues to grow shorter before I shall be with you and maybe I won't be happy!

As I said I shall try to let you hear from me as often as possible while I am on tour but please don't worry about me for we are travelling deluxe. Tell all the folks howdy. I received Gladys [Crawford Hawkins][32] letter and

32. Gladys Crawford Hawkins was Matt's sister.

FIGURE 7. Members of *Black and White* film group with Soviet friends in Central Asia, 1932. Louise is in the front row, fourth from left; Matt and Langston are in the back row, fourth and fifth from left, respectively. (Louise Thompson Patterson papers, Special Collections & Archives, Robert W. Woodruff Library, Emory University.)

was certainly glad to know that things are going along pretty good. I won't have time to write her before I leave.

Next time you hear from your daddy babe he will be away out in Asia.

Love,
Matt

LOUISE TO NEBBY, SEPTEMBER 30, [1932]

Tashkent

Sept 30

Greetings Neb dear from Central Asia

Matt and I are having a real honest to goodness "ball". This is the most interesting place in the world. I am sure the extremes meet and the tremendousness of the social changes is amazing. Of course the old order will not die out at once but it is sure to do so under the stimulus and guidance of Soviet power.

Love to you,
Weez

FIGURE 8. Cover of the Russian edition of Langston's novel *Not Without Laughter,* 1932. (Matt N. and Evelyn Graves Crawford papers, Special Collections & Archives, Robert W. Woodruff Library, Emory University. Copyright (©) 2015 by The Estate of Langston Hughes, Arnold Rampersad and Ramona Bass Kolobe Co-Administrators. By permission of Harold Ober Associates Incorporated.)

MATT TO NEBBY, [OCTOBER 17, 1932]

Dnieperstroy Dam, U.S.S.R

Babe:

We arrived this morning at the Dam. Our car was left on the track just opposite the Dam, it was a spectacle I shall never forget. When I looked out of the window and saw the 47 spillways of silver sheets of water dashing into the river below. Later in the day we visited the electric power station with its 9 huge turbines—5 of them in operation. We also walked over the dam. This is an appropriate ending of our trip throughout the Union. We have seen the beginning of socialism in Uzbekistan and the other Asiatic republics and now the height of accomplishment of the Soviet Union Dnieperstroy Dam and Hydroelectric station. We leave [for] Moscow tomorrow night, arriving the 22.

Love, Matt

TO MATT, OCTOBER 23, 1932

1st Dom Soviet
Ashkabad, TCCR,

October 23, 1932.

Dear Matt:

By now, you must be back in dear old Moscow enjoying the hospitalities of Meschrabpom again, and discussing the scents of the various cheeses you have for breakfast. Tell me how the trip finished up, and when you'll be leaving for home. . . . . Down here, big doings are about to come off. Kessler [Arthur Koestler], the only writer who accompanied the Graf Zepplin[33] to the North Pole, is here getting together a book on the USSR; also a film director from Moscow making a Komsomol[34] picture; so the lot of us, with the Turkmen head of the writers' union, are due to leave tomorrow for Merv (accompanied by sundry technicians and a newspaper man or so); and from Merv into the country for some days; and then out into the desert looking for Nomad tribes, which ought to be interesting. . . . . I seem to have seen most of the local high spots, and have a book full of notes. The great difficulty here is getting in touch with the native life. The Turkmens

33. The *Graf Zeppelin* was a hydrogen-filled German passenger aircraft similar to a blimp.
34. "Komsomol" was the Russian name of the Young Communist Youth League of the Soviet Union.

sort of step aside, and let the Russians take charge of all the visitors. But this is the official town, whereas Merv, (like Bukhara) is the native center, so I trust that, through the Turkmen writer, I will get to know some real Turkomans there—If we can escape the more dynamic Russians. . . . . If [it] weren't for my mail, and a wire from Anissimov saying he has sent some money here, I'd move on to Bukhara from Merv, but as it is, I'll have to come back, so I'll be here for the [November 7th] Celebration.[35] Tell Loren not to send any more mail here, though, (after this letter is received) and to ask Meschrabpom to hold everything until I wire them an address, probably from Tashkent in late November. (Wires can reach me at Ashkabad until Nov. 9.) . . . . . What about the Scottsboro Case? Yesterday's paper here reported Hoover's campaign tour as meeting with lots of opposition, street-demonstrations against him by farmers, etc. . . . . I heard a swell shouting here the other day. The movie director and another fellow have a room rented from a woman who used their bread card, but resold a part of the bread, so they took the card back. The woman, in retaliation, took the mattress off their bed, and left only the springs and the sheets, so when they pulled back the cover to go to bed, they had nothing but springs to lie on. This was about 2 A.M. The shouting then began, and lasted all night, and was still going on the next day when I went down to see about our trip to Merv. The fellows refused then to pay their rent. So yesterday the woman sealed up the door. Last night they invited several guests to a party, had to get the GPU[36] to open the door, and when we got to the party, the woman had taken away the lamp, so we had to drink by candle light. I am awaiting new developments today. Out of it all, I've learned some swell new cuss words in several minority languages. The point of the story is . . . but why be obvious? All my best stories are subtle! . . . . . Well, I must now go to dinner. In case some of my previous letters didn't get to Moscow, (they say the mail is rather irregular down this way) I'll repeat once more: that I sent you-all some Turkmen Childrens books which I trust you have by now; and that I asked for a Russian-English dictionary so I can talk to folks. . . . . Also, if you have time, please try to find out how much it would cost to return to America via the Trans-Siberian and across the Pacific. If I can do it, I'd like to consider coming home that way next spring. To see you and Nebby on your native heath again, for one thing. And, to see a little of the Orient, as one would have to go by Japan and the Philippines. . . . . Regards to Chalito

35. Langston was looking forward to the celebration of Lenin's Russian Revolution (described in note 26), which was held on November 7 in Moscow's Red Square.

36. GPU (Gosudarstvennoye politicheskoye upravlenie, or State Political Directorate) was the Soviet intelligence service and secret police.

[Frank Montero], Lydia [Filatova], Loren [Miller], Louise [Thompson], Dot [Dorothy West], Mollie [Lewis], Mildred [Jones], Juanita [Lewis], George [Sample], Katherine [Jenkins], Sylvia [Chen], etc. and so on, including Otto [Huiswoud]. . . . . Wire me your date of departure. . . . . Hope you'll enjoy the rest of your time in Russia, and that your trip home will be interesting and pleasant. And that you'll do what you can for the furthering of the movement when you get home.

Sincerely,
Lang

Tell Chalito no pictures came from Tashkent for him here.

FROM LOREN MILLER, [OCTOBER, 1932]

Dear Lang:

Got both your letters and have been delayed in answering due to the general rush and hurry that always afflicts this gang at the end of a trip. True, Lydia [Filatova] got burned slightly at Baku and had to miss Tiflis; nothing serious and the patient is expected to recover. See Baku: it is a grand city of oil and technical triumphs and workers' clubs and all of the new social manifestations. And go to Tiflis and see the Georgian theatre. In many ways it is the most excellent one in the whole USSR. Beside that, the sight of Georgian girls is more than restful to the eye. Beautiful!! And fairly bubbling with friendliness. There must be something about Georgia's [Georgians] that make them produce good looking gals. And then go and see Dnieprostroi and its Socialist city. The story of the building of the dam and the dam itself is worthy of a great movie. After Hoover Dam it will be welcome. I had the impression that I was blasé as far as technical triumphs went but nobody can fail to be taken aback at this project.

Saw Anicimov [Julian Anissimov] after some effort. It seems that he was getting off a street car and some woman in back of him shoved him out with disastrous consequences to one leg, one shoulder and one of his spectacles. But he is definitely on the mend and will be OK. The greatest difficulty is that he has been unable to go out with me and the money—if any—is lying dormant. He says he sent you the dough for your novel and I hope that you have got it by this time. He gave me 1000 roubles from Persov (of yours) and many thanks. We are planning to go out tomorrow and see what we can collect. He will send you whatever we can get. The anthology is ready and the preface has been accepted. Anicimov says that I may be able to get my money but I doubt it like hell and it doesn't make any difference

FIGURE 9. From left: Louise, Loren Miller, Otto Huiswoud, and Matt in Tashkent, USSR, 1932.

anyhow. Meschrabpom got all big hearted and is keeping the gang here for the celebration and so we eat and sleep and what else is there? Mac [Alan McKenzie] and Matt and I are living in an apartment that is swell. We have two rooms and parties and good neighbors for whom we shop. In turn, the neighbor woman cooks our breakfast and you should see us eating ham and eggs and kasha and anything else dictated by our jaded appetites. Sorry you aren't here for we have all kinds of privacy and all kinds of food and all kinds of whatever else that appeals to our petty bourgeois sense of good-living. But what I started out to say is that if I do not get the money I will leave it here for you in case you need it and if you do not, then leave it and we will spend it when we return to the SU [Soviet Union]. Am going to Trud [37] tomorrow and see if I can get that money and likewise may leave that for you. How is the writing coming on? I have a contract to do a pamphlet for the International Publishers and the Cooperative Publishers here on the trip but the damned things will not get going and it may be that I will not write until I get to America. Either through laziness or through something-or-other I can't make the pamphlet click.

The Yard Apes[38] got back to New York and are raising hell as you will see from the papers I sent you if you ever get them. I don't get many of my papers because of Meschrabpom's quaint old custom of opening them and keeping such as they want. I even found papers here for as far back as July which had been hidden in the marvelous inefficiencies of our sometime employer. What a company! But the boys, they sent out a story from Berlin saying that the Soviet had betrayed us for big money and Friend Thurston [Lewis] spilled his guts to the inane Floyd Calvin when he got back to the breadlines of New York and are the papers having fun! The Amsterdam News had a story, an editorial and a cartoon in one fell swoop. And the Daily Worker rushed into the breach with you and me and some four interviews (via Myra Page) and the whole affair is going merry-hell. [H. W. L.] Dana of the committee[39] is here and his doddering mind accepts the original yarn about the pressure of Americans. The way the story goes now is that Cooper said that either he [Cooper] or the damned niggers would have to go. Then, the tale says, Stalin got scared and bowed and said "Yessah, Boss", and the Colonel stayed. Dana takes such tripe seriously. Ironically enough, Meschrabpom has just finished a film of the American intervention which gives America a Black Eye in the Grand Manner and out to incense the American capitalists no end and defer recognition until hell freezes over but it won't. But no amount of pointing to this fact would move the simple minded who take this betrayal seriously. And again, Meschrabpom has put out a short cartoon film of Mayakavsky [Vladimir Mayakovsky]'s "Black and White",[40] which you translated. Why in hell

37. *Trud* was a workers' newspaper published in the Soviet Union. *Trud* is the Russian word for "work."

38. "The Yard Apes" was a title Langston, Matt, Loren, Louise, and others used to refer to Ted Poston, Henry Moon, Thurston Lewis, and Laurence Alberga.

39. The committee Loren Miller is referring to is the Co-Operating Committee for Production of a Soviet Film on Negro Life.

40. Soviet poet Vladimir Mayakovsky's (1893–1930) famous poem "Black and White" was inspired by his trip to US-dominated Havana, Cuba, in 1925, where he witnessed American racism toward Black Cubans.

don't you send it to the dear Crisis or Opportunity and send a slight foot note that the film was made. Or better still, I shall say in one of my news dispatches to ANP [Associated Negro Press] that such a film was made and that you are translating the [Mayakovsky's] poem and if you never get the poem translated everybody will say that nigger newspapers are unreliable anyhow. Which reminds me that ANP is bubbling over with thanks and what-have-you for my reporting over here and wants to know what it can do for me. Suppose I should ask [Claude] Barnett for money! O yes, the Baltimore Afro[41] sent me a check for three bucks for some article that I sent them and the hell of it is that I do not remember what kind of a thing it was and if I did I could get more dough by writing the same sort of thing again. Life is difficult in this Russia!

Saw [Lydia] Filatova a day or two since and had a long and (blacked out) heart-to-heart talk with her in which she expressed dissatisfaction with some of Anicimov's translations, claiming that he had maltreated the ending of Waldorf Astoria and further saying that the translation of Good Morning, Revolution is so bad that many Russian have disliked it. Then when I saw him he said that some of the Russian poets were jealous and that some of them had said something or other which he interpreted as mere crabbing at him as a translator and at you as a poet. What the truth is, God alone can tell and he has been banished from Russia. Maybe it would be well for you to get some expert opinion from some place. I rather think that Filatova is more or less correct and that Anicimov has been turning out his work too fast to do as well as he could.

Am also going tomorrow to the Drama Union. It seems that they have taken the music of the protest songs and put them in the hands of Russian composers for some strange reason but are holding up publication of the words through some sort of fear that the songs may not be genuine. I plan to pull a McKenzie on them and shout all over the place. I do not know what is the matter with the damned fools, as it seems to me that the fact that you gave them the songs is good enough proof that they are not spurious. And why they should want to the Russian composers to fool around with the folk music is more than I can tell. Will tell you more when I have seen them.

Oh yes, the publishers took the anthology all apart and poor Anicimov had to put it back together. It seems that the administration changed and the old administration forgot to tell the new gang that the book

41. The *Baltimore Afro-American* was founded by John H. Murphy Sr., an ex-slave, and it is the longest-running Black family-owned newspaper in the United States.

had been accepted so the new set of genii censored it anew with the results that half of your poems were out as well as many more. The way I gather it is that nothing much was left but my preface and a few other things. So Anicimov got Dinamov and he called them up and told them to gotohell and publish the book and god knows when it will get out. What a life!

Louise is planning to leave Moscow the 8th and will not go to Paris but Matt and I will go and hope to sail for America on November 28 on the Bremen. I shall not remain in the East for long—only a week or so and then to Los Angeles and to my novel. The damned thing is just about all in my mind and if the words look as good as the idea (which they won't) I will like it despite the fact that I will probably be the only one in the world who will. When you do come to the USA come on out to the Golden West where there is plenty of good warm weather and sunshine and cheap rent and all of the other things that delight the hearts of the author and those who like leisure.

You had better wire subsequent addresses to Meschrabpom and I will tell Shallito [Frank Montero] to see that your mail is forwarded to you at given places. He is the only man who is apt to do anything.

Be Seeing You
lorenmiller

TO MATT, NOVEMBER 4, [1932]

[Handwritten postcard c/o Meschrabpom in Moscow]

Bukhara,

November 4

Boy—Have been in the desert, and yesterday interviewed one of the Emir's wives. Going back to Ashkabad today.

Lang

The trip home must have been bittersweet. A majority of the group had spent several weeks on a "consolation" tour of the USSR, which had been organized by the Meschrabpom Film Company after the production of *Black and White* had been put on hold. At every stop they were greeted and treated like VIPs and welcomed and entertained by new hosts. But when they returned to Moscow and prepared to leave for the United States, they were again confronted with the conflicting versions of why the film had been stalled and where the responsibility lay. Some members of the group maintained a half-hearted hope that they would be able to return to the Soviet Union the following summer when conditions would be favorable for resuming the production of *Black and White*, although this was not to be. For those like Matt and Loren Miller, who returned to the States via Paris, there were the late-autumn pleasures of the French capital to enjoy.

FROM MATT TO NEBBY, [NOVEMBER 21, 1932]

[Postcard]

PARIS, FRANCE

Babe:

We arrived in sophisticated Paris Saturday: its reputation is not exaggerated at all. Went through the famous Montmartre Saturday evening and saw gay Paris in all its splender. Sunday I went to the horse race and in the evening to the Latin quarters. We planned to tour the city to-day but it has been raining since early morning so I doubt if we shall make it. Everything is very expensive here compared to things in Berlin, and it is difficult to get a good meal for less than $.75. I shall wire you tonight for I guess it has been several days since you received the last letter I wrote.

Love
Matt

TO LOUISE, DECEMBER 30, 1932

Tashkent,

Dec. 30, 1932

Dear Lou—I'm back where colored are. Have lots of swell material, but too much company to ever get my work done. Am going to Moscow in 10 days. Write me there. How's mother?[42]

Langston

42. Langston is referring to Mother Thompson, whom he knew well and had great affection for, as he had been a frequent guest at the Thompson home in Harlem. Langston asked for news of her because he knew she was ill.

FIGURE 10. Shortly before his death in 1967, Langston inscribed this 1933 cover photo to Matt as a reminder of their time together in Tashkent, USSR, in 1932. (Matt N. and Evelyn Graves Crawford papers, Special Collections & Archives, Robert W. Woodruff Library, Emory University.)

Tashkent, Soviet Asia

January 4, 1933

Dear Matt—

Somebody fooled me. It's as cold here as Seattle, and snow every other day. I've bought myself a wagon-load of wood. Am living with 2 Uzbeks in a big room that is also a sculpture's studio by day. She's very pretty and Georgian. Happy New Year!

Lang

Louise did not linger in Moscow at the end of the tour. On November 8, upon receiving news that her mother's health had worsened, she rushed back to New York. After surviving the vicissitudes of the events surrounding *Black and White* in the Soviet Union, she nonetheless steadfastly clung to her belief that the film was only postponed. Once back in the United States, she strongly refuted the published anti-Soviet commentaries of Henry Lee Moon, Theodore Posten, and others who had lashed out against the Russians. In February 1933 the NAACP's magazine, *The Crisis*, published Louise's rebuttal to an editorial that had appeared in the magazine the previous month, wherein the editors expressed skepticism about the film having been postponed due to technical problems. In part, she stated:

> I am sure you realize that the capitalist press is especially eager to discredit in the eyes of American Negroes the one country in the whole world which gives them complete equality—the only country that has successfully solved the national question. . . . The matter of the postponement of a film is something which occurs daily in Hollywood or other film centers. Scenario and technical difficulties are not mysterious, political intrigues in any place but the Soviet Union. In the case of this film [*Black and White*] the facts of its postponement are very simple to understand, once one divorces them from the entanglement of bourgeois propaganda against the Soviet Union.

These words were written through a veil of tears, because although Louise bravely insisted on the probable resumption of the *Black and White* film project, her deepest preoccupations were elsewhere: her mother was dying. Four months after returning from the Soviet Union, she wrote to Langston with sad news.

[Handwritten]

February 26, 1933

Lang dear:

Mother slipped quietly on away last Thursday morning at seven o'clock.[43] Services were Friday at three and Howard Thurman conducted a most beautiful ceremony which was a tribute worthy of "Mother Thompson".

I have a great sense of peace now and quiet happiness—for my Mother is no longer suffering. She suffered such intense agony, and particularly during the last ten days it was so terrible for her. So that anyone who loved her could only be glad when her suffering had ended.

Everyone has been most kind. Your Mother came frequently and stayed many of those last nights with us. We had a nurse for Mama when she became so low—but your Mother and others came each day and night to do what they could. So that the experience I had dreaded most of all in my life became relatively easy—on the one hand because, since there was no other relief for Mama, I wanted her to go, and on the other hand, those about us helped so much.

I have no plans for making any change at present. Mary is here with me—then Doris and Emily have been with us and will continue for a while any way. Tomorrow morning I shall return to work. In other words, I shall go ahead living as I know Mother would wish it—missing her very much— but indulging in no morbidity. The Scottsboro boys and Angelo Herndon must be saved and one must sublimate his personal problems to the great struggle.

I received your cable and finally your letter from Moscow. I am glad to think that it may not be so long before I shall be seeing you again. There is so much to do here, Lang, and we need you. In Harlem we have succeeded in stirring a number of intellectuals and petty bourgeois elements on Scottsboro and Herndon. We have a Sunday nite forum at Augusta [Savage]'s and have begun a Marxian study circle. Then there are many other things and now I shall throw my every minute into the thing. We held two large mass meetings on Scottsboro at Abyssinian and St Philips Churches and had about one thousand Harlem Negroes at each meeting.

I hear that Matt is doing very good work up North and Loren wrote that he was trying to interest L.A. people in Scottsboro. Also that he was trying to begin a left wing magazine for Negro intellectuals.

---

43. Mother Thompson died on February 23, 1933.

Lang, I wish you would try to bring something definite back with you from Meschrabpom concerning the film. Go to them about it—Ford has asked that I ask you to do this. I would like to write more but have no time now.

Love to you,
Your pal Lou

THREE

Horror in Scottsboro, Alabama, and War in Spain

MAY 1933–NOVEMBER 1937

From 1933 to 1937 one of the major focuses of the lives of all of the five correspondents was the Scottsboro case. By 1933 Louise and Matt had returned from the trip to the USSR. Matt, Louise, Langston, and Loren Miller had been deeply impressed by the developments they had seen in Central Asia, results of the 1917 Russian Revolution. The oppressed colored minorities of the region had developed written languages, opened schools of higher education, introduced education for girls and women, reversed the obligatory wearing of paranja (a traditional garment similar to a burkha), built hospitals and housing for the people. Matt gave talks about the trip to groups all over the Bay Area. When speaking to Black audiences, he asked them to imagine what changes like these would mean for their lives and those of their people.

Louise had decided not to resume her work at the Congregational Education Society. Instead she joined the National Committee for the Defense of Political Prisoners, which was successfully organizing around the Scottsboro case. She and Augusta Savage formed a successful political salon in Harlem called the Vanguard Club.

On February 23, 1933, Mother Thompson closed her eyes for the last time. Louise was devastated by the loss, as she and her mother had been extremely close, yet she welcomed her mother's release from the unbearable pain she had suffered during the last months of her life. She threw herself into action with all the passion and energy she had, knowing that it was what her mother would have wanted her to do. In May, she helped organize a march from New York City to Washington, DC. The demonstration picked up supporters all along the route, bringing four thousand people to the capital to demand freedom for the Scottsboro Boys and other political prisoners, such as Tom Mooney in Northern California. Louise was one of the main speakers at the event.

Pat joined the International Labor Defense and was busy organizing the mass national and international movement to free the Scottsboro Boys. He was convinced there could be no victory in the courts without outside pressure.

Meanwhile in Carmel, California, at Noel Sullivan's country home, Langston was writing and speaking out about the Scottsboro case as well. He was also involved in social life and political struggles in the Bay Area.

In December 1934 Langston's father died. In spite of the fact that the two had never been close, Langston went to Mexico to tie up his father's affairs. Wallace Thurman, Louise's ex-husband, also died that December. Matt and Loren joined the National Council of the League of Struggle for Negro Rights.

In 1935 Harlem's first race riot broke out. Louise got involved and was called to testify before a mayoral committee that was investigating the riot. Langston's play *Mulatto* opened on Broadway and ran through 1936, although Langston barely earned a dime from the production. In 1936 the Negro National Congress was formed. All five friends were involved with it. To earn some money, Louise started working as a clerk for the International Worker's Order, and in early 1937 she got the organization to publish a selection of Langston's revolutionary poems under the title *A New Song*. It sold for ten cents a copy.

TO MATT, MAY 17, [1933]

> Meschrabpom, Moscow,
> May 17.

Dear Matt:

Glad to get your letter and all the news. It is spring here again and swell sunshine. Mil [Mildred Jones] and Dot [Dorothy West] left yesterday, via London. And I am leaving in a couple of weeks via Far East,—so fatten up a calf, as I'll probably be broke and hungry when I get to the Golden Gate with all the suitcases I have to carry around. Meet me with a truck and a beefsteak. I be there in July, I reckon. I'm staying for the Theatre Olympia here this month . . . May Day was tremendous— several hundred planes and tanks and a million people. I had a seat on the square.[1]

> LANG.

---

1. Red Square in Moscow. A viewing tribunal was always erected on the square so that officials and visiting dignitaries could view the May Day parade.

[Pages 2 and 3 of a four-page letter; pages 1 and 4 were lost.]

one story to Scribners almost immediately. All the Left writers in Moscow recommend him [Maxim Lieber][2] very highly as they say he has been most successful in disposing of stories and novels of proletarian life. I think I shall let him handle all of my magazine work from now on as it will save me keeping track of it myself.

I guess you are anxious to know about what happened in Japan and I want you to know because some of the newspapers carried very untrue versions of the affair, making up out of the clear sky situations that did not take place and statements that I did not issue. Here is the whole story in outline at least. When I came from Russia to Japan I spent a very delightful week there, visiting the beauty spots of the island and then stopping for three or four days in Tokyo. I met in Tokyo many of the literary people and all the artists of the Tokyo Left Theatre (the only modern theatre in Japan doing O'Neill, Shaw and Russian plays and other foreign dramas, as well as Japanese). Then I went to Shanghai where I spent two weeks, met very few Chinese Liberals or Radicals, as most of them are in hiding, living in terror of their lives. I did meet Mrs. Sun Yat Sen, however, and twice had dinner at her home. Since she is the head of the Anti-Imperialists League[3] in China and has spoken openly against Japanese oppression there I do not doubt that she is watched all the time by Japanese spies. In any case upon my return to Japan they knew there that I had met Mrs. Sun Yat Sen and immediately began to question me, even at Kobe, where I did not intend to land. At Tokyo, where the boat on which I was coming to America remained in port for two days, I was allowed to go ashore after relating the entire history of my life to the Immigration Authorities on board ship. A group of Japanese writers had arranged a luncheon for me the following day that I might meet other literary people that I had not met before. As I was waiting in the lobby of my hotel for some of the writers to come and take me to luncheon two gentlemen came up to me and presented their cards. When I looked down at the cards they said "Metropolitan Police Bureau". They informed me that their chief wished

2. Here Langston expresses his interest in hiring Maxim Lieber, who would eventually become his literary agent and champion in the publishing world.

3. The Anti-Imperialist League was an international organization founded in Brussels in 1927 to create an anti-imperialist movement on a world scale. It was considered, by the forces it opposed, as a front for the Comintern. Its formation was due in part to the anti-imperialist movement in China, which started in 1926.

to see me. When I said that I had a luncheon engagement and could not see their chief at the time they, with extreme politeness replied, "but the chief must see you". Anyway, I went with them to police headquarters and there I was questioned for the rest of the day. I learned from reporters that evening that a number of Japanese writers were also detained and questioned so I presume they must have arrested all those in attendance at the luncheon. And as Japanese may be held twenty-nine days in Japan without charges being put against them I expect that most of these fellows are still in prison. Some of them were quite conservative people too and not what you would call proletarian. The police were most interested to know why I would come from Russia, go through Japan and then go to China. They seemed to feel that I was carrying messages and that I had much more important connections that I have. They even seemed to feel that I might know Stalin. They ended by demanding to search all of my baggage and asking me to swear that I had brought no messages from Moscow to Japan. The whole thing was more or less amusing as most of their questions seemed very naive to me and as I had nothing to hide I could answer all of them truthfully, so in spite of the continual repetition of the same forms of questions I never became confused and eventually I suppose they decided that I was telling the truth. There are lots of amusing things to tell you about the dialogues that went on between myself and the police but it would take me all day to write them down so I shall wait until I see you. The only exciting evidence they found in my baggage was a fan from the Left Theatre which the members of the cast had autographed for me, writing their names on both sides of the colored paper. The police went to great pains to copy down every single name on the fan as though they had discovered a list of conspirators. You see what a dangerous person they thought I was. Anyway they forbade me to see any more Japanese, two detectives accompanied me everywhere and walked beside me to the very door of my cabin on the boat. Of course you know the extent to which suppression of freedom of speech goes in Japan. Hundreds of students are arrested there every year and there is strict censorship of thought, speech and writing. I have many facts from American observers, teachers and missionaries who have lived there for some time and I hope to do an article about conditions there soon. Japan, as well as China labors under a militaristic dictatorship that crushes without shame anyone opposing the rain of bullets they have let Asia in for.

I suppose you have gotten direct information about Black and White from comrades lately returned from Moscow so I will not go into details here. It seems to me best, at least, to stop making public statements of any sort in regard to the picture as it will perhaps not be made for some time. You know how slow the Russians are anyway and although I do not doubt but that our picture will be made eventually, I think the years will roll on there a little while before it is completed.

Why don't you come out here for a vacation or a speaking tour or any other good reason this fall? Nebby and Matt and all of your friends (me too) would be mighty glad to see you and ... [rest of letter missing]

TO MATT AND NEBBY, [OCTOBER 10, 1933]

Carmel, Wednesday, 10th

Dear Matt and Nebby,

Loren and Juanita [Miller] say they can come up (they think) a week from this Saturday, which would be the 21st, wouldn't it? Could you all come down then? I hope so. And stay over Sunday when we can have a picnic at Point Lobos. Plan to arrive Saturday in time for evening dinner. Let me know. . . . . I seem to have eating on my mind. . . . . I think I will have to buy a new belt. The one I have is getting too short. I am getting fat. . . . . If it isn't one thing to worry about, it's another. A few months ago I was worried about being undernourished in Tashkent. Now, I['m] worried about being over-nourished in Carmel. Who's knows what the correct line is? Anyhow, if you can't come down then, come any time you want to, only let me know so I'll be looking out for you. . . . . Thanks a lot for those colored papers. They are still keeping me company.

Sincerely,
LANG

TO MATT AND NEBBY, [DECEMBER 23, 1933]

[Handwritten Christmas card]

Dear Matt and Nebby—

Hope you have a grand time. I have a bottle of old wine for you, but am scared to mail it—so I'll either keep it or drink it till I see you again.

Lang

FIGURE 11. Nebby, Langston, and his dog Greta on the beach in Carmel, California, 1933.

TO NEBBY AND MATT, [APRIL 25, 1934]

Carmel, Wed.

Dear Nibby, also Matt,

Wally [Wallace Thurman] and Fay [Jackson]⁴ got married today and will be up this week-end—so come on down Sat. Nora Holt is here. See you. Lang

TO MATT, [OCTOBER 1934?]

Dear Matt,

Sorry, but I can't speak. And if, when I get in jail, nobody speaks, I won't say a word.

I had a nice letter from Pat and Vera,⁵ and the kid is a year old and is learning to walk.

4. Wallace Thurman was only pretending to have married his friend Fay Jackson. At the time he was suffering from tuberculosis, and he died a few months later.

5. Pat and Vera are Lloyd and Vera Patterson. Lloyd went to Moscow with Louise, Langston, and Matt in 1932, and he stayed in the Soviet Union. He married Vera, who was a stage and movie costume designer. They had three sons together.

Swell, heh? And Pat's mother came over, is living with them, and likes it very much, he says. Pat says he has been reading my poems over the radio. . . . . But I wish to God I had never written anything if I am going to have to speak all the time. . . . . I think I have a chance to get a job in a barbecue place. I think I will take it and go back to normal. The literary life is getting me down. . . . . I wish I could buy a plane and commute between Harlem and the Metropol.[6] Sylvia [Chen] says Jack [Chen] and his wife have a baby, but it is too white. She wants one with more colored blood in it/////Boy, you ought to fly once. You'd never ride on the ground any more—except when you didn't have the money to ride in the air. I had to pawn my watch this time—but I flew right on. I got back to Frisco with fifty cents.

Tell Nebby HY!

Lang

Louise was tested in a dramatic way in the summer of 1934. She joined the staff of the International Workers Order (IWO), a left-wing fraternal and insurance organization headquartered in New York that was closely aligned with the Communist Party. While on an organizing trip in Alabama, she was arrested in Birmingham and jailed for several days for associating with white radicals.[7]

TO LOUISE, [1934]

[Christmas card]

To Lou—ise:

Felices Pascuas y Prospero Ano Nuevo (Merry Christmas and a Prosperous New Year)

Lang

San Ildefonso 73

6. The Metropol Hotel in Moscow.

7. None of Louise's letters concerning this incident survive. However, she wrote a fearsome article about her experience in Birmingham, titled "Southern Terror," which appeared in NAACP's *The Crisis* magazine in November 1934.

Dear Louise:

I tried so hard to find a card that didn't have a church on it. The Patinos[8] insisted that I send you the Virgin of Guadalupe. They remember you with much pleasure, and all three of them send regards. It seems that your visit to Mexico was one of the highlights of the past decade in their and my father's life. They hope you will come back again.

TO MATT AND NEBBY, [1934]

[Christmas card]

San Ildefonso 73
Mexico, D.F.

Dear friends, pals, and comrades in struggle—Here am I, safe and sound, after being held up 4 days on the border because my permit didn't say I was colored. I finally pulled a Jean Toomer[9] on them and said my papa was an Indian anyhow, so they put me down as <u>mixed</u>!

Lang

TO MATT AND NEBBY, JANUARY 31, 1935

San Ildefonso 73
Mexico City, Mexico

January 31, 1935

Dear Matt and Nebby,

Today it is so cold down here that I am writing to you with all the clothes I have on my back, but I had determined not to permit the thirty-second year of my life to end without writing you a letter. I have been thinking of you all often and wondering if you've moved yet and if you've heard from Louise and if Nebby ever sent her letter on to Wallie [Wallace Thurman] before he went on[10] . . . With me, of course, nothing has happened yet as regards my father's estate. Everything takes a long time down here. He left all his belongings to the three elderly old Catholic ladies[11] with whom he

8. Langston is referring to the Patiño sisters, three elderly Mexican women who lived with his father in Mexico.
9. Langston is referring to Toomer passing as white.
10. Wallace Thurman died of tuberculosis in New York City on December 22, 1934.
11. The three Patiño sisters (see note 8).

lived, but they want to share a fourth of it with me. The government takes a 20% tax, and when the lawyer is paid and a few debts, I hope there'll be enough left to pay you back your ten. I think it'll just about almost cover the trip, so I've decided to stay down here and have a good trip while I'm at it. I've begun to read DON QUIXOTE in four volumes (with a teacher) so you can imagine how long I will be here! .... I, too, live with the three Catholic old maids, who are really awfully nice, and are spoiling me terrible, waiting on me hand and foot, and preparing all sorts of Mexican dishes and desserts of tropical fruits for me every day, and taking me to mass and praying for my soul—among others—because there are so many more devils in Mexico beside me! And the church is having a hard time, and I am hearing all about their side, at least.... So far I haven't met any writers or artists, thank God, and so have been having a nice quiet time doing quite as I please, with nobody asking me to make a speech, or attend a tea, or read their manuscripts, or make a statement. And it's got so good to me that I don't think I'll ever let anybody down here know I'm a writer. Everybody just thinks I'm an unusually dark-complexioned American who's lost his father—and so I get a lot of sympathy.... I belong to an "explorers" club of fellows and girls called the Dragones who make semi-monthly excursions to out of the way places like the Desert of the Lions and the Pyramids; and occasionally give dances. And every Sunday so far I've been to the bullfights. This Sunday it ought to [be] extra good as one of the most famous of the Mexican fighters makes his first appearance of the season, having pulled a Babe Ruth on them and held out for ever so many thousands up until now. I guess they agreed to pay him, and they are making a festive occasion of his first appearance, with specially decorated tickets and all. Ortega, great Spanish bullfighter, has been a flop in Mexico this year, and last week it took twenty cops to get him out of the plaza whole after the crowd had pelted him with insults, cushions and beer bottles just when he was trying his best to make a kill. The proletarians on the sunny (and cheaper) side of the plaza especially dislike him, and used to yell every time he would side-step the horns of a bull, "What's this for twenty-thousand pesos, you capitalist, you?" . . . But the most hair-raising fights are to be seen, not in the big ring where the great professionals perform, but in the suburban plazas where they have the novilleros—the young and unknown fighters who are out to make a name for themselves. Here you see the most dangerous gyrations in front of the bull's horns; you see kids butted and trampled and gored; silken suits slit wide open, horn and sword both hitting the mark at the same time—all for the dream of the big plaza, El Toreo, and 20,000 pesos a fight, and Madrid and Sevilla—if they live to see it. You can see what it takes for a bullfighter to get where he wants to go, in the Novilleros.

Trying to decide which ring to go to on Sundays has now about got me down—whether to watch the great and skillful, or the unknown and brave. . . . . Anyhow, with all this, I've written four stories. Imagine the <u>New Yorker</u> publishing OYSTER'S SON![12] I know there's something wrong with the line, now! Anyhow, Joe North wrote me it was about my best story and I should have given it to the NEW MASSES. (Did I tell you Loren [Miller] says Joe North is the guy Louise is in love with and vice versa?) . . . . I went to a big I.L.D. [International Labor Defense] Meeting here on the anniversary of [Julio Antonio] Mella's death.[13] It was about the only big mass meeting lately here that hasn't ended in shootings, head-breakings, and the coming of the fire department to drench everybody with ice water. The Catholics and the Red Shirts[14] have been raising hell—and pistols are playthings! . . . . I should have written you before now to warn you that I might have to ask you to do me a favor. On Dec. 1, I sent mother, Mrs. Carolyn Clark (then 117 South Main St.) Oberlin, Ohio a money order for $20.00 from the Ferry Building Office. She never received the order, and so we are trying to trace it. I sent her the receipt, and wrote her that should she be unable to make use of it on her end, to send it to you with the request that you ask the S.F. Ferry Buldg. Office to trace it and repay, if not found. I don't know whether mother has sent it on to you or not, but if she does, please see what you can do about it for me on your way to or from work. . . . . . Best regards to all, Leland, Gladys, your mother, Arcie, Charlie, Irene and so on to yourselves.[15] Write me all the news. I am now about to go to a dance. They have swell big public dance halls down here from five o'clock on with Cuban rumba bands playing and the lights going dim and colorful like in the Savoy in New York. There you will find me struggling. One has to keep warm somehow these cold Mexican days . . . .

12. "Oyster's Son" was one of Langston's short stories. It was published in *The New Yorker* magazine on January 12, 1935.

13. Julio Antonia Mella (1903–1929) was the founder of the "internationalized" Cuban Communist Party. Mella was assassinated on January 10, 1929, while in exile in Mexico. His killer remains unknown. Some scholars believe he was shot by Trotskyites; others claim the murder was a crime of passion committed by Italian revolutionary Vittorio Vidali because of a love triangle between the two men and the radical Italian photographer Tina Modatti. He is a mythic and heroic revolutionary figure in Cuba today.

14. The Red Shirts was an anti-Catholic paramilitary organization of the 1930s, founded by Tomas Garrido Canabal, the governor of Tabasco, Mexico, during his second term.

15. These are members of Matt's family in Berkeley and Oakland: his brother-in-law and sister Leland and Gladys Hawkins; his mother Mrs. Emma Crawford; his brother Artice Crawford; and his brother and sister-in-law Charles and Irene Sears Crawford.

IMITATIONS OF LIFE[16] opened here with a big play from the critics, all of them rating Louise Bevers [Beavers] as the star of the film. And one of the papers even said, "Among the other players are Claudette Colbert, etc." ......!!!!!!..... Also 3 colored fighters have been here this month: Armstrong, Cocoa Kid, and Chalky Wright.[17] I would do a piece about them for the papers but I'm [the rest of the letter is hand written in the margins around the bottom and sides] scared the line wouldn't be right and you all might say, like you did about my piece about the Reno mail-man—"What's the big idea?" I know Nebby wouldn't though. She's my pal. Anyhow every time I sit down to write the piece it's time to go to the dance! Love.

[Note in margin] *Enclosures—stamps for the young one, and a clipping for old atheists! Don't show it to your mother—nor mine either. (See both sides).*

TO MATT AND NEBBY, MAY 20, 1935

San Ildefonso 73
Mexico, D.F.

May 20, 1935

Dear Matt and Nebby,

Alright for you, you dogs! You won't write to me, heh? Are you dead or alive? Have you moved or not? Don't tell me because I'll be back in no time, and will find out for myself. I didn't come back sooner because I was scared to return with my debts unpaid! Especially my Uncle John! But now I'm on my last go round down here. Up to my neck in work as usual, having translated some thirty Mexican and Cuban short stories this last month to make an anthology. Six to go, but one is almost as long as a novel. And I haven't seen a thing in Mexico—but the night clubs and dinner parties, etc. Must try and get down to Taxco and Puebla before I leave. So I'm not telling anyone I'm departing. They just got through welcoming me, and if the farewell parties were to start, I'm sure I would die before I got on the train. Besides I have to be in New York by the end of June. I shall probably have to speak my way across the country. Have Kansas City already booked. And

16. *Imitation of Life* is a movie that was released by Universal Pictures in November 1934, based on a book by Fannie Hurst. It's the story of a young, very light-skinned Black woman who passes for white, abandoning her mother in the process. Claudette Corbert was the star.

17. Henry Armstrong (1912–1988) held three boxing championships at one time. The Cocoa Kid, born Herbert Lewis Hardwick (1914–1966), was an Afro-Puerto Rican welterweight boxer. Albert "Chalky" Wright (1912–1957) was a featherweight boxer from 1928 to 1948.

the American Youth Congress[18] in Detroit. If you know anybody in Jalapy who wants to hear a good bad speaker at $100 bucks an hour or an evening—if they insist on it—let me know. For the moment, I'm renting my eloquence out by the night. I hope I can think of something to say. I think I shall take my text: Whether The Black Man? Or would: Whither America? Give me more scope? For a hundred dollars it ought to be something profound! Maybe merely, Whither? Which takes in everything. . . . . Well, anyhow, I hope to see you all again before I start East. Which will be about an hour before I'm due in Kansas City, I'm sure. Time goes faster and faster, and I get later and later starting out for anywhere—especially with my watch almost continuously in the pawn shop. I hope to get it but once and for all tomorrow. . . . . I think you'll like my Mexican-Cuban stories. They are swell. Lots of Indian and Negro characters. Almost all the authors in these countries are left. And some are even lefter than left. . . . I've been working on this business of Negro tourist and Mexico, now that the new road is open-ing. I think it's about o.k., and according to the Secretary of Immigration, orders have been sent to the Mexican Embassy at Washington that Negroes are to be granted the same entrance privileges as other Americans. Sue Bailey was just down here, had a hard time entering, so we went around and raised sand about the rights of the race—with the above results. Thanks for this ten. Tell Nebby to put it back in her pocket book. I don't know how ART would get along if it wasn't for nice people like you all. ART has a hard time.

Sincerely,
Lang

TO MATT AND NEBBY, NOVEMBER 9, 1935

[Letterhead: New York Central System]

en route to Indianapolis, November 9, 1935

Dear Matt and Nebby,

How are you-all? I am on the run as usual. Don't seem to do anything but pack up and go places. The day I got to New York (to my great amazement) my play went into rehearsal. I had about a week there before I had to go out to Minnesota where I lectured to 4,000 students, also to two Urban League

---

18. The American Youth Congress, founded in 1934, was the first national progressive youth organization in the United States. During the New Deal years it lobbied for jobs and against racial discrimination and the draft.

groups, and twice over the air. Then back to New York for the opening and now out to Indiana for my aunt's funeral. Then back to Cleveland next week for a reading at the Woman's City Club. After that I think I shall retire!

Boy, you ought to see the play![19] It's melodrama with a big M. It has murder, rape, suicide, and insanity in it, and a mob with hounds as the curtain falls! It got so changed in rehearsals and beforehand by the producer that it's only about half mine now. Some of the reviews were good— but most were not so hot. Audiences seem to go for it though, and it may have a run. Anyhow, it's still there at present and Rose McClendon has made a great personal success as the mother, one critic terming her one of the three great actresses on the American stage . . . Well, I have learned a lot and lost ten pounds during rehearsals. There's nothing like a play to bring you down . . . I went to see Ethel Waters the night my show opened. She was swell in "At Home Abroad."[20]

Loren [Miller] is fine. Says he's going home this month. . . . Louise was all excited when I told her Nebby might come to New York for a vacation. Lou makes speeches from a step ladder [drawing of ladder] and is great . . . Ted [Posten] and [Henry] Moon and all the "News" staff are on strike. I did my first picketing. Ted gets married Wednesday. Write me at once, will you.

Lang

[Note in left margin] *c/o Knopf, Inc., 730-Fifth Ave, New York*

[Note in top margin] *Made my first speech at Soviet Russia Today[21] Banquet last week*

TO MATT AND NEBBY, JANUARY 4, 1936

2. A.M. Morning
January 4, 1936

Dear Matt, and Nebby: Hy!

Wish you and Nebby could have been here for this Congress.[22] Great opening mass meeting tonight, ten thousand people, the largest crowd I

---

19. The play was *Mulatto,* Langston's first Broadway production, which ran for 373 performances at the Vanderbilt Theatre.

20. *At Home Abroad* was a musical revue by Arthur Schwartz and Howard Dietz that ran on Broadway.

21. *Soviet Russia Today* was a pictorial monthly magazine published by the Soviet Union for distribution in other countries.

22. Langston is referring to the Third US Congress Against War and Fascism, which took place in Cleveland, Ohio, on January 3–4, 1936.

ever spoke to—outside that Scottsboro demonstration at the Park of Rest and Culture. There're lots of Negro delegates—even one I've met directly from Los Angeles. [James W.] Ford and [Angelo] Herndon and Newton are here, lots of colored youth delegates. Louise is said to be saving herself for the Negro Congress[23] in Chicago in February, so she didn't show up . . . You ought to see me stopping at this swell hotel, broke as a fool. Even with a lawyer I can't so far collect from MULATTO which is still running, but which the Dramatists Guild will close shortly if the man doesn't come through with my royalties. Nobody knows what makes Broadway producers such rascals . . . Why don't you-all write me a card and let me know if you're still alive? Eula [Eulah C. Pharr] says you are.

Sincerely,
Lang

TO MATT, [FEBRUARY 1936]

BALLAD OF OZIE POWELL[24]

Red is the Alabama road,
Ozie, Ozie Powell,
Redder now where your blood has flowed,
Ozie, Ozie Powell.

Strong are the bars and steel the gate,
Ozie, Ozie Powell,
The High Sheriff's eyes are filled with hate,
Ozie, Ozie Powell.

The High Sheriff shoots and he shoots to kill
Black young Ozie Powell,

---

23. The National Negro Congress (1935–1940) was formed at Howard University in 1935. Its first national meeting was held in Chicago on February 14–16, 1936. Over 800 delegates from 558 organizations attended. It grew out of discussions between Communist Party delegates to the Joint Committee on National Recovery conference in May 1935 about the economic status of Negroes under the New Deal.

24. "Ballad of Ozie Powell" is a poem Langston wrote evoking the plight of one of the youngest Scottsboro Boys. Ozie Powell cut a prison guard in the neck with a penknife, and the guard then shot him in the face, leaving him with permanent brain damage.

The law's a Klansman[25] with an evil will,
Ozie, Ozie Powell.

You're one of the nine in the law's lean claws,
Penniless Ozie Powell,
<u>Not</u> one of the nine who pass the laws,
Ozie, Ozie Powell.

Those nine old men in Washington,
Ozie, Ozie Powell,
Never saw the High Sheriff's gun,
Ozie, Ozie Powell.

Nine old men so rich and wise,
Ozie, Ozie Powell,
They never saw the High Sheriff's eyes,
Ozie, Ozie Powell.

But nine black boys know too well
Heh, oh, Ozie Powell?
What it is to live in hell,
Ozie, Ozie Powell.

Where the devil's a Kleagle[26] with an evil will,
Ozie, Ozie Powell,
A white High Sheriff [^who] shoots to kill
Black young Ozie Powell.

And red is that Alabama road,
Ozie, Ozie Powell,
But redder now where your life's blood's flowed,
Ozie! Ozie Powell!

Langston Hughes

[Note in left margin] *Dear Matt, you old N.A.A.C.P.er you! Happy to have your letter, of course! Are you coming to the Congress [Third US Congress*

25. A Klansman is a member of the terrorist, racist, anti-Communist, anti-Semitic, and anti-Catholic organization the Ku Klux Klan. Klansmen wear white robes and pointed hoods that cover their faces, with small openings for their eyes. They terrorize, murder, lynch, bomb, torch, and otherwise intimidate. They also burn huge crosses, usually at night.
26. A "Kleagle" is the title of an officer in the Ku Klux Klan whose job is to recruit new members.

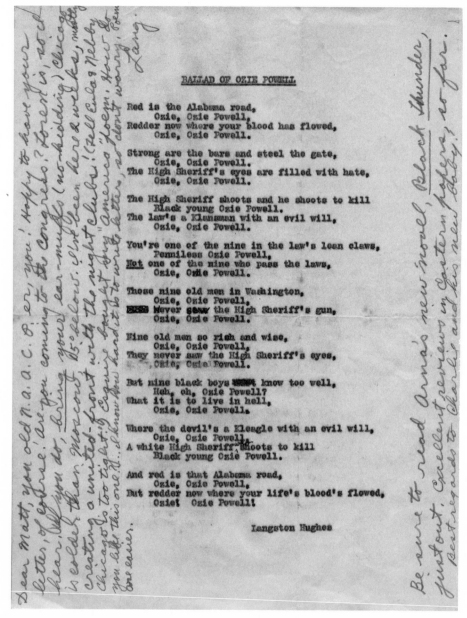

FIGURE 12. A letter from Langston to Matt with a draft of his poem "Ballad of Ozie Powell," 1935. (Matt N. and Evelyn Graves Crawford papers, Special Collections & Archives, Robert W. Woodruff Library, Emory University.)

Against War and Fascism]? Loren [Miller] is, so I hear. If you do, <u>bring</u> your ear-muffs (no kidding) Chicago is colder than Moscow, 15° below. I've been here 2 weeks, mostly creating a united-front with night clubs! (Tell Eula [Eulah Pharr] & Nebby Chicago is too tight!) Esquire bought my "America" poem ["Let America Be America Again"]. How do you like this one? . . . . I know how hard it is to write letters, so don't worry. Poems are easier.

Lang

[Note in right margin] *Be sure to read Arna [Bontemps]'s new novel, <u>Black Thunder</u>,[27] just out. Excellent reviews in Eastern papers, so far. Best regards to Charlie [Crawford] and his new baby!*

TO MATT, [JUNE 4, 1936]

[Postcard of Lorain Carnegie Bridge, Cleveland]

Dear Matt,

I just sent your JOHN HENRY[28] book back today. Who says I don't return books? MULATTO is now the longest running play of the season! You ough<u>tn't</u> to see it.

Lang

FROM MATT, NOVEMBER 29, 1936

Nov. 29, 1936

Dear Lang:

It's the same old story—been so damn busy I just haven't had a minute to write. However I decided I wouldn't let the year get away before writing to you. This is the first free Saturday afternoon I have had for months, and this happened because a guy didn't keep an appointment I had.

Weez told me, when she was here, that you wanted to know if I had received the check and the book. I did, and thanks very much. I knew you would get the cancelled check, and clear that up and Weez said she would see you and give you a message for me, so I know you would at least know that I had received both of them.

---

27. Arna Bontemps's 1936 novel, *Black Thunder,* tells the story of an ultimately suppressed slave revolt led by Gabriel Prosser that took place in 1800 in Virginia.

28. It's not clear who wrote the book on John Henry that Langston refers to here.

We all were very glad to see Weez and enjoyed her visit very much. As she has no doubt told you she really had a vacation while she was here. I think she spoke at <u>only</u> two meetings the whole time. There were very few parties that she had to go to, so when she and Nebby were not at Santa Cruz or some other place out of town, we just stayed at home and generally relaxed. Among the few places we did go was to Sullivan's to see Eula [Eulah Pharr]. Sullivan came in before we left and he and Louise had quite a discussion about the Party. It began with a discussion of some of your recent work. His opinion was that your revolutionary writing did not express your real ability, that it gave the impression that you were doing something that you did not really feel, etc. etc. He talked more than I had ever heard him talk about anything. All sympathy he had for the party had gone and he had become very conservative—to say the least. I believe that there are several reasons for his new attitude; his sympathy may have been abused by some people in the movement, probably some-one made a stupid mistake with him. But more important, I believe that his family and his business advisers have put a great deal of pressure on him and all together he has come to realize that the revolution is a very serious business. It was all rather sad to me for the whole thing seemed to affect him very much, his conviction seemed as sincere on his changed attitude as his sympathy had previously been. It must be hell for a liberal to be rich, catholic, and have a very conservative family all at the same time.

Our work on the Negro Congress has gone along steadily but difficultly since I returned from Chicago. At first there was an enthusiastic response from the community generally, then the boys in the NAACP began red-baiting[29] in a big way and many sincere people were frightened away. However there has been a faithful few who continue to work very hard for the building of the congress and we are gradually winning the confidence of the people. John Davis was here a few weeks ago and he helped a great deal to create interest in the idea, so I am optimistic about the possibilities of building a real mass movement here. Last week we had a meeting on the waterfront situation as it affects Negroes. Revels Cayton, who is a member of the Joint Strike Committee, and a white fellow spoke very well on the whole fight of the maritime unions.[30] The congress endorsed the strike and

29. "Red-baiting" is the practice of creating suspicion or fear about a person or institution by claiming that she, he, or it is Communist (i.e., "red"). It dates to the 1917 Russian Revolution, although it became widespread during the period leading up to World War II and into the Civil Rights era of the 1960s, when anti-Communist witch-hunts targeted left-leaning individuals and organizations of various political stripes.

30. The 1934 West Coast Waterfront Strike had won longshoremen unionization rights, non-discrimination clauses, and other concessions from the shipping companies. The

issued a joint statement with the Strike Committee on the position of the Negro maritime workers in the strike and urging the people in the community to support the unions. There has been no attempt to recruit strikebreakers yet but if it lasts much longer efforts certainly will be made to get Negroes to help break the strike. The report Revals [Revels] gave about the number and conditions of Negroes working on the front was very well received by the people at the meeting, so I hope we will be able to give some effective assistance to the unions.

There has been real advancement made among Negro maritime workers since 1934. Approximately 800 Negroes are in the various unions on the coast. A number of them occupy important positions in the unions.

It is impossible to say how the strike will pan out, there is no question that the ship owners are trying to starve the unions out and break their strength once and for all. However, the unions are maintaining absolute unity up to now and it looks as though they will be able to hold out for quite a spell yet. They are far better prepared than they were in 1934. There has been no disturbance even of a minor nature during the month the strike has been on. There are effective committees coordinating the work of all the unions. There has been a break in the ranks of the ship owners and it looks quite possible that agreements may be reached with some of the smaller lines very soon.—I hope.

Loren [Miller] was up to the Western Writers Congress[31] week before last, he read a very good paper on Negro writers and their various difficulties. It was the first time I had seen him since we came home from the Soviet Union, he was very busy so we had only a short time together.

We have an I W O branch here now, Nebby and my brother's wife are very active in it, we have about 15 members, all Negroes, we are trying to establish a real organization before we expand in all directions, if you get what I mean. Mulatto is opening at the Curran [Theatre][32] Monday, as you probably know. It has gotten a great deal of advance publicity, so I am eager to see the reviews of it next week. I shall see it before it leaves.

Well Lang I think I have told you most of the important things that have occurred in these parts. I shall again make the pledge that I shall not wait so long before I write to you again.

---

companies were, however, slow to implement them, so in 1936 a new strike was called, which became known as the 1936–1937 Maritime Union Strike. It lasted ninety days and was won by the workers.

31. The Western Writers Conference was held November 13–14, 1936, in San Francisco. It was organized by a group of liberal and left-wing writers, including John Steinbeck.

32. The Curran Theatre is a major theater in downtown San Francisco.

I hope your mother is getting along better now, give her my best regards.

All of the folks here are getting along pretty well, they often ask about you. One thing I did not say, by the time you get out again our house will be finished. After many delays, we are just about ready to begin building. So you will have an additional "home in the west"[.]

Sincerely
Matt

TO MATT, [DECEMBER 18, 1936]

[Christmas card]

My very best to you and Nebby. Greatly enjoyed your letter. Louise is here in Cleveland. Tell Nebby to come on and go to Europe with me this summer. I'm conducting a tour for Edutravel[33]—6 countries including U.S.S.R.!!!! I'm still hustling free boat rides!! And food!

Lang

Has or hasn't the Loren Miller's a child?

FROM LOUISE, JANUARY 8, 1937

[Letterhead: International Workers Order]

January 8, 1937

Mr. Langston Hughes
2256 E. 86th St
Cleveland, Ohio

Dear Lang,

Happy New Year to you and household!

Since my return to these parts I immediately took up the matter of getting your revolutionary verse into a volume. And since we in the I.W.O. are interested in such things, I took it up right at home. The result is that our Educational Department is anxious to publish these through independent auspices and have asked me to write you under what conditions you would be willing to have this done.

33. Edutravel was the name of the travel bureau at Columbia University in New York.

Their idea is to get out an attractive little paper bound volume which could sell for about ten cents. That is should be illustrated as much as such a low price would permit. Therefore, whether this is possible or not would depend on what you would require as your royalty.

Also they want to know if you have other poems. I know of two which I did not get—Open Letter to the South, and Waiting on Mr. Roosevelt. You may have others. I am sending you under separate cover the current issue of our monthly magazine in which we have printed Our Spring, as you told me we could reprint any of them we wanted to.

I hope that you will agree to have these poems published so that they can be available en masse for wide distribution. So please let me know AT ONCE as they are on my ear about the matter, and I have put off writing you because I have been pretty rushed.

Hope you had a nice holiday time. I am sure you did for you have the capacity of enjoying yourself wherever you are.

Love to you and to your mother,

Lou

TO MATT, [FEBRUARY 1, 1937]

Dear Matt,

I can't tell you-all how much I enjoyed your holiday gift, as did all the rest of the family. It looked so good we kept it on the mantle-piece a long time for decoration. In fact the box is still there. Thanks to you and Nebby. It was pretty swell. . . . Mason [Roberson] is here as you know working on one of our local papers, and is rooming next door to us, so we see him all the time. He just left a while ago to go bang his typewriter. I've got two typewriters now. Purchased a noiseless to write plays on since nobody seems to appreciate playwriting after one o'clock in the morning on an ordinary machine. . . . . . . Today is my birthday so I'm sending you a poem on Spain just finished an hour ago. . . . Also an anti-lynching playlet the N.A.A.C.P. juniors are doing here Feb. 12. If it's of any use to anybody in the Bay Region, let them use it, and welcome. . . . I couldn't resist having a little fun with it at the very end!. . . . . Lou's I.W.O. is going to bring out my proletarian poems in a booklet[34] to sell for a dime or less. Isn't that swell? . . . . Don't worry about answering this. Your recent letter was welcome enough and

34. The booklet was titled *A New Song* and was published by the International Workers Order in 1938.

good enough to last a year. But give my best regards to everybody, and if anybody wants to go to Russia this summer tell them to go with me, as it seems I'm conducting a tour for Edutravel sailing July 1st for eight weeks: London, Scandinavia, Russia, Poland, Paris and home.[35] $500 bucks. White and colored. I'm to be the leader, so I've written Louise asking her where she found her comrade shoes. I'll probably need a pair.

Sincerely,

Lang

February 1, 1937
At the age of 35,

2256 E. 86th St.,
Cleveland, Ohio.

FROM LOUISE, FEBRUARY 10, 1937

[Letterhead: International Workers Order]

February 10, 1937

Dear Lang:

I don't like your remark about being as old as you; it sounds like a dirty crack. However, tho belated, let me extend to you all best wishes for not only this birthday, but a hundred to come.

Now about the poems. I am certainly glad that both you and [Maxim] Lieber like the idea. I am enclosing a list of those we have. OPEN LETTER TO THE SOUTH I am sure we can get from the New Masses as it was printed there in 1930 or '31, was it not? You can go over this list and make your suggestions as to those which you think should be included. The WALDORF-ASTORIA one is so long we may have to cut it out, and then, it is sort of dated.

It seems to me, Lang, that a good title might be A NEW SONG. I like the poem itself and I think it might set the right tone for such a volume.

I went up to see Doug [Aaron Douglas] the other night to ask him if he might do the illustrations. He was not cold to the idea. He wanted me to leave the poems with him so he could go over them and see whether he

---

35. Edutravel canceled the trip. Langston went to Spain to cover the civil war there instead.

could get into the mood. His idea was, if he did them, that they be sort of mass outlines in black and white.

So in the midst of writing operas, arranging tours to Europe, going to parties, and sleeping, try to get these things re-arranged so we can go ahead with it as quickly as possible.

I wouldn't mind travelling along as your secretary, valet, or something—how about it? I'd even volunteer to find some comrade-shoes for you. If you haven't any proposals to make, about as far as my possibilities can extend for the summer is to the West Indies. I haven't any money so far, but the idea lingers.

Love to everybody. Let me hear from you as soon as possible.

Lou

FROM LOUISE, FEBRUARY 16, 1937

[Letterhead: International Workers Order]

Feb. 16, 1937

Langston Hughes
2256 E 86th St.
Cleveland, Ohio

Dear Lang:

Received your letter and we had quite a discussion about the matter of illustrating the book of poems.

Your idea of actual photographs is one well worth considering. The thing is whether or not we would be able to get the proper pictures. They would have to be especially fine studies. Maybe we might combine both pictures and some illustrations. When you send in the additional poems and your proposals as to how many and which ones should be included we can consider the matter of a section on translations.

By the time you get to New York we can probably have a final conference on the whole set-up. Everybody is very enthused about it and has some swell ideas about the publicizing of it. What we want to do is get as broad a distribution of it as is possible.

I am leaving for Boston and will be gone until the 22nd. I hope when I get back to find a letter from you telling me when you are going to be in New York.

I have to be out of town quite a good deal next month and want to be sure that when you are here I shall be here also if possible.

I believe that the publication of this volume of your poems can be used as a means of bringing Negro culture to the masses of people and I cannot tell you how enthusiastic I am about the whole idea.

Love to you and your mother.

Sincerely,
Louise
LT/SS
BSAU
12646

TO MATT AND NEBBY, JUNE 10, 1937

En route to Denver, June 10, 1937

Dear Matt and Nebbie,

I was certainly sorry not to have time to run up to San Francisco to see you-all, but I had booked lectures on my return East, had to leave California last Sunday, so the best I could do was a day at Carmel just before departing. . . . . I spoke Tuesday in Salt Lake at the Unitarian Church and afterwards the minister gave a party for me. Everybody there was at least United Front[36] except two Trotskyists[37] who had to take an awful hauling over the coals, especially when they claimed that the USSR was fostering anti-Semitism in that most of those recently executed were Jews! Something I had never heard before. . . . . . I had a long letter from Homer Smith who was about to leave for the Negro soviets on the Black Sea. He wants me to bring him a number of things over, including two good pipes and some tobacco.

So Loren thought it might be nice if the original group of "22 Nègres"[38] would perhaps each contribute a dollar to a kind of gift or remembrance fund and I could then take Homer and perhaps Pat [Lloyd Patterson]'s babies a few things from us all as a whole. If you agree, and have said dollar, send it on at once to me [at] 634 St. Nicholas, New York . . . I was

36. United Front, also called Popular Front, was an alliance between radicals and socialists on the one hand and liberal Democrats and progressive trade union leadership on the other. It was founded by the Communist Party in the struggle against rising fascism.

37. Trotskyists, often called "Trots," were followers and advocates of Leon Trotsky, who believed in worldwide revolution. Trotsky participated in the Russian Revolution with Lenin but soon after broke with him and Stalin. As a result he was exiled to Mexico, where he was assassinated in 1940.

38. Langston playfully uses French to refer to the "22 Negroes" who went to Moscow to make *Black and White* in 1932.

delighted to hear about your new house being almost done, and certainly wish I could see it. But I will no doubt be out again, I hope next winter. I hate this Eastern cold. This morning there is snow along the tracks here in Colorado . . . Loren and Juanita [Miller] were fine, and the baby is cute and worried looking, as though he were taking the struggle on his shoulders already, but perhaps that is because he is so young. Mike Gold's baby, who is older, is as round and jolly as can be, and has probably been clarified by this time. They plan to Octoberize[39] him for the benefit of Spain soon . . . I tried to call you by phone from Carmel, but no one was at home that evening at all. But drop me a line, if you have time, before I sail, and a snap shot of the new house if it is done. . . . I hear you're both taking your vacation together this year, and here's hoping it will be a very pleasant one. All my best wishes to you,

Sincerely,
Lang

Both Langston and Louise traveled to Spain in the latter half of 1937. Langston went as a foreign correspondent for the *Baltimore Afro-American* newspaper, although he also sent reports to other Black press organizations. He traveled to Paris, and then went by train to Spain on July 24, 1937, with the Afro-Cuban poet and writer Nicolas Guillen, whom he knew from visiting Cuba. Their first destination was Barcelona, and they subsequently traveled to Valencia and then on to Madrid.

Langston's articles from Spain paint a vivid picture of the experiences of fellow foreign journalists reporting from the front and on the efforts of foreign fighters of many nationalities. Langston traveled to the front lines to view the combat firsthand and was caught in the fascist bombardments of Madrid. Langston not only reported on the horror of the war but also told the personal stories of the many ordinary Black Americans, Africans, and others from the Black diaspora who felt compelled to fight fascism by joining the International Brigade to fight alongside the Spanish Loyalists. He praised the bravery, skills, and military pursuits of these Black fighters and emphasized the "lack of a color line" in Spain. In the essay "Fighters from Other Lands Look to Ohio Man for Food," published in the *Baltimore Afro-American* on January 8, 1938, Langston quoted Abraham Lewis, a young member of the International Brigade, from Cleveland, Ohio, who rose to the rank of quartermaster

39. "Octoberize" is a made-up word combining the words "baptize" and "October" (in reference to the October Russian Bolshevik Revolution).

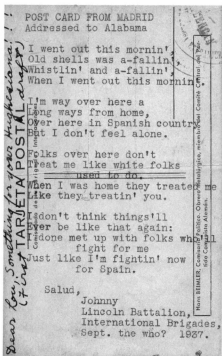

HONOR A LOS HÉROES DE LAS
BRIGADAS INTERNACIONALES
CAIDOS EN LA LUCHA POR LA PAZ

Hans BEIMLER
Comisario Político

POST CARD FROM MADRID
Addressed to Alabama

I went out this mornin',
Old shells was a-fallin',
Whistlin' and a-fallin',
When I went out this mornin'.

I'm way over here a
Long ways from home,
Over here in Spanish country
But I don't feel alone.

Folks over here don't
Treat me like white folks
used to do.
When I was home they treated me
Like they treatin' you.

I don't think things'll
Ever be like that again:
I done met up with folks who'll
    fight for me
Just like I'm fightin' now
    for Spain.

Salud,
    Johnny
    Lincoln Battalion,
    International Brigades,
    Sept. the who? 1937.

FIGURE 13. A postcard from Langston to Louise with the first draft of his Spanish Civil War poem "Post Card from Madrid: Addressed to Alabama," 1937. (Louise Thompson Patterson papers, Special Collections & Archives, Robert W. Woodruff Library, Emory University.)

in the Abraham Lincoln Brigade:[40] "Here nobody sneers at a colored person because he is in a position of authority. Everybody tries to help him everybody salutes him."

Langston hoped to use his reporting to impress upon Black people in America the need to support struggles for liberation wherever they occurred. Every victory, no matter where, represented a victory for all in the face of a common enemy. After spending almost five harrowing months in Spain witnessing the civil war, he returned to New York in January 1938.

Louise left New York for Europe in September 1937. She stopped first in Paris to attend the Second World Congress Against Racism and Anti-Semitism,[41] which

40. The Abraham Lincoln Brigade was a contingent of 2,800 North Americans who joined the International Brigade that fought on the Loyalist side, against General Franco, in the Spanish Civil War. They were a racially integrated troop.

41. The Second World Congress Against Racism and Anti-Semistism was held in Paris in 1937. Louise, Pat, and Thyra Edwards attended.

FIGURE 14. From left: Afro-Cuban Loyalist Captain Basilio Cueria, Langston Hughes, Commander Valentín González González (El Campesino), and Louise Thompson in Madrid, Spain, 1937.

was held from September 10 to 12. Chicago's most prominent African American social worker and relief activist, Thyra Edwards, was also at the congress. Louise saw Pat, who was attending as well. Louise and Pat had known each other since the 1920s. They had both spent their formative years as members of the African American communities of Oakland and San Francisco, California. Later, in New York, they were active in the political campaigns of the Communist Party, and they both organized in defense of the Scottsboro Boys of Alabama, beginning in 1932.

Louise and Pat visited the 1937 International Exposition of Art and Technology in Modern Life, where they ran into Howard University professor, and later diplomat, Ralph Bunche. Louise then traveled to Spain, where she met up with Langston. She spent three weeks in Spain investigating the Black American volunteers who were fighting on the side of the Loyalists and learning about the humanitarian needs of Spanish civilians. She returned to New York in time to attend the October meeting of the National Negro Congress in Philadelphia, after which she set out on a six-week speaking tour to raise funds for the Spanish Loyalists' humanitarian relief campaign.

Langston and Louise corresponded regularly during the Spanish Civil War. When Louise had returned to the United States, Langston would send his articles and poems to her, and she would forward them on to various newspapers. However, the following letter is the only one that survives from this period.

Pittsburg, Pa.

November 13

Dearest Lang:

At last, at last, at long last this letter is being written. I have been getting to it for so long. But between the hecticness of getting home, and now of jumping about [all] over America I had no time for anything.

I am now touring about the country, lecturing on Spain. I have been at it for over three weeks now, and have three more to go and I am plenty tired. My head is so full of train schedules and bus schedules, and times and places of meetings, that you will have to forgive me any disconnectedness in writing. I love Spain, but I am rather [^fatigued] telling others how much for I only speak well and enjoy it when I can feel the spirit and the enthusiasm, and boy, both are wearing thin under this strain. But the reception my talks get in most places keep me going rather well. Particularly am I pleased to get before so many Negroes, and find that they can be aroused. On the side, I am trying to stir up enthusiasm among them in each city to get a fund together to send an ambulance to Spain in the name of the Negroes of America. They seem to like the idea and I believe we will be able to do it. What do you think of the idea?

Pittsburgh, Chicago, St. Louis, Detroit, Cleveland, and way points. Philadelphia and New York. Come, all ye Negroes, hear the tale of Spain. See the blight of the fascist touch, hear the roar of bombas and obuses.[42] Be inspired by the morale of the Spanish people. Learn the lessons of unity and "one command". Keep fascism out of America by keeping it out of Spain. Aid yourselves by aiding Spain. Ole! Salud!

Your stories are swell, Lang, and I like the idea of the pamphlet. I have them all with me and can't discuss it with anyone until my return to New York which will be about December 5. I shall use the poems in my talks. I have seen some of the stories in the Afro [*Baltimore Afro-American*] and they have given them swell front page spreads. Which means that Afro-America is learning about Spain, about those Negro fighters who stretch the bond of solidarity across the sea of the ole Atlantic and of race, about a Negro girl who nurses Spanish wounds, and marries a son of Erin, about the Moors whose cries for freedom are clogged up in mouths filled with blood, about that ole debbil fascism. In brief, you are doing a swell job,

---

42. *Bombas* and *obuses* are the Spanish words for "bombs" and "cannon shells," respectively.

Lang, and I am so glad that you are there in that city of cities, Madrid, and plugging away in the house of the Marquis, mingling the click-click of your typewriter keys with the whistle and thud of obus and machine gun. I wish I was there, too, boy. But the ole debbil is reaching across, and has caught hold of the Amazon and Brazil,[43] and his appetite is whetted for more of America, and there is much to do, and I am trying to do, tho the road gets a little steep and one wishes to stop for breath.

Your mother came to see me the day I was in Cleveland. She was worried to death because she has not heard from you. I tried to reassure her through the knowledge of the letters I had from you and some <u>duros</u>.[44] She says you have quite some money in the bank but of course she can't draw on it, and there is rent to pay and food to buy. Gwen [Gwyn "Kit" Clark][45] is working, but just started. I will be there again and I shall see that she is taken care of until you return. She says she has written often but feels that you did not get her letters.

The National Negro Congress[46] was swell, boy. Some 1218 of us, more resolute, more mature in thought, more militant. Fine representatives from the steel mills, mines and farms. Splendid young people, eager to move ahead. And every one was there, from William L. Patterson of Scottsboro fame to Frederick Patterson from Massa's Tuskegee. (I wonder what you would have said, old Booker T. [Washington], if you had been there?) Even Franklin Delano [Roosevelt] sent a telegram of greeting. And 5000 gathered every night to hear what the Negro is thinking, and to applaud all moves for unity. This Congress demonstrated, I think, that this movement is here to stay, that it expresses the longing of the Negro toilers for unity and militant action, that it can impel even those who would hold back progressive action to move ahead.

Some sad news. A letter from Ralph tells of the death of his mother in Cincinnati. She died the day after he got there and was too far gone to recognize him. But his letter makes me feel, that though it has shocked him and the sense of loss is intense, he is not too despondent. He is now in Dayton at 47 Gold Street. I have written Mary [Savage] to forward your

43. Louise is referring to the Estado Novo, or the "New State," a period of dictatorship in Brazil that was started when the country's president, Getulio Vargas, declared a ninety-day state of emergency because of a supposed impending coup d'état by Communists and then dissolved congress and reappointed himself president.

44. *Duros* was the word for hard currency in Spain during the civil war.

45. "Gwen" is a misspelling of Langston's stepbrother's name, Gwyn "Kit" Clark.

46. The National Negro Congress held its second meeting in Philadelphia from October 15 to 17, 1937.

letter to him. I hope that, though, I don't go to Dayton, I shall manage to meet up with him somewhere in Ohio during the next week.

As soon as I get back to New York I shall gather up all the stuff you have sent me, which I have all with me now, and get in touch with all the magazines and papers and try to get them circulated. There is nothing I can do of value while I am on the road except to use the stuff in talks. I shall also get in touch with [Maxim] Lieber on the Garcia Lorca translations you mentioned in your last letter.

Tragic fate seems to haunt the pamphlet the I.W.O. is to bring out. When I got back I raised hell because nothing had been done. It seems that in working with the Workers Publishers, who were collaborating with us in the publication so that we could print the volume in larger quantities, the guy there had fallen down on the job. He reported to Roberts that it was set up to print. Then he went off to California, and when I left New York a desperate [^search] was being made to catch [^up] with the manuscript as well as the guy. I was exceedingly put out about it, and our new educational director, Levine, gave Roberts plenty hell for his carelessness and I promised to get along with it, even if it took the Central Control Commission to find out what had become of the manuscript. I am exceedingly sorry, Lang, over the damn mess it got into. I am writing to Levine again today about it. I agree with you about including some Spanish stuff, if it is not already printed.

Thyra [Edwards] is back but of course I have not seen her. Mary says she got in last Monday, the 8th. And says that Thyra says that you will be coming home December 1.[47] Verdad, camarada? I'll be on hand to meet you at the station, or rather the boat. And will I be glad to see you once more. And what are your plans? I know that you will be lecturing as I have been told that the date is already set for your coming to Pittsburgh, February, I believe. Your mother says there are all sorts of letters about speaking dates, and your attorney wants to know what to do about Mulatto. She says you have no agent on the job and no money is being collected. And she also says that everybody under the sun has been writing her how to get in touch with you.

I wish you would do something for me before you leave. I brought home a pair of Toledo earrings, you know that Toledo gold,[48] and by gosh if I didn't lose one at a dance in Chicago the other week. Would you please, sir,

47. Langston did not return from Spain until January 1938.
48. The city of Toledo in Spain is famous for products made using the Damascene method, a Moorish style of inlaying gold and silver threads in decorative patterns into black steel.

buy me a pair, the loveliest you can find and bring them home to me. And if you have enough pesetas, you can bring me two or three pairs, and I will remit on the dotted line upon your return. Also if you see anything else I would like and have the dinero, ditto. I found so many wanting something from Spain when I returned, that they picked me bare of the few little things I brought back.

Well, darling, if I am to write any other letters today I must sign off. It's such fun, writing to you, that I could keep on going for several hours. But I am about snowed under with correspondence which has piled up as I rush about making trains, making meetings breathlessly, talking and talking and talking until my throat is dry and my tongue tired. But I am glad to do it. To talk to Negroes, to steel workers, to miners, to auto workers like the meeting I had in South Bend, Indiana, the first of its kind, where 2200 auto workers from Studebaker, Chevrolet and Ford turned out.

Hasta luego, companero. Salud!

Lou

Luisa

FOUR

A People's Theatre in Harlem and Black Anti-Fascism on the Rise

JANUARY 1938–DECEMBER 1939

By early 1938 Pat was in Chicago working as a coeditor of the Communist Party–sponsored *Midwest Daily Record* newspaper.[1] Pat wrote to Langston[2] in Madrid, praising his dispatches from Spain in the *Baltimore Afro-American* newspaper. The articles, written in late 1937 and early 1938, number a score.

Although Pat enthusiastically approved of Langston's reporting, he strongly believed in the need for a broader distribution of information about the Spanish struggle. He wanted to bring news of the fight against fascism in Spain to a mass audience. This was one of his primary goals in his editorial role at the new *Midwest Daily Record*.

FROM PAT, [JANUARY 5, 1938]

Langston Hughes
Madrid
Spain

Dear Lang:-

Am following your Afro-American articles with not only the deepest interest, but with great appreciation—the simplicity mingled with great depth of human feeling and understanding, which they disclose. Such

---

1. The *Midwest Daily Record* was the CPUSA's Midwest newspaper, headquartered in Chicago. It was started in 1938, and Pat moved to Chicago that year to be one of the coeditors. The party had two other established newspapers, *The Daily Worker* in New York and *The People's World* in San Francisco.
2. Langston and Pat had met in Harlem during the 1920s, likely introduced by their mutual friend Paul Robeson.

writing deserves a still broader audience. Not only is this true, it is equally true that they should be a weapon in the forging of the United Front, the American People's Front and the Negro People's Front. They should and can be a force to help merge these Fronts into an irresistible power in the struggle for Democracy.

I am here in Chicago,—one of the three editors of the MIDWEST DAILY RECORD—which will be born on the anniversary of the birth of Abraham Lincoln, February 12, and two days before the anniversary of the other great American of that era, Frederick Douglas [Douglass].

Please send greetings to us before that date. However, I am looking forward to more, a series of articles by you.

The attack upon Roosevelt grows sharper. It is the spear-head of the assault upon Democracy here and a powerful first aid to Fascism internationally. Your voice will reach out still more through us and augment the value of everything you write for the Negro press.

My love to the boys in the trenches. Tell them that we want their greetings through Dave Doran and any other leader.

May victory rest this year upon the banners of the Republican forces and may world Fascism receive a mortal blow on Spanish fields.

Comradely yours,
Pat
WILLIAM L. PATTERSON

As he sailed back to New York from France on the Cunard liner SS *Berengaria*, Langston jotted a newsy postcard to Matt and Nebby to keep them updated on his travels.

TO MATT AND NEBBY, [JANUARY 15, 1938]

[Postcard]

S.S. Berengaria

Dear Matt and Nebby,

This is where I came out, way up in the Pyrenees. If you look closely you can see me on skis! Saw Johnny Davis in Paris on his way to see Haile [Selassie]. Paul [Robeson] is going to Spain. Are you in your new house? I wish I had a new house too!

Salud! Langston

Langston was politically reenergized by what he witnessed in Spain. Back in New York, he met with Louise and told her he wanted to found a theater. He envisioned a company that would combine a political message with a popular form—a radical avant-garde, agitprop approach. He described it as "a people's theatre that has its roots in the masses of our people."[3]

Louise willingly offered her assistance and also asked the IWO to help. She had been working at the organization for several years at that point and had risen from office worker to vice president. She suggested that he write a play based on *A New Song*, a collection of his radical poems soon to be published by the IWO.

Langston quickly produced a draft of a one-act play with blues and spirituals that would eventually be called *Don't You Want to Be Free? A Poetry Play: From Slavery through the Blues to Now—and Then Some!—with Singing, Music, and Dancing.*

Louise recruited the players and found the space for the new theater, and the IWO agreed to sponsor the project. They then launched the Harlem Suitcase Theatre, which Langston sometimes refers to in his letters as H.S.T. and Suitcase. A company of players was soon rehearsing and performing in the second-floor loft of the IWO Community Center at 317 West 125th Street, in the heart of Harlem.

The Harlem Suitcase Theatre premiered its first production on April 21, 1938. It was a two-part program featuring Langston's one-act play, with Robert Earl Jones playing the central character. *Don't You Want to Be Free?* was mounted three times a week, with tickets at thirty-five cents. A reviewer for the *New York Amsterdam News* called it "a significant proletarian drama" and announced that Earl Jones was "a brilliant new star." The season closed that July. Some 3,500 people (the vast majority of them Black) had seen a total of thirty-eight performances.

In June of 1938 Langston was preparing to go on a lecture circuit, organized by Louise and sponsored by the International Workers Order (IWO). The theme was "A Negro Poet Looks at a Troubled World." Before he set out, he wrote a sad personal note to Matt, who had been visiting New York.

TO MATT, JUNE 3, 1938

634 St. Nicholas Ave., Apt. 1D, New York

June 3, 1938

Dear Matt,

Sorry I wasn't able to see you off. I came by Lou's again, but could find no one. And my mother was very ill that day. She died last night and we're

3. Quoted in an interview with Langston published in the *Daily Worker* on April 20, 1938.

having the funeral Sunday. Wish I could have seen more of you. There are many things I would have enjoyed talking over with you.

My best to Nebbie,
Sincerely,
Langston

FROM MATT, JUNE 10, 1938

[Handwritten]

June 10, 1938

Berkeley, Calif
1399 Delaware St.

Dear Lang:

We were awfully sorry to hear of your mother's death. Deaths in ones family are always difficult to face regardless of how inevitable we realize they are, however I hope you do not have too difficult a time adjusting yourself to this loss. I too was very sorry we were unable to have more time together, but I was very glad to be with you for the short time we had. Weez and I have often remarked that it seems we always get to see one another every few years, regardless of how far apart we get during the interval, this I am beginning to believe (I hope it continues as in the past) and although we may have but a short time together at any one time it may not be very long before we find ourselves in the same place again.

I like your play [*Don't You Want to Be Free?*] very much Lang. It was like meeting a group of old and very dear friends all at one time, hearing the experiences they had gone through over the years, which had given them a very mature and sound perspective for the future. My opinion is that the play is another demonstration of the excellent character and rock bottom soundness that your work has maintained over a long period of time.

Nebby is feeling very well under the circumstances. The baby is scheduled to arrive about July 17, so there isn't very much time left. If you feel in the mood for California relaxation it would be swell to have you greet the baby this summer.

Sincerely,
Matt

TO LOUISE, JULY 12, 1938

July 12, 1938

Dear Lou,

Figure this out! I'm still amazed. But Theodore Dreiser and I are off to Paris on the Normandie tomorrow to represent the League of American Writers[4] at a Peace Congress[5] there. All very sudden, but I reckon true. Will be back no doubt, in due time, if I don't go to Madrid. Loved your letter. Theatre is going along swell.

I love 'em all. Plus you. Will write from boat.

Langston

Wish I had your front-yard brook to cool off in. Now 2 A.M. and not packed yet.

TO MATT, JULY 14, 1938

A bord, le Normandie

July 14, 1938

Dear Matt,

On three days' notice, I'm off to Paris with Theodore Dreiser[6] (as delegates from the League of American Writers) to attend a Peace Congress there, against the bombing of open cities. I didn't have a chance to write you before sailing, but I left word for Lou (who's in the country) to let you know. I shall be most eagerly awaiting word of the baby. And be it boy or girl, shall do my best to bring it a baby-something from Paris. I wish I could fly on out to California on my way back. I have a feeling that baby is here now, and I want to see it.

Thanks immensely for your letter. My very best to Nebby.

As ever,
Lang

4. The League of American Writers was an association of American writers, launched by the CPUSA in 1935. It included most of the prominent writers of its day, including Langston. It was terminated in 1943.

5. The Congress for Peace Action and Against Bombing of Open Cities was held in July 1938 in Paris.

6. After the meeting, Theodore Dreiser went to Spain.

Langston was away a lot during 1938, in Europe or working in Los Angeles, so the running of the Harlem Suitcase Theatre fell to Louise and others, and without Langston to hold them together and help raise money, it wasn't easy going. The theater faced many internal and external challenges, and Louise tried her best to hold down the fort during Langston's long absences from New York.

TO LOUISE, JULY 16, 1938

[C/o American Express 11 rue Scribe, Paris]

A bord, le Normandie

July 16, 1938

Lou, my dear, here I am again on the high seas, just as surprised as I can be—but it looks like I'll be in Paris tomorrow! Dr. [Herman] Reissig is aboard. Also Leland Stowe whom I met in Spain last year. And only one colored, a valet to the head of Dunn & Bradstreet. A couple of Japanese and one Chinese. Otherwise just various kinds of assorted white folks.

When I left, our theatre seemed to be all right. Leigh Whipper got the Apollo[7] to give us a jail door for Scottsboro—which now has a new ending commuted to life imprisonment. Dorothy [Peterson], Leigh, and [Hilary] Phillips also went to see Sufi's[8] theatre, which they declare to be swell, stage, 300 seats, etc. that they will let on %. But I said I saw no need to move until our public was overflowing into the street, and our treasury capable of furnishing sets for a real stage . . . Leigh wants to direct "Chip Woman's Fortune"[.][9] And Miss [Angelina Weld] Grimke would like to be on our play-reading committee. Both of which I said O.K. And the Youth Group wants to do their own production of "Don't You Want To Be Free" which I said was O.K. too. . . Did you get the songs I sent you? Also a copy of Dorothy Johnson's story about the burro that talked? I wish he [^*the burro*] had also told me how to make a fortune. Here I am Paris bound with $21.00. Just $14.00 more than I had when I first went to Paris in 1924. So I seem to have cleared $14.00 in 14 years! Which is pretty good at that, I reckon, on literature!

7. The famous Apollo Theater was on 125th Street in Harlem.
8. Militant Harlem labor and religious leader Sufi Abdul Hamid (1903–1938) owned a large meeting space at 103 Morningside Avenue, called the Universal Holy Temple of Tranquility. It was used variously as a mosque, meeting hall, and theater.
9. *The Chip Woman's Fortune* was a play by the Black playwright Willis Richardson (1889–1977). It was produced on Broadway at the Frazee Theatre in March 1923 and ran for one week.

[Nathan W.] Levin has 4 lectures for me beginning September 22nd. I'll no doubt be on hand. They're in New England.

How am I going to know when the baby comes? Please let Matt know where I am. I didn't have a chance to write him before I left. Nor do I have his new home address.

News (you may or may not have heard by now): André has gone back to Mexico. Thyra [Edwards] did not go abroad. I was an usher at James Weldon [Johnson]'s funeral. (Forgot you were still in town then!) Brownie lost an eye, they say, on the 4th. Firecrackers. Henri Cartier [Bresson]'s sister, Jacqueline, died in Paris. The Victrola is in pawn. At last I am going to see "Blockade".[10] It is being shown on shipboard today. Mr. Phillips plans to open the first State Theatre in Liberia in a year or so. I told him we would exchange companies—do a New York and a Liberian season both. How about it? Yours till our Suitcase is a Trunk.[11]

Langston.

Langston anxiously awaited news of the arrival of Nebby and Matt's baby. She was born in San Francisco on July 28, 1938. They called her Evelyn Louise, but she was swiftly nicknamed Nebby Lou.

TO MATT AND NEBBY, SEPTEMBER 1, 1938

[Handwritten]

Paris, September 1, 1938

Dear Matt and Nebby,

Just heard the good news! I must come out soon and see the kid. Kiss her for me. How lucky you-all are! Mighty nice!

Paris is beautiful this summer. Fine weather. Lots of tourists—even from California. I'm home-bound next week.

Salud! Lang

10. *Blockade* (1938) is an independently produced film about the Spanish Civil War, starring Henry Fonda. It was written by John Howard Lawson, who later became one of the Hollywood Ten.

11. This is a reference to the Harlem Suitcase Theater, a proletarian theater-in-the-round that Langston and Louise founded in 1938. It had a mission statement and a constitution. The name comes from a requirement that all the props and scenery for each play had to fit into a suitcase. It was the first theater-in-the-round in New York.

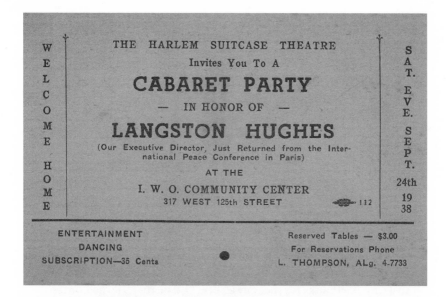

W
E
L
C
O
M
E

H
O
M
E

THE HARLEM SUITCASE THEATRE

Invites You To A

CABARET PARTY

— IN HONOR OF —

LANGSTON HUGHES

(Our Executive Director, Just Returned from the International Peace Conference in Paris)

AT THE

I. W. O. COMMUNITY CENTER
317 WEST 125th STREET   112

S
A
T.

E
V
E.

S
E
P
T.

24th

19
38

ENTERTAINMENT
DANCING
SUBSCRIPTION—35 Cents

Reserved Tables — $3.00
For Reservations Phone
L. THOMPSON, ALg. 4-7733

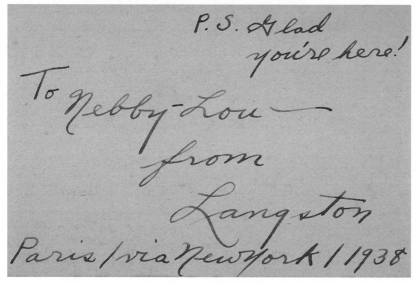

P. S. Glad you're here!

To Nebby-Lou — from Langston

Paris / via New York / 1938

FIGURE 15. An invitation to a Harlem Suitcase Theatre party thrown in Langston's honor, 1938. Langston wrote a greeting to Nebby Lou on the back.

[Printed at the bottom of the stationery: La guerra no es desesperación, sino esperanza: maldita, si es de demonio; grande y noble, si es de libertad y de por duradera.— Enrique Díez-Canedo.]

TO LOUISE, SEPTEMBER 2, 1938

Paris, September 2, 1938

Dearest Lou—

So delighted to hear from you that I'm writing you before breakfast!

Because I thought maybe you had disappeared in the wilds of Wallkill, and never got back to Harlem at all![12] But now your note. Swell about Nebby-Lou. I wish I wasn't broke (as usual) I'd like to bring her her first Paris gown. Also Mollie [Moon]'s Henry! Time works wonders! . . . I didn't go to Spain, but have seen lots of the boys here. Vaughn [Love] is O.K. and back at the front, they say. Everybody needs food, so let's get that foodship[13] off to them. . . . Thanks for the tour leaflet.[14] I'll be there, if the Lord is willing. Leave here for London Wednesday, if the English permit. Joe North's just been denied a visa. . . . I hear that the Chicago production of "Don't you Want to Be Free" is coming along swell. . . . . Let's go to Old Colony!

Lang

[Printed at the bottom of the stationery: La guerra no es desesperación, sino esperanza: maldita, si es de demonio; grande y noble, si es de libertad y de por duradera.— Enrique Díez-Canedo]

After Langston returned from Europe, he went to Los Angeles to work in Hollywood. Meanwhile, Louise and others continued to get the Harlem Suitcase Theatre up and running in New York.

12. Louise has been on vacation in the village of Wallkill in upstate New York.

13. Langston and Louise supported Spanish Civil War relief efforts, which included sending ships with food and other supplies ("foodships") to the Loyalists.

14. Louise had organized an IWO-sponsored speaking tour for Langston to talk about the Spanish Civil War. It was due to begin once he returned from Spain, where he had spent five harrowing months reporting on the war.

[Letterhead: International Workers Order]

Dec. 17, 1938

AIR MAIL
Mr. Langston Hughes
1379 E. Washington Boulevard
Los Angeles, Cal.

Dear Lang:

Indeed I was glad to get your letter. I realized of course that you were probably on the go every minute but I was anxious to know how your trip turned out and what your plans were.

I cannot say that I am really surprised at your decision to spend more time out there, nor that I am surprised at your resolution to turn over a new leaf. We shall do all we can to keep things going here in the Theatre though I must say that it will be a happy day for us when you return.

We are now laying plans to hold a patrons tea and to start a serious effort to raise funds. However, we can't do anything until after the holidays are over.

We have gotten a decision that the sponsorship of the Theatre should be broadened and we intend to use the patrons tea to begin a broadening of our base. I am confident that once we get this started we will be able to raise the funds necessary to carry on our work and to cover the expenses of our director. We all agreed that if when you do return you will be willing to assume this post it will be the thing really necessary to get our Theatre launched.

There is one thing I wish you would do and that is to write Toy [Harper]. She is somewhat disturbed feeling that we are trying to take the Theatre away from you. I think you should write her a nice letter and tell her that you have heard from me giving you an idea of our plans and that you feel they are O.K. This will help to set her straight. I don't think she realizes that anything I propose, or any of the rest of us for that matter, we do only in consultation with you and with your approval.

The Opera[15] is meeting with a few obstacles. At one rehearsal the singers did not appear in sufficient numbers and at the subsequent two rehearsals [James P.] Johnson was absent I think because of a number of things he had to do. But we intend to plug away and try to keep it going.

15. Louise is referring to *De Organizer,* a folk-blues opera in one act, written by Langston, with music by James P. Johnson.

We have the house all sold out for the month of January.

The rehearsals of the other two plays seem to be going along fairly well.

I presume you have seen by now the fine article [Edward] Lawson did for us in "Opportunity". We are thinking of using this article in subsequent material we intend to get out on the theatre.

I will be writing you again but I wanted to get a note off to you now. Thanks for sending me the check.

Tell everybody "hello" for me and in your next letter tell me about Dot [Dorothy Johnson] and some of the others. I hope you don't stay too long. I miss you and we all need you.

Vaughn Love should be home from Spain next week. He did not come in with the first group.

Love,
Louise

LT/SS
UOPWA-No.16

FROM LOUISE, [JANUARY 13, 1939]

[Letterhead: International Workers Order]

January 13, 1939

AIR MAIL
Mr. Langston Hughes
1379 E. Washington Boulevard
Los Angeles, Cal.

Dear Lang:

I have been intending to write you all this time, first of all to thank you for your nice California Santa Claus, then to let you know how we are getting along with the Theatre. I am going to have a lot of hard luck to tell you so be prepared.

First of all we have been forced to move out of our 125 Street headquarters by the Fire Department and the Department of License. We are not permitted to give any more performances there without a license and they tell us that we can't get a license there because of the fire hazard. Last Sunday we gave our performance in the YWCA. This coming Sunday it will be in the Finnish Hall. From there I don't know where we go because as yet we have not been able to get a permanent place but we are working on it very hard and I hope to have some good news to report on it soon. This is problem number one.

As far as the license is concerned I am working through Bob Elzy to try to get permission for us to continue our work without it because once we need a license we will be in for many things that we as a non-professional group would not be able to stand. Next week Elzy and I are going to see [Herbert] Delaney about it.

Otherwise things are not so good. The main problem is that Hillary [Hilary Phillips] is so weak that we are always in a chaotic state.

We were forced to suspend rehearsals on the "Organizer" during the holidays because [James P.] Johnson was tied up with a number of other things, one of them being a play on Broadway "Policy Kings"[16] which got lambasted and closed very quickly. I have seen him since then and he is willing to go ahead with rehearsals but now we have to find a place in which to rehearse. Meanwhile John Hammond called me today and told me that Johnson had brought the opera to Columbia Broadcasting Company. John Hammond is working there now and is very enthusiastic about it and feels that they may be able to use it with some very prominent singers. They are to have an audition on Monday morning and I will let you know further about this.

"A Young Man of Harlem"[17] is also meeting with considerable difficulty. I have not been able to see Toy [Harper] because I was sick through all the holidays, but I know they have had to postpone their rehearsal date and Lindsey [Powell Lindsay] is supposed to be doing some re-writing on the third act. It is my frank opinion that this play is too weak a vehicle for us to follow "Don't You Want To Be Free" with. It seems to me that in order to live up to the reputation we have earned we must follow it with something like the "Organizer".

I can't write you at great length now because I am on my way to the train and have but a minute or two to finish this.

The one thing I want to raise with you though, is the matter of your coming back. Unless you come back soon and take hold of things, or we are able to get somebody stronger than Hillary, I feel we will just muddle along and not get any place. It is almost impossible to organize the work unless we have a competent man at the helm. If you are not planning to come back soon then we may have to think of someone else. The thing that distresses

16. *Policy Kings* is a 1939 play by Michael Ashwood. Policy is an illegal gambling game that was especially popular in Harlem and other working-class urban communities in the United States. It is also called "playing the numbers" because one must guess a specific number, which is selected randomly, to win. In most instances it was run by the mafia.

17. *A Young Man of Harlem* is a play by Powell Lindsay, written in the late 1930s. It was due to be shown at the Harlem Suitcase Theater, but the theater closed before it could produce the play.

me so much is that I hate to see this splendid start we have in the Theatre lost. George [Murphy Jr.] and I have had a long talk about it and we are both convinced that until we do get the right person in charge of the Theatre we will not get any place.

I will write you again next week. Meanwhile I would like to hear from you as regards your own plans.

Give my regards to everybody in Los Angeles.

Sincerely,
Louise
LT/SS
UOPWA-No.16

TO LOUISE, JANUARY 14, 1939

Lou, darling,

Head over heels in work, as usual, but profitable work at last! I've just signed for my first picture job, only a couple of weeks writing, but a beginning anyway.[18] And the first hundred goes to you, enclosed! (I told you I was going to turn over a new leaf!) Signed last week with the Federal Theatre, too, to revise ST. LOUIS WOMAN. And in six days have had five lectures in the local high schools, and Pasadena. So I see my debts dwindling steadily. Only trouble is, I can't sleep late any more. High School assemblies all seem to be early in the morning, and miles out in places like Verduga Hills and Beverley [Beverly Hills]. . . . Besides, all this, the colored I.W.O. lodge has gotten together a fine group of players (and Dot Johnson has secured 50 patrons already at a buck each) to put on DON'T YOU WANT TO BE FREE. So I'm helping them two nights a week on rehearsals. They want to open for the National Negro Congress meeting here in February. . . . Plus that, I've been making some headway on SOLD AWAY which I've promised the Gilpins for February, and which I think will be a good play for us in New York, too, written to be done in the manner of our present production without sets, and with spirituals. (And the leads for Earl [Robert Earl Jones] and Edith [Jones], who'll be our Lunt and Fontaine.) . . . . . What's news about our SUITCASE, anyhow? Have our

18. Langston had been hired to cowrite the screenplay for the 1939 film *Way Down South*. He collaborated in writing the script with the well-known African American screen actor Clarence Muse. When the film debuted it was sharply criticized for its stereotypic depictions of the Black characters, and in the end the project became an embarrassment for Langston.

official secretary write the Ex. Dir. a new bulletin, because I am way behind. . . . . . Len Zinberg called me up the other day. He says we've had to vacate the hall, and are performing in the Y.W.C.A. So gimme the why and wherefore. And don't let it keep you awake at nights! I'll bet you-all are having a wonderful, wonderful time. . . . . . I haven't had a chance to write Toy [Harper] yet, but will. This is the first time I've been home ten minutes for ten days, and I have to rush out now to Hollywood. So will tell you more later. . . . . Also will send my I.W.O. dues shortly, (if I'm not put out) and the money for the pictures. Trying to get the big debts out of the way first, then I'll take up the matter of the little ones. And they are legion! . . . . . I'm taking engagements in the East for April since I have some in Middle West the first half of that month. Had to cancel Philadelphia Feb. 12th, and I have quite a few out here still in February. . . . . Are you coming out for the Fair?[19] I phoned Nebby during the holidays. All O.K . . . . Loren [Miller] is in Washington for NYA Conference, and you'll probably see him in New York. Take care of yourselves. Write soon. Who's back from Spain? How's MAMBA'S DAUGHTERS?[20]

Salud, camarada!

Lang

1372 E. Wash. Blvd., Los Angeles,

Jan 14, 1939.

TO LOUISE, [JANUARY 16, 1939]

Dear Lou,

Just wrote you yesterday, but was delighted [to] hear from you today, although sorry to hear of the troubles of our theatre. Does that mean that we can't even REHEARSE in the Center anymore? Why not? Even if we have to perform elsewhere. And if we haven't the Center, do we lose Miss Allerhand, or what? And how is the Dance Drama going anyhow? Wish you'd have our Secretary or somebody write me a detailed letter about all the little things, such as who's playing what roles, how our debts are being paid off, etc., if somebody can do that. I know you're about as busy as me, which means that you don't get your proper rest, but I DO. The more I

19. Langston is referring to the Golden Gate International Exposition, a World's Fair held on San Francisco's Treasure Island for several months in 1939 and again in 1940.

20. Langston is asking for Louise's review of the 1939 Broadway production of *Mamba's Daughters,* staring Ethel Waters.

work the deeper I sleep. I always figure that there's no real need of worrying, because the world is always here the next morning anyway, and if it isn't who cares? So don't let this here theatre get you down.

Seriously, however, since I won't be able to come back until spring, in any case, if you can find a capable person to take over please don't hesitate to get them for the job. In fact, you-all there run the theatre and do whatever you feel needs to be done in my absence, <u>carte blanche,</u> as you know I can't begin to direct it from way out here. What about Suffi [Sufi Abdul Hamid]'s old place? But I know you must have thought of that.

That would be swell if our Blues Opera [*De Organizer*] was purchased by Columbia. Try to get "A Harlem Suitcase Theatre Production" into the announcement over the air. Tell them we will furnish them with lots of other original things if they want them, and will announce them as ours! Even if we lose that for the theatre, SOLD AWAY promises to be lots better, and is a full length production which we can do instead with our group, singing and all. And there seems a possibility that the Pasadena Playhouse might sponsor its production out here with George Garner and other local singers and actors, into which we could perhaps get Kenneth [Spencer] as the lead. But by all means (or any means) hold our group together, even if we are temporarily without headquarters. How about the YMCA little theatre? Or one of the church auditoriums? Maybe the Lennox Players would permit us the cooperative use of their place. A tie-up with one of the churches might not be bad, since they have audiences, money and everything, usually that one needs, since we are going to broaden our front <u>anyhow</u>.

This month ought to see most of my bills (the big ones) paid off. They are already cut in half. And this very week I shall finish with Mrs. Pratt. In my <u>last</u> letter to you, I enclosed a $100 draft. Which settles us up, doesn't it? Thanks a million. A friend in need is a friend indeed. And truer word never spoken. If the movie job continues beyond next week, (depending on a million things, since movies are worse than the theatre) I shall get myself a few sport shirts and a pair of tan shoes, also discard that hat you-all don't like.

I lectured last night again in Pasadena, the second time recently, to an overflow audience, three hundred turned away, in a Negro church. Said everything about Spain I usually say, intelligent discussion period and questions afterward. Which leads me to believe that the churches after all are probably the places to appear. Besides they can <u>afford to pay</u>. And do. And they can always get much better Negro crowds than the movement so far seems able to attract. Even if the collection afterwards all goes to the minister, the people at least have heard something new that might take effect on some. What do you think about that?

Did you see Loren [Miller]? How's Mason [Roberson]? How's Dorothy [Fisher-Spencer]?

I guess Matt will be down next month for the Negro Congress.

Tell everybody the Director says HY!

Tell George [Norford] Salud!

Sincerely,

Langston

Please ask Edith [Jones] to let me know what my I.W.O. dues are—and I'll pay them all up at once, now. Will even pay ahead!

TO LOUISE, JANUARY 29, 1939

Dear Lou,

Rushing off to Hollywood these days, instead of the Suitcase Theatre! Did I tell you I had a job doing a picture for Bobby Breen which has now been extended four weeks with an option on four more—since they liked the original outline Clarence Muse and I submitted. So I'm coming out of the red at last! Thank God and Capitalism, the later of which is, nevertheless, a dirty dog... Enclosed please find check for $15 which, if you'll kindly do me a favor and apply toward my I.W.O. policy, (if they haven't put me out) I'd appreciate immensely. Also, please let me know how much I owe for books, NEW SONG, and I'll pay it at once. Also the photographer's bill. But since I don't know how much I owe, either, but if this doesn't cover it, please ask Edith to let me know exactly... Saw Loren for a moment the other day, first time after his Eastern trip, and he says the show [*Don't You Want to Be Free?*] was not so hot when he saw it at Finnish Hall, actors coming in late, others missing, etc. So I think maybe the best thing to do would be to close down until you're able to get a permanent place again for rehearsing and performances. Do you think so? And the Ex. Com [Executive Committee]? Or just what? Awfully sorry I'm not there to help out in the present crisis. Perhaps a temporary suspension would be better than slowly going to seed for the rest of the winter..... I hope to be back in April, unless I'm unnaturally lucky and get further movie work, in which [case] I shall simply retire and rest the rest of my life. NOTE FOR MURPHY [George Murphy Jr.] AND OUR PUBLICITY DEPARTMENT: Two members of Harlem Suitcase Theatre are now screen writers in Hollywood, Len Zinberg and myself... Also, that the play [*Don't You Want to Be Free?*] is about to be done out here under I.W.O. leadership, but probably community sponsors. We have Hot

Shot Evelyn Burwell (formerly choir leader for Hall) to direct and play the music. First cocktail party today to raise funds with me and Hattie McDaniels as guests of honor. BUT BELIEVE YOURS TRULY, I AM NOT HEADING IT THIS TIME. Name of group is NEW NEGRO THEATRE.[21] Estelle Sherewood, Ex. Director. (Give her your sympathy and support!) Loren, publicity director. Dorothy Johnson and Juanita [Miller] are organizing sponsors. Enough people for three casts already. All we need is you out here now! SO COME ON . . . Matt will be down next week for N. Negro Cong [National Negro Congress] . . . Just wrote a swell song last night about the refugees. Muse is doing music today so we can introduce it at Anti-Nazi League meeting out here sometime soon . . . Say, what about the ORGANIZER. I guess Jimmy Johnson, Dorothy Peterson, Toy [Harper] and every human think I am dead. Please tell them I'm not, but Hollywood has got me! Getting to studios at ten in the morning is just about to lay me low. That alone is worth all the contract pays. The rest is nothing. But the man killed me when he said Story Conference at 10 A.M.!!!!! And Hollywood from where I live is like going to Kansas City . . . Did you get the check for a Hundred I sent you week or so ago? When you have a chance, let me know how things are, who's back from Spain, what you're having for dinner, how Mason [Roberson] is, say Hy to Mary [Savage], and write soon. Miss seeing.

Love,
Lang

1379 E. Wash Blvd.
Los Angeles
1/29/39

FROM LOUISE, MARCH 30, [1939]

[Letterhead: Hotel Detroiter; handwritten]

March 30

Lang darling:

Arrived here yesterday after a week of frantic rushing about in Chicago. Friends are grand to have but when one is in a town for a short time can

---

21. A group of Langston's Los Angeles friends organized the New Negro Theatre, a Los Angeles company loosely modeled on the Harlem Suitcase Theatre.

overwhelm one to the point of exhaustion. Here, thank goodness, I know few people and am in a hotel just across the street from my office. So I shall sleep much, rest a-plenty and catch my breath before moving along Saturday.

Mary forwarded your letter to me in Chicago. I had spent a day in Toledo and found out from Tommy [Thomas Richardson] and Bill that you are to be there in April.

Went to see "Don't You Want To Be Free" in Chicago and did not like it as well as our production. [Carroll C.] Tate may have been a thorn in our side and made a sieve of our purse—but he certainly was and is an asset to our blues. This, I felt, was a very weak spot in the Chicago group's production. I met with Lilian Summers—also Fannie McConnell and [Ligon] Buford and find they are having their troubles too. Disciplinary problems—personality problems—and others with which we in NY have been afflicted. Now here you come, talkin' 'bout <u>discipline</u>. Maybe that's inherent with a Little Theatre. Mary wrote me that she was writing you— so you probably have all the news about the H.S.T. by now. Am anxious to know how the opening was in L.A. so write me all about it.

When do you leave and what is your itinerary and when will you reach NY? I do hope you will return to Calif. since I am to be there this summer. I am not so eager about bringing the theatre along tho. For I am coming for a rest—doctor's orders. Nor to start one in S.F. I don't want to go into the <u>decline</u> and I think the theatre is one way to accelerate it. But, high ho, what care I as long as I get there. How about going to Carmel—I yearn for its <u>restful sands</u>.

I didn't get to see Arna [Bontemps] in Chicago. He has no phone and I just didn't have time to get over. Tommie told me he would be in Toledo with you. Your good friend Zora is in Cincinnati on the radio but I didn't try to look her up.

Kenneth Spencer arrived in Chicago at the same time I did. But he only stayed one day and should be in NY by now.

I'll be back in NY next Wed. and shall be looking to hear from you soon. I hope you will tell me you are to be in California this summer as I know we can have a ball out there. In any event don't come to NY this summer as everyone you have ever known or heard of will be there for the Fair. Am I not glad to be away—and how!

I am sleeping much better since I have been out of NY. Last nite I chalked up nine hours' sleep and don't I feel like a human being today!

Will you get up to see Nebby-Lou before leaving. Do try to as I know Nebby is expecting you.

Give all the gang my regards and tell them to look for me this summer.
Write soon,

Love,
Lou

FROM LOUISE, MAY 14, [1939]

[Handwritten]

May 14

Lang dear:

I want to let you know my plans which have changed a little.

I will be leaving May 25 and will not come thru Chicago as I am taking Mary to Cincinnati to visit her mother. She will come back May 31 on the train.

So I am wondering if I will get to see you. Arna [Bontemps] was by one night but I wasn't home. He told Mary he didn't think you would get here until the writers congress.[22] If this is so then I won't see you until you come to Calif. When are you planning to come out there?

I'll be in L.A. on June 9–10 after spending a few days in S.F. I'll stay there until July 2 and then return north. I plan to take my vacation about the first of August and then I might go down to Carmel. How about you joining me there?

We are trying to get the theatre straightened out. Main problem is to have someone take over. Hilary [Phillips] just can't. Tonite we are talking with Theodore Ward to see if he can help us out.

Whatever happened to "Sold Away"? I wrote you and wired you about it—but so far you have been mum. Let me hear from you before the 25th.

Love, Lou

Saw Pat last weekend.

Langston wrote to Matt and Nebby from Carmel Valley, where he was living at Noel Sullivan's retreat, Hollow Hills Farm. He had recently visited the Crawfords in Berkeley. Enclosed in the letter was an early draft of "Note From a Worker" for Nebby Lou, who was with him when he wrote it.

---

22. The Third American Writers' Congress was held June 2–4, 1939, at the New School for Social Research in New York.

TO NEBBY AND MATT, AUGUST 21, 1939

August 21, 1939

Dear Nebbie and Matt,

Naturally, I carried off the key, but here it is, and forgive! I've never had a more pleasant few days than that visit with you all and I wrote Louise a line about being present on that historic morning when Nebby-Lou took her first step! She certainly is a sweet child.

Eulah [Pharr] is fine, and it is fair and warmer down here and I've seen lots of my old friends already—but I'm starting to work tomorrow, now that my trunk full of notes has arrived from Los Angeles.

When hair-cutting time comes I'll be up looking for a cullud barber shop—so in a few weeks, I'll be seeing you.

Until then,
Sincerely,
Langston

[The poem "Note from a Worker" was enclosed with the letter.]

NOTE FROM A WORKER

I believe it to be true,
You see
That Tomorrow belongs to me.
And so
Let not too many tears
Water our unhappy years.
Being poor and black
Today,
I await my First of May,
Certain
As this final rhyme,
It will come—
In due time.

Matt's house,
August 16, 1939,
4 p.m. Third draft
In the presence of Nebby-Lou.

FIGURE 16. Matt and Langston with Nebby Lou in Berkeley, California, 1939.

TO LOUISE, [AUGUST 28, 1939]

Dear Lou,

Seems you're back just in time for the war! How was the trip, and how is New York after God's Country.[23] Personally, I think New York is another little God's country, providing you can live up to it. Otherwise, it sure can beat you down . . . Well, I have the whitest of white little houses, Mexican style with a walled garden, on the side of a hill above the pear orchard, all to myself here on this very charming play-toy farm, where I shall stay, I hope, until my book is done.[24] I only have to come out for meals—which makes me wish I had my only summer suit back—which is in pawn in Los Angeles—since we're having baronesses and movie stars to luncheon practically every day. Today I sat next to the Baroness del Gido who told me quite a little about Mussolini who is her personal friend and a brilliant person. She also told me this country was overrun

23. By "God's Country," Langston is referring to California.
24. Langston was working on the manuscript of his first autobiography, *The Big Sea,* which was published by Knopf in 1940.

by reds lead by Mrs. Roosevelt! But a few days ago Ella Winter and the Melvyn Douglasses [Melvyn Douglas and Helen Gahagan Douglas] were up, which sort of balances things. The see-saw of world politics seems to rock even in this canyon in the deep country, where flowers scent the air and snow-white sheep roam the hillsides. . . . . Dot [Dorothy Fisher-Spencer] was down for a short visit. She's back in L.A. now . . . Dr. Kenneth Johnson and his wife were also down . . . So many guests poor Eulah hasn't yet been able to get off on her vacation . . . Carlton Moss has sent me a couple of wires for lyrics for a new show to go into Café Society, lyrics with some light social meaning. Inquire around (without saying I said so) and see if you hear anything of it. Anyway, I've sent him a half dozen lyrics or so, including this one, NEWSBOY SHOUT, which I wrote today . . . Wish you would see if you can get Dorothy [Peterson] or Tommy [Richardson] to send me a copy of FRONT PORCH for our theatre out here. (Left one with Tommy Richardson and another with Dorothy to consider for the Suitcase— but need one for L.A.) . . . Also, dear darling Louise, if you're not broke, and will pay my I.W.O. dues for me before I get put out, I'll send it back to you when my musical ship comes in on the waves of LOUISIANA or some other song . . . BY the way, if you see any New York clippings about my picture [*Way Down South*], please send them to me . . . And having asked you to do all these things for me, I will be, Madame, eternally at your service . . . Look what a good job Juanita [Miller] has . . . DON'T YOU WANT TO BE FREE has just been performed at Atlanta University summer session! Is in rehearsal in New Orleans! And will be put on in Nashville this winter! Hurrah for the South, and you who inspired said epic! I hope I can get on SOLD AWAY soon . . . Have you resigned yet . . . Any chance of keeping Tommy on throughout the year? . . . If no, YOU and no TOMMY, WHO? How about possibly Owen Dodson if he is back in Brooklyn and not at Yale any more? Ask Dorothy . . . Give my best to Mary [Savage] and Grace [Johnson] and Moko and Waring [William Waring Cuney].

> Be good, be careful,
> Be practical and prayful, PEACE!
> Be gentle, be kind,
> And if you lose your all,
> Don't mind!

> Langston

*[Letterhead: The Association for the Study of Negro Life
and History, Incorporated]*

September 9, 1939

Lang darling:

Back in ole NY I swing into my old habits of being a bad writer but I cannot let my birthday pass without saying hello to you and wishing I could join you today in that Mexican casita. I swung right into action the minute I hit the city and have been going steadily since.

You're awfully good about writing. In fact, you are so good that my conscience is troubling me awfully—but you know what this town can do to you. And I must confess that I am not glad to be back at all. The subways worry me, the bustle and hurry jars me, and all I can wish is that I would like to be back in California. I enjoyed the lyrics. I like especially "How Can I Fall in Love" and the one I received today—"Solid". They should be swell with the right music setting.

I know you want to know all about the theatre, so I shall swing into it right here and now. I haven't been up to the library but I met with the executive the other night. We didn't pull any hair, but it was a meeting to try one's patience. Tommy [Richardson] was supposed to give a report of his stewardship, and all he did was to give us a talk about how we should organize our theatre, like he did that first time he came to one of our meetings. The exec asked him to prepare a real report—in writing—which he is supposed to have at our next meeting which is tomorrow. The two new plays—Mighty Wind and Plant in the Sun, and the speech choir, all to be the first production, <u>are</u> about ready, so Tommy informed us. They wanted to open on Sept. 17, but we felt it was too early as there is no promotional apparatus to carry the show along. And the experience of the summer should teach us never to try to get along as they did this summer. They had eight Sunday evenings—took in $92.00—and put us about $200 in the hole. The total debt, according to the report Muriel gave the other evening— is around $312. George [Sample] and Muriel [Unis] are adamant on the subject of Rita [Romilly]—swear that they are going to throw her off the exec. We had a few words about it the other night, particularly Grace [Johnson] and George. He accused her of pulling a Chamberlain—appeasing. They state she Rita held back Tommy's money, tho she sent a letter of explanation, which they don't accept. I don't think that I shall put up any opposition, tho I think they are wrong. Rita is a difficult person, but I think that before they cast any one aside they should have other forces to suggest.

Muriel states she is resigning and George went to work with the citizen's committee.

Larry Gellert has made a proposal to us, which if it could materialize would solve our financial headaches. He states that Paul Robeson promised to give a concert of his new work songs, which are coming off the press and that he is willing to let the Suitcase Theatre sponsor it and reap the proceeds. It sounds too good to be true and we have no way of knowing yet whether Paul actually promised to do it—I have my doubts. But we hope to contact Robeson, in fact have already written him a letter which he may not receive as I suspect he is already on the high seas. But we shall see.

Tommy is supposed to leave on Sept. 18. He thinks that Hilary [Phillips] is the one to carry on. Certainly he has developed no one else as far as I can learn. Which leaves us exactly in the position we were in before we acquired a "Guest Director." I really don't want to be too sharp on the subject of Tommy, for he probably did the best he could. But it doesn't make our plight any the happier.

We are to meet tomorrow and work out reorganization. I hate to get out now when everything is so much up in the air, but I don't see how I am going to work along with George and Muriel much longer. But you can rest assured that I will do all I can. It hurts so to see our beautiful dream—which could be a reality—being smashed by such stupid and bungling tactics. But things may not be as bad as I am picturing them. I don't know what the mood of the players is. Evidently they are cooperating in the new productions. And we may be able to find the new people for leadership which is our primary concern.

I am taking care of your IWO dues. You asked me to do something else, I think, but I can't find your letter here. I must have taken it to the office. So I shall get it Monday.

Haven't seen many people. I just go to work every day, come home and that's all. Went to the Fair last Sunday—there were only a half million there—and Dot [Dorothy Fisher-Spencer], Mary [Savage] and I walked our feet off trying to get someplace that the crowd wasn't. We have been sitting on top the radio, of course, trying to fathom what's next in Europe. Right now it looks like another grand sellout. France and England negotiating and contacting until Hitler gets all he wants of Poland. What a mess!

The Harry-Mary-Ted [Harry Haywood, Mary Sangigian, and Theodore Ward] mixup is too much for me. I have been busy consoling Harry, who, by the way is now in the Veteran's Hospital with angina pectoris. According to him he felt bad to see her desert him when he is down, and feels that she doesn't mean Ted any good. Meanwhile, as I understand it, Ted has swallowed her line, hook and all, and is stepping out as the protector of a very much misunderstood woman. Meanwhile she walked off with all the theatre's promotional materials and no one can find her. Personally I feel that she has simply born out all the things I've thot of her all these years but felt it would be too evil to say.

Love

Lou

Lou

FROM LOUISE, OCTOBER 13, 1939

October 13, 1939

Things are moving very badly with the theatre. I think I can say without exaggeration that Tommy [Richardson] left us in a worse state than he found us. We have no money and are having all kind of costume troubles with Plant in the Sun, also with Mighty Wind. It is hard for me to see any way out but we are doing our best to hold the thing together. Kenneth Spencer just came in yesterday and I guess will go into the cast of John Henry which is supposed to begin rehearsing next week.[25] I understand that Robeson is back. I am enclosing a receipt for your dues. I will see that they are kept up until you are able to take care of them. Kit [Gwyn "Kit" Clark] called me the other day and wanted to know whether I could lend him $10. Bearing in mind what you said about him I told him that I could not.

I guess you know about Matt's undergoing an appendectomy. I haven't heard from Nebby yet as to how he is getting along. She told me the operation was to have been last Tuesday. She also told me that you came up every so often and how much it means to them to have you.

I still have not run down the reviews on your picture but I heard lots of comments and all of them are uncomplimentary. Everybody says they cannot understand how you could have written such a scenario or if they changed it why you permitted it to come out under your name. I tell you this unpleasant news because I know you want to know what they are saying about the picture here. I understand one review in the [New York] Post stated that the film had set the cause of the Negroes back a number of years and in general all the papers panned it.

25. Opera and concert singer Kenneth Spencer was Paul Robeson's understudy in the 1940 Broadway musical *John Henry*.

Well, that is all for now. Write and let me know how you are getting along with the book.

Sincerely,
Louise
Louise

FROM LOUISE, OCTOBER 25, 1939

October 25, 1939

Mr. Langston Hughes
Hollow Hills Farm
Monterey, California

Dear Lang:

Are you so engrossed in your book that you can't take time off to write a fellow? I am interested in getting your reaction to the report I made to you on the opinions expressed here on your movie. I thought afterwards that I might have been too abrupt in what I said but I still think I should have told you the word that is going around.

We are still struggling to get somewhere in the theatre. At the present time we are suspending all production activities and going to concentrate on getting new plays. We gave one performance of "Mighty Wind" for the Spanish Committee but we never yet succeeded in getting together a full cast for "Plant in the Sun" and we can't put "Mighty Wind" on the boards by itself. Furthermore, I am convinced that we are going about the whole thing wrong. I don't see any point in putting on productions per se. It seems to me that if we haven't anything worthwhile and original to present we should keep quiet until we have something to do. This opinion is shared by other members of the Executive Committee so we are just about where we were a year ago. I still feel that the next production which follows "Don't You Want To Be Free?" will have to be as significant and as original. Therefore we are very interested to know if at this time you can give us any new production. In this connection we would like to know whether you would need any money for this. I am wondering what you have in mind to do about "Sold Away". Also I should like to know if you think any of your old plays done by the Gilpins might be suitable for us.

We had in mind something else to do. You know the fad now is for adapting and swinging the classics. The latest announcement is a swing version of "Midsummer Night's Dream". By the way, [Robert] Earl Jones got a nice part in this. I believe he is to play opposite Maxine Sullivan. We are thinking about the adaptation of some of the classical satires like "Alice in Wonderland", "Gulliver's Travels", etc., or the possibility of using some of the fairy tales. The idea is still quite nebulous and we haven't investigated but I think if we could think of something novel and new to do, it would mean as much for us as these things are meaning for Broadway. What do you think about it and would you be interested in exploring any such possibilities? I am frank to confess that I don't want to spend any more time worrying or trying to raise any money unless we have something worthwhile to offer. Tommy left us in a hell of a mess and there is just no point in trying to go ahead as is. Yet our Suitcase Theatre has meant something and can mean something if we stick to our original idea. Otherwise it becomes just one of those things that pass in the night. Have you seen Matt since his operation? I have had just one card from Nebby saying he is getting along all right.

Have you finished your book yet? And, when do you think you will be wending your way back to these parts? Kenneth is waiting around for John Henry to get into rehearsal. Paul Robeson is back but as yet they haven't set the date to start.

Please write.

Sincerely,
Louise
Louise
LT/SS
UOPWA-No.16

TO LOUISE, [NOVEMBER, 1939]

Dear Lou:

This is one of those last days at the Fair, when, remembering that cold night we were there, I took my top coat—and then it turned out to be the hottest day of the year, and all the check stands were full to capacity and you couldn't find any place to park your coat. And if you did succeed in checking it, it took an hour in line to get it out!

Are you all having turkey for Thanksgiving? Wish I were there.

I'm outlining my spring lecture tour. Antioch is to be March 19th. I have a couple in Kentucky and one at the Book Fair at West Virginia State. If you know any good places for dates down there, wish you'd phone them to

Miss Wills (Frances) at the Y—or 370 Manhattan Avenue—as she is doing all the letter writing for me and arranging the dates.

Ballet Caravan is here tonight. And 20 for Thanksgiving dinner.

I keep on getting swell ideas for a Suitcase Review. Even if the theatre evaporates, we'll have to get together and work out that show—you, Waring [William Waring Cuney] & Co., (like we did the skits) then we'll probably have to stage it in your parlor.

L.H.

FROM LOUISE, NOVEMBER 29, [1939]

Cleveland

Nov. 29

Lang dear:

The nite before I left NY on this barn storming tour your Thanksgiving remembrance came. (This darn pen refuses to act right.) And this is the first time I have had a free moment to tell you how nice it was to have you think of me.

I spent Thanksgiving in Chicago. Marcella [Walker McGee] and I had dinner at Horace [Cayton]'s. He has a grand Capehart and a grander collection of blues and other Negro records. Stop there some time when you are passing thru Chicago—I know you will enjoy it.

I shall be on the road until Dec. 9 travelling thru Ohio and upper NY State. I was in Toledo yesterday and had dinner with Myra Wheeler. She is treasuring a copy of "A New Song" which you autographed when you were there last year or last spring.

I wasn't in Chicago long enough to learn anything much of the theatre there. I imagine tho that they are struggling along like the other groups. When I left NY we were discussing with Powell Lindsay his coming into the H.S.T. He has in mind some three things he would like to do right away. "Bury the Dead"— "Young Man of Harlem" and a Political Cabaret on the order of Tac [Theatre Arts Committee]. He wants to do Bury the Dead because of its timeliness and because he has done it successfully in Conn. We were discussing the possibility of combining it with a dramatization of your poem on The Negro Soldier. He wants very much to work with us. I don't know what has happened since. But I do know that unless we can get some one to head up the theatre we can't go anywhere. Our trial of Tommy was a miserable flop but that was a mistake in selection I think. One thing is clear to me—we must get rid of Hilary. He is still up to his old tricks of gossiping and cliquing (how do you spell it?) and has no idea whatsoever for developing the theatre. We told Powell of what a hole we are in—no money—lots of debts—and no possibility of raising any money until we have some thing to offer. But he wants to work with us any way—or at least said that he did. If we don't get him, or some one else, then I don't think we can go ahead until we do have some one. The Rose McClendon's[26] are successful because they do have a good organization and Dick Campbell is a darn good promoter. But I think their success will be ephemeral unless they do some thing worth-while. I heard conflicting reports of their Father Divine play but don't think it was any great achievement.

I haven't read as yet any of the new Spanish books. I intend to when I return, especially Constancia de la Mora's new book.[27] It has received splendid reviews as you have read no doubt. I saw [Eugene Victor] Gavin[28] the other day in Detroit. Did you know he lost an eye? He has a glass one which gives the impression of moving. He wanted to know if you wrote anything about him and used his picture—and if so where and when.

I have thot a lot about your reaction on Way Down South—that is on the criticism[.] I wrote you about it. You know, Lang, you will have to expect such attacks I think because you have built up for yourself very high standards, artistically and in content, too. People will therefore not be tolerant with you—in fact will even be unkind when you turn out some thing that doesn't measure up. Of course I am still talking as an outsider for I haven't yet been able to run into the picture. It was advertised all over Detroit to start this coming Friday. Oh, what a job I'll face when I return. We are moving! Back to 409 Edgecombe. Dot [Dorothy Fisher-Spencer] and Kenneth [Spencer] and Grace [Johnson] are joining us. In other words we are opening up a dormitory. Don't you want to join? We hope to be moved by Xmas so I'll have to start packing as soon as I get back.

Kenneth has started rehearsals. He doesn't have much to do—understudying Robeson and a walk on role. Colored seem to be getting a good break in the show. Dean Dixon will direct the orchestra—white I believe (that is the orchestra.) The asst stage manager is Negro. Leonard [De Paur] has the choir. And there is one white character. Ruby Elzy is playing opposite Robeson.

26. Louise is referring to the stage productions of the famed African American actress and theater director Rose McClendon.

27. The book is *In Place of Splendor: The Autobiography of a Spanish Woman*, which was published in 1939.

28. Oklahoma native Eugene Victor Gavin was an African American who fought in the Spanish Civil War. He was severely wounded and lost an eye in the Battle of Teruel in 1938.

[Robert] Earl Jones was walking on air for a while. He got the part of Oberon in Swinging the Dream. I don't know just the how or why of it but I learned that he was out and Rex Ingram would do it. He had already begun rehearsals but evidently had no contract.

I can't think just now Lang of any groups in Ky. or W.Va. If I think of anything I'll call Frances [Wills].

When will you reach NY? Do you expect to finish the second volume of your book first? Any chance of my reading the manuscript of the first volume? I have the pictures for you. Your brother has a new job—marriage seems to have been good for him.

Love,
Lou

TO LOUISE, DECEMBER 4, 1939

Hollow Hills Farm,
Monterey, California

December 4, 1939

Hy, Lou:

Delighted to hear from you from Cleveland. Who did you see in my old home town that I know? I'll be there on Easter, I think. Engagements are coming in pretty good so I shall be barnstorming, too, this spring. If I can barnstorm up three months' livehood, I'll write a novel. From now on I'm going to try to do two books a year, & one play thrown in. . . . . I think it might be a very good idea if we could get Powell Lindsay. Why not start off by letting him stage his own play, YOUNG MAN OF HARLEM on which (because it is his own) he'd probably work very hard. . . . . . BURY THE DEAD, remember, is a royalty play.

It also requires scenery—a trench, expert lighting, and soldiers' costumes. All of which costs MONEY. Besides it is non-Negro. Personally, I am against anything white, anything expensive, and anything already done on Broadway. Seems to me we're not prepared to do things of that sort either financially or spiritually. . . . . The political cabaret idea I like very much however, WITH NEGRO MATERIAL—not warmed over downtown stuff. . . . . . So you-all are going up in the world again—409. Nice, though. We'll be neighbors. . . . . Sorry about Earl [Robert Earl Jones] being out of SWINGING THE DREAM.

IN LOOKING THROUGH MY OLD LETTERS I FIND A GUY WHO'S BOUGHT AND PAID FOR AN AUTOGRAPHED COPY OF A NEW

SONG MONTHS AGO, AND I'VE NEVER SENT IT TO HIM. SO
WOULD YOU BE SO KIND AS TO PHONE DOWN AND ASK EDITH
TO MAIL ME TWO OR THREE COPIES OF A NEW SONG RIGHT
AWAY!!!!!!! AND WHEN MY SHIP COMES IN I WILL REMEMBER
YOU ALL.

Did you hear about Dick Wright's book[29] being the January Book-Of-
The-Month? Mighty nice, huh! I hope it has a BIG sale and makes lots of
money for him so he won't have to write for Hollywood like a lot of white
party members do. . . . John Bright[30] is in Carmel and I had dinner with
him the other night. He said he never writes any Negro parts into his
pictures because he feels that it is better the Negro actors don't have jobs
than that they conform to the patterns of Hollywood. All of which is very
sweet of him. I suppose being the most downtrodden, we ought to be
willing to starve and die first. Do you believe in anihilization, amalgamation, or compromization? Or should we give up the arts all together and go
in the Post Office. (The W.P.A. is overcrowded). . . . . I seek clarification?

Erskine Caldwell is due here at any moment.

I hear the Trotskyites are proposing a united front now just to be
contrary! . . . . . What all went on at that Spanish Med. Meeting in
Harlem? Ted [Poston] must have had a grand time writing it up for the
cullud papers.

Su seguro servidor.

Lang

[The sentences about Richard Wright are bracketed, and a line labeled
"Times Square shuttle—Follow The Line" connects them to the following
bracketed sentences in the top right margin] *Is it true Dick married the
white girl, as we hear out here? Nebby wants to be clarified on that point.*

[Note in top left margin] *Why don't some of the colored lady leaders
marry white, too? Say Mrs. [Mary McLeod] Bethune and [Harold] Ickes?
Otherwise the rank and file get mad, and are filled with bitter thoughts. 1. 10¢
Shoot the shoots*

[Note in left margin] *Luna Park [drawing of people in water] THE BIG
SEA 45¢*

29. Richard Wright's blockbuster 1940 novel, *Native Son*.
30. John Bright (1908–1989) was a left-wing journalist and screenwriter, who was blacklisted in Hollywood during the 1950s.

[Note in bottom left margin] *How come they let the white actors compromise? It seems like white chauvinism to me! (Plus a nice income.) Are only white folks due to make a living? Not cullud?*

[Top of reverse side] *1. The key to this symbol is found on reverse side.*

[Middle of reverse side, encircling a Christmas ornament] *a Bitter Ole Thought*

Langston is using code when he asks Louise to "clarify" him in the following letters. He wanted to understand why the prominent English Marxist writer Ralph Bates left the Communist movement. Bates cited the Soviet invasion of Finland as his reason for "getting off the train." In her Christmas greeting to Langston, Louise "clarified" Langston and expressed her continued commitment to the revolutionary cause, while allowing that there would be other "dissenters" who would abandon the party and the Soviet political line in light of events such as the 1939 Nazi-Soviet Non-Aggression Pact and the USSR's military invasion of neighboring Finland.

TO LOUISE, [DECEMBER, 1939]

Dear Lou,

What's happening to folks in New York? Clarify me, will you? Guess you saw the Ralph Bates article in this week's NEW REPUBLIC [December 13, 1939]. He's the first person I really know and like [^*to come out*] on the present change and crisis! Golly! Wish you'd tell me something.

Have you-all moved? Where are you getting your Christmas cards at? Have a little tiny gift for you (broke as usual) which I guess I'd better send to 500 not knowing where you're at.

I've got a new book of poems ready, too, that I think Knopf will like.

Too broke to even go to the city and shop, so haven't seen Matt or Nebby. After this year I give up art and literature and either go in for commercial writing or go back to being a bus boy. Maybe then I'll get re-discovered on the money making side. . . . . It's such a bore being flat every Christmas!

HEY*HEY! I'm going to the village and drink some gin!

Sincerely,
Lang

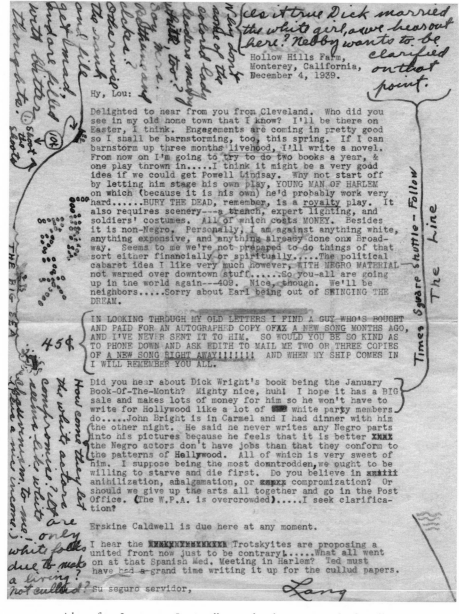

FIGURE 17. A letter from Langston to Louise, illustrated in the margins with a few of his comical notations, 1939. (Louise Thompson Patterson papers, Special Collections & Archives, Robert W. Woodruff Library, Emory University. Copyright (©) 2015 by The Estate of Langston Hughes, Arnold Rampersad and Ramona Bass Kolobe Co-Administrators. By permission of Harold Ober Associates Incorporated.)

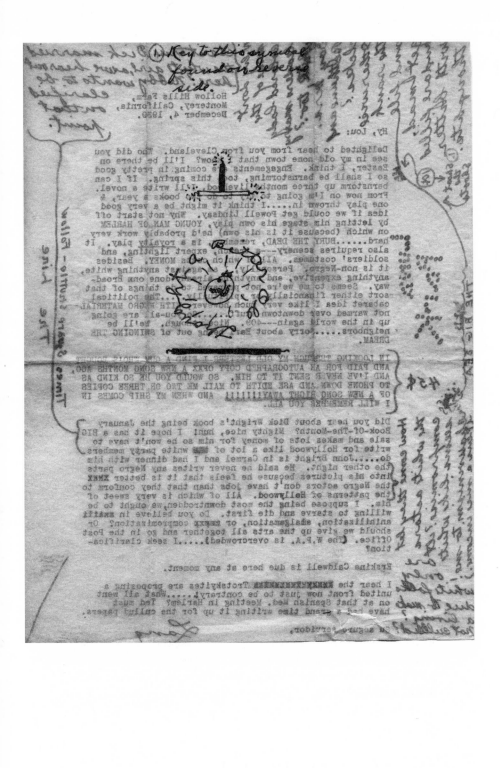

Hollow Hills Farm,
Monterey, California,
December 4, 1939.

Hy, Lou:

Delighted to hear from you from Cleveland. Who did you
see in my old home town that I know? I'll be there on
Easter, I think. Engagements are coming, in pretty good
so I shall be barnstorming, too, this spring. If I can
barnstorm up three months' livelihood, I'll write a novel.
From now on I'm going to.... to do two books a year. A
one play thrown in..... I think it might be a very good
idea if we could get Powell Lindsay. Why not start off
by letting him stage his own play, YOUNG MAN OF HARLEM
on which (because it is his own) he'd probably work very
hard.....BURY THE DEAD, remember, is a royalty play. It
also requires scenery------and, I expect lighting, and
soldiers' costumes. All of which cost MONEY, besides
anything non-Negro. Personally, I am against anything white,
anything expensive, and anything else not done one Broadway. Seems to me we're poor folk and good things of that
sort either financially or ... LIFE.... The political
cabaret idea I like very much too....our HARLEM NEGRO MATERIAL
not warmed over downtown stuff....those...you-all are going
up in the world again----40¢. Nice going. We'll be
neighbors.....Sorry about Harlem. Lose out of SWINGING THE
DREAM.

IN LOOKING THROUGH MY OLD LETTERS I FIND A CLIPPING REGARDING
AND PAID FOR AN AUTOGRAPHED COPY OFXX A NEW SONG MONTHS AGO.
AND I'VE NEVER SENT IT TO HIM. SO WOULD YOU BE SO KIND AS
TO PHONE DOWN AND ASK EDITH TO MAIL ME TWO OR THREE COPIES
OF A NEW SONG RIGHT AVAILIIIIIII AND WHEN MY SHIP COMES IN
I WILL REMEMBER YOU ALL.

Did you hear about Dick Wright's book being the January
Book-Of-The-Month? Mighty nice, huh! I hope it has a BIG
sale and makes lots of money for him so he won't have to
write for Hollywood like a lot of white party members
do.....John Bright is in Carmel and I had dinner with him
the other night. He said he never writes any Negro parts
into his pictures because he feels that it is better
the Negro actors don't have jobs than that they conform to
the patterns of Hollywood. ALL of which is very sweet of
him. I suppose being the most downtrodden, we ought to be
willing to starve and die first. Do you believe in small
antinihilation, amalgamation, or compromation? Or
should we give up the arts all together and go in the Post
Office. (The W.P.A. is overcrowded!)....I seek clarification?

Erskine Caldwell is due here at any moment.

I hear the Trotskyites are proposing a
united front now just to be contrary......What all went
on at that Spanish Med. Meeting in Harlem? Ted must
have had a grand time writing it up for the daily papers.

Lang dear:

Santa Claus is on his way but I fear won't reach you come Xmas. What with moving, just getting home and plenty else I am just getting the old guy off today. But he's on his way—<u>believe</u> me! My dear your search for clarity is going to tax my capacity for writin' I fear. First of all—re Dick Wright yeah—your information is correct. He's done crossed the color line! He and his wife (white) live up in Mohegan Colony. I guess it was love—he was supposed to marry colored once but something happened after the wedding invitations went out. So he didn't try a second time.

Now getting to more political matters—re Bates, Hicks 'n company. I am enclosing the Redfield cartoon which I think explains all. Some folks just can't swing that ole curve. I guess we were all surprised at Bates. But Lang, when you read this article, and I read it several times, I think you see through his argument and can't read into it anything but a desire to get off that ole train. He seems to have swallowed (indigested) all the propaganda which has flooded the pages of our daily press. How does he know that the Soviets actually bombed civilians. The cap press says yes—the U.S.S.R. denies it! Certainly if Bernard Shaw concedes Finland's being used as a cat's paw by his own and our imperialistic governments certainly Bates, who has been considered a Marxist, should. Is it conceivable that Finland would dare or want to provoke a conflict unless she was being egged on by greater powers than herself. Wouldn't anyone who had thru the past years watched with bitterness the destruction of Ethiopia, Spain, China view with at least an ironical smirk the sudden concern of the Hoovers, Roosevelts et al. over poor little Finland. They sure didn't start a nationwide campaign for Ethiopia or Spanish refugees—nor offer either of them $10,000,000. There will probably be more dissenters as the going gets tougher—and from all appearances it is likely to. Regrettable—yes—but inevitable—still yes. Some just can't take it.

Well, as for me—I am just marching along with the ole Red Army. Too bad the Union Army didn't do a similar job in the Civil War. If that 40 acres and a mule had been realized for our folks like the granting of land to the peasants in Polish Ukraine and Byelo Russia we wouldn't have those sharecroppers starving along the roadside today in Arkansas. In fact I just wish we would just "sit back" and wait for that Red Army to come march-ing thru Georgia today. But of course we can't—so if we have the guts we just gotta keep on fighting.

Well, Lang dear, you asked me to elucidate—so here it is, according to how I sees it.

Yours to keep on the train as long as we can hold tight.

Love,

Lou

Wish you were here. When will you come—before or after your tour?

We move this Thursday—the Lord willing. It is sure a mess—and will I be glad when it's over. Merry Xmas.

(If you want some money—just say so. I am not the Chase Nat'l but I got a few pennies which are yours for the asking.)

PART II

The Far-Reaching 1940s

As the United States finally began climbing out of the frying pan of the Great Depression, only to end up in the fire of World War II, the 1940s swung pendulum-like from hope to disaster, resistance to repression, and fascism to freedom. All the while, Langston and our parents remained at the fulcrum of progressive political struggle. The eighty-four pieces of correspondence we discovered from this decade not only offer a window into the personal trials and tribulations of war, anti-fascism, repression, mobility, work, childbirth, and the difficulty of maintaining friendship under extreme duress, but also reveal what was at stake for the American Left and African Americans as they struggled for justice, democracy, and basic citizenship rights in this rapidly changing era of waxing US global dominance and Cold War anti-Communism.

The prevailing image of the 1940s is that of fighting the "Good War"; it was an era of national unity, when old grievances were transcended to fight for an Allied victory. But for many Black people, it was an age of defiance, violence, and deferred dreams. In 1943 African American journalist Roi Ottley noticed a profound change in the sound of Black voices: "Listen to the way Negroes are talking these days! . . . Black men have become noisy, aggressive, and sometimes defiant."[1] They had good reason to be defiant and restive. African Americans were challenging a federal government that was seemingly indifferent to the fact that Americans were called upon to crush Nazis in Europe while white supremacy reigned in the United States. Black leaders understood the war as a battleground for racial justice, and thus

1. Roi Ottley, *New World A-Coming: Inside Black America* (New York and Boston: Houghton and Mifflin, 1943), 306.

started the Double V Campaign, calling for a double victory: against fascism abroad and racism at home.

The domestic terrain became more embattled as wartime industrial demands drew about a million black workers from the South to the sprawling factories of the urban North and West, as well as to Southern metropolises tied to the war economy. In places like Mobile, Alabama, and Philadelphia, white workers waged "hate strikes" to protest the hiring and promotion of Black men and women workers, and African Americans frequently retaliated with their own wildcat strikes to resist racism. These battles often spilled out into city streets. Dramatic incidents of racial violence occurred in cities across the country, prompted by acts of police brutality, shop floor rumbles, or scuffles on a bus or a streetcar. By June of 1943, race riots had erupted in Los Angeles, California; Detroit, Michigan; Beaumont, Texas; and Mobile, Alabama, and a Black man was lynched in Marianna, Florida. As US troops invaded Normandy, France, and bombed Okinawa, Japan, African Americans fought their own war at home in the urban ghettoes.[2]

The upsurge in Black militancy swelled Black organizational capacity. The NAACP enjoyed a tenfold increase; new organizations, such as the Congress on Racial Equality, came into being during the war; and trade-union membership skyrocketed.[3] In 1941, over a year before the Japanese attack on Pearl Harbor that lead to the United States joining World War II, activists declared war against racism when a Black woman delegate to a civil rights conference proposed that labor leader A. Philip Randolph lead a march on Washington. Randolph took up the challenge, warning President Roosevelt that if he did not issue an executive order banning racial discrimination in

2. Herbert Shapiro, *White Violence and Black Response: From Reconstruction to Montgomery* (Amherst, MA: University of Massachusetts Press, 1988), 301–48; Dominic J. Capeci Jr., *Race Relations in Wartime Detroit: The Sojourner Truth Housing Controversy of 1942* (Philadelphia: Temple University Press, 1984); Dominic J. Capeci Jr., *The Harlem Riot of 1943* (Philadelphia: Temple University Press, 1977).

3. Neil A. Wynn, *The Afro-American and the Second World War* (New York: Holmes and Meier Publishers, 1975); Harvard Sitkoff, *A New Deal for Blacks: The Emergence of Civil Rights as a National Issue* (Oxford and New York: Oxford University Press, 1978), 298–325; Robert Korstad and Nelson Lichtenstein, "Opportunities Found and Lost: Labor, Radicals, and the Early Civil Rights Movement," *Journal of American History* 75 (December 1988), 786–811; Herbert Shapiro, *White Violence and Black Response: From Reconstruction to Montgomery* (Amherst: University of Massachusetts Press, 1988), 301–48; George Lipsitz, *A Rainbow at Midnight: Labor and Culture in the 1940s* (Urbana, IL: University of Illinois Press, 1994), 14–28; Nelson Lichtenstein, *Labor's War at Home: The CIO in World War II* (New York and Cambridge: Cambridge University Press, 1982), 124–26.

hiring, selection for employment training programs, and union membership and desegregating the armed forces, one hundred thousand Negroes would march on the nation's capital. While not all the demands were met, Roosevelt did issue Executive Order 8802, creating the Fair Employment Practice Committee (1941), which led to the President's Committee on Fair Employment Practice (1943), and ultimately persuaded the National War Labor Board to abolish wage differentials based on race.[4]

The Communist Party and its allied organizations also became a force to be reckoned with during the war. Young Black Communists founded the Southern Negro Youth Congress (SNYC) in 1937, which became a major precursor to the modern Civil Rights movement during its eleven-year existence. Under the slogan "Freedom, Equality and Opportunity," SNYC leaders fought for Black voting rights, job security, the right of Black workers to organize, and general improvement in the health, education, and welfare of Black citizens. They also challenged segregation in public spaces and police brutality. Likewise, the SNYC's parent organization, the National Negro Congress, indirectly supported the Double V Campaign, despite the fact that the Communist Party's official stance opposed the slogan in favor of a complete united front against fascism.[5]

Indeed, what may be most revelatory in the correspondence between Pat, Louise, Nebby, Matt, and Langston during the 1940s is the extent to which the five, along with other Black Communists, expressed a radical political vision that was often independent of the Communist Party at large. They worked hard to sustain strong ties between the Left and Black workers and artists, and they remained attentive to the politics of popular culture. Between 1939 and 1940, for instance, Black Communists led a boycott of the film *Gone With the Wind,* initiated a campaign to end Jim Crow in Sports, and collected ten thousand signatures to demand the integration of Blacks in Major League Baseball (an initiative spearheaded by Pat), organized numerous plays and jazz concerts, and persuaded blues composer W. C.

---

4. Paula F. Pfeffer, *A. Philip Randolph: Pioneer of the Civil Rights Movement* (Baton Rouge: Louisiana State University Press, 1996); Herbert Garfinkel, *When Negroes March* (Glencoe, IL: Free Press, 1959); Harvard Sitkoff, *A New Deal for Blacks* (New York: Oxford University Press, 1978), 298–325.

5. Robin D. G. Kelley, *Hammer and Hoe: Alabama Communists During the Great Depression* (Chapel Hill: University of North Carolina Press, 1990); Erik S. Gellman, *Death Blow to Jim Crow: The National Negro Congress and the Rise of Militant Civil Rights* (Chapel Hill: University of North Carolina Press, 2012).

Handy to lecture at the New York Workers School, an institution run by the Communist Party USA. When Communists eventually abandoned their support of the Nazi-Soviet Non-Aggression Pact and shifted to a pro-war position after Germany invaded Russia in 1941, it was the Black Communist Party leadership that adopted an uncompromising stance vis-à-vis the war effort, embracing the principles of the Double V Campaign. Often in defiance of the Communist Party's Central Committee, American Black Communists continued to fight on the civil rights front throughout the war, demanding the full integration of the armed forces and implementation of the Fair Employment Practices Committee.

The decade opened with Langston living in Los Angeles, trying to make his way into the Hollywood film industry and hopefully into some money. Yet promising plays and musicals he worked on failed, exhausting and dismaying him. On January 19, 1940, Langston wrote to Louise that he was "laying off political involvement." Yet he never completely withdrew from politics, nor did he abandon the Left. He continued to write political poems like "To the Red Army" and "Good Morning, Stalingrad," and, about a year later, when he returned to Los Angeles after a tour promoting his autobiography, *The Big Sea,* he initiated collaborative film projects with Paul Robeson and the dancer and choreographer Katherine Dunham, although these projects fared no better than his earlier efforts.

In 1940, Langston was condemned and attacked by the evangelist Amiee McPherson over his poem "Goodbye Christ." The assault was an example of the fears that had already begun to take hold of American politics and served as a precursor of what was to come. The Red Scare began before Joseph McCarthy joined the Senate in 1947 or Winston Churchill delivered his infamous "Iron Curtain" speech in Missouri in 1946. In 1940 Congress passed the notorious Smith Act—also known as the Alien Registration Act. It essentially outlawed any organization alleged to advocate the overthrow of the government, which included the Communist Party, and required all non-citizen residents of the country to register with the federal government.[6] Two years earlier, Texas congressman Martin Dies had launched the House Un-American Activities Committee (HUAC). Its purpose was initially to investigate pro-Nazi activity, but it soon pivoted to rooting out alleged Communists and their

6. Michael R. Belknap, *Cold War Political Justice: The Smith Act, the Communist Party, and American Civil Liberties* (Westport, CT: Greenwood Press, 1977).

"fellow travelers."[7] In other words, what is often referred to as the "Little Red Scare" was in full swing by the time McPherson and others took aim at Langston's "Goodbye Christ." Still, Langston would not back down, and he stayed close to Louise and Pat, who were known Communists. He dedicated his 1942 collection of poetry, *Shakespeare in Harlem,* to Louise, and began drafting the second part of his autobiography, in which he unequivocally acknowledges his respect and admiration for Pat's intellect and political opinions. Indeed, through the early 1940s the two men often worked and conspired together. In 1940, when Pat launched the Abraham Lincoln School[8] in Chicago, Langston was happy to offer his services.[9]

Contrary to what might be expected, political repression deepened rather than strained the friendships between Pat, Louise, Matt, Nebby, and Langston. Life, love, and even some normalcy often prevailed. At some point between 1939 and 1940, after many years of friendship, Louise and Pat had started a romantic relationship. They had first met during their formative years in San Francisco and Oakland, where the small Black communities on both sides of the San Francisco Bay interacted in church and social settings. Later, both of them had moved east and become active in political campaigns in New York and Chicago. By the 1940s, both had been previously married, Louise once and Pat twice. Having known each other for years, they were drawn closer through their mutual passion for the political work they dedicated their lives to and a shared group of interracial friends. They had long been partners in "the struggle," and in the autumn of 1940, they tied the knot, deciding to become partners in life as well.

They honeymooned in California, where they spent time in the Bay Area with Nebby and Matt. In 1943 Matt was appointed assistant director of the

---

7. Kenneth O'Reilly, "The Dies Committee v. the New Deal: Real Americans and the Unending Search for Un-Americans," in *Little Red Scares: Anti-Communism and Political Repression in the United States, 1921–1946,* ed. Robert Justin Goldstein (Surrey and Burlington: Ashgate Publishers LTD, 2014), 237–260. This important collection of essays demonstrates the nearly unbroken history of anti-Communist repression in the United States since the birth of the Third International.

8. The Abraham Lincoln School for Social Science was a "people's" school founded by Pat. It was created in the spirit of the Popular Front and sought to suspend all militant and antiracist struggle to create the broadest possible coalition against the then critical enemy—fascism. The school taught European immigrant and African American workers about political economy, democracy, and the principles (and limits) of citizenship in the United States.

9. Gerald Horne, Black Revolutionary: William Patterson and the Globalization of the African American Freedom Struggle (Urbana: University of Illinois Press, 2013), 87–88.

California CIO Council Minorities Committee. In March of 1943 Mary Lou was born, and despite an increasingly hectic schedule for all of them, Langston took time to welcome his new "niece" into the world. He never missed an opportunity to congratulate, encourage, and cajole his friends. As the war intensified and the organizing demands of the five increased, letters were often their only mode of communication. Langston traveled extensively to support the war effort, speaking primarily to white audiences and on the radio. At a massive pro-Allied Forces rally at New York's Town Hall, Langston read his poems "Salute to the Red Army" and "Lenin" (the latter of which he had written as an anthem to be set to music for the opening of the Southern Negro Youth Congress in 1944).[10]

For the first time in his life, Langston began to make a decent income. He entered into ventures with conductor and composer Leopold Stokowski and the Left-leaning owner of New York City's famed Café Society, Barney Josephson. He penned a successful campaign jingle for Democrat Adam Clayton Powell's first congressional run in 1944 and also found time to collaborate with the great Duke Ellington. By 1945 he had saved enough money to buy a house on 127th Street in Harlem together with his adoptive "aunt" and "uncle" Toy and Emerson Harper, enabling him to finally lay down serious roots. Pat and Louise, on the other hand, found themselves financially downsizing and facing a precarious existence. Pat's writings in the *Chicago Defender* and his editorial position at the *Midwest Daily Record* came to an inauspicious end when the paper was shut down, and he turned his attention to internal Communist Party matters and to leading the fight against the use of racially restrictive covenants to deny Black Chicago homebuyers access to better neighborhoods.[11]

The defeat of the Axis powers in 1945 did not usher in a new era of peace, security, or stability for Black America. On the contrary, the war for racial justice on the home front was intensifying. Black workers, and especially Black women, were the first fired to open up jobs for returning white male war veterans. A housing crisis left many poor Black families in dilapidated homes, and middle class Black families who tried to move into white neighborhoods often faced firebombs, burning crosses, and death threats. Yet African Americans continued to fight. They persisted in pressuring the fed-

10. Arnold Rampersad, *The Life of Langston Hughes,* vol. 2, *1941–1967* (New York: Oxford University Press, 1986), 95.
11. Horne, *Black Revolutionary,* 98.

eral government and the courts to extend the promises of democracy to their own backyard. For Black people all over the country, from returning veterans to underpaid maids, steel workers to musicians, the world had changed irrevocably. The fight for racial justice on the home front eventually gave rise to one of the most important civil disobedience campaigns in modern history, the Montgomery Bus Boycott of 1957.

That struggle, however, was fought on the minefields of another battle: the global Cold War. The United States had ramped up its long war against Communism—both at home and abroad. America's Cold War ostensibly sought to "contain" the Soviet Union and its Eastern bloc allies, buttress free-market capitalism (particularly when it benefitted sales of US commodities, opened markets for US investments, and ensured US access to raw materials), spread "democracy" around the world, and secure a lasting peace through military, economic, political, and cultural hegemony. The reality was quite different. The Cold War gave rise to a massive national-security state and led to a dangerous and unpredictable arms race involving nuclear weapons, covert wars against sovereign nations, support for authoritarian regimes over democracies, targeted assassinations, an interventionist foreign policy, and the increased power of military and intelligence institutions (such as the CIA and the NSA), which became free to operate without Congressional oversight. The Cold War was hardly cold. Germany was divided into East and West, the United States, spearheaded by the CIA, intervened in the Greek Civil War to defeat the Left, and by 1950 the United States was embroiled in the era's first full-scale proxy war in Korea.

At home, genuine Communists or anyone expressing opinions critical of US policies or sympathetic to a planned economy, workers rights, and racial justice faced a phalanx of institutions and forces prepared to silence dissent. The scope and powers of the FBI and HUAC were significantly expanded. The Senate created the Subversive Activities Control Board in 1950, and several states passed their own anti-subversion laws. Michigan, for instance, imposed a life sentence on anyone "uniting or speaking subversive words." Tennessee upped the ante by mandating the death penalty for anyone convicted of espousing Marxist ideas. Public employees, scientists, and scholars were required to sign loyalty oaths, and many were summarily fired on suspicion of Communist Party membership. In 1947, in the name of anti-Communism, Congress passed the worst anti-union legislation since the Gilded Age, the Taft-Hartley Act. This act restricted workers' right to strike, infringed on their freedom of speech by requiring loyalty oaths, prevented unions from contributing to political campaigns, outlawed sympathy strikes and secondary boycotts by unions, and made union officials vulnerable to fines and imprisonment for refusing to condemn wildcat strikes.

To compound matters, the Communist Party was dealing with internal problems. In 1944 General Secretary Earl Browder issued a directive effectively dissolving the CPUSA and replacing it with loosely structured Communist Political Associations. This stunning decision was prompted by the successful Tehran Conference in late 1943, a meeting of the leaders of the United States, Britain, and the Soviet Union, the three main Allied powers, in which the countries decided to collaborate more closely to fight the Nazis. For Browder, this proved that a future of peaceful coexistence between capitalist and socialist countries was on the horizon.[12] With Communist Party membership at an all-time high, Browder envisioned turning the traditional cadre-based organization into a mass movement. However, the new Communist Political Associations came to an abrupt end in 1945, when French Communist Jacques Duclos published an article sharply criticizing Browder's strategy. The subsequent expulsion of Browder from the party and the ascension of William Z. Foster to power in 1946 generated an internal crisis in the party, resulting in a wave of expulsions prompted by charges of Trotskyism, Browderism, and "Negro Nationalism."[13]

As one of the highest-ranking members of the party, Pat was smack in the middle of the shake-up. He pushed for Browder's expulsion and backed the decision to restore the party's earlier stance that Black Americans in the South constituted a nation with a right to self-determination.[14] As the United States moved farther to the Right under the cloak of McCarthyism, the Communist Party moved farther to the Left and farther into isolation under Foster, although popular front-style coalition politics continued to find expression through Henry Wallace's 1948 presidential bid on the Progressive Party ticket.

Langston publicly praised Wallace but never went so far as to endorse him. Pat, Louise, and Nebby openly supported Wallace's bid, and Matt worked

12. Earl Browder, *Tehran: Our Path in War and Peace* (New York: International Publishers, 1944).

13. Thomas W. Devine, *Henry Wallace's 1948 Presidential Campaign and the Future of Postwar Liberalism* (Chapel Hill: University of North Carolina Press, 1948), 1–20; Edward P. Johanningsmeier, *Forging American Communism: The Life of William Z. Foster* (Princeton: Princeton University Press, 1998), 293–313.

14. Horne, *Black Revolutionary*, 93–96.

directly on his campaign. Having served as Secretary of Agriculture, Secretary of Commerce, and vice president under Roosevelt, Wallace was a loyal Democrat and a solid bureaucrat—not fitting the profile of America's first civil rights and antiwar candidate. And yet these two issues were precisely the ones that galvanized the country and defined the presidential elections of 1948. With America selling itself to the non-white world as the exemplar of freedom and democracy, the persistence of Jim Crow laws undermined US legitimacy and became something of an international embarrassment. The Truman administration formed the President's Committee on Civil Rights. In 1947, the committee issued a report titled *To Secure These Rights,* which documented cases of racial violence and discrimination and offered recommendations to mitigate racial inequality. Southern Democrats, who at the time represented the most powerful, most senior force in the federal government, were none too happy about the report or Truman's statements about addressing racism. Despite Truman's conciliatory efforts, they broke with the Democratic Party in 1948 and formed the States' Rights Party, popularly known as the Dixiecrats, running Strom Thurmond, who was the governor of South Carolina, as their presidential candidate.

To Truman's left stood Henry Wallace and the Progressive Party. Wallace broke from the Democratic Party primarily over its Cold War foreign policy, warning that treating the Soviet Union as an enemy would inevitably lead to nuclear war or, at best, a never-ending arms race. The Progressive Party called for a radical shift to cooperation and for détente and disarmament. Wallace also called for an even more robust civil rights policy than Truman had implemented, attracting a significant percentage of the Black vote. In a radio address delivered in September 1948, Wallace told his listeners,

> The eyes of the world are upon us: the colonial peoples of the world are watching us, assessing us by our treatment of Negroes and other minorities. And they ask: "What do Americans really mean by democracy?" Do we mean the democracy of Mississippi where three-tenths of one percent of the Negro citizens vote? Do we mean the democracy of Tom Dewey who would restore the Italian bankers to their former positions of empire as rulers of the colored people of Africa? Do we mean the democracy of Harry Truman, who proclaims a non-segregation policy for the Army, and sits by while his Southern secretary of the Army deliberately violates the policy? Which is the true policy, the world is asking—the words or the deeds?[15]

15. Henry A. Wallace, "Radio Address," given at the Wheat Street Baptist Church, Atlanta, GA September 13, 1948, www.blackpast.org/1948-henry-wallace-radio-address.

Realizing that he could not win back the Dixiecrats, Truman recognized that Black votes would matter in the election. Although the vast majority of African Americans in the South remained disenfranchised, massive Black migration to the north and west, the 1944 Supreme Court decision to strike down white-only primaries, and a federal law waiving poll taxes for war veterans significantly increased the Black electorate all across the country. Truman swiftly issued two executive orders to demonstrate his commitment to civil rights, creating a fair employment practices board and desegregating the armed forces.[16]

But neither Truman nor Wallace nor the Supreme Court bare responsibility for birthing the Civil Rights Movement. Rather, African American demands for equality under the law created the political crisis in Cold War liberalism and bent national policy slightly toward justice. But Jim Crow laws, racial violence, and a regime that regularly denied Black people basic constitutional rights still prevailed. So in the year of the 1948 presidential elections the Pattersons moved from Chicago to New York, where Pat took over as head of the Civil Rights Congress (CRC). Founded in 1946, the CRC was the product of a merger between the International Labor Defense (ILD), the National Negro Congress, and the National Federation for Constitutional Liberties. As the new executive secretary, Pat was committed "to the defense of victims of racist persecution and of those who were hounded for advocating peaceful co-existence," and he was "determined to follow the course established by the ILD and make of the CRC a fighter for Black Liberation."[17] In addition to legal defense, the CRC investigated and challenged incidents of police brutality, housing discrimination, and a range of other civil and human rights violations. One of its first national cases was the defense of Rosa Lee Ingram of Georgia, a Black tenant farmer and widowed mother of fourteen children, who in 1947, along with two of her sons, was convicted and sentenced to death for the murder of their neighbor, Stratford, a white tenant farmer who had assaulted and harassed her. A third Ingram son had

---

16. Devine, *Henry Wallace's 1948 Presidential Campaign*; Michael J. Klarman, *From Jim Crow to Civil Rights: The Supreme Court and the Struggle for Racial Equality* (New York: Oxford University Press, 2004), 237–253; Richard M. Valelly, *The Two Reconstructions: The Struggle for Black Empowerment* (Chicago: University of Chicago Press, 2004); Zachary Karabell, *The Last Campaign: How Harry Truman Won the 1948 Election* (New York: Alfred A. Knopf, 2000).

17. William L. Patterson, *The Man Who Cried Genocide* (New York: International Publishers, 1971).

been acquitted for lack of evidence. On appeal, the sentences of Ingram and her eldest son, Wallace, were commuted to life in prison.[18] After a long fight by the CRC and other organizations, Rosa Lee and Wallace Ingram were finally paroled and released from prison in 1959.

Toward the latter half of the decade, Langston's correspondence with Pat, Louise, Nebby, and Matt dropped off considerably. However, given the political environment they were living in, the lull in their correspondence should not surprise us. Many Communists and suspected Communists were hounded by the FBI, jailed for violating the Smith Act, or ultimately forced underground. As the red-baiting of Langston escalated, he began to limit his public support for radical activities, although he continued to publish articles praising the Soviet Union in the pages of *New Masses* and the *Chicago Defender*. Matt, who suffered a near-fatal car accident in Oakland in 1946, kept Langston abreast of the political situation on the Left with thoughtful and detailed reports on news and events within labor and civil rights circles. Langston's speaking tour of the West and South in 1946, as well as a four-month teaching gig at Atlanta University in 1947, kept him face-to-face with the realities of Jim Crow laws. The following year, the Pattersons left the Windy City for New York, and Langston taught at the University of Chicago's Laboratory School and collaborated with African American composer William Grant Still on a New York stage production of his play about Haiti, *Troubled Island,* which he had written some eighteen years earlier.

But the frigid winds of change were blowing strong. That year Langston's poems "Goodbye Christ" and "One More S in the USA" were entered into the *Congressional Record,* and he was labeled a Communist. By 1950 HUAC had referred to him in its documents.

18. Gerald Horne, *Communist Front?: The Civil Rights Congress, 1946–1956* (London and Toronto: Fairleigh Dickinson University Press, 1988).

FIVE

Early Political Repression

JANUARY 1940–NOVEMBER 1941

By the 1940s, Langston had become the most famous Black poet and playwright. However, as he confessed to Matt in a January 2, 1941, letter, he was "broke and ruint." In February 1940 he set off on a grueling speaking tour of thirty-five cities in eight states to promote his autobiography, *The Big Sea*, reviews of which were mostly favorable.

By 1940 Pat had moved to Chicago to start a worker's school. Louise was in New York keeping Langston abreast of the news and gossip and trying, unsuccessfully, to salvage the Suitcase Theatre. Matt and Nebby were in Berkeley, working and raising Nebby Lou, who Langston declared the "prettiest child in the world."

TO MATT, JANUARY 15, 1940

> Hollow Hills Farm,
> Monterey, Calif.
>
> January 15, 1940

Dear Matt & Nebby,

Enjoyed your little Christmas note so much, and had been hoping to get up to the city but the week before Christmas both Eulah [Pharr] and Mr. [Noel] Sullivan were ill in bed with colds all the week, then I got one. And then holiday guests began to arrive. And the holidays are just beginning to be over now. I'm behind in my work (as usual) and broke (as usual) and have got to get done with everything this month as I have to shove off for the East in February and resume my career as a lecturer. They tell me it is cold back there, so I shall put on two undershirts and three sweaters.

Lou has moved, you know, up to 409 Edgecombe Avenue,[1] right around the corner from me. Practically everybody I know lives in that house.

Louise has clarified me on the current situation[2] on the back of her Christmas card—which is another reason why I don't have to rush up to the city now to confer with you-all.

But I sure would like to see you, and shall, I hope, before I go. Give my best to Nebby-Lou, and tell her not to eat those hens and chickens [animal-shaped soaps], but to wash her hands with them instead.

Eulah says to tell you she got your letter and will write soon, meanwhile she sends love.

Lou sent me IN PLACE OF SPLENDOR for Christmas, swell book about Spain.

My book[3] is almost done. Looks like books never get really done though. I'm still revising. I guess I told you it was accepted, didn't I? Now I've got to do the second volume as soon as I can.

Sincerely,
Langston

P.S. Wasn't Mr. Sullivan that had the accident but Eulah who turned over three times New Year's Eve and didn't even faint. Just a few bruises and one little cut on her finger. So she climbed on out and went to the party and had a Happy New Year.

FROM LOUISE, JANUARY 18, [1940]

[Handwritten]

Philadelphia

Jan. 18

Lang dear:

Here I am in the sleepy city for a few days—will be going home tonite. So in the midst of its peace and quiet I am getting off a few letters which despite good intentions I never seem to get to in New York.

1. 409 Edgecombe Avenue in New York's Harlem is a famous apartment house where many prominent Black professionals, intellectuals and artists (including the Pattersons) lived over many decades.
2. Langston is referring to the writer Ralph Bates renouncing the Communist movement.
3. Langston was working on *The Big Sea,* his autobiography, which was published in 1940.

Thanks for my Santa. I just needed a compact hankie case to take with me when I go a travelling. And I shall be going out the first of February for a month in Ohio.

What are your plans? From Zell [Ingram] I hear that you may be in NY before going on your lecture tour. It will be just my luck to miss you like I did in L.A. Let me know any way. Maybe you will be coming thru Cleveland in February.

Well at long last we got moved—just before Xmas. So you can imagine what the holidays were like. But despite all the chaos and furor we had a nice time.

Now to tell you about John Henry.[4] It has came and went according to my last information which was on Monday when I left NY. They did their best to fix it up during the try outs in Phila. and Boston. But despite Robeson, an excellent cast, good voices and $80000—they just couldn't make it with [Roark] Bradford's book and Wolf [Jacques Wolfe]'s music. They both failed to catch the spirit and vitality and significance of this marvelous folk character. Robeson struggled in vain—the cast tried to fill in the gaps—but it wasn't in the cards. I am sending the reviews I have to Nebby and shall ask her to pass them on to you.

I have seen Jacques Romain [Roumain] a few times and like him so much. He is really a swell person. He speaks often of you too. He will be in NY for at least a year I believe so you will be seeing him when you come. I am hoping you will be doing some more translations of his things.

It is so cold here now I imagine you won't be liking to leave good ole California. What are you working on and what about your book. Has Knopf accepted it?

I have thot many times of your comments on art vs. making a living. It's a real problem I know, Lang. Yet in you I feel one whose whole life has been a dedication to the things you have believed in and wanted to do. And that has resulted in the high place you hold today, Lang. On every side there are those who do prostitute themselves before the great god Mammon—not to [be] praised for it even if it is understandable. But the things you are doing I am confident are bringing to you that sort of satisfaction that can't be measured in dollars and cents.

Love,
Lou.

4. *John Henry* was a Broadway musical that premiered in 1940. It was based on the novel of the same name written in 1931 by Roark Bradford.

Hollow Hills Farm,
Monterey, California,

January 19, 1940.

Dear Lou,

Your Christmas gift was the very ONE book I wanted, since I had already gotten the two about the Brigades. Constancia's [de la Mora] makes my SALUD collection complete. It was mighty sweet of you to send it to me. . . . . Also thanks for the clarifying. That is also a great help. I'm laying off of political poetry for a while, though, since the world situation, me thinks, is too complicated for so simple an art. So I am going back (indeed have gone) to nature, Negroes, and love. ESQUIRE has just bought SEVEN MOMENTS OF LOVE and I think intend to have [Elmer Simms] Campbell drawings with them. Golly! What a welcome check it was, too. . . . . The old book drags along just like the old novel did, and just won't seem to get itself done. But I've only got about three more weeks to work on it before leaving, so I've got to make a Titanic effort. Shouldn't take more than a week or so now though for final polishing. . . . . I had also hoped to finish SOLD AWAY but it looks like I won't get to it at all. My first lecture's a month from tonight in Downingtown, Pa., and I've got to spend a few days in L.A. before I leave. Had also hoped to get up to Frisco to see Nebby-Lou once, too, but I'm not sure about that. . . . . I had a swell Christmas and got some very useful presents, pajamas, ties, travelling cases, etc. And from Dot and Ivan [Johnson] a dozen swell white handkerchiefs with my name across one corner L-A-N-G-S-T-O-N. . . . . The Indian youth leader Rajni Patel arrived for New Year's with a letter to me from Paul Robeson, so we learned quite a bit about what's going on in India. He'd spoken in New York, so perhaps you heard him. Just out of Cambridge, and now on his way home via China. . . . . . New Year's Eve Eulah, on her way to a party, skidded and turned over three times. But she didn't even faint. She just climbed on out and came on to the party with only a tiny cut on one finger. And a few bruises that came out a day or two later. Strangely enough there was a plaque of the Virgin Mary in the car and she fell right on it—and neither was hurt. But she was good and scared. . . . . You ought to see the excitement right now among the feminine portion of Monterey Peninsula's colored population. About Fifteen Hundred Negro soldiers have arrived for the spring maneuvers! Mostly newly enlisted kids from big towns like Chicago with pin stripe suits and full of jive. . . . . There was an "air attack" on Monterey at dawn today that sounded too much like the

real thing for me to enjoy it. Such a roar of planes you never heard. . . . .
How's 409 [Edgecombe Avenue]? If Molly [Mollie Lewis Moon] and
[Henry] Moon move up there then practically everybody I know will be
living in the same house. . . . . And that would be very nice. . . . . How's
JOHN HENRY? Hope it's in for a run. Too bad about THE DREAM
flopping. . . . . Tell Mary [Savage] thanks for her amusing Christmas
card. . . . . And thanks to you for your comforting offer of water when the
well runs dry. I think I must be letting my bucket down in a desert. But I'll
yell for help if it comes up full of rocks on my birthday cause I'll just about
be packing for that long trans-continental haul. Sure, I've got to come to
New York to see what you and Harlem look like before I start carrying
po'try to West Virginia. . . . . Our theatre down South has a director at last!
How about Harlem's fate? . . . . The Jelliffes will be in New York next week
campaigning for the Gilpins. Say a good word for them to Johnny
Hammond if you see him. . . . . Drink some gin for me.

Love,
Langston

TO LOUISE, [JANUARY 20, 1940]

To Lou—

SOUTHERN MAMMY SINGS

Miss Gardner's in de garden,
Miss Yardman's in de yard,
Miss Michealmas is at de mass
And I am getting tired!
Lawd!
I am getting tired.

The nations they is fightin'
And the nations they don fit.
Sometimes I think that white folks
Ain't worth a little bit.
No, m'am!
Ain't worth a little bit.

Last week they lynched a colored boy.
They hung him to a tree.

That colored boy ain't said a thing
But us all should be free.
Yes, m'am!
Us all should be free.

Not meanin' to be sassy
And not meanin' to be smart—
But sometimes I think that white folks
Just ain't got no heart.
No, m'am!
Just ain't got no heart.

TO LOUISE, APRIL 10, 1940

[Handwritten postcard]

W. Va. State College

April 10, 1940
On lecture tour.

Dear Lou—

Look where I am and look who's here: *Larry* [signed by Larry Brown]

Lang

TO LOUISE, APRIL 18, 1940

[Picture postcard]

Louisville, April 18, '40
On tour.

Dear Lou:

If this horse were mine
I'd ride him right straight to you!
But this horse ain't
mine
So there's nothing
I can do!

Yours sincerely,
Lang

Langston was in Chicago preparing for the American Negro Exposition, a two-month-long event celebrating "75 Years of Negro Achievement." He was contracted by the organizers to write the script for a musical revue, *The Tropics after Dark*.

FROM LOUISE, [JULY 12, 1940]

[Western Union telegram]

THREE RIVERS MICH 1940 JULY 12 PM 11 20

LANGSTON HUGHES =

CARE TROPIC AFTER DARK AMN NEGRO

EXPO COLISEUM 16 AND WABASH CHGO =

BEST OF LUCK TONIGHT SPIRIT WITH YOU BUT FLESH IS WEAK I
NEED GOOD COUNTRY AIR LOVE =

LOU

TO LOUISE, AUGUST 11, 1940

Hotel Grand
5044 S. Parkway,
Chicago, Illinois,

August 11, 1940

Dear Lou,

Delighted to have both your letters, and called up Helen [Glover] immediately about your coat and offered to come after it, but she said she had it already wrapped up to mail you and was going downtown anyway today and would take it. I carried her THE BIG SEA, but had to leave it with the Williams next door since, both times I passed, there was nobody home. They leave for Idlewild on Wednesday so they'll have the book to read on their vacation. I asked Knopf to post Doug [Aaron Douglas] and Alta [Douglas] one, too, and trust they have it by now. I managed to give away only 50 this time, which still leaves out some of the people I love.

I guess I forgot to take up that matter of petitions with you when you were here but I've already informed most of my friends of the left that I'm not signing anything this year—except those of the Writers League for refugee writers, which might possibly be of some actual assistance to someone. But, having signed several thousand statements and petitions in the last ten years—and the more I sign the worse the world situation becomes—I've come to the conclusion that they are just about the least effective of weapons, especially when they contain the same old names over and over and over. Do you think they do any good? If I did I would keep on signing them—even though they come thicker and faster than ever these days accompanied by so many documents it would take one's life to read them and be sure you were signing the right thing. So I give up. Let those sign who will. Me, *niet*.

[Editors' note: The remainder of this letter is handwritten.] Thyra [Edwards] is back at work. Pat I see almost every day. In fact, had dinner with him last night. I thought I'd found a good point for argument over a portion of the Defender's excellent editorial on Paul Robeson—but it turned out we were in agreement on the basic issues. However, Pat can certainly be as inflexible as the early Christians at times—even when faced with the facts of life in the form of a square peg against a round hole. But probably with enough hammering, even a square peg will fit, somehow or 'nother.

Exposition so far gives up no cash. Say they'll need a Hundred Thousand more customers to come out of the red. They owe gangs of people, so probably no use to sue, but I'm leaving it in the hands of a lawyer anyhow, ere I depart.

Horace [Cayton]'s father is very ill. (I'm having dinner with them tomorrow). . . . Margaret, my most charming of cousins, is here from Louisville. . . . . My California cousins started East, had a blowout in Nevada, turned over, so turned around and went back.

I'm in the midst of great letter-writing preparatory to leaving. But determined to leave nary one unanswered—so reckon I won't leave soon. Might even see you on the 30th.

The Catholics supported the Expo beautifully—full house all week—largest attendance so far (in return for refusal of Birth Control Exhibit) with lots of Catholic clubs, choruses, nuns and priests, coming from all around the Middle West. Because one of their children's bands played, the union pulled out the "Chimes Of Normandy" orchestra for a night—which further aroused union antagonisms down there. Some of the exhibits are not lighted yet because the electricians (apparently all white) demand that the diorama wired by WPA be torn down and rewired at a union cost of several hundred dollars—so they won't touch anything else. This whole thing, unfortunately, has helped to make a lot of the colored intellectuals out here more anti-labor than ever. Lord help us.

A most timely check from the Afro [*Baltimore Afro-American*] for serialization of "The Big Sea" has saved my life. But thanks anyhow.

Hope you've gotten all rested from your vacation. See you soon.

Love,
Lang

*[Letterhead: Hollow Hills Farm / (Carmel Valley) Jamesburg
Route / Monterey, California]*

November 3, 1940.

Dear Lou,

Would you like to have a book of poems dedicated to you? Such is
SHAKESPEARE IN HARLEM, the present collection I'm assembling
for Knopf. Folk, blues, and lyric verse in the lighter manner—but not
too light.

How are you and where are you? Did you come out of the hospital
O.K.?. . . . . I saw Matt, Nebby, and Nebby Lou. All fine. Nebby is
working again. And Nebby Lou is the prettiest child in the
world.

Loren and Juanita [Miller] are about to move into their new house. . . . .
I'm bound for Los Angeles again tomorrow for a month or so,
bookshop appearances and work with the revue, too, I guess. They sent
me half a dozen wires this week about it. But I'm not clear yet what the
set-up is.

How was BIG WHITE FOG? And CABIN IN THE SKY?⁵ Way out
here and nobody lets me know a thing. Or has Hitler invaded New York
and no letters can come out?

I'm living in a new little house by myself with enormous windows—a
view of cows on one side and sheep on the other—and the whole valley
below. Very sunny and quiet and fine for writing and sleeping. All the
Filipino help have departed the first of the month and a very nice Negro
couple are coming—which will be company for Eulah. . . . . Best to Pat.
Write soon.

Love,

Lang

5. *Big White Fog* is a play by Theodore Ward, who in 1940 had joined with Langston, Paul
Robeson, Richard Wright, and others to form the Negro Playwrights Company in New York
City. Their first production was a revival of *Big White Fog* at the Lincoln Theatre in Harlem.
Cabin in the Sky is a 1940 musical by Lynn Root and Vernon Duke. It was choreographed
by Balanchine and Katherine Dunham, who also starred in the show, which featured an
all-Black cast.

[Handwritten]

Hotel Vincennes
601 E. 36th St.
Chicago.

Sunday

Lang darling—

I was just-a-thinkin' about writing you when your letter came forwarded on from NYC. I've been here about three weeks—had a spell of illness when I first came but am now feeling great—the rest was good for me. So now I am beginning to find my way around this big ole sprawly Chicago.

Would I like to have a book dedicated to me? My dear—I'd be so thrilled I'd want to buy up all the copies just to look at such a dedication!!! Maybe that's an idea—huh? Write a lot of books and dedicate them to folks who would buy out whole editions. Only, Lang, you'd better pick out folks with dough and not your po' friends whose only assets are pride in your accomplishments and high hopes for your success. Do let me know how you come along and what other projects you are undertaking.

I am sending on to you the clippings of Big White Fog and Cabin in the Sky. They both opened after I left NY—in fact, Lang, I left Harlem the day you left here—How come we are always just missing each other—kismet or what have you—The cullehd theatre doesn't seem to have gotten off to a very good start. It seems that Cabin in the Sky is carrying on in the tradition of the ill-fated <u>Swingin' The Dream</u>[6] and <u>John Henry</u>.

I wonder if Broadway will learn or change its line. Mary [Savage]'s reaction to Big White Fog was more or less like the reviews. I do hope the Playwrights will make it. Let me know how the Negro Theatre[7] comes along out there.

How are the sales of The Big Sea coming along and are you as yet starting Volume 2. Have you seen Claude McKay's Harlem[8]—Henry Moon was here and had a copy which I read. It is quite bad I think—not only because of its serious anti-communist bias but also for its entire

---

6. *Swingin' the Dream* was a 1939 musical adaptation of Shakespeare's *A Midsummer Night's Dream*, starring Louis Armstrong, Butterfly McQueen, and "Moms" Mabley. It did poorly, closing after just thirteen performances.

7. The American Negro Theatre of Harlem was a part of the Federal Theatre Project.

8. Claude McKay's novel *Home to Harlem* was first published in 1928.

ideological perspective. According to Claude the Sufis[9] and Garveys[10] are our national heroes—all else is to be damned. I think the guy is bankrupt.

We have moved over here to the [Hotel] Vincennes and are fairly comfortable in two rooms. It is the only thing I could find in a furnished place and it's not bad tho not luxurious. I don't know yet whether I shall be here permanently but I shall be here for the next few months at least. The gang will keep the 409 [Edgecombe Avenue] apartment until the end of the year—then I imagine it will be broken up and I shall have to do something about my junk there. I'm glad Nebby is working. What is she doing? I haven't heard from her as yet.

Give all the L.A. gang my regards. I haven't written anybody out there so will you tell them all hello for me and tell them where I am.

Helen [Glover] and Marcella [Walker McGee] told me all about your reception here. I haven't seen Thyra [Edwards] as yet—I hear she is not well at all. I shall plan to see her this week. Did you know that Irma [Jackson Cayton Wertz] got her divorce from Horace [Cayton]? Quick work, eh?

Since you didn't give me any L.A. address I shall send this note on to Carmel, hoping it will be forwarded. Tho you will be busy I shall be looking to hear from you soon. Try to see Irma and Norman Hopkins, won't you and give them my best—also to Dot and Ivan [Johnson] and Loren and Juanita [Miller]. I bet the latter's new home is swell, no?

Love to you,
Lou

TO LOUISE, DECEMBER 4, 1940

Dear Lou,

Enjoyed your nice long letter no end. And many thanks for the clippings about the shows. I'm glad BIG WHITE FOG is making a significant run anyhow—and hope they will come out from under. I see where they have met and reorganized! That's what they're still doing out here, too—meeting and re-meeting and re-organizing! I will have no part of it—confining my activities entirely to the creative end of the revue. Enclosed is one of the songs[11] I've done for the show, to be a part of a skit built around the Joe

9. The followers of Sufi Abdul Hamid were often called "Sufis."

10. "Garveys" or "Garveyites" were followers of the Jamaican Black nationalist leader Marcus Garvey.

11. Langston is probably referring to the song "America's Young Black Joe," which he wrote the lyrics to, extolling boxer Joe Louis.

Louis-Schmelling fight. How do you like it? Whatever social and protest significance is lacking (tell Pat) therein, is amply made up for in other songs and skits we have in the show, such as YOU DON'T HAVE TO GO SOUTH TO FIND DIXIE, etc. . . . . Just got the contract for your book of poems[12] today. Knopf seems to like it. . . . . Loren and Juanita [Miller] move into their new house next week. . . . . Mrs. [Charlotta] Bass has a nice editorial defending me against Aimee [McPherson] in this week's [California] Eagle. And one of the colored ministers has invited me back to Pasadena to his church. I hope another Gary doesn't develop before I can get there. . . . . For the curtain of our show we're having heads of all the Negro celebrities, including the one and only candidate for Vice-President [James W. Ford] thereon. It's a killer! Only hitch now is funds as the [Hollywood] Theatre Alliance lost plenty in their ill-fated ZERO HOUR which closed after two weeks. It was a bad play—largely a walking editorial on civil liberties. Important, but unfortunately not drama. . . . . How is Horace [Cayton]? Sorry to hear Thyra [Edwards] is still ill. . . . . . Arna [Bontemps] writes that it is six below zero in Chicago! Please, Lawd, lemme stay out here. . . . . . I hope you-all are warm. . . . . Saw Harry [Haywood] the other day all dressed up in tan sport clothes and looking like a million dollars. I reckon rest does anybody good. I'm gonna look for me some soon.

Sincerely,

Lang

Clark Hotel,

Wash. & Central,

Los Angeles,

Dec. 4, 1940.

P.S. If you see Johnny Hammond, ask him if he would like to record YOUNG BLACK JOE? The music is a killer—swing march tempo.

In December of 1940 *The Saturday Evening Post* magazine reprinted Langston's poem "Goodbye Christ" without his permission or any clarification as to when he wrote it, deliberately creating the impression that he had just penned it, when in fact he had written it during his one-year stay in the Soviet Union in 1932–1933. Langston was on tour promoting *The Big Sea* at the time, and during an engagement in Los Angeles, the popular evangelist Aimee McPherson openly denounced him, backed

12. Langston dedicated his book of poems *Shakespeare in Harlem* to Louise.

by an angry crowd of her supporters. This was not the first attack on "Goodbye Christ," but it was the worst, and Langston was forced to flee the event through a side door for his safety. An earlier attack saw him defended by writer Melvin Tolson, but this time he was advised by several people, including Pat, to defend himself publicly, which he did in a press statement that some considered an apologia.[13] Around this time, unbeknownst to him, Langston was placed on the FBI's watch list.

Soon after the scandal, Langston became physically ill and retreated to the comfort and security of the cottage his patron, Noel Sullivan, kept for him at Hollow Hills Farm, his estate in California's Carmel Valley.

TO MATT, JANUARY 2, 1941

> Hollow Hills Farm,
> Monterey, California,
>
> January 2, 1941

Dear Matt,

S.O.S. Broke and ruint—having just come back from Los Angeles working on another show that didn't come off as yet. (I must be crazy!) But have you got a Twenty—or a Ten—or a Five you could lend me until royalties or something or other come through? At the moment I'm just getting over flu which had Eulah and the houseman down in bed most of the week, too. Between that, the show business, Aimee [McPherson] and the SATURDAY EVENING POST, the New Year came down like a ton of bricks. I'm writing a statement on the poem[14] now, out-dated as it is. Like our movie, won't down! I have a dog for Nebby Lou—half daschund and half cocker—very cute and black, if you-all think you'd like it. Will bring it up next time I come. Just old enough to be house broken. (I think.) And hope.

Trust I shall see you shortly. Due back in L.A. in February for a lecture, but will be up North first.

Happy New Year to you all,

> Sincerely,
> *Lang*

13. Notwithstanding Langston's defense, J. Edgar Hoover, the director of the FBI, vilified the poem at a Methodist Ministers conference in 1947.

14. See Langston's statement "Concerning 'Goodbye Christ'" on page 147 of Faith Berry's *Good Morning Revolution: Uncollected Writings of Langston Hughes* (New York: Carol Publishing Group, 1992).

Hollow Hills Farm,
Monterey, California,

January 6, 1941.

Dear Lou,

Been meaning to write you for the longest time (and especially during the holidays as I came back here to the farm just before Christmas) but what with the flu that laid Eulah, me and the houseman low, toothache, Aimee and the SATURDAY EVENING POST, and six weeks in L.A. working on <u>another</u> show that didn't come off—the New Year came down on my head like a ton of bricks!!! It'll probably take me until 1942 to recover. . . . . Well, you and I both know what happens when Negroes, white folks, the theatre, and the movement all get mixed up together—add Hollywood and you really have a scramble! Between the New Negro Theatre[15] and its committees and the Hollywood Theatre Alliance and its committees, and their respective boards—each with as many and varied opinions as there are members on each—and the customary interminable meetings—it would take I don't know who or what to bring them together in any unity of opinion. How social or un-social, liberal or not liberal, left or left-or-right of left, all black or half-black or white and black to make the show seemingly cannot be decided upon. When I left the producer in charge, Charles Leonard (who produced Wally [Thurman]'s HARLEM[16] in New York) had taken to his bed, and was able to sleep less than you in the hey-day of the SUITCASE [Harlem Suitcase Theatre]. His wife said he was walking the floor at night! . . . . . Anyhow, with enough good material for three shows on hand, that is the state I left things in. But I hope they will snap out of it for they really can have an excellent Negro revue once they get together. . . . . Meanwhile, Aimee was after me. And then out comes the POST with their spread of GOODBYE CHRIST which started the [American] Legion. So, under the circumstances, it seemed wise for me to make some sort of statement on the poem—which is quite out of line today anyhow. And in the light of the various statements the Hollywoodites have been issuing (as Pat explained to me, under dispensation) I judge I am correct in doing so, too. But my special reason for attempting to calm the waters is that a series of lecture recitals of SONGS AND POEMS OF THE NEGRO PEOPLE have been and are being arranged here on the coast with myself and Ivan Browning, Dorothy Johnson's club sponsoring one

15. Langston founded the New Negro Theatre in 1939 in Los Angeles. It was patterned on the Harlem Suitcase Theatre.
16. Wallace Thurman's play Harlem premiered on Broadway in 1929.

at the Hotel Biltmore on February 2. The POST business naturally frightened some of them. And, in the light of the fact that Browning has been having <u>such</u> a hard time since his return from Europe, and is looking forward to these recitals to sort of get himself and family on their feet, I felt badly about that and them. I had intended, as usual with me in controversial matters, to simply say nothing—and, left to myself, wouldn't—but it seemed that something had to be stated—since GBC ["Goodbye Christ"] like our movie [*Black and White*] just won't down. Statement [concerning "Goodbye Christ"] is herein enclosed for you to see. How does it strike you? Lemme know. . . . . Just heard from Matt who has had flu, too (as did Loren, Juanita, and Pete [Miller]— which kept them from moving). But worst of all Nebby Lou has been in bed with it nearly three weeks, poor little kid. (I have a dog for her—real live one—to take next time I go to the city. But being broker than broke, Lord knows when that will be. I am really weary no end of New Year's that start out in the same old way: broke! I have certainly seen a mighty lot of them!). . . . . . What's news with you-all? Is it still 16° below in Chi? How's Helen [Glover], Marcella [Walker McGee], Thyra [Edwards]? . . . . . . Give my best to Pat. . . . . . Write soon . . . . . .

Love,
Lang

TO MATT, [JANUARY 20, 1941]

[Handwritten]

Peninsula Hospital,
Carmel, Cal.

Dear Matt,

Meant to write you long ago but kept feeling worse and worse and finally about a week ago, ended up in bed here where I have been in <u>some</u> misery— arthritis[17] pains in left leg, etc. Today temperature has broken so can write a little—not much. Was on verge [of] coming up to see you 10 days ago to bring puppy, thank you for such a welcome check, and discuss my poem statement with you. Wasn't able. Troubles have beset me since holidays. Too much and too weak to tell now—but last, on day I took to bed, was word from New York that the guys who have my apt. let their own rent get

---

17. Langston was less than candid with Matt and other friends about what ailed him. He was actually suffering from gonorrhea and was probably embarrassed about this. See Arnold Rampersad, *The Life of Langston Hughes*, vol. 1, *1902–1941* (New York: Oxford University Press, 1986), 394.

so far behind (expecting to catch up) that although I sent mine promptly—all evicted—with all my mans. [manuscripts], books, and stuff.—Just one many in row. So I am knocked out. Give up for dead! But ain't.

Mr. Sullivan, Eulah, everybody here swell and looking out for me, so guess I'll be O.K. and back to farm in a week or two. Would love to see you-all.

Sincerely,
Langston

P.S. Now that I can't work, revue in L.A. is all set to go and sends contract! This is a sweet little hospital and everybody is so kind. Beautiful food—that only now I am able to eat.

TO LOUISE, JANUARY 25, 1941

[Letterhead: Hollow Hills Farm; handwritten]

Peninsula Community Hospital
January 25. 1941

Carmel, Cal.

Dear Lou,

Well, for the past two weeks now I've been flat on my back here in the hospital—a kind of arthritis like infection of one leg—very painful, and unable to set foot to floor, so just lie here mostly in a fog from pain-pills. You can hear me moaning and groaning for miles. Too much trouble all at once, I guess. Then Zell [Ingram] wrote Artis got so far behind on rent all were being evicted. I wrote Knopf for check, but before it could get here, I landed in hospital. With it I paid my last week's bill, $73.00 (not including Dr.), so at this rate, guess I'll be mortgaged for life. Mr. Sullivan's away, but Eulah and others have been coming in to see me. Today my fever's down, so I am trying a few letters. I wrote Mary [Savage] a note and sent her some money for my IWO insurance—which she wrote me was behind. Poor darling says she can't lose her cold, and she was sad about the house breaking up. In fact all my mail from the East has been so sad and full of trouble. Reckon the whole world is wrong. Or all's out to England and nothing left here . . . .

My best to Pat, and hope all goes well with you. Regards to Helen [Glover], Marcella [Walker McGee], Thyra [Edwards], Horace [Cayton], and all.

Love,
Lang

[Letterhead: Hollow Hills Farm; handwritten]

Community Hospital

January 25, 1941

Dear Matt and Nebby,

Feel a thousand times better, and the sciatica-arthritis like pain I had has lessened considerably. Still haven't been out of bed, nor set foot on the floor, but doctor says I will be up and back to the farm this coming week. Hope so, as the bill here is terrific and I don't want to be mortgaged for life. They serve beautiful meals all under silver covers—and what has hurt me is I've been able to eat practically nothing—so you know I must have been bad off! And such rain, rain, rain the like of which I've never seen, so much and so long.

Haven't heard from Louise but a letter from Mary [Savage] says all her furniture is being sent to Chicago the end of this month. Lawd, what will New York be without Louise? I hear Kenneth [Spencer]'s concert was excellent and the critics good, but haven't seen any clippings so far.

Fisk [University] is using our song America's Young Black Joe for commencement with full male chorus. They're still undecided about it for show down South. Can't make up minds how nationally militant to let Negroes be. I don't think a blackface "Meet the People" is enough—just general working problems, etc. Colored show must have own special problems, too. But then, I'm laid up now and can't do anything more about it.

Best to you-all,

Lang

[Letterhead: Hollow Hills Farm; handwritten]

Feb. 4, 1941

Dear Matt,

Just out of the hospital, in bed at home, and seeing all my mail—a vast pile. From the East just came [James W.] Ford's splendid comment, from The Daily [*Worker*] 1/29/41, in answer evidently to [Ben] Burns in People's

World of Jan. 15th.[18] I didn't see his (Burns) article. Could you please send it to me?

Golly! How I hate all this controversy! Deluged with letters from everybody, left, right, colored, and Christians.

Did you get my note from the hospital? I'm much better now and hope to be up and out soon.

<u>Done</u> with statements. Sorry any had to be made. Knopf's and lawyer in East have whole matter. They felt [the *Saturday Evening*] <u>Post</u> required a comeback and explanation. So, in light of Pat's comment that poem was now out of line, since there's no point in a quarrel with church today, I did best I could on it. If you haven't seen complete statement, will send you copy I have for you, soon as up and able to find it.

Best to Nebby. Will repay your latest kindness soon. Write when you can.

Lang

TO MATT, FEBRUARY 13, 1941

February 13, 1941

Dear Matt,

Knowing how busy you are, I doubly appreciate your taking time out to write me, and I was very happy to have your letter. I think I told you I was on my way up to see you that week after Christmas when I was struck down with flu which prevented my bringing the puppy (which must be a full grown hound now—I have not seen it of late) and talking over all this business with you before I said anything. The Sat. Eve. Post printed the poem in its Christmas Issue, centered in big spread, almost a page, with no comment, as if it were a new poem. My problem was to get over the fact that it was not new, and that (according to the left even) it was no longer a correct poem, as the quarrel at the moment is not (according to Pat) with the church. Think out what would have been the proper way to clarify all that, and let me know next time I come up, since I need clarification. I am, as you know, quite used to attack—but always heretofore the attack against me has been on the basis of something for which a fight back was right and

---

18. Langston is referencing two opposing and contradicting newspaper articles that appeared in the Communist press about his statement "Concerning 'Goodbye, Christ.'" The first, by Ben Burns, was printed in the West Coast paper *People's World* and was highly critical of Langston's statement. The second, by Black Communist leader James W. Ford, was published in New York's *Daily Worker* and applauded Langston's statement.

correct. This time it came on the basis of an obsolete anti-religious position out-moded and incorrect from any viewpoint except the Spanish anarchists—who gave the fascists ammunition when they burned the Barcelona churches in the Civil War in Spain. When Aimee [McPherson] made her attack not a single left paper so far as I know contradicted her or defended the poem. And it is not a poem which any liberal publication would publish today since tactics have changed. So. . . . . . ?! What to say? . . . . . I figured he who fights and runs away lives to fight another day. There is certainly no use breaking a lance on a religious windmill, is there? . . . . . . In any case, I've had long and helpful letters from Thyra [Edwards], Pat, Hermie [Hermina Huiswoud], you, and other friends. And dozens of unknowns. . . . . . Paul [Robeson] called from S.F. the other day. . . . . It was a surprise to see Mason [Roberson] and good to have all the news from the East. . . . . I'm at work again and making some headway on my book [I Wonder As I Wander]. Am now in Central Asia where you-all niggers left me standing in the middle of the desert without guide or guidance! But, thank God for the OGPU,[19] I was saved, fed and looked after. So I shall expose the lies concerning that organization. . . . . . My song, AMERICA'S YOUNG BLACK JOE, is being used by lots of the Southern schools during Negro History Week. I have just writ another one called: MESSAGE TO THE PRESIDENT, An American Negro Defense Song.

> In your fireside chats on the radio
> You've been telling the world
> What you want them to know.
> I've been listening attentively.
> Now this is what I want you to say for me:
>
> Mr. President, let me hear you say:
> No more segregation in the U. S. A.
> For our land's defense—if we have to fight—
> Let's stand side by side then, black and white.
> (No Jim Crow for you know that's not right.)
> In the name of American Democracy
> How can anybody want to Jim Crow me?
> So, Mr. President, let me hear you say:
> No more segregation in the U. S. A.

19. The OGPU, or the Joint State Political Directorate, was the foreign affairs branch of the Soviet secret police during Langston's stay in Russia in the 1930s.

Hey! Hey! Plus several more verses and patter. . . . . . Syncopated. . . . . . Eulah returns your kind regards. Poor girl, she is down with a cold again. Too much rain here. . . . . Mr. Sullivan is hoping to leave for New York next week. I'm plenty better and expect shortly to move from the Big House to my own cabin in the pines, providing it stops raining. To transport my book notes over here would require a van. . . . . . HTA [Hollywood Theatre Alliance] writes that Duke Ellington is to be in the show down there, band and all. I hope it doesn't turn out like the Chicago Negro Exposition where plans were equally grandiose. Duke was to participate, Etta Moten, Abbie Mitchell, etc. Maybe (since I've gone back to the church) God is with the left more so than he is with cullud. I hope He's with all—cause if somebody don't pay off shortly, I'll have to go teach at Tuskegee! . . . . . So glad Nebbie Lou is O.K. Did you see on Kenneth [Spencer]'s Town Hall program he sang a song called "Nebbie"? Do you-all know it? . . . . . Thanks again for writing. Hope to be up before the month ends. Or early March anyway.

Sincerely,
Lang

Read IN PLACE OF SPLENDOR for wonderful entertaining background on Spain.

TO LOUISE, MARCH 10, 1941

Hollow Hills Farm,
Monterey, California,

March 10, 1941

Dear Lou-ise:

Overjoyed with your letter! Who knows how hard it is to write is me—so there was nothing to forgive. (I have a box full of three year old unanswered letters.) Only thing was I hoped you wasn't mad. . . . . Both Pat's and your letters are most helpful. Naturally I don't think I am anywhere near as important as you make me out to be. Your friendship and kindness of heart have always given you the ability to say nice things. Anyhow, at the moment my main interest is centered on trying to get a brown suit. I see such swell ones in the windows in Carmel and Monterey, and never having had one, I would like you-all to see me in it before HR1776[20] passes and we all have stripes. I don't want no house on Sunset, all I want is a brown suit just

20. H.R. 1776, also known as the Lend-Lease act, was enacted March 11, 1941. It allowed the United States to prepare for World War II while officially remaining neutral.

once. . . . . So arrayed, I will fight anybody who tries to take it away from me. . . . . . But who could have been in a fighting mood with influenza, arthritis, a New Year's hangover, an HTA [Hollywood Theatre Alliance]-revue-committee-plus-committee-argumentation-ideological-white-colored-show-no-yes-no-indigestion, and minus $000.00 plus debts plus doctor's bill plus a temperature plus an eviction notice plus Aimee [McPherson] plus no brown suit feeling? Plus lack of clarification? Plus just naturally being tired? Plus still having less sense than I was born with? . . . . . Anyhow, AMERICA'S YOUNG BLACK JOE is being sung lustily at Tuskegee, Wiley, Texas College, Downingtown, and points South. At which I am delighted, but still amazed at how I can turn out more non-profitable hits than anybody now writing. Which is why I'd just as well go back to waiting table and get a suit on credit. You know, being a "great" author doesn't even give one the credit rating of a guy with a $12 a week job. . . . . I know you can't have your cake and eat it too,—and I have done et my cake up! Which is what gives me <u>pause</u>. . . . . Anyhow, I have just written an article for THE CRISIS on the need for heroes in Negro literature. To read it you would almost think I was a hero myself. Such is the power of literature to deceive. . . . . If you want to read a book that will outline for you beautifully the viewpoint of the Southern aristocratic plantation owner, read LANTERNS ON THE LEVEE, a beautifully written book, one third about cullud and how sweet and criminal, better than poor whites but burden no end, used to [^be] servants but now are problems—but still the best mannered people in America, we are. It is really a most interesting book, admirable in its frank statement of a frightful but evidently sincere viewpoint. The man is an excellent writer and a southern gentleman, William Alexander Percy, who presided at my reading years ago in Greenville, Mississippi, and was most cordial to me there. You and Pat be sure to read the book. Hope the left press reviews it. A chapter from it is in Harper's this month. . . . . . We've just had a delightful week-end visit from Dorothy Maynor who sang in Carmel with great success Saturday night. She stayed here at the farm and Mr. Sullivan rushed back from New York especially to greet her. She is a charming person with lots more sense than most singers and says she is a great friend of Max Yergan. Do you remember her at Hampton? I first met her there. She is travelling with an entourage: coach, manager, and pianist. . . . . Noel Sullivan saw Kenneth [Spencer] and Dot [Fisher-Spencer] in New York and went to Cafe Society to hear him sing. Saw lots of other cullud including Miss [Ethel] Waters and has invited various out for the summer. . . . . Did I tell you we have a new butler from New York who used to live in 409 [Edgecombe Avenue]? Floyd Fisher. His father runs a very nice tea-chicken house in Carmel, the only colored business there. . . . . The influx of colored army men is playing havoc with domestic peace hereabouts. Practically all wives have been beat by irate husbands and Carmel has had almost as many fights as Percy describes on his Mississippi plantation. But surely he wasn't telling the truth in that book? (Read it and see if Miss. is anything like Ark.) Mrs. Vanderbilt's[21] butler here in Carmel Valley just blacked both his wife's eyes over a soldier! I saw her fleeing at the bus station yesterday. Poor Mrs. Vanderbilt! (The last colored couple she had pawned her gold-brick paper weight, got fired, and took half her pure linen sheets and opened a sporting house in Monterey for the army. The army is a killer around here!) . . . . Dorothy Johnson was up for the week-end and the Maynor concert. Says hopes you-all come out this summer. Best to PAT.

Sincerely,
Lang

[Note at bottom of first page] *Why did Constancia [de la Mora] leave Campesino [Valentin Gonzalez Gonzalez] out of her book? Did he stray the wrong way?*

[Note running up left margin of first page] *Just got royalties check so shall have* brown suit *[circled in letter]. Also a small gin!*

[Note running up right margin and across top of first page] *Did you read For Whom Bell Tolls? I just borrowed it. Know most of his Madrid characters. Salud!!!*

[Note running up left, across top, and down right margin of second page] *Nice letter from Mary [Savage] today—delighted with your visit to N. Y. Huh! If you was mighty nigh 40 and broke—I would be sorry for you! → O.K. I'll get back at you! Will tell in next book how you-all left me in the middle of the track in the desert in Turkmenia too!!!*

TO MATT AND NEBBY, MARCH 23, 1941

Hollow Hills Farm,
Monterey, California,

March 23, 1941

Dear Matt & Nebby,

I certainly enjoyed my visit with you, and one result which begins a new phase in my life is that from Matt's example, I am inspired to garden, and

---

21. Muriel Vanderbilt Phelps Adams was a New York-born socialite who owned and bred racehorses in the Carmel Valley in California.

have bought two packages of seed, but haven't found out where the spades are kept yet. . . . . Yesterday a skunk got under my house and it smelled to high heaven. One of the week-end guests went to get the hired man to get it out, but in doing so, left the gate open and all the dogs (except Greta) six dachshunds, got in and ran the poor skunk out, caught him, and tore him limb from limb. Result: all the dogs smell terrible today, even after baths and toilet water. . . . . I got back to find Eulah in bed ill again with a kind of pleurisy. Mustard plasters on her back and chest. But she is up today. Won't lie a-bed even when she should. . . . . . The weather is beautiful down here and the whole valley in front of the farm is just turning white with pear blossoms. Wish you-all could drive down here some Sunday soon and see the spring. Just send a wire ahead so we'll have something to eat and a small bottle ready. . . . . Well, next time I come to town, I will bring half my new book to show you, especially so Matt can read about himself—and Nebby can read about Matt. (I will tell all!). . . . . You ought to see Santa Fe Trail, the movie about John Brown. It is pretty good, even if only half-and-half. . . . . Take care of your selves and that beautiful child. . . . . See you again soon.

Sincerely,
Lang

TO LOUISE, [MARCH 1941]

Dear Lou,

I enjoyed your letter no end. . . . . Verdict accepted. . . . . . Matt working in his front yard has inspired me to garden, too. This morning I stuck a piece of ice plant in the earth. They tell me it grows by itself. . . . . . I'm having all my revue material re-typed—32 skits written in L. A. (Enough for a whole show if anybody wanted to put them on.) I came across these extra copies (2nd drafts) that I thought might amuse you and Pat. If there's anything any group might want to put on, go ahead. If any of the I.W.O. groups would like to sing AMERICA'S YOUNG BLACK JOE let me know and I will send you the music, or else borrow it from Thyra [Edwards] to whom I sent a copy for the Lincoln Center. . . . . Got brown suit, shoes, sox, shirt, belt, drawers, and tie! Thus armoured I return to the struggle. Your book, SHAKESPEARE IN HARLEM will be out May 5th. Hope you like it. It contains:

Levee, levee, how [^*high*] does you have to be
To keep them cold muddy waters from
Washing over me?

FIGURE 18. Matt, Nebby Lou, and Nebby in San Francisco, 1941.

You can take that for a text to say: "Our levee has to be so high the exploiters can't get over it, neither can they get under it, neither can they get through it. It has to stretch so far they can't get by it, and they can't do nothing about it. It has to be built with the sandbags of the working class. Can't nobody else build a levee that won't break down."

Amen!
Lang

THE MITCHELL CASE
   By
   Langston Hughes

I see by the papers where
Congressman Mitchell[22] won his case.
Down South the railroads now
Must give us equal space:
Even if we're rich enough
To want a Pullman car,
The Supreme Court says we <u>get</u> it—
And a diner and a bar!
Now, since the Court in Washington
Can make a rule like that,
If we went to court enough we might
Get Jim Crow on the mat
And pin his shoulders to the ground
And drive him from the land—
Since the Constitution ain't enough
To protect a colored man—
And we have to go to court to make
Dixie understand.
But for us poor people
It's kinder hard to sue.
Mr. Mitchell, you did right well—
But the rest of us ain't you.
Seems to me it would be simpler
If the Government would declare
They're tired of all this Jim Crow stuff
And just give it the air.
Seems to me it's time to realize

22. Arthur Wergs Mitchell (1883–1968) was a US congressman from Illinois, who served as a member of the US House of Representatives from 1935 to 1943. He was the first African American Democrat to be elected to the US Congress. In 1937, while traveling from Chicago to Arkansas, Mitchell was pulled off a first-class train car and forced to sit in the Negro car. He successfully argued a segregation case before the US Supreme Court on April 28, 1941, but it was not until 1955 that the Interstate Commerce Commission prohibited segregation on interstate railroads, train and waiting room accommodations.

That in the U. S. A.
To have Jim Crow's too Hitler-like
In this modern age and day—
Cause fine speeches sure sound hollow
About Democracy
When all over America
They still Jim Crowing me.
To earn a dollar sometimes
Is hard enough to do—
Let alone having to take that dollar
And go and sue!

TO LOUISE, MAY 8, 1941

Dear Lou,

I enjoyed your letter immensely. . . . . Is that true that Mary [Savage] might come out here for her vacation? Swell! I just saw Matt and Moko and baby Nebby and her mama in town. . . . . I thought maybe the enclosed poems might amuse you. They tickle me! Hey! Hey! . . . . . My book of poems has been postponed until August due to illness of the artist doing the decorations. I'd just had proofs, too, and was looking for copies shortly. . . . . . A very interesting Indian fellow named Babulal Singh [Jagjivan Ram] is spending a few days here at the farm on his way back to India and jail. I met him last year in Dayton. He's representing the Indian National Congress. . . . . Is a friend of [Max] Yergan's and Paul [Robeson]'s. . . . . . Too bad about Gwennie [Bennett] losing her job, isn't it? Think of poor me with no job to lose! Anyhow I got a [Julius] Rosenwald [fellowship] and am going to use it to read the Fred Douglass autobiography, as I imagine it will take me about a year to read such a big book. . . . . Give my best to Pat. . . . . And don't worry about being so slow in writing. You can't beat me. . . . . AMERICA'S YOUNG BLACK JOE was sung at the APM [American People's Mobilization] meeting in Los Angeles with great success, they tell [^me]. And Singh tells me he heard LET AMERICA BE AMERICA AGAIN sung at Orchestra Hall in Chicago with a chorus of 150. Did you hear it? It's set to music by a young fellow at Elmhurst College and I suppose it was their Glee Club that sang it as they have been doing it on tour this year. And Hermie [Huiswoud] writes that she heard the NEGRO MOTHER sung on the IWO's Fiesta program. . . . . Too bad I can't sing myself. What a

program I could give! In fact I would make a one-man show out of the
ORGANIZER which I guess will never get on otherwise. . . . . Best to Pat. I
got to go to tea-e-a-e-ae-a for the Indian gentleman!

(I am in society.)

Sincerely,
Lang

Hollow Hills Farm,
Monterey, California

May 8, 1941.

P.S. Why don't you ring up Arna?

TO LOUISE, [AFTER MAY 18, 1941]

Hollow Hills Farm,
Monterey, California

Dear Lou,

Just back from town where I saw our friends and had some wonderful
fried chicken at Nebby's and was there for Matt's birthday Sunday when
they had a little small party. Moko was over and is waiting to give a party
for Mary when she comes out, being under the impression that it would be
in June. All are anxious for you-all to arrive, and the baby, you wouldn't
know her, she is walking and talking and going next door to play by herself.
And is perfectly beautiful.

You better stop fooling around with theatre and get your rest. It will give
you insomnia! It is my intention not to go anear another one for years. . . . .
I do not think it is a good idea for the Chicago group [Chicago Negro
People's Theatre] to revise DYWTBF [*Don't You Want to Be Free?*] as they
have wore it out, and people don't want to come to see the same old play
over and over again, even with new parts in it. They ought to do something
brand new, I should think. I will write something for them—in due
time—in fact this summer.

Nicolas Guillen has been refused permission to enter the country from
Havana to attend the forthcoming Writers Congress in New York. . . . .
And Jacques [Roumain] has just sailed back to Haiti from Havana. . . . .
And Dorothy Peterson is going to Puerto Rico to see her new little
niece. . . . . . And the oldest of my dear old ladies [the Patiño sisters] died in
Mexico.

Out here the white folks are still ahead. And in Ethiopia the Duke of Aosta retains his pistol.

What did you put in your Bundle For Britain?

Que te vaya bien,
Lang

How is Nelson and Helen [Glover]? Saw dear Mrs. Allen[23] and she looked fine, about to go to Portland for a week.

Langston sent this sardonic poem to Louise the spring of 1941, several months before the United States entered World War II. In it he appears to mock the British for their retreat from Dunkirk, France, in May 1940, when threatened by advancing Nazi German forces, and their withdrawal of troops from Crete, which left the Greeks to fight the Nazis alone.

TO LOUISE, [MAY 26, 1941]

[Envelope postmarked San Jose, California]

THE BRITISH RETREAT
Calypso
By
The Prince of Gales

The British retreated victoriously:
They left the field so gloriously.
They turned their backs to the enemy
And yelled, "Heroic! Look at me!"
The British at Dunkirk backward ran,
Left their equipment on the sand.
When they got to England they said, "Hey! Hey!
Look how the British have won the day."
The British on the island of Crete
Ran into the water to the British Fleet.
The British said, "You Greeks fight on!
Thank God A-Mighty! We are gone!"
Oh! The sun never sets on the British flag—

23. Oakland resident Mrs. J. T. (Emma) Allen was a close friend of Louise's mother, Lula Thompson.

But that's become an old-time gag,
Cause the British will to "do and die "
Has turned into "turn tail and fly "
Sill the British send us cablegrams,
AMERICA, SEND GUNS AND HAMS.
Looks like to me tain't guns they lack.
They need to learn to stop backing back.
The British retreat victoriously.
They leave the field so gloriously.
The turn their backs to the enemy
And yell, "America, come help me!"
But Europe's a long ways to go.
Why I should go there, I don't know.
To tell the truth, I've got no desire
To pull British chestnuts out the fire!
No, no! No, no, no!
Let them British chestnuts go.
Yes, yes! Yes, yes, yes!
Tell the British to—
Station XYZ signing off

TO LOUISE, [MAY 1941]

Dear Lou,

Did I tell you I heard from Mortelia Womack and she is the only colored worker in the social services division of the Austin State Hospital in Texas. . . . . It is feeding time for animals and tea time for humans here on the farm. Outside my window the caracules [lambs] are all rushing for the fold at the hired man's approach (who's an Okie) and the houseboy has just brought me a nice big hot piece of chocolate cake and a glass of goat's milk. . . . . So all is well at the moment at Hollow Hills. . . . . Loved your Lincoln card. As to my plans, I'm doing my best to get my book done, but am far from it, so will probably be here well into July or maybe longer, but at the same time will begin my Rosenwald [fellowship] reading. And shall do a series of ballads about all the characters, too, along with the plays. How did you like the ballads I sent you? They are fun to do. . . . . Did you ever meet Sam Solomon?[24] Notice what big play [Arthur] Koestler's

24. Solomon was the subject of one of Langston's ballads, "The Ballad of Sam Solomon."

anti-soviet novel is getting? He's the guy was with me all the time in Bokhara and Tashkent. I was just writing about him in my book when I saw last Sunday's TIMES Book Review. I remember how the dirt of USSR got on his clean German nerves. But Hitler caught him there and he couldn't go back home. But he must be somewhere else now!

Pjalsta!
Lang

[*New York Times* article from May 25, 1941, enclosed.]

TO LOUISE, JUNE 4, 1941

Is this here too nationalist?

POEM TO UNCLE SAM
by
Langston Hughes

Uncle Sam
With old Jim Crow
Like a shadow
Right behind you
Everywhere
You go.

Uncle Sam,
Why don't you
Turn around,
And before you
Tackle Hitler—Shoot Jim down?

TO LOUISE, [JUNE 17, 1941]

[Envelope postmarked Monterey, California]

Dear Lou,

Delighted to hear the good news of your impending arrival with all the gay companions you're bringing! A keg of nails is due to be opened! The Ethel Waters show is in San Francisco next week and I am going up for that. Might even be there when you come. Or if not, will surely come up to see you-all and plan for you to spend a day down here in the country. Looks like I'm here for several weeks yet, as I'm nowhere near done [with] my book and I don't want to leave until a draft is finished. Besides I'd like to see the Salinas Rodeo in mid-July, which I have never seen. . . . . Also it seems the Duke Ellington show is going to have in it my GOING MAD WITH A DIME (at least it is in rehearsal now) and I'd like to see the opening of that, also in July in L.A. At which rate I reckon it will be August before I start East. If then. . . . . . You will love Nebby Lou more than ever. Besides, she can now communicate with you! . . . . Best to Mary [Savage], Pat, Dot [Fisher-Spencer], and all.

Sincerely,
Lang

Tuesday

TO LOUISE AND PAT, JULY 17, 1941

Tuesday July 17, 1941

Dear Lou and Pat,

It was swell seeing you-all the other day! And I wish I had thought to tell you that the Salinas rodeo was being held this week. I've just come from the opening this afternoon and it was very colorful and exciting. And quite international too. There was one colored cowboy in it, and another colored fellow in the band. And a Japanese soldier on one of the six horses pulling a big army artillery piece. Not to speak of numerous Mexicans and Indians and Chinese in the parade. (Which seems to make democracy, bad as it is, slightly better than Hitler—who's too Nordic for any color at all.). . . . . Just got W. C. Handy's autobiography, which is having swell reviews. Arna worked with him on it and is credited as editor. . . . . . Did you see where I was mentioned in Mrs. Roosevelt's column the other day where she was reading poetry to students and some of them asked for mine? . . . . . The League of American Writers just sent back my check for [a] copy of the Congress Report they'd announced. Told you! They're not publishing it as they say it was fully covered in the papers! #"&*%! . . . . . Literature sure has a hard time keeping up with the line! I reckon writers better go back to love and the moon—much as I have denounced such trivia in the past! . . . Tell Mary she should have seen those cowboys riding broncos this afternoon, and wrestling steers by the horns. Eulah [Pharr] and I are going again tomorrow after which we are invited to a pig foot supper. . . . . Happy trip and drop me a card on the way home.

Sincerely,
Lang

[Enclosure]

For IMMEDIATE Release
Exclusively for ANP

GOVERNOR FIRES DEAN
  by
  Langston Hughes

I see by the papers
Where Governor Talmadge[25] got real mad
Cause one of Georgia's teachers
Thinks Democracy ain't bad.
The Governor has done had him
Kicked plumb out of school
Just because that teacher
Believes the golden rule.
Governor Talmadge says that white folks
And black folks cannot mix
Unless they want to put
The sovereign state of Georgia
In a awful kind of fix.
The governor says equality
(Even just in education)
Is likely to lead us all
Right straight to ruination—
So I reckon governor Talmadge
Must be a Hitler man
Cause that's just what Hitler*d say
If he ruled the land.
Ain't it funny how some white folks
Have the strangest way
Of acting just like Hitler
In the U.S.A.?

25. Eugene Talmadge (1884–1946) was a staunch segregationist and white supremacist. He was twice elected governor of Georgia, serving from 1933 to 1937 and from 1941 to 1943.

[Postcard from Cheyenne, Wyoming; handwritten]

Hollow Hills Farm
Monterey, Calif.

Wednesday

Howdy Lang!

There's a big rodeo here too—but the kind of travel schedule we have forces us to refrain from enjoying the treats of road travel.

Got your nice farewell letter—I'm hoping to see you soon in Chi,

Love,
Lou

TO LOUISE AND PAT, NOVEMBER 5, 1941

Hollow Hills Farm,
Monterey, California,

November 5, 1941.

Dear Lou and Pat,

How're yuh?. . . . . Eulah and I are having a cocktail party in the garden by the pool tomorrow afternoon and you-all are cordially invited. One of my farewell parties—I'm leaving for Chicago next week—sure enough. Have to speak for the Book and Play Club on the 21st so I won't write the news. Will bring it. . . . . Mary [Savage] looked well when I saw her a few days ago. And Nebby-Lou is so lovely she probably intends to be an international beauty! Have you seen Arna [Bontemps]'s anthology for children, GOLDEN SLIPPERS? Or the big one from the pilgrims on, THE DEMOCRATIC SPIRIT? Seven Negroes therein—including me. Some swell stuff on slavery and abolition. Pat would find that interesting. . . . . . . And looky here! Just today my clipping bureau sent me a big box of old clippings, evidently from their files—and in it were a number of reviews of A NEW SONG I'd never seen. Maybe you haven't either, so here they are. Just keep them for me until I come. . . . . . SHAKESPEARE IN HARLEM has finally gone to press for good. The artist recovered and the book is due out in January. I hope the pictures have some hair on their heads. The delay enabled me to strengthen the social content of the book. I put in ten more poems, including:

Where is the Jim Crow section
On this merry-go-round,
Mister, cause I want to ride?
Down South where I come from
White and colored can't sit
Side by side.
Down south on the train
There's a Jim Crow car.
On the bus we sit in the back.
But there ain't no back
To a merry-go-round.
Where's the horse for a kid
That's black.

Which is the best poem I ever wrote—next to MIDNIGHT CHIPPY'S LAMENT—next to KIDS WHO DIE—next to WAKE.

Please tell Horace [Cayton] and Erma [Irma Jackson Cayton Wertz] I'd be delighted to accept their kind invitation to stay at Good Shepherd [Community Center] provided they protect me from teas, manuscripts, and free speeches. Also if they will let me play their record machine that plays twelve all at once. Revels [Cayton] has gone to China.

Mosquitos are legion out here this fall and I am bitten all over the arms.

There's a new two dollar edition of NOT WITHOUT LAUGHTER out. And Schirmers have published the SONGS TO THE DARK VIRGIN that Marion Anderson sings.

And MR. GEORGE'S JOINT has just about the lowest-down Negroes in it that have yet appeared in fiction! . . .

Best to you,
Lang

P.S. They're doing our DON'T YOU WANT TO BE FREE in Newport News!

FROM LOUISE, [NOVEMBER 9, 1941]

[Handwritten]

Lang dear—

It was grand—hearing from you after so long a time. And better still to know you would soon be here.

Dot [Fisher-Spencer] has been here for about three weeks and will be going on to NYC probably this week. So if you come on next week I won't be so lonely.

I wish you could stay here at the [Hotel] Vincennes with us. I will get you a comfortable room and you can spend all your other than sleeping hours in our apartment. It's nice and quiet. And I have a phonograph-radio. It's not as grand as Horace [Cayton]'s but you can play 12 records at a time. And I do cook home and we could have so much fun together. It's been so long since we have had much time together—so won't you say yes— please, sir.

There is so much to talk about, Lang dear. And I couldn't begin to write everything. And then when you don't want to talk you won't have to. And I'll protect you very well from teas, manuscripts, speeches ad infinitum— cause we have few visitors and I don't see many people. Horace's place is a beehive of activity. And Horace is more and more on the other side of the fence—so I haven't seen him for a long time. But first and last I would like to have you close by so we could get together as much as possible.

I'm glad the book is finally coming out. And I liked your "Merry-Go-Round" but think your "Uncle Sam" doesn't strike the right note now. You know, Lang, if we don't stop Hitler, we will not be able to "shoot Jim down". But I haven't time enough to talk now—so will save it till you come.

Please come on down here to the old Vincennes. I want you to meet Mrs. Barnett [Elizabeth Barnett-Lewis]. She is nice and fat and the only Negro in Chicago actually running a Negro hotel. She is hard as nails but [a] most interesting character.

And we have an elevator that trembles and gasps—but does run. And maids and bellboys who change every week—so there is no monotony. And transients on Sat. nite who don't bother or make noise. And plenty of quiet.

I'll be looking to hear from you. If you let me know when you are arriving, I'll be there to give you the key to Chicago.

Love,
Lou

TO LOUISE, NOVEMBER 11, 1941

Dear Lou,

So sorry! It would be nice to be at the Vincennes—I've stopped there before and know Mrs. Barnett—but I've already accepted Horace [Cayton]'s invitation and just had a letter from him yesterday that he's expecting me and is making the guest room ready. Arna [Bontemps] tells me that Richard Wright stayed there and found it most comfortable and protective. The main thing is it's near the L and on the bus lines—and you know how hard it is to get about in Chicago in the winter. The Vincennes is miles from anywhere—except you-all, which, of course, cancels most of its other disadvantages.

But I will be down to see you and play that 12-record Victrola 12 twelve times.

I heard Dick [Wright]'s new picture book of 12 MILLION VOICES is marvellous! More beautiful even than the prose of Du Bois at his best. I am most anxious to see it.

I just wrote a strong letter of protest to Dutton's about MR. GEORGE'S JOINT that they sent me for comment.[26] It is as low-down a picture of Negro lumpen-proletariat as has ever come out, yet they are advertising it as "A magnificent picture of Negro life as it is—," in the New York Sunday Times.

Eulah has a soldier-boy boy friend. Did I tell you about our party the other day? It was supposed to be a cocktail party from 3–6, but it went on until 3 in the morning and everything in the house was eaten and drunk up and the music was mellow. Nobody fought, only thing was that one girl took and tore all the wires out of a former boy-friend's car when she found out he was taking another girl home—which, since it was [^a] big car, left seven stranded high and dry way out here in the country in the early morning and they had to [^be] sent home in our station wagon. She also took his radio antenna and twisted it around like a boomerang and broke it off. But she did not break no glass.

Tell Pat HY!

Sincerely,
Lang

November 11, 1941.

P.S. Tell Dot (if she's still there) that Mr. Sullivan wrote Kenneth a letter to New York but it came back. What is their address now?

26. Langston was troubled by the negative stereotypes of Blacks depicted in *Mr. George's Joint,* a novel published in 1941 by Texas writer Elizabeth Lee Wheaton, and complained to E. E. Dutton, the book's publisher.

TO MATT, NOVEMBER 19, 1941

[Letterhead: El Capitan / Santa Fe; handwritten]

Wednesday,

November 19, 1941

Dear Matt,

What a pleasant, surprising, totally unexpected, amazing, and delight-fully unusual event it was receiving a letter from you!! And just the day I'm leaving too. (I missed the first train—naturally. But caught the next—and here I am crossing Kansas—and thinking of a certain distinguished American from here—at the moment locked up. Otherwise "sedit."

I guess I'll be in Chi [Chicago] a couple of weeks or so. Speak there on Friday. And on to New York for the holidays.

So sorry all the women-folks have had colds. Give my best to Mary, Nebby, and Nebby Lou. This train is rolling too much to write. More on land later.

Lang

[Note in left margin] *[James Weldon] Johnson and [Countee] Cullen antholo-gies are best for poems. Claude [McKay]'s "If We Must Die" most widely known single poem probably.*

SIX

World War II and Black Radical Organizing

JUNE 1942–JULY 1944

Langston had returned to New York, and Harlem, in mid-December 1941. In the summer of 1942 he was attending the Yaddo writers' colony in Saratoga Springs, New York, where he was working on the second part of his autobiography, *I Wonder as I Wander*. He would return to Yaddo in 1943.

In 1942 he started his column "Here to Yonder" in the *Chicago Defender*, the nation's largest Black weekly newspaper at the time, and in 1943 he introduced its readers to his everyman character, Jesse B. Semple, often referred to as "Simple." In March 1943 Mary Lou was born in Chicago.

TO MATT AND NEBBIE, [JUNE 10, 1942]

[Postcard, Café Society, New York City; handwritten, and signed by Kenneth, Arna, and Langston]

Dear Matt & Nebbie-

Wish you were here tonight (late) with—Kenneth [Spencer], Arna Bontemps and Langston. Hy, Jack!

TO MATT, OCTOBER 11, 1942

Hy, Matt—

JIM CROW'S LAST STAND[1]
  by
  Langston Hughes

There was an old Crow by the name of Jim.
The Crackers were in love with him.
They liked him so well they couldn't stand
To see Jim Crow get out of hand.
But something happened, Jim's feathers fell—
Now that Crow's begun to look like hell!
    DECEMBER 7, 1941,
Pearl Harbor put Jim Crow on the run—
That Crow can't fight for Democracy
And be the same old Crow he used to be.
Although right now, even yet, today,
He still tries to act in the same old way.
But India and China and Harlem, too,
Have made up their minds Jim Crow is through:
Nehru said, before he went to jail,
Catch that Jim Crow bird, pull the feathers out his tail.
Walter White told Hollywood,
Your Uncle Tom's ain't no good.
Marion Anderson said to the DAR,
I'll sing for you—but drop that color bar.
Paul Robeson said, out in Kansas City,
To Jim Crow my people is a pity.
Mrs. Bethune told Martin Dies,
You ain't telling nothing but your Jim Crow lies—
If you want to get old Hitler's goat,
Abolish poll tax so folks can vote!
Frederick Douglass said, years ago,
Old Jim Crow has got to go.
Joe Louis said, we gonna win this war

1. Langston sent Matt this early draft of "Jim Crow's Last Stand." He later toned down some of the most strident phrases for the published version of the poem, which appeared in the *Baltimore Afro-American* on October 24, 1942.

Cause the good Lord knows what we're fighting for.
When Dorrie Miller grabbed that gun,
     DECEMBER 7, 1941,
From Harlem to India to Africa's land,
Jim Crow started his last stand.
Our battle yet is far from won,
But when it is, Jim Crow'll be done.
Bury that bird, feathers and all,
And never dig him up a-tall—
But first we got to beat Jim's head
Until that lousy Crow is dead.
Come on and help us beat his head!

Lang

Yaddo,
Saratoga Springs, N.Y.
October 11, 1942.

TO PAT, OCTOBER 26, 1942

Dear Pat,

   That was a splendid criticism you gave me on STALINGRAD.[2] Thanks
immensely. I understand from my agent NM [*New Masses* magazine] has
taken it. I thought their Negro Issue very good, particularly the [Earl]
Browder article. . . . . How is this one? Too strong?

TOTAL WAR

The reason Dixie
Is so mean today
Is because it wasn't licked
In the proper way.

I'm in favor of beating
Hitler to his knees—

---

   2. "Stalingrad: 1942" was a poem Langston wrote lauding the Soviet defeat of the
Nazis at the city of Stalingrad in the USSR. It was published in the anthology *War Poems of
the United Nations,* edited by J. Davidman (New York: Dial Press, 1943).

Then beating him some more
Until he hollers, *Please!*

If we let our enemies
Breathe again—
They liable to live
To be another pain.

Or is it wrong to link up Dixie so definitely with fascism?......I think
the army has near about got me!

Sincerely,
Lang

634 St. Nicholas Avenue, Apt, 1-D,
New York, October 26, 1942

FROM LOUISE, NOVEMBER 5, [1942]

November 5

Lang dear—

I've been enjoying your frequent contributions and should have written—but you know my weakness.

I think <u>Jim Crow's Last Stand</u> can be made into a good popular mass song. Haven't the slightest idea here who could put it to music. Have you done anything with it? We're featuring <u>Freedom Road</u> on an International night of the dances and songs of many nations at our IWO Center in the Loop. Margaret Goss [Burroughs] is getting it put on for us. I'll write you how it comes out.

I suppose you have been told you will soon be an uncle again.[3] Are you as surprised as me? I'm feeling fine—but right now am rather disappointed because I'm not on my way to NY tonite. The [I.W.O.] board meets this weekend there. I wanted to see you-all and to be at the American-Russian Friendship Congress. But the doctor said <u>NO</u>—so here I am writing letters instead.

Are you really about to be taken in hand by Uncle Sam? Tell me more about it and when.

What are you working on now and did you get your book finished while in Saratoga?

---

3. Louise is referring to being pregnant with Mary Lou.

I read your last poem <u>Total War</u> you sent Pat. No, I don't think it too strong, Lang—it's not strong enough! While writing this note I just happened to glance at a clipping on a meeting in London's Albert Hall where the Archbishop of Canterbury spoke on Nazi pogroms, saying about it "such an eruption of evil as the world has not seen for centuries."

What I think is missing from your poem is that grim, stern note of hate which we must feel toward Hitler and Hitlerism abroad and home. We must destroy or be destroyed! I think that it wasn't incorrect to bring Dixie in—if we show what must be done always to such malignant cancers—must be cut out—destroyed. It seems to me, Lang, that what we must get is that burning hatred that the Spanish manifested—that the Russians have. And I'd like your poem to arouse this burning indignation.

Have you seen Mary [Savage] and how does she look. How are Toy and Emerson [Harper]. How are you and why don't you come see us. What is Zell [Ingram] doing and what is Harlem like in war time.

Last I heard from Dot [Fisher-Spencer] and Ken [Spencer] they were still in L.A. but expecting to leave soon. Matt is working in a defense plant.

And I guess that's all I know. I go [out] little and see few. Helen and Nelson [Glover] always ask of you,

Much love and write soon,

Lou

Pat's out—but I imagine he'll be writing you on his own. That's why I include no message from him.

FROM MATT, NOVEMBER 24, 1942

[Handwritten]

Nov. 24, 1942

Dear Lang:

I know you have called me all of the "so and sos" for not writing to you long before this—and you are more than justified. Each time I received a poem from you—resolved anew to write the very "<u>next</u>" day but it remain[ed] the "next" day.

I have enjoyed your poems very much and I am truly thankful to you for sending them to me. I will not attempt to give a critical opinion of any of them at this writing for there are many other things I want to say, however my general reaction is that both the poems and your songs have been progressing firm and positive in content and for me altogether enjoyable.

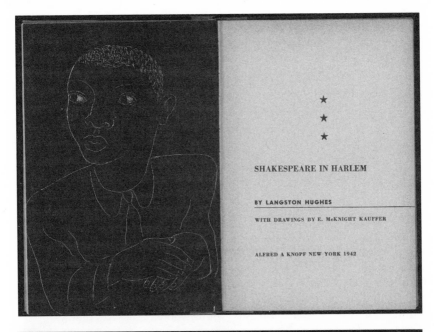

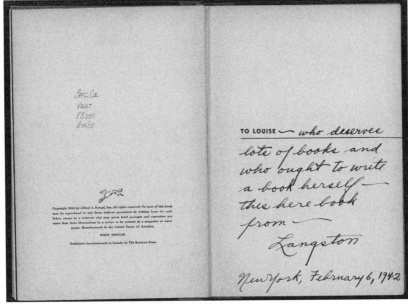

FIGURE 19. Langston's book *Shakespeare in Harlem,* with a personal dedication to Louise, 1942.

You may have heard through Lou or Mary that I am now a "machinist" or more correctly a lathe operator. I have been working in a machine shop here in Berkeley since July and like it very much. It is a small plant (employs 60 workers) and unlike some defense work it is plenty tough. For the first month I had to spend about 12 hours in bed getting over the effects of 8 hours' work. However I finally got accustom[ed] to the work and for about two months worked a 10 hour shift without too bad effect although I didn't do anything but work, eat and sleep. I am now back on an 8 hour shift and feeling fine. The only drawback is I have to work days one week and nights one week which makes it pretty difficult to have a regulated life. But this is war.

Nebby is home from work for a while. The baby hasn't been well and it was impossible to get anyone to care for her as she had to be cared for during this time. At the moment she is getting along very well and I am hopeful that she is gradually getting strong enough to resist the attacks of throat infection which have been the main source of her trouble. Nebby is very well, at the moment she is in the midst of preparing Thanksgiving dinner. Her sister and her two girls (young women now) are coming for dinner to-morrow. I don't know whether you heard that Lloyd, Nebby's brother-in-law, died last August (or maybe it was earlier in the summer).

All of my family are well. The only casualties have been both Charles and Artice [who] are separated from their wives. Artice was married about 6 months and his wife ran off with a soldier.

Dot is up from Los Angeles for a few days. Kenneth just completed Cabin in the Sky[4] and has signed a contract for a new picture since Dot came up; he didn't say what the picture would be about Dot said.

We were delighted with the surprise at Weez's prospective mother-hood—Boy that is really going to be something—Weez with a baby. Well I guess that about exhaust[s] the personal news.

The Bay Area is really seething with war activity. The place is overrun with shipyard workers. There are literally thousands of new people here now Negro and white. The general bar against Negro employment has been broken, the number working in the shipyards is estimated at about four thousand however there is still a great deal of discrimination as to the type of work Negroes are given. The number of skilled and semi-skilled workers has increased but the majority are doing laborers' work and have difficulty

---

4. *Cabin in the Sky* is a 1943 MGM musical that starred Ethel Waters, Eddie Anderson, Lena Horne, and Kenneth Lee Spencer

getting anything else. Negro women are going into industry in increasing numbers. At the last meeting of my union (United Steel Workers, C.I.O.) of about 25 women initiated 8 were Negro women. These were from plants outside the shipyards. Moore's shipyard in Oakland has begun to hire Negro women as welders, electricians and similar types of work. This is the bright side but there are a host of concealed barriers that still prevent Negroes from fully participating in the war effort. We have been unable to develop a strong united campaign to smash the remains of job discrimination here, although some very good work is being done by the Bay Area Council Against Discrimination which is made up of a number of "big" names including Walter Gordon as chairman and directed by people like Aubrey Grossman, one of [Harry] Bridges' lawyers. The main trouble however is that there is not a "grass root" movement of Negro people to really give substance and character to a general anti-discrimination campaign; the housing question here is terrific and nothing is done about it. The [National Negro] Congress has very little effect on the situation here. About all we can do is maintain a skeleton of an organization and participate wherever we can. The NAACP conducts itself as usual. Paul [Robeson] and Max [Yergan] had a meeting here that was actually the most successful ever attempted in Oakland.[5] It was in the Oakland Auditorium theater which was literally jammed and about a thousand people were turned away. Both Paul and Max made fine talks. We are trying to develop something from the basis laid by the meeting (if any).

Well boy it looks as though the tide of war has turned in our favor, at long last. I am restraining too much optimism over the new offensive around Stalingrad but it really looks like the "[real] McCoy". The best guarantee for real victory in the war and after is still a strong Red Army. The African campaign adds much weight to the future decision of the whole war and particularly the prospect of knocking Italy out. Well Lang it is about time for me to go to work. I am really going to try [to] write again soon.

Sincerely
Matt

5. The meeting Matt is referring to was held on September 22, 1942, and was sponsored by the Citizens for Victory Committee and the Bay Area Council Against Discrimination. Speakers called for the United States to open a "second front" in World War II to fight discrimination in the war industries.

TO MATT, [DECEMBER 1942]

[Postcard, handwritten]

Dear Folk:

Seasons Greetings.

We motored to Carmel to visit Eulah [Pharr] for Xmas. N.S. [Noel Sullivan] is out of town. Eleven of us went and we had a very lovely old fashioned one. It reminded me of those you see pictured in Magazines.

Please tell Nebby Lou to drop me a line sometime and tell me the list of Dolls that she has. I heard she was making a collection of Dolls of Other Lands. I would like to add to the collection. I intended writing when I first heard it but you know old man delay—that's me!

TO MATT, NEBBY, AND NEBBY-LOU, [1942]

[Postcard, Café Society, New York City; handwritten and signed by Louise, Dorothy Fisher-Spencer, Alta and Aaron Douglas, and Kenneth Spencer]

Nebby—Matt—Nebby-Lou

Celebrating Alta's birthday and the birth of Lang's swell new fighting song—sung by Ken [Spencer] tonite—"Freedom Road"
Love to you-all from us-all
Weez—Singer swell—song better—will see you definitely—Hold on!
Dot
Hello Alta. All the Best—Doug
Hy! Langston

[In top margin] Kenneth

TO MATT, [JANUARY 12, 1943]

TO CAPTAIN MULZAC
Negro Skipper of the Booker T. Washington
by
Langston Hughes

Dangerous
Are the western waters now,

And all the waters of the world.
Somehow,
Again mankind has lost its way,
Down paths of death and darkness
Gone astray—
But there are those who still hold out
Both chart and compass
For a better way—
And there are those who fight
To guard our harbor entrance
To a brighter day.

There are those who, too, for so long
Could not call their house, their house,
Nor their land, their land—
Formerly the beaten, and the poor
Who did not own
The things they made—nor their own lives—
But stood, individual and alone,
Without power—
They have found their hour.
The clock is moving forward here—
But backward in the lands where fascist fear
Has taken hold,
And tyranny again is bold
Yes, dangerous are the wide world's waters still,
Menaced by the will
Of those who would keep or once more make
Slaves of men.
We Negroes have been slaves before.
We will not be again.
Alone I know no one is free.
But we have joined hands—
Black workers with white workers,
I, with you! You, with me!
Together we have launched a ship
That sails these dangerous seas—
But more than ship,
Our symbol of new liberties.
We've put a captain on that ship's bridge there,

A man, spare, swarthy, strong, foursquare—
But more than these,
He, too, is a symbol of new liberties.
There's a crew of many races, too,
Many bloods—yet all of one blood still:
The blood of brotherhood,
Of courage, of good-will.
Of deep determination geared to kill
The evil forces that would destroy
Our charts, our compass, our bell-buoy
That guide us toward the harbor of the new world
We will to make—
The world where every ugly past mistake
Of hate and greed and race
Will have no place.
In union, you, white man and I, black man
Can be free.
More than ship then,
Captain Mulzac, is a BOOKER T., And more than captain
You who guide it on its way.
Your ship is mankind's deepest dream
Daring the sea—
Your ship is flagship
Of a newer day.
Let the winds rise.
Let the great waves beat.
Your ship is Victory,
and not defeat.
Let the great waves rise
And the winds blow free,
Your ship is
Freedom,
Brotherhood
Democracy!

[Note in top margin] As read at the C.I.O. dinner to Captain Mulzac at
the Hotel Commodore, New York, Jan. 12, 1943.

[Handwritten]

Jan 16, '43

Dear Lang,

Louise showed me the poem to Capt. Mulzac. I have read it several times each time being the more pleased with it.

The futility of individual effort, the efficacy of unity within a nation, on an international scale, in fact the essence of the concepts of National Unity and International Solidarity are there—yet so simply, so strong.

Splendid Lang splendid.

Then there is a question of style, which perhaps by reason of the content, seems so much better than that of other recent things.

More of such is needed Lang a great deal more which lifts the hopes and faith of youth. More that shows the illimitable possibilities opening up before youth and peoples.

You alone of all poets are equipped to do things in the People's language. So often I have tried to make myself clear to you, now you have made it clear that you saw the course, only you were slow to embark upon it.

The positive note that does not ignore objective difficulties but which sees their solution in the powerful force of unity and WILL is there too.

My sole criticism is that "mankind has NOT lost its way[.]" No Lang! It has been consciously driven from its course.

The Soviets are the vanguard of mankind. They have not lost their way. They sought to steer the destinies of mankind along a clearly defined course but they were snubbed, defiled and ignored until they could be ignored no longer.

More power to you Lang—and still more power.

Pat

On January 23, 1943, Duke Ellington held a jazz concert in Carnegie Hall in New York City. He played before a mixed Black and white audience. Langston wrote a "Here to Yonder" column about the concert and sent a copy of the column to Louise.

THE DUKE PLAYS FOR RUSSIA

There must be something wrong with a guy who feels like crying all the way through a concert by a jazz band. But that is the way I felt the other night when the Duke gave his first Carnegie Hall concert in New York in celebration of the Twentieth Anniversary of Duke Ellington's Orchestra. The concert was for the benefit of Russian War Relief. Tickets were sold out a week in advance. Great crowds of people at both the front and back doors of Carnegie Hall were turned away. A fellow I know was offered $20.00 each for a pair of $2.20 seats he had. He wouldn't sell them. There was a big sign in the lobby that said entirely sold out, no stage seats, no standing room. In other words, no nothing.

The program listed various famous people as box holders—Marian Anderson, Benny Goodman, John Hammond, Count Basie. Celebrities were pouring down the orchestra aisles as early as eight o'clock. I never saw people come so early to a concert. I was even early myself.

The audience seemed to be almost half-and-half—half colored and half white. The tiers of stage seats behind the musicians were jammed with all kinds and colors of people, and all mixed up, from blonds to our own types of brunettes. Some wore evening gowns, some wore sweaters, white jitterbugs in sport clothes, colored jitterbugs in tuxedoes, and everybody in a mellow mood. What the French would call, a *soiree de gala,* minus the formality.

It was nice to see so many colored and white folks, famous and not famous folks, so mixed up and happy together—and nobody the worse for it. I couldn't help thinking about the more backward and barbarous regions of our country where people are prevented from sitting together in concert halls by law. And thought, if they just know what they're missing, seeing how happy people are here tonight at Duke's concert, they wouldn't be that way.

That was one of the things that got me to feeling like crying thinking how a simple thing like music—and not high-brow music, but popular music— the people's music—could bring folks together, like at the Savoy Ballroom in Harlem where everybody dances with everybody else, white, West Indian, Filipino, Mexican, Negro, and nobody's the worse for it. Then I got to thinking how this music was Negro music, and how Negro music had influenced all American popular music to such a great extent that it is now pretty hard to draw any color line at all in popular music. From George Gershwin up or down, white American composers have been influenced by, have improvised on and borrowed from the Negro composers and the folk songs of the Negro people, until our American popular music is flavored through and through with the sad-happy honey of the Negro soul.

The Duke is not only conductor and arranger for his band (pianist, too) but a great composer of popular music as well. The other night, he played many of his own compositions. As his orchestra came onto the stage the individual members were each given a hand by the audience for, even in the vast reaches of Carnegie Hall, the jazz addi[c]ts could recognize their favorite artists—Rex Stewart, Johnny Hodges, Sonny Greer. And when the Duke came on, as they say in theatre parlance, "the house fell in."

The band went into BLACK AND TAN FANTASY. Then, with scarcely a pause, into a regular good old down home blues—by another name. Then into two pieces by the Duke's son, Mercer Ellington, who was just inducted into the army. By that time, I was thinking about the army, anyhow, and how this concert was being recorded by OWI [United States Office of War Information] for rebroadcast to our boys overseas. And I got to thinking about some other boys—only somehow people never say boys" in referring to the Red Army—fighting on the coldest front in the world—and the most active—the Russian Front, and how the Duke was here playing his BLACK AND TAN FANTASY, his PORTRAIT OF BERT WILLIAMS, his PORTRAIT OF FLORENCE MILLS, and his JACK THE BEAR for the Russian War Relief. And got to thinking how the Russians had lately driven the Nazis—who hate Negroes—back from Leningrad. And how they had driven the Nazis—who hate Jews—back from Stalingrad. And how they were driving the Nazis—who hate colored and white people sitting together listening to music—back in the Caucausus [Caucasus], back, back, back, in the cold and the snow of the Russian night, under the dive bombers and artillery fire—the Russian people driving the enemy back with their own lives so that never again will they be able to say, "Aryans over all! Hate and Hitler over all!"

About that time, the Duke and his band started to play a new composition of his own, a musical tone poem about the history of the American Negro. And the first part of the music had in it slavery time and a little old colored woman standing outside the windows of the white folk's church who kept saying over and over to herself on the trumpet, "Jesus is my Savior, too!" She was not supposed to be near the slave-owner's church. Certainly they wouldn't let her in. And the slave-owning preacher wasn't preaching for her. But she kept saying over and over, anyhow, "Jesus is *my* Savior, too!" Decency and kindness and life and happiness are *mine,* too!" MY right, too! I can sing, too! Live, too! Walk on the earth free, too!

Democracy! Freedom! All the fine words in the papers and on the radio today, the fine words that sometimes the insincere use so carelessly and so cheaply—that even senators from Texas where I can't vote use—they are my words, too! Freedom! Liberty! Democracy! Are my words, too. The guns on the Russian Front driving the Nazis back, back, back into their own lair of death and darkness, those guns speak [for me, too. And the Duke's music—music reaching down into the hearts of millions of all colors all over the world—affirms for me, and for Russia, and for the common people everywhere, the right to life and joy and happiness, too. Harlem to Stalingrad!

From the Duke to Shastakovitch! From the mixed audience in Carnegie Hall to the great Republic of the USSR with its many varied races working and fighting together! A long way—but not so far in terms of the human heart, of human needs, and the basic unity of human beings.

FROM PAT, FEBRUARY 23, 1943

[Letterhead: Abraham Lincoln School]

February 23, 1943

Mr. Langston Hughes
634 St. Nicholas Avenue
c/o Harper
New York, N.Y.

Dear Lang:

I have a favor to ask you, one to which I hope you will find it possible to give a favorable response.

We have been working now for several months seeking to bring into being the Abraham Lincoln School. It has been a herculean task yet despite some very considerable organizational weaknesses, we have made splendid progress. We have often despaired that the whole task would not be accomplished, but now I begin to feel that it will be realized and the school opens March the First. I am sending you under separate cover most of the material which has been mailed out so far so that you may see for yourself what our objectives were and possibly also get some understanding of the size of the responsibilities we have taken on.

Difficult as things have been, no one associated with the school has for a moment slowed down. In fact I believe the more trying the situation was, the more zealously did all throw themselves into the struggle. It has been a struggle.

What I want you to do is to devote a column to the school. I am enclosing among other materials a column that Herb Graffis of the Chicago Daily Times gave us February 23. It will give you a feeling of the prestige that the school, although not yet opened has already acquired. But on the South Side it is still almost an unknown quantity.

You will pardon me I know if I make some suggestions as to the line I should like you to follow. I think the school is destined to be one of the truly effective weapons on the cultural front here in the Middle West against reaction in general and the McCormick-Hearst-Green and Curly Brooks cabal[6] in particular. It is for this reason that I believe that some of my own activities in the school should be featured in the Negro press.

For some time I have felt very definitely that history had placed this school on the order of the day. I felt that the progressive school that we had here in Chicago had exhausted its potentialities for penetrating the broader circles of national unity, for clarifying them, for giving them a concept of their responsibilities to themselves, to their country, to humanity in the people's war and for giving them guidance as to their practical programs of action.

It seemed to me clear that in the period of a people's war, not alone was it necessary for them to be moved politically and to appreciate the necessity for great economic changes but that a real understanding came not alone through political activity and increased production but also from a fundamental understanding of the basic reasons why these are necessary. It was clarity, more clarity, and still more clarity that was needed.

It was necessary to give thorough enlightenment as to the character of national unity, as to its basic content. The nebulous phrases with which we dress up our Fourth of Julys were not enough. Now

And so I initiated the struggle for the school. You know I have an impression that this was something like the activities of the Negroes that helped to create Wilberforce University—like the black men who coming out of slavery together with the poor whites built up the public school system of the Southern states. I hope you don't think I am without modesty if I put this school on a political level of the educational institutions that came out of that other great struggle for human freedom.

I think Negroes should know something about this, not only the Negroes in Chicago but others in the country because they so often think of people like myself as having only a destructive program.

I know of no one who could present the picture of what we are doing here to the public more graphically and forcibly than you. I hope that I am not asking too much.

Sincerely yours,
Wm L. Patterson
Wm. L. Patterson,
Asst. Director

6. The McCormick family owned a company that became International Harvester. They were strongly anti-union. Publishing magnate William Randolph Hearst owned the *Chicago American* and the *Chicago Examiner* newspapers. Charles W. "Curly" Brooks was Republican U.S. Senator from Illinois, who served from 1940 to 1949.

P.S. I think that your poem[7] in the Digest was extremely powerful, still more extremely bitter, too bitter. It was like gall and wormwood so bitter Lang, that it became defeatist and not positive. It showed the terrific power that is yours[. H]ad it been more positive, it would have been a great poem. WLP.

FROM LOUISE, MARCH 15, 1943

[Birth announcement for Mary Lou]

Dear arrived	Mary Louise Patterson
Date	March 15, 1943
Time	9:15 P.M.
Weight	7 lbs. 9 oz.
Hair	Black
Eyes	Brown

(Louise Patterson)

TO MARY LOU, MARCH 23, 1943

March 23, 1943,

New York, New York,
634 St. Nicholas Avenue.

Miss Mary Louise Patterson,
Hotel Vincennes,
Chicago, Illinois.

Dear Mary Louise,

This is for your first collection of original manuscripts. By the time you are old enough to read, I hope this war will be over. And by the time you are a big girl, I hope the red star will be shining everywhere, and that you

---

7. It is unclear which poem Pat is referring to here. We found no poems by Langston in the *Negro Digest* magazine during this time period.

will be here a long time to enjoy all of its blessings. So be a nice baby and take your cod liver oil and grow up strong.

With love from
Langston

[First and second drafts of the poem "Where the Armies Passed" enclosed.]

Mama, I found
   this soldier's
   cap
Lying in the
   snow.
It has a red
   star on it.
Whose is it?
Do you know?
         1st draft
         March 2, 1943

WHERE THE ARMIES PASSED
By
Langston Hughes

Mama, I found this soldier's cap
Lying in the snow.
It has a red star on it.
Whose is it, do you know?

I do not know whose cap it is, Son.
All stained with wet and mud.
But it has a red star on it!
Are you sure it is not blood?
I thought I saw red stars, mother,
Scattered all over the snow.
But if they were blood, mother—
Whose?

Son, I do not know.
It might have been your father's.
Perhaps it was your brother.
See! When you wipe the mud away,
It IS a red star, mother!

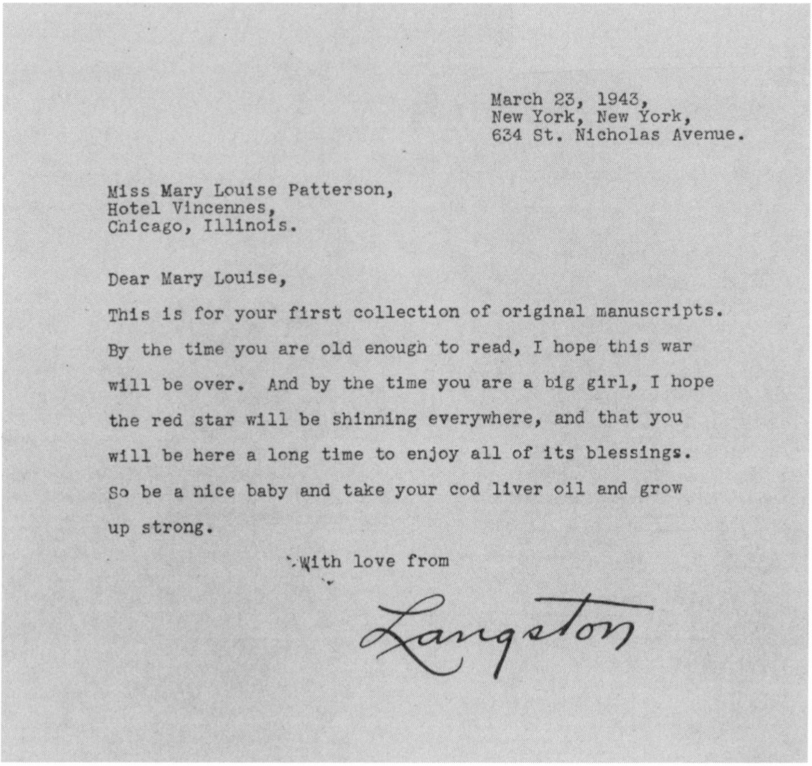

```
                                        March 23, 1943,
                                        New York, New York,
                                        634 St. Nicholas Avenue.

Miss Mary Louise Patterson,
Hotel Vincennes,
Chicago, Illinois.

Dear Mary Louise,

This is for your first collection of original manuscripts.

By the time you are old enough to read, I hope this war

will be over.  And by the time you are a big girl, I hope

the red star will be shinning everywhere, and that you

will be here a long time to enjoy all of its blessings.

So be a nice baby and take your cod liver oil and grow

up strong.

                        With love from

                            Langston
```

FIGURE 20. A letter and a poem (opposite) from Langston to Mary Lou welcoming her into the world, 1943.

FROM LOUISE, APRIL 12, [1943]

April 12

Lang dear—

MaryLou—her dad and mother were quite excited and pleased to have you dedicate a poem to her. She says it isn't every little girl that can start out in life collecting original manuscripts. And she is taking very seriously your admonition about growing up strong for she eats all we will give her—takes her vitamins, sleeps according to the book, and can cry, and only cries, when it's time to eat and we are a little slow.

She really is very nice, Lang, and I am glad you are coming so soon to visit her.

Mama, I found
this soldier's
cap
Lying in the
snow.
It has a red
star on it.
Whose is it?
Do you know?

1st draft
March 2, 1943

I [am] really thrilled over <u>Freedom's Plow</u>. It's beautiful, Lang—I like it even better than <u>Let America Be America Again</u>. I missed hearing [Paul] Muni do it—I was sick then—and had not seen it until your copy arrived. Pat liked it very well too, and he was very pleased also with the comments on your column. I know he has meant to write you but the school is literally running him ragged.

Mary [Savage] left Sat. after being here two weeks. You will probably see her and she can regale you with tales of our first week with a new baby. She did everything and was really the mother. And I certainly miss her.

I am excited over your doing the pageant and await hearing about it from you. So hurry on out here, boy.

Love,
Lou

[Letterhead: Abraham Lincoln School; handwritten]

April 12, 1943

Dear Lang—

Thanks for the advance news of the columns and the poems. The poem done by [Paul] Muni was splendid. The Langston who is satisfied that art belongs to the people and in the throes of a people's war must become for them a driving spiritual force wrote that poem.

On the Hollywood column I should be somewhat critical of some of my supporters if I were you. Some of them are in responsible positions but have shown little fundamental understanding of the character of the struggle— and less responsibility.

Hollywood reflects more perhaps than any other channel of artistic expression the gigantic clash of forces in our country. Forces opposed to the annihilation of Hitler and Hitlerism are strongly entrenched there. The words of the Wallaces, Edens, Wilkies', Roosevelts'[8] and their sincere supporters are anathema to these people. But they are the ones upon whom the batteries must be turned.

Negro artists must be made to appreciate that they speak not as individuals but as representatives of a people. But our William Hasties'[9] and other political figures don't understand that yet else we would have a united Negro people, Langston Hughes seems at times to forget it even.

Negro artists must be made appreciative of the great political, economic and cultural contributions the Negro has made to the development of democracy in our country. When they are aware of this they will hesitate to aid reaction both through fear of the wrath of others, contempt of others, and because they will know the role they play and their responsibilities to America.

There must be sharp criticism but most constructive criticism of the Negro in Hollywood. Without some political content the artist you seek to help will not be clarified. "Pure" national pride appeals won't do. You make great artists when you make artists politically conscious people. Not that all politically conscious artists are great. Great ability placed at the service of reaction only makes its master the more ignoble,

8. Matt is referring to liberal politicians such as Henry A. Wallace, Wendell Willkie, and Franklin D. Roosevelt, contrasting them with reactionary political forces in Hollywood.
9. William Hastie was a prominent African American lawyer and judge.

These Hollywood people must be helped to understand that true cultural expression is an expression of struggle for freedom. Langston can help them appreciate this. Gorky did in Russia.

But to end. The letters you get are further proof that Lang is an object of the people's attention. The forces opposed to progress want him no less than do his friends the fighters for progress. Having made your choice you must reveal the reasons for making it. This is the essence of Robeson's greatness. You have power Lang—great power.

You are writing Lang as a responsible, a politically responsible artist. You are the leading poet of your people, a leading poet of America, a leading poet of humanity. More power to you. Carry on.

Very sincerely,
Pat

TO MATT, [JULY 1943]

What's news, man?

Did you hear my song on the CIO-Robeson broadcast a few Sundays ago?

How's the family?

Lang

TO MATT, [JULY 30, 1943]

From Yaddo

THE BLACK MAN SPEAKS
By
Langston Hughes

I swear to the Lord
That I still can't see
Why Democracy means
Everybody but me.

I swear to my soul
I don't understand
Why Freedom don't apply
To the black man.

I swear, by gum,
That I really don't know
Why in the name of Liberty
You treat me so.

Down South you make me ride
In a Jim Crow car.
From Los Angeles to London
You take your color bar.

Jim Crow army,
Navy, too—
Is Jim Crow Freedom the best
I can expect from you?

I simply raise these questions
Cause I want you to state
What kind of a world
We're fighting to create.

If we're fighting to create
A free world tomorrow,
Why not end right now
Old Jim Crow's sorrow?
Facts and figures
All agree,
You're not acting
Right by me.

[Note in margin] *Drop a guy a line once in awhile. Lang*

Yaddo
Saratoga Springs,
New York

TO PAT, [1943]

JUST AN ORDINARY GUY
By
Langston Hughes

He's just an ordinary guy.
He doesn't occupy

A seat of government
Or anything like that.

He works hard every day,
Saturday brings home his pay—
He may take a glass of beer
Sometimes at that.

He never had his name in lights.
He's never front page news.
He stands up for his rights,
Yet doesn't beef, or sing the blues.

But when his country gets in trouble
And it's time to fight and die,
He doesn't ask for a deferment—
He's just an ordinary guy.

Listen, Hitler!
About this ordinary guy,
You may wonder why
He's taken such an awful
Hate to you.

[Note in margin] *I hear you-all have moved. What's your new address, Pat?*
Best to Lou and the baby. Lang

[Editors' note: The second page of the typescript, which contained the remaining four
stanzas of the poem, is missing.]

FROM PAT, AUGUST 2, 1943

[Letterhead: Abraham Lincoln School]

August 2, 1943

Mr. Langston Hughes
Yaddo
Saratoga Springs, New York

Dear Lang:

The new address is 5341 South Maryland, telephone Midway 4641.

I have gone over the poem and like it. I look forward anxiously to the
collection of your poems, "Jim Crow's Last Stand."

There are two things that I hope you might be able to do which I think would be helpful to the country as a whole. One is a real article on the [Abraham Lincoln] School for P.V. [*The People's Voice*],[10] the other is a column in which you deal with the [A. Philip] Randolph thesis that Negroes can go it alone. Maybe this could be in the form of that conversation between you and your friend. I am satisfied that both of these things done at once would pay dividends.

I have spoken to Thyra [Edwards] on the School article and she is ready for it as soon as it comes. If you feel you have insufficient material I will get some for you.

Mary Lou is coming along fine. Paul [Robeson] and Larry [Brown] were in to visit her the other day and she is constantly asking, "When is Mr. Hughes coming to see me?" She always says, of course, "Uncle Lang."

Sincerely,

Pat

William L. Patterson

WLP/ew uopwa:24

FROM PAT, SEPTEMBER 17, 1943

[Letterhead: Abraham Lincoln School]

September 17, 1943

Mr. Langston Hughes
Yaddo
Saratoga Springs, N.Y.

Dear Lang:

Thanks for the plug for the School. I am sending you enclosed in this letter a full page ad which we had in the Chicago Sun which you might be interested in looking over.

In answer to your question, I am graduated from Hastings Law School of the University of California and had two years pre-law at U.C.

To clarify the record a little bit, neither our School nor the School for Democracy is a workers' school. Their vitality lies in the fact that they are people's schools bringing education to the people in a people's war. It is my

10. *The People's Voice* was a weekly Harlem newspaper edited and published by Adam Clayton Powell Jr.

opinion that at this moment a worker's school could only have vitality, if anywhere at all, in such a city as New York.

Incidentally, I showed that card to my secretary, and she was very much put out. She very promptly told me that she didn't see the point. You will have to send a card that is a little clearer next time.

Sincerely,
Pat
William L. Patterson
WLP:r
Enc.

[Note in right margin] *Jay Jackson's HERE IT IS!! IN BLACK AND WHITE. L.H.*

FROM PAT, SEPTEMBER 27, 1943

[Letterhead: Abraham Lincoln School]

September 27, 1943

Dear Lang,

Your last poem[11] in the New Masses was a gem, keep that work up.

Sincerely,
Pat
William L. Patterson
WLP/ew
uopwa:24

Mr. Langston Hughes
Yaddo
Saratoga Springs, New York

11. Pat is probably referring to the poem "The Underground (To the Anti-Fascists of the Occupied Countries of Europe and Asia)," which was published in *New Masses* on September 28, 1943. See Arnold Rampersad, *The Collected Poems of Langston Hughes,* ed. Arnold Rampersad and David Roessel (New York: Alfred A. Knopf, 1994), 279.

[Letterhead: Abraham Lincoln School]

October 1, 1943

Mr. Langston Hughes
Yaddo
Saratoga Springs, New York

Enclosed is a little booklet which was sent to me by Lawrence Martin, who was at one time chief editorial writer of the Chicago Times. The author is a Jamaican Negro boy. Martin, who is now in South America, heard his name there for the first time and was of the opinion that the youngster should be brought to the attention of the American public. I am sending you this volume because you might be able to do a review of it somewhere or in some wise get notice of it in the press. If there is nothing you could do, I would suggest that you send it on to Mike Gold.

I should like you, if you found it possible, to treat of it in one of your columns.

Sincerely yours,
Pat
Wm. L. Patterson
WLP/ew
uopwa:24
Enclosure

[Langston later typed the following onto Pat's letter]

"AND MOST OF ALL MAN"
by Roger Mais
27 ½ Central Road, Kencot
Halfway Tree, P.O., Jamaica, B.W.I.

L.H.

TO MATT, [JANUARY OR FEBRUARY 1944]

SALUTE TO THE SOVIET ARMIES
by
Langston Hughes

Mighty Soviet Armies marching to the West,
Red star on your visor, courage in your breast!

Mighty Soviet Armies, warriors brave and strong,
Freedom is your watchword as you forge along!
The eyes of all the people, poor upon the earth,
Follow your great battle for mankind's rebirth.
Mighty Soviet Armies, allies, comrades, friends,
We will march beside you till Fascism ends.

Mighty Soviet Armies, guard your Fatherland!
The earth of your Union warms the hope of man.
Fascist foes surround you with their ring of steel,
But your warriors crush them with a workman's heel.
Never will the people let them rise again.
Death to Fascist tyrants! Death to Nazis' reign!
Mighty Soviet Armies, Allies of the free,
We will fight beside you until Victory!
Mighty Soviet Armies, now as one we stand,
Allies all together for the cause of man!
Salute to the Soviet Armies—from our land!

[Note in margin] *Hy, Matt! Flying to Ok tomorrow for USO [United Service Organizations]. Wish I could fly out to sunshine! Lang*

FROM PAT, [JANUARY 28, 1944]

[Letterhead: Abraham Lincoln School]

Mr. Langston Hughes
634 St. Nicholas Avenue
New York, N. Y.

Dear Lang:

The last poem which you sent was splendid. I have looked for its publication, but have not seen it anywhere as yet. Please let me know where it is published.

Do you remember that I sent you a copy of a book by a young boy in Jamaica, B.W.I. named Roger Mais? I am wondering if you got in touch with him. His address, if you have lost it, is 27 1/2 Central Road, Kencot, Halfway Tree, P.O. Jamaica, B.W.I.

If you have not written to him, I think you should, and if you could get someone to review his book, I am satisfied that it would strengthen his morale a great deal. You know, those youngsters look upon you as one of their great leaders and great inspirations—and rightly so. If you were to contact him personally, I am sure that it would be a deep source of assistance to him.

Keep up the good work.

Very truly yours,
Pat
Wm. L. Patterson
WLP:ag
uopwa-24

FROM PAT, FEBRUARY 8, 1944

[Letterhead: Abraham Lincoln School]

February 8, 1944

Mr. Langston Hughes
634 St. Nicholas Avenue
New York, N.Y.

Dear Lang:

It is true that Roger Mais' book is not what we would order, but his relative isolation from a developed movement has to be taken into consideration. That is why I thought a letter from you to him would be helpful.

There is hardly any need for you to return the book to me. I think it would be preferable if you could send it directly to [W.E.B.] Du Bois' Phylon, using my name if you wish, if it would in any way help.

I am particularly glad to hear that you are working on the British Broadcasting script. It should be a splendid salute and should be particularly heartening to the Negro people within the British empire.

Very truly yours
Pat
uopwa/24/cio
wlp/bm

[Handwritten]

February 20, 1944

Dear Langston,

I heard your speech on Town Hall[12] last night and was inspired out of my long delay in writing to you.

Your talk was swell Lang! I certainly agree with you that Federal action is the only solution to the "problem". Furthermore now is the time to get such action. The very fact that Town Hall could present such a program is the best proof that there is an important section of the American people who are either convinced or are fast becoming convinced that the government must move nationally.

I suppose you have heard by now that I am working for the California State C.I.O. [Congress of Industrial Organizations]. My official title, which sounds quite important, is "Assistant Director, California CIO Minorities Committee." Revels Cayton is the Director. I have been on the job since last August and the work has taken all of my time and energy. The work of the Committee has two main objectives; they are briefly,

1. To further consolidate the ranks of the CIO unions to prevent any division on race questions. This includes eliminating any remains of discrimination in admittance into CIO unions, discrimination in hiring by any employers who have contracts with the CIO. A very important and vital part of the program is the full integration of Negroes and other minorities into the activities of the unions, such as officers and committee members.

2. Participation of the CIO in community effort to establish real unity and cooperation of all sections of the people. Our approach in community work is to develop the understanding that problems of Negroes, Jews and others are not separate group or race problems but that they are the vital concern and interest of every last person who has an honest interest in the protection of his own right and the future security of

12. Matt is referring to NBC Radio's *America's Town Meeting of the Air.* The subject of the program was "Let's Face the Race Question," and the panel speakers were Langston; progressive journalist and author Carey McWilliams; conservative white Southern journalist John Temple Graves II; and Black conservative James Shepard, who was president of the North Carolina College for Negroes.

all Americans. There is nothing new of course in placing the question in this manner but it is possible to bring into the struggle many people who considered it a "Negro Question", that could be solved only when Negroes learned how to behave. Also it is possible to get action from people who have been afraid of "race relations." Once they understand that this is a bogy used by the worst of reaction to strike at ~~their own~~ interest of the great majority of people, white and black, they will go along.

Your talk last night was particularly effective because it did expose the manner in which this is done. Although there is nothing new in approaching the whole question from this angle it is possible to bring this home to people—white people—now more than ever before. The war has revealed so much that was hidden and confused in the past.

The cry of "white supremacy" in an effort to kill the soldiers vote for 10 million white soldiers sounds a little too much like the "Aryan master race" mouthing of Hitler to growing numbers of people. As the war progresses the deadly nature of race incitement and race divisions will become clearer.

Since I have been working in the union and in the community on minority problems I have realized as never before the complexity and confusion that must be broken through to make the necessary progress. However the best results have been achieved when the issues are clearly tied into the interest of everyone concerned.

In the last two years Los Angeles and the Bay Area have really gone through big changes. Both places are buldging with people. There are more than 90 thousand Negroes in L.A. and over 50 thousand in San Francisco, Oakland & Berkeley. The most acute problem is housing—and I mean acute. There have not been any serious outbreaks in the Bay Area, but several tense situations have developed from time to time. The most serious was last summer when the papers carried on a full-dress anti-Negro campaign around the "Green Glove Rapist". A series of eight or nine rape cases were blamed on an alleged Negro who wore green gloves. At the height of the campaign a thousand cops roamed the Fillmore district every night looking for the "Negro rapist." After weeks of terrorizing the community there a white man was arrested for the rape cases. He was finally convicted and sentenced last week.

One of the important things we are attempting to do now is to get the cities in the Bay Area to establish official committees on "Home Front Unity". Los Angeles has already set up such a committee.

Nebby and the Nebby Lou are well. Nebby Lou is growing very fast—you would not recognize her now. She has been in kindergarten almost a year now and will be going into the 1st grade this summer. I look at her now and realize how old I am getting. I also feel how old I am these days. Time was when I could go night after night and work all day without much trouble—but no more. I really have to take my rest now.

History sure has moved in the last few years, Lang, and from the way things are shaping up now there are going to be many more changes in the next few years of even greater importance. What do you think of Teheran?[13] The proposal of dropping "party" from Communist? What are your thoughts about what will happen to Negroes after the war?

You had better plan to come to California this year so we can have time to kick some of these questions around. It is really about time you came out again. Why don't you arrange a speaking tour or something out here?

Thank you for the poems. I always enjoy them and appreciate your thoughtfulness in sending them to me.

Nebby and Nebby Lou send love.

Sincerely,
Matt

TO MATT, JUNE 23, 1944

LENIN
  by
  Langston Hughes

Lenin walks around the world.
Frontiers cannot bar him.
Neither barracks nor barricades impede.
Nor does barbed wire scar him.

---

13. Matt wants to know Langston's thoughts about the Tehran Conference, a meeting held between Allied leaders Franklin D. Roosevelt, Joseph Stalin, and Winston Churchill in Tehran, Iran, from November 28 to December 1, 1943. The aim of the summit was to develop a coordinated war strategy against Hitler's Nazi forces in Europe.

Lenin walks around the world.
Black, brown, and white receive him.
Language is no barrier.
The strangest tongues believe him.

Lenin walks around the world.
The sun sets like a scar.
Between the darkness and the dawn
Rises a red star.

[Note below poem] *Man, I have been to St. Louis, Detroit, Chicago, as Narrator for the Music Festivals. Travelling with maestros and prima donnas!!! Sure did!*

Lang
6/23/44

FROM LOUISE, JULY 24, 1944

[Postcard from Torrington, Connecticut]

Mr. Langston Hughes
634 St. Nicholas Ave.
New York City

We're having a most perfect vacation—isolated, plenty of food and drink, sunshine & cold nites. Hope to see you when I pass thru NY Aug 1.

Love,
Lou

FROM PAT, JULY 25, 1944

[Letterhead: Abraham Lincoln School]

July 25, 1944

Dear Lang:

Thanks for giving me a preview of the Lenin poem. How are you coming along on the matter we discussed at Helen [Glover]'s?

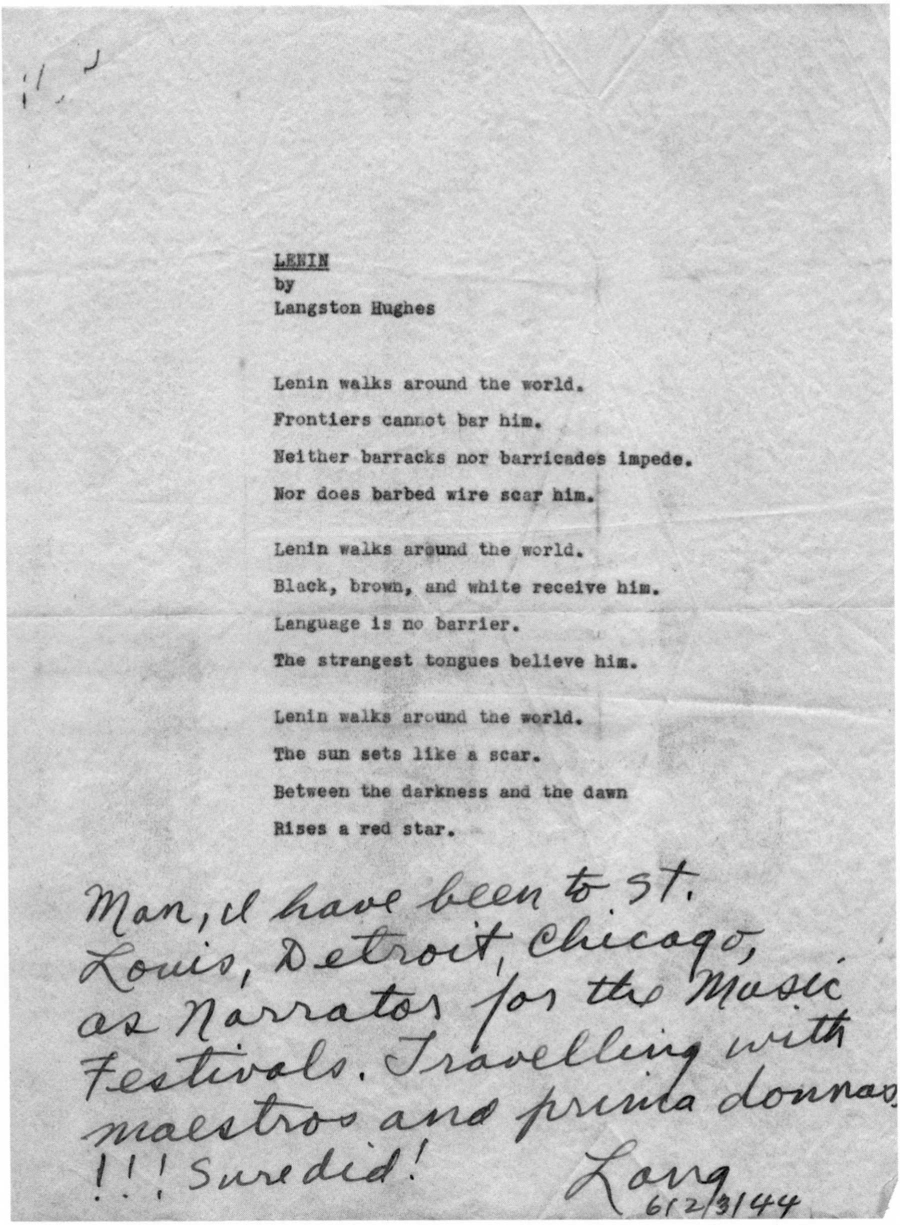

```
LENIN
by
Langston Hughes


Lenin walks around the world.
Frontiers cannot bar him.
Neither barracks nor barricades impede.
Nor does barbed wire scar him.

Lenin walks around the world.
Black, brown, and white receive him.
Language is no barrier.
The strangest tongues believe him.

Lenin walks around the world.
The sun sets like a scar.
Between the darkness and the dawn
Rises a red star.
```

Man, I have been to St. Louis, Detroit, Chicago, as Narrator for the Music Festivals. Travelling with maestros and prima donnas. !!! Sure did! Lang 6/2/3/44

FIGURE 21. A draft of "Lenin" and a few words from Langston about his recent travels, sent to Matt, 1944. (Matt N. and Evelyn Graves Crawford papers, Special Collections & Archives, Robert W. Woodruff Library, Emory University. From *The Collected Poems of Langston Hughes* by Langston Hughes, edited by Arnold Rampersad with David Roessel, Associate Editor, copyright © 1994 by the Estate of Langston Hughes. Used by permission of Alfred A. Knopf, an imprint of the Knopf Doubleday Publishing Group, a division of Penguin Random House LLC. All rights reserved.)

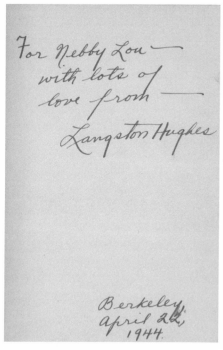

FIGURE 22. Cover of *Popo and Fifina,* a children's book by Langston and Arna Bontemps, 1944, with an inscription from Langston to Nebby Lou. (Copyright (©) 2015 by The Estate of Langston Hughes, Arnold Rampersad and Ramona Bass Kolobe Co-Administrators. By permission of Harold Ober Associates Incorporated.)

May I make a suggestion for a column? "The Negro Soldier"—treating its production as a high point in development of the cultural revolution which in our country has never paralleled the development of new political institutions or the industrial revolution. That is one of the major differences between the manner in which we and the Russians conduct this war. For the Soviets the industrial, the political, and the educational-cultural are inseparably linked together. They thereby secure a clear understanding in the masses of the fundamental economic and political changes. If we make changes economically and politically while the idea of racial superiority is not fought on the cultural front, no stable base for economic and political changes is realized.

"The Negro Soldier" is a departure from the old and should be praised as such, it seems to me. It is a blow at the domination over our cultural-educational life assumed by the South after 1876 and maintained up to the present time.

Sincerely,
Pat
Wm. L. Patterson
WLP/cw
uopwo:24

Mr. Langston Hughes
634 St. Nicholas Avenue
New York, New York

FROM PAT, JULY 25, 1944

[Letterhead: Abraham Lincoln School]

July 25, 1944

Mr. Langston Hughes
634 St. Nicholas Ave. New York, N.Y.

Dear Mr. Hughes:

On behalf of the Abraham Lincoln School I wish to express our deep appreciation for your contribution. It is only through the financial contributions of friends of the School, such as yourself, that we are able to do the work which we have begun and which must continue. Again many thanks.

Sincerely yours,
Pat
William L. Patterson
uopwa;24;cio Encl. 1

TO MATT AND NEBBY, [1945]

GIVE US OUR PEACE
  by
Langston Hughes

Give us a peace equal to the war
Or else our souls will be unsatisfied,

And we will wonder what we have fought for,
And why the many died.

Give us a peace accepting every challenge—
The challenge of the poor, the black, of all denied,
The challenge of the vast colonial worlds
That long has had so little justice by its side.

Give us a peace that dares us to be wise.
Give us a peace that dares us to be strong.
Give us a peace that dares us still uphold
<u>Throughout the peace</u> our battle against wrong.

Give us a peace that is not cheaply used.
Give us a peace that is no clever scheme.
Give us a peace for which men can enthuse—
A peace that brings reality to our dream.

Give us a peace that will produce great schools—
As the war produced vast armament,
A peace that will wipe out our slums—
As war wiped out our foes on evil bent.

Give us a peace that will enlist
A mighty army serving human kind—
Not just an army geared to kill the body,
But an army trained to help the living mind:

A mighty army trained to work for good
To bring about a world of brotherhood.

SEVEN

Ebb and Flow—To Chicago, New York, San Francisco, and Back

JULY 1946–NOVEMBER 1949

Many of the letters from the mid to late 1940s have a lighthearted tone that belies the personal and political challenges facing Langston and his friends. They lived with constant anti-communist harassment and FBI profiling. In the summer of 1946 Nebby and Nebby Lou traveled by train to Chicago to meet Mary Lou for the first time and share their vacation with Louise, Pat, and Dot (Dorothy Fisher-Spencer). By the fall of that year Louise, despite suffering a leg injury, was busy fundraising for the Abraham Lincoln School and the Du Sable Center. Langston and Matt exchanged letters about Matt's near-fatal car crash on the San Francisco Bay Bridge. They also discussed Langston's upcoming Broadway show, *Street Scene*. As winter approached, Matt had recuperated enough to begin planning statewide political campaigns and cultural events for the California National Negro Congress (NNC). Paul Robeson visited Berkeley and Oakland to hold mass meetings with the aim of boosting local membership in the NNC. In San Francisco, Nebby was back at work at the US Civil Service Commission.

In January 1947 Langston began teaching at Atlanta University in Atlanta Georgia, where Jim Crow life was ever present. In California, Matt was working as an organizer in Henry A. Wallace's 1948 presidential campaign. In Chicago, the Abraham Lincoln School was experiencing financial problems, and toward the end of 1949 Louise and Mary Lou were back in New York while Pat remained in Chicago to close the school.

FROM NEBBY, [JULY 22, 1946]

[Postcard from Chicago; handwritten]

Dear Lang—

Had to wait until we came to Chicago to get your address to let you know we rec'd the ring & ceramics & love them. Weez, Dot, Mary-Lou &

FIGURE 23. Nebby Lou and Mary Lou meet for the first time in Chicago, 1946.

Nebby-Lou & I are having a glorious visit in spite of the heat which is really something.

Love,
Nebby

FROM LOUISE, [OCTOBER 14, 1946]

[Handwritten]

Friday

Dear Lang

You oughta see me. I'm sitting in a wheel chair in the hospital with the biggest cast on my right leg—from toe to hip—you ever saw. I had so much trouble with my leg—the doctors finally decided to put it in a cast. So here I am—I will be going home later this p.m. ~~Then~~ I'll have to wear this thing for at least 3 weeks.

About the picture. Lang I haven't seen or heard of it for so long. There is an outside chance that it is in my big trunk—but I'll have to go into the storage room to find out—and I haven't been able to navigate our crooked basement stairs to go down to find out. So, I've been carrying these cards around in my pocket hoping I would soon be better. Now it seems I will be more circumscribed for some time. So I'll just send these cards along.

The doctor just came in to say he would probably make me wear this longer than 3 weeks. So I have a long sojourn at home to face tho I'll be able to learn to scoot around on the cast.

Give my regards to Toy [Harper] and everybody.

Lou

TO MATT AND NEBBY, OCTOBER 29, 1946

ONE WAY TICKET
  by
  Langston Hughes

I pick up my life
And I take it with me
And I put it down in
Chicago, Detroit,
Buffalo, Scranton,
Any place that is North and East
And not Dixie.

I pick up my life
And take it on the train
With me to Los Angeles,
Bakersfield, Seattle, Oakland,
Any place that is
North and West—
And not South.

I am fed up
With Jim Crow's laws
And people who are cruel
And afraid—
Who lynch and run,
Who are scared of me
And me of them.

I pick up my life
And take it away

On a one-way ticket—
Gone up North,
Gone out West,
Gone!

[Note in top margin] *For Matt and Nebby—*

Who have been North, lo these many!

Lang

Oct.29,

1946

TO MATT, [OCTOBER 1946]

[Letterhead: 634 St. Nicholas Avenue / New York 30, New York; handwritten]

Dear Matt,

What's this I hear about you being in an accident? Dot just told me as she departed Sunday for Mexico. Let me know how you are.

Eulah [Pharr] is here for a visit—our house guest.

"Street Scene" has me beat down. Rehearsals start the 14th.

Yours,

Lang

FROM MATT, NOVEMBER 1, 1946

[Handwritten]

Berkeley, Calif.

Nov. 1, 1946

Dear Lang

I was very glad to hear from you. Only yesterday I had been talking about you with Rose Segure, whom I think you know, and told her that I was going to write to you today (and that's not jive). More about that later.

Yes boy, I had one of those "all-out" accidents. A head-on collision on the S.F. Bay Bridge. It happened Sept 10 as I was coming home from a meeting. My car was totally wrecked. I received a brain concussion, a nasty cut on the top of my head, several cuts on my face and on my knees. Fortunately there were no internal injuries nor any broken bones, how I escaped the latter I'll never know. All of my injuries have healed satisfactorily and there will not be any major scars visible. The shock was pretty terrific but I am now recovering from it fairly well.

I was in the hospital one week and was confined to bed at home four weeks. I am now up and around but have not returned to work. Regaining my strength is a slow process and I am forced to take it pretty easy. At the present time I am swimming an hour three times a week (YMCA pool) as a part of the rehabilitation process. This has been very helpful and if I continue the present satisfactory progress I hope to be able to return to work in about a week or ten days.

The car (a Cadillac) that hit me was driven by a soldier with a second soldier riding with him. They have admitted falling asleep and losing control of the car. Their car was insured thank the Lord—so I don't expect too much trouble regarding damage settlement. Well I guess that's about the story Lang, with the exception of a footnote in bold letters "I was one lucky dog".

You probably heard that Paul Robeson and Revels Cayton were out here last month speaking for the Negro Congress. I was unable to attend any of the meetings, but all reports indicate that they were very successful. Paul and Revels were over a couple of times and they were both very pleased with the attendance and response to the meetings. The purpose of their tour was to stimulate organization of the Congress in California, and they succeeded in creating interest and activity in that direction.

I plan to do considerable work in the Congress as soon as I get on my feet good. If it is at all possible to do so I am going to devote full time to Congress work in the near future. This will of course depend on how much dough we can raise to maintain a staff and office. We have already opened an office in San Francisco with a part time office girl.

Rose Segure who is the sister of a fellow who worked with you on a song for Mig Williams some years ago is helping on the preliminary organizational work of NNC. She and I were talking about money raising ideas and I mentioned that you might be coming this way some time the early part of next year on a lecture tour. I told her I would write to you to-day to find out what your plans are, if any, for a tour. We discussed the idea of arranging a series of affairs presenting Negro artists in San Francisco and Oakland. In addition to you we thought of Kenneth Spencer, Josh White, Pearl Primus and Lena Horne. If possible we would like to start the series the latter part of December and run it for about six months, one appearance a month. Aside from the money angle I am convinced that there is a real desire, to say nothing of the need, for cultural events by Negroes in this area. We also have a basis for this type of activity which did not exist before the migration.

If you are not planning a lecture tour for next year what are the chances of you making a short trip out here for an appearance for the Congress— for pay of course? You know boy it will be getting pretty cold in New York soon and I know you would enjoy a couple of weeks in the glorious weather of the Bay Area—between fogs of course.

I would like your opinion regarding the possibility of securing the characters I mention for such a series—and any others you might suggest. We can't pay top fees but it would be a good opportunity for a few shivering New York artists to get thawed out in California sunshine. We could throw in plane or train fare and a decent per diem for good measure. Seriously Lang I would like you to consider the idea and let me know what you think of it.

Nebby and Nebby Lou are well. I suppose you know they were in Chicago this summer visiting Louise and Dot. From what Nebby said all of them had a swell time. It was particularly enjoyable for Nebby and Nebby Lou for it was the first time they had seen Mary Lou.

I read the very good piece which Arna [Bontemps] did on you for Ebony.

We are in the final phase of the campaign to pass a State FEPC [Fair Employment Practices Commission].[1] It will be voted on in the Nov. 5 election. Altogether it has been a good campaign, as always there were many more things which could have been done. The opposition has really opened up against the bill. They have dumped $72,600 in the effort to defeat it. The opposition has been confined in the main to Chambers of Commerce, merchants and manufacture asso., Associated Farmers etc. etc.

The campaign for its passage is supported by a very broad and repre-sentative group of organizations and individuals, including the State AFL [American Federation of Labor], League of Women Voters, Catholic and Protestant church groups. Unfortunately for me the final drive for the FEPC started just at the time of the accident and I haven't been able to do a

1. The bill failed to pass in the California State Legislature.

FIGURE 24. Matt and comrades on the picket line at a demonstration demanding jobs for African Americans during the Oakland General Strike, Oakland, California, 1946.

thing in this most important phase of the campaign. From reports I have been able to get from those who are active in the work the bill has a 50–50 chance to pass.

Give my love to Eulah [Pharr], if she is still there.

Please let me hear from you as soon as possible.

Nebby and Nebby Lou send love.

Sincerely yours,
Matt

[Letterhead: Du Sable Lodge 751]

International Workers Order
6200 Cottage Grove Ave.
Chicago 37—Midway 3805

Mr. Langston Hughes
640 St. Nicholas Ave.,
New York, New York.

Dear Lang:

I am sending you with this note our brochure on Du Sable Community Center. Also an invitation to our Founders Luncheon[2] next week which I know you won't be able to attend, but I wanted you to know about it.

We are moving ahead on the campaign for the Center with very hopeful signs. We have gotten support from the unions, the various I.W.O. groups, and Business and Professionals, both Negro and White. If the present development continues and expands we can rightfully say that we are building a real people's Center.

There is one thing that you could do for us now if you will, I would like to have a telegram from you by the time of the Luncheon next week, pledging your support and wishing us success. How about it?

I'm still at home but I have set up shop right here, using the phone, the typewriter and other people's legs to carry on the work.

I should like to know also, when you will be here in January and what free time you have. We would like to organize something around you. I don't think the Center will be opened by then officially so we will not be able to have a big public affair, but we could have a private party aimed at big donors such as we are doing with Paul [Robeson] on November 14 at the Stevens Hotel. What do you say to this?

If Eulah is still in town give her my best regards and the toy [Toy Harper?].

Sincerely,
Louise

---

2. Paul Robeson was the honored guest speaker at the luncheon.

[Telegram, handwritten]

MRS. WILLIAM PATTERSON

2ND FLOOR

5341 SOUTH MARYLAND

CHICAGO, ILLINOIS

EVENING OF JANUARY NINETEENTH IS OK. HAPPY NEW YEAR

LANGSTON

(CHESTERFIELD-311)

FROM MATT, JANUARY 17, 1947

[Handwritten]

January 17, 1947

Dear Lang:

I just read Billy Rose's column commenting on "Street Scene"[3]—
Congratulations! I know you must be very happy that the show turned out to
be a "bust-in-the-nose" as Rose phrased it, particularly after it apparently had
such rough going in Philadelphia. I hope the show continues to be a hit.

I read your own column in the [Chicago] Defender just after the show
went into rehearsal. I understood very well after reading it why I had not
heard from you regarding the possibility of you coming to the Coast for the
Negro Congress.

We all had a very pleasant holiday season. Nebby-Lou is quite a young
lady at 8 years now and was a real joy to us this Christmas. She is taking
piano lessons now and likes it very much.

Conditions are getting tough here as I imagine they are all over the
country. The Congress is getting established again; so far there has been
enthusiastic response from people to the Congress [National Negro
Congress] program. We did a fairly good job on the Oust Bilbo petition
campaign.[4] Paul is going to speak for us when he comes out here in March.

---

3. *Street Scene* was a 1946 American folk opera based on Elmer Rice's award-winning play of
the same name. Langston wrote the lyrics for the opera, and German composer Kurt Weill wrote
the music. The production was successful on Broadway, running from January 9 to May 17, 1947.

4. Matt is referring to a nationwide campaign that was launched to prevent segregationist Mississippi politician Theodore G. Bilbo from taking his second-term seat in the US
Senate in 1947. Bilbo was ousted from the Senate after he made the following inflammatory

FIGURE 25. Louise, Mary Lou, and Pat in Chicago, 1946.

Well Lang I wanted you to know that we were happy about the show, and I wanted you to get this letter before one of the thousand and one things kept me from writing you, so I decided to write <u>to-night</u> and not <u>to-morrow</u>.

As ever,
Matt

FROM LOUISE, FEBRUARY 15, 1947

*[Letterhead: Du Sable Community Center, Inc. / 62 E. 49th Street, /
Chicago 15, Illinois / Irvington 7365]*

February 15, 1947

Mr. Langston Hughes
Atlanta University
Atlanta, Georgia

Dear Mr. Hughes:

First, we should like to apologize for this delay in thanking you for the wonderful contribution you made to Du Sable Community Center by

---

campaign statement: "I call on every red-blooded white man to use any means to keep the niggers away from the polls. If you don't understand what that means, you are just dumb."

giving us an evening of your valuable time on January 19. We are still getting responses from the party in Wilmette where you appeared on our behalf.

Second, we want to thank you for your generous contribution of $25 toward your Foundership of $100.

We wish you much success in your new post at Atlanta University and are confident that the students and faculty will gain a great deal by having you as part of the faculty. We do appreciate and thank you for your generosity.

Cordially yours,

Luther S. Peck
Luther S. Peck
Chairman, Sponsoring Committee

Louise Thompson Patterson
Louise Thompson Patterson
Campaign Director

Rhea Pearce
Co-Director

LTP:mas

FROM PAT, MARCH 4, 1947

[Letterhead: Abraham Lincoln School]

March 4, 1947

Langston Hughes
Atlanta University
Atlanta, Georgia

Dear Lang:

Chicago is very much worked up about a Salute to Paul Robeson affair organized for April 27th. It will be a tribute to his vision, courage and self-sacrifice in coming still more prominently into the fight against the people's enemies.

The affair will be held in the Chicago Civic Opera House under the auspices of the Abraham Lincoln School. They have asked me to see if you could do a poem to Paul which could be used on this occasion.

Lang, I don't know anyone in the country who is better equipped in every way to handle this job. There are several people here ready, willing and able to put it to music. The time seems adequate. You can't say no—and answer soon. These music people have to know. Wire at my expense.

Sincerely,
William L. Patterson
William L. Patterson

Per em
W.L.P.:e
enc.
uopwa #24

FROM PAT, [EARLY MARCH 1947]

[Handwritten]

Langston Hughes
Atlanta Georgia University
Atlanta, Georgia

Dear Lang:

Got your leaflet. You are in a hot area fellow. But you surely have some reserves in that youth. Really it must be a great pleasure to work with them. And you have so much to give them. Of all the fighters on the cultural front I know of none other whose presence on that spot could be more helpful to the young guard now moving into action.

You will inspire them Lang that is for sure and they will inspire you. I wish I could trade places with you for a period.

You know I wrote you at Fisk [University] the other day. We are holding a people's night in tribute to Paul Robeson and I hoped you would have time to do a poem in his honor. The date is April 27th but we have musicians here who would set it to music so we need it early.

Incidently your column in this last [Chicago] Defender is splendid, splendid. Maybe a note of fight back should have been injected but it was fine indeed.

Best of luck to you. Carry on the good work.

As Ever,
Pat

March 13, 1947

Mr. William L. Patterson
Abraham Lincoln School
180 W. Washington Street
Chicago 2, Illinois

Dear Pat:

I was delighted to hear from you and to learn about the Salute to Paul Robeson being held in Chicago in April. As usual, I am up to my neck in activities of one sort or another here on the campus where I teach four days a week, and my week-ends are practically all taken up with out-of-town trips to places like Birmingham, Mobile, and New Orleans for lectures. Students and town people are flooding me with manuscripts to read, and I am continually behind trying to wade through them so it is very difficult for me to promise to take on anything else, especially something that requires several hours of quiet contemplation to achieve.

However, if I can get any inspiration for the kind of song you would need, I will certainly put it down and send it to you, but it is not possible for me to make a definite and iron-clad promise that I will be able to do so. It is even hard for me to get my Chicago Defender column down these days, as these Negroes down here are really keeping me busy.

With all good wishes to you and Lou, as ever.

Sincerely yours,
Langston Hughes
LH:wmb

April 11, 1947

Langston Hughes
Atlanta University
Atlanta, Georgia

Dear Lang:

Excellent column. Its content has to be emphasized and re-emphasized, and broadened and deepened I think.

Broadened by including Eastern European countries, the new democracies which will welcome the Negro professional and specialist to the same degree as will Asia and where the need is historically greater because of the more compelling tasks facing these countries, i.e., strengthening their industries at post haste, preparing for any eventuality.

Deepened by bringing in the Anglo-Saxon psychology which is as peculiar as the German which is as pronouncedly white-supremacy as the German is anti-non-Germanic.

At the same time it seems to me the question must not be put one-sidedly. There is need too to fight here for the positions which now are only available to Negroes elsewhere than the U.S.A.

Keep the good work up.

Sincerely,
Pat
PAT

TO MATT AND NEBBY, MAY 19, 1947

[Postcard]

Atlanta University,
Atlanta, Georgia,

5/19/47

Dear Matt & Nebby,

I've just about worn out that wonderful brief-case you-all gave me for Christmas going back and forth to classes here, but only two more weeks to go so guess I can make it. I go to Miami for the S.N.Y. [Southern Negro Youth] Congress on Memorial Day. Then to Chi after Graduation. And on home to Harlem. I've enjoyed the campus but you can have Ga [Georgia].

Sincerely,
Lang

TO MATT, NOVEMBER 4, 1947

New Orleans, Nov 4,

Hy, Matt—

I'm just back from a month in the West Indies, full of rum and coconut water!

Lang

[Letterhead: Civil Rights Congress]

Aug. 17, 1948

Mr. Langston Hughes
27 East 127th St.
New York, N.Y.

Dear Lang:

I do not know whether you had heard that Louise and the family will again be residents of your fair and unfair city. I am here now as the National Executive Secretary of the Civil Rights Congress, 205 East 42nd Street. I have been here since the latter part of July. Louise will be here for a few weeks after Thursday, the 19th. We are up at 409 [Edgecombe Avenue].

But what I wrote specifically about is a reception being given for me by way of a farewell in Chicago, the 19th of September. They want me to bring you. They will pay the fare. Is it possible?

As ever,
Pat
WILLIAM L. PATTERSON
WLP:jn
uopwa 16–47

[Letterhead: Civil Rights Congress]

Oct. 8, 1948

Mr. Langston Hughes
20 East 127 Street
New York, N.Y.

Dear Langston:

I think this is grounds for action on your part. Perhaps you can make Mr. [William Randolph] Hearst pay you some money.

As ever,
Pat
WILLIAM L. PATTERSON
WLP:jn
uopwa 16–47

[Handwritten]

January 3, 1949

Dear Lang:

Thank you very much for "One-Way Ticket." Nebby, Nebby-Lou and I are all reading and enjoying it very much. Nebby-Lou likes "Madam Alberta K",[5] especially. She remembered them from your recital here last year. I hope "One-Way Ticket" has a large reading and <u>Sale</u> which it most certainly deserves. We do appreciate your always kind consideration in honoring us with your new books.

The cards we receive from you from time-to-time help to keep us informed as to some of your activities. I also read your article on Jamaica which was in Ebony, and found it extremely interesting. Your article which must have warmed the heart of every Jamaican who read it—including the Jamaican Chamber of Commerce or its counterpart—(no offense) and Paul [Robeson]'s recent article in the Guardian[6] on his trip to Jamaica has kindled for me a new interest in that country.

We had a very pleasant—though quiet—holiday. We went to Nebby's sister's for Christmas dinner and to my sister Gladys' for blackeyed peas and ham hocks New Years day. Gladys said that she intended to have the traditional "hogshead" with the blackeyed peas but hogshead was too damn high to be lucky this year.

Christmas is of course, an especially happy time for us because of Nebby-Lou. It sorta focuses the changes that have taken place in her growing process since the last Christmas. She is now ten years old and this has been the first Christmas that she has not wanted a doll. Her first choice this year was a bicycle; her other requests were for things to wear and very particular about styles and colors. We were a little afraid of the bicycle because of the automobile traffic. Nebby-Lou is not the most careful child in the world—so we compromised with [a] radio for her bedroom. She is growing very tall—just a little shorter than her mother—now. Along with her physical growth she also changes considerably in temperament from year to year and at times faster than that. All of which is to be expected but it

5. Madam Alberta K. Johnson was one of Langston's fictitious Harlem characters. She was a high-spirited, independent, and irreverent woman who took on the world on her own terms. She appears in Langston's book of comic poems *One-Way Ticket*, published in 1949, which he sent to Matt and Nebby.

6. The *National Guardian* was an American socialist newspaper that was published from 1948 to 1992.

certainly taxes all the "paternal guidance," persuasion and patience we can muster to keep up with her.

I haven't worked since the end of the election campaign. I think you know I was in the Wallace campaign organization in San Francisco. I was there from the beginning of the petition drive to put the [Progressive] party on the ballot until Nov. 9th. I don't know whether it was a particularly rugged campaign or that I am just getting a bit too old to stand the gaff. But I was pretty well washed out when it was over. I have been resting and going to the doctors trying to get myself in shape again. I am beginning to feel pretty good now and plan to start looking for work in a few days. I am going to try working in a machine shop again if I can get a job doing the sort of work I did when the war first started. It may be a bit heavy for me for a while but I just don't feel like doing any kind of organizational or office work for awhile.

Conditions generally are about the same here as in other parts of the country. Jobs are getting hard to find and everything is high as hell.

We will soon be able to know what 1949 will bring both to America and to other important sections of the rest of the world. The indications at home are not too hopeful for a really happy New Year. But in China, especially the year opens with great prospect for "A New Day".

Are you planning a tour for California this year? If you do let us know a little in advance.

Thanks again Lang and best wishes for 1949. Nebby and Nebby Lou send best regards.

Very Sincerely Yours,
Matt

TO NEBBY LOU, [JANUARY 19, 1949]

[Postcard]

20 East 127th Street, New York 35,
N.Y.

Dear Nebby-Lou,

I am delighted to hear from your daddy that you got a radio for Christmas. Now I can have music in your guest room when I come out to visit! ...... Tell Matt to note above that I have a new address—a big house with a yard for you to play in when you come to New York.

Love to all,
Langston

FROM LOUISE, [MARCH 1949]

[Letterhead: Council on African Affairs / 23 West 26 Street / New York 10, N. Y.;
handwritten]

Dear Lang—

Well here I am—Mary Lou, baggage et al. back in the Big Town. Have been thinking of you and wanting to get in touch with you. But it's been quite a problem, getting settled in a new place, altho it is temporary, getting Mary Lou in school, and getting adjusted once more to the tempo of New York.

And I am already at work here at the Council [on African Affairs].⁷ Had hoped to loaf for a while but that's hard to do these Days, if not impossible.

We are living at 474 Central Park West but have no phone, which has added to my difficulties.

So if you are in town won't you call me at the Council at [the] above number. Or drop a note with your phone number so I can call you.

Have read about the coming production of "Troubled Island"⁸ and was thrilled.

Love from us all,
Louise

TO LOUISE, MARCH 24, 1949

March 24, 1949

Dear Lou:

Shortly after I got to Chicago I went by your house only to learn that you had moved to New York, but the man who answered the door did not know your address. So I was delighted to find your note here and if I did not have to fly right back to Chicago, I would see you. But I will be back next week for the opening of TROUBLED ISLAND on March 31, providing the flying weather is good that day.

---

7. Louise was the office manager and secretary for the Council on African Affairs (CAA) for several years. The CAA was founded in 1937 to provide support in United States for anti-colonial struggles in Africa. Both Paul Robeson and W. E. B. Du Bois served as officers in the organization. Under the weight of anti-Communist attacks during the Red Scare of the 1940s and '50s, the CAA closed in 1955.

8. *Troubled Island* was an opera with music by William Grant Still and a libretto by Langston. It opened at the New York City Opera on March 31, 1949, and ran for one month.

As you probably know, I have just taken up my duties as "poet in residence" at the Laboratory School of the University of Chicago, but a few little difficulties came up (as usual in relation to show business) concerning TROUBLED ISLAND, so I had to hie myself over here. That show is costing me more in travel expenses than I will make in ten years—since it is an OPERA. But it looks pretty good in rehearsal, and being based on man's eternal fight for freedom it might help the cause a little bit—particularly since it has some very high notes in it.

My best to Pat.

Sincerely yours,
Langston Hughes
LH:HHS

[Note in top margin] *For Nebby and Matt— Same was sent For Pat and Lou— Lang*

[Langston sent clippings of the poems "Low to High" and "High to Low" to both couples.]⁹

LOW TO HIGH
Langston Hughes

How can you forget me?
But you do!
You said you was gonna take me
Up with you—
Now you've got your Cadillac,
You done forgot that you are black.
How can you forget me
When I'm you?

But you do.

How can you forget me,
Fellow, say?
How can you low-rate me
This way?
You treat me like you damn well please,
Ignore me—though I pay your fees.
How can you forget me?

But you do.

9. "Low to High," *Midwest Journal* 1, no. 2 (summer 1949), 25; "High to Low," *Midwest Journal* 1, no. 2 (summer 1949), 26.

HIGH TO LOW
  Langston Hughes

God knows
We have our troubles, too—
One trouble is you:
You talk too loud,
cuss too loud,
look too black,
don't get anywhere,
and sometimes it seems
you don't even care.
The way you send your kids to school
stockings down,
(not Ethical Culture)
the way you shout out loud in church,
(not St. Phillips)
and the way you lounge on doorsteps
just as if you were down South,
(not at 409)
the way you clown—
the way, in other words,
you let me down—
me, trying to uphold the race
and you—
well, you can see,
we have our problems,
too, with you.

TO LOUISE, [1949]

[*Handwritten*]

Hy!

   Guess who I just saw up at Hamilton College—drove over from Rome
to see me—Mildred Jones! almost fat now—but looks fine.

                                                              Lang

[Letterhead: Civil Rights Congress]

Sept. 12, 1949.

Langston Hughes,
20 E. 127th St.,
New York, N. Y.

Dear Lang:

It was good to see you and to talk with you yesterday, even though there were only a few moments, and what with Henry Moon raising all of that political chatter, much time was wasted.

I believe, however, that Daniels is a very sympathetic person and I was glad to hear that he had not seen George Padmore when he was in England, for Padmore and Moon were cut from the same cloth.

I was very happy also to meet Mr. [Emerson Harper] and Mrs. Toy [Harper].

I cannot find a copy of the letter I sent you. However, it dealt with a suggestion that you do a column on Walter White's calcimining business. I don't think anyone could do a better job than you.

Enclosed is a copy of a release we put out on it, but as compared to your writing it is stiff. Am also enclosing a copy of two pamphlets and an editorial on the Civil Rights Congress which was printed in the Compass.[10]

I am hoping that on some occasion you will be able to bring the Civil Rights Congress and its work into your column.

As ever,
Pat
WM. L. PATTERSON.
WLP/ss.
uopwa/16–17

Keep up the good work
W.L.P.

10. The *Compass* was a New York City leftist newspaper.

November 28, 1949

PUBLICITY RELEASE:
OPERA DERIVED FROM POEM

ON JANUARY 18TH AT THE BRANDER MATTHEWS THEATRE, COLUMBIA UNIVERSITY, THE COLUMBIA THEATRE ASSOCIATES ARE PRESENTING THE WORLD PREMIERE OF "THE BARRIER", A NEW AMERICAN OPERA, LIBRETTO BY LANGSTON HUGHES, SCORE BY JAN MEYEROWITZ, WITH MURIEL RAHN IN THE LEADING ROLE. THE GERM IDEA OF THIS MUSICAL TRAGEDY OF MISCEGENATION DERIVES FROM THE POEM, "CROSS" BY LANGSTON HUGHES IN THE KNOPF BOOK, "THE WEARY BLUES":

> MY OLD MAN'S A WHITE OLD MAN
> AND MY OLD MOTHER'S BLACK......

THE TWELVE LINES OF THIS POEM DEVELOPED INTO THE PLAY, "MULATTO", WHICH RAN FOR A YEAR ON BROADWAY, INTO THE SHORT STORY, "FATHER AND SON" IN THE BOOK, "THE WAYS OF WHITE FOLKS", (KNOPF), AND NOW INTO THE LYRICAL LIBRETTO OF "THE BARRIER", THREE QUITE DIFFERENT VARIATIONS OF A POETIC THEME. THE MUSICAL VERSION, A FULL EVENING'S ENTERTAININMENT, IS IN TWO ACTS WITH A PROLOGUE.

[Note in top margin] *How's everything on the Western Front? Rugged out this way!... Still working hard—this show; another under way; new book scheduled for March, SIMPLE SPEAKS HIS MIND; and a song in a forthcoming revue, DANCE ME A SONG...... Do you still have the paper?..... Pat, Lou and the kid were by recently..... Regards to Nebby.*

Lang

FROM LOUISE, [1949]

[Western Union telegram]

DEAR LANG. AS SOON AS YOU REACH TOWN WILL YOU PLEASE CALL ME AT MURRAYHILL 3–6209. VERY URGENT.

LOUISE T PATTERSON

PART III

The Fearsome 1950s and the Promising 1960s

Depending on where one stood, the decade of the 1950s was an era of promise, prosperity, and expanding democracy or one of war, repression, and impending doom. Many Americans experienced both realities. Post-World War II demobilization, the Cold War intensified America's domestic conflicts and entanglements abroad. America's newly established national security regime declared the world its battlefield, and this new fight even extended to the US domestic sphere, where a wide range of political, cultural, and sexual activities were deemed subversive and became subject to criminal prosecution. Postwar peace turned into domestic turmoil, as anti-Communist witch-hunts and demands for conformity in the name of "Americanism" divided the nation, generated fear, and undermined democracy. The US Department of State, the military, labor unions, think tanks, and corporate interests were also seeking to Americanize the world against Soviet and Chinese Communism, the nationalism of the member countries of the Non-Aligned Movement,[1] and other influences thought to be inhospitable to American interests.

In 1950 the Truman administration approved the development of the new hydrogen bomb, a nuclear weapon more powerful than the bombs the United States dropped on Japan in 1945. Within two years, the United States claimed a nuclear arsenal of some thousand bombs, the largest of which possessed twenty-five times the explosive force that had wiped out the city of Nagasaki. The administration developed a policy to justify such terrifying destructive

---

1. The Non-Aligned Movement consisted of newly formed states that had been liberated from their former colonial rulers. They did not formally ally themselves with any power bloc, but the US government believed they leaned toward supporting the Soviet Union.

force. A then-secret report known simply as NSC-68, produced in 1950, stated that the United States now saw the Soviet Union as a threat to Western civilization and an enemy of the United States. In light of this, it proposed shoring up Western Europe's defenses, identified Asia as a critical theater where Communism needed to be contained, and called for a substantial increase in spending on military and economic assistance programs, covert operations, psychological warfare, and a massive buildup of nuclear and conventional arms.

The Cold War wasn't so cold—at least not in the Third World. The Soviet Union and the United States often fought their battles through proxy wars in developing nations, with the United States backing coups or insurgencies against socialist-oriented regimes or propping up undemocratic governments to fight Communism. Iran, Guatemala, Korea, Vietnam, Guyana, Malaysia, Algeria, Cuba, the Congo, and South Africa were just a few of the "hot spots" where this fighting was taking place. The Non-Aligned Movement was conceived as an alternative for countries that wanted to stay independent of American/European and Soviet power, but this proved to be incredibly difficult, if not impossible. In West Africa, for example, most of the former French colonies that had newly become independent countries in the 1950s opted to remain in France's sphere of political and economic influence. A notable exception was Guinea, where President Sekou Touré said *non* to his French counterpart de Gaulle and instead allied his country with the Soviet Union and socialist countries of Eastern Europe.[2]

On the domestic front, the 1950s opened with the advent of television, which contributed to unifying and homogenizing US cultural identity into a mythical image. The space race took off. Dr. Jonas Salk invented the polio vaccine. The construction of federally subsidized interstate highways mushroomed, along with the car and oil industries, enabling suburbanization and bringing about urban decline. Black music began to reach well beyond Black communities and national boundaries. A new upsurge in the Black struggle for civil rights took off, emboldened by African decolonization and Third World liberation movements. At the same time, the vice grip of the Second Red Scare tightened, producing the longest and severest period of political repression in US history outside of the dismantling of Reconstruction. The trial and execution of Ethel and Julius Rosenberg and the case of Alger Hiss

2. See Vijay Prashad's excellent book, *The Darker Nations: A People's History of the Third World* (New York: New Press, 2007).

were among the most dramatic examples of the anti-Communist frenzy, which led to a climate of fear among liberals and leftists—both Black and white. Joe McCarthy's congressional witch-hunts were nationally televised, creating a hysteria-saturated atmosphere of "a Red under every bed." Friends spied on and denounced friends, marriages were torn asunder, people committed suicide, jobs were lost, and children were harassed. A cloud of paranoia hovered over the country. This anti-Red campaign had a special focus on Black radicals: Communists and anti-Communists alike. Our parents and Langston were not spared.

The force of Cold War anti-Communism and the ongoing quest for full civil rights during the 1950s compelled some prominent African Americans to close ranks with US nationalism and distance themselves from Africa and the struggles of colonized people. Some genuinely believed in the American empire's democratizing project, while others acted out of fear of repression. Journalist Roi Ottley, NAACP leader Walter White, Congressman Adam Clayton Powell, and many others praised the material abundance and liberties African-Americans presumably enjoyed. Although they acknowledged persistent racism, these Black men nonetheless proclaimed America a beacon of freedom against the tyranny of Communism. When Congressman Powell attended the historic meeting of non-aligned nations in Bandung, Indonesia, he defended his country against allegations that the persistence of segregation rendered the United States a hypocritical freedom fighter, at best. "Second class citizenship is on the way out," Powell told his critics. "To be a Negro is no longer a stigma."[3] A year later, when Martinican poet, politician, and critic Aimé Césaire characterized racism in the United States as an extension of colonialism in a speech he gave before the Congress of Black Writers and Artists in Paris, several Black Americans in attendance protested. Political scientist John A. Davis, founder of the American Society for African Culture, rejected the analogy, insisting that America itself has a long and distinguished *anti*-colonial history. Even James Baldwin, a sharp critic of US policy, dismissed the colonial analogy, arguing that there was something exceptional about being an American Negro that was a result of living in a "free" country.[4]

3. Richard Iton, *In Search of the Black Fantastic: Politics and Popular Culture in the Post-Civil Rights Era* (New York: Oxford University Press, 2008). Also see Ingrid Monson, *Freedom Sounds: Civil Rights Call Out to Jazz and Africa* (Oxford: Oxford University Press, 2007), 145.

4. Iton, *Black Fantastic*, 50.

Our parents, along with Paul and Eslanda Robeson, Alphaeus and Dorothy Hunton, W. E. B. Du Bois and Shirley Graham, and other Black Leftists who circulated in their orbit, refused to defend US policy or distance themselves from Africans who were struggling against their colonial rulers.[5] Louise, for example, worked directly with Paul Robeson and W. E. B. Du Bois, serving as secretary for the Council on African Affairs.[6] Pat fearlessly continued his work directing the Civil Rights Congress (CRC).[7] In 1950 Pat was subpoenaed by and appeared before the House Select Committee on Lobbying Activities, led by acting chair Henderson Lovelace Lanham of Georgia. Pat provoked Lanham into a verbal sparring match, during which a furious Lanham called him a "Black son-of-a-bitch" as he charged around the Committee table towards Pat, breaking past the hold of two attendants. A pair of Capitol police finally stopped Lanham before he was able to reach Pat. In the end, Pat, not Lanham, was indicted for contempt of Congress.[8]

Pat was not deterred. A year later, he and Paul Robeson presented to the United Nations a CRC document entitled "We Charge Genocide: The Crime of Government Against the Negro People." It chronicled the work the organization was doing to fight lynching and the violations of Blacks' civil

5. Lisa Brock, "The 1950s: Africa Solidarity Rising," in *No Easy Victories: African Liberation and American Activists over a Half Century, 1950–2000*, ed. William Minter, Gail Hovey, and Charles Cobb Jr. (Trenton, NJ: Africa World Press, 2007), 59–62; Brenda Gayle Plummer, *Rising Wind: Black Americans and U.S. Foreign Affairs, 1935–1960* (Chapel Hill: University of North Carolina Press, 1996); Penny M. Von Eschen, *Race Against Empire: Black Americans and Anticolonialism, 1937–1957* (Ithaca: Cornell University Press, 1997); Hollis R. Lynch, *Black American Radicals and the Liberation of Africa: The Council of African Affairs, 1937–1955* (Ithaca: Africana Studies and Research Center, Cornell University, 1978); Carol Anderson, *Eyes Off the Prize: The United Nations and the African-American Struggle for Human Rights, 1944–1955* (Cambridge: Cambridge University Press, 2003); David H. Anthony, *Max Yergan: Race Man, Internationalist, Cold Warrior* (New York: New York University Press, 2006).

6. The Council on African Affairs was a progressive international organization dedicated to supporting African decolonization and ending foreign economic exploitation of the continent's resources. It disbanded in 1955, a casualty of Cold War repression.

7. The CRC took on many famous civil rights cases, such as those of Rosa Lee Ingram (a Black woman given a death sentence for her alleged involvement in the murder of her white neighbor), Willie McGee (a Black man from Mississippi who was sentenced to death for allegedly raping a white woman), and the Trenton Six and the Martinsville Seven (Black men accused of murder and rape, respectively). They also campaigned on behalf of Smith Act defendants.

8. Gerald Horne, *Black Revolutionary: William Patterson and the Globalization of the African American Freedom Struggle* (Urbana: University of Illinois Press, 2013); William L. Patterson, *The Man Who Cried Genocide* (New York: International Publishers, 1971).

rights and liberties. The report cited, among other things, the continuation of racist terror in the South, segregation, unemployment, poverty, police violence, and disfranchisement. Pat went to Paris to present the petition to the UN Secretariat, while Robeson presented it to the UN Human Rights Commission in New York. Not surprisingly, American UN representatives used their influence to block the Human Rights Commission from even discussing it.[9] The two men paid an enormous price for their audacity. Upon leaving Paris, Pat was detained for hours at the London airport and then strip-searched at New York's Idylwild Airport, where his passport was confiscated. Their actions also resulted in loud denunciations at home by the likes of the anti-Communist columnist Walter Winchell. Concert halls across the country canceled Robeson's performances—denying him his livelihood, and Pat and his family endured constant harassment. Robeson, W. E. B. Du Bois, and others also had their passports revoked during the 1950s.

These were difficult times, to be sure. Nebby and Matt were suddenly faced with the prospect of taking in Mary Lou if Louise and Pat were imprisoned. Nebby Lou was thirteen at the time; Mary Lou was only eight. Pat successfully dodged the contempt charge, but in 1954 the IRS went after the CRC and Pat. When he refused to cooperate he was sent to jail for three months for contempt of court. The CRC was forced to close down for good in 1956, so Pat went to work at the *Daily Worker* for several years before retiring. But he continued to maintain vital contacts within the Civil Rights Movement, especially with members of the Black Panthers.

9. This was not the first such petition submitted to the United Nations. In 1946, as soon as the UN established its Commission on Human Rights, the National Negro Congress presented a petition on behalf of the entire Black world, seeking "relief from oppression." It emphasized issues like poverty, schooling, housing conditions, high Black mortality rates, and segregation, and it compared the conditions of African Americans to that of colonized populations elsewhere in the world. Less than a year later, the NAACP submitted its own petition to the UN. W. E. B. Du Bois was central to this effort. The petition, titled "An Appeal to the World: A Statement on the Denial of Human Rights to Minorities in the Case of Citizens of Negro Descent in the United States of America and an Appeal to the United States for Redress," was submitted on behalf of 14 million Black people and was endorsed by Black organizations and leaders from around the world. The 155-page document was a detailed list of grievances against the US government. For more information, see Azza Salama Layton, *International Politics and Civil Rights Policies in the United States, 1941–1960* (Cambridge: Cambridge University Press, 2000), 48–58; and Patterson, *The Man Who Cried Genocide.*

FIGURE 26. Louise, Matt, and Nebby in Berkeley, California,
1951.

The beginning of the 1950s found Louise as the breadwinner for her family.
She was still working at the International Workers Order (IWO), where she
had begun as a secretary in the 1930s, but was now one of the organization's vice
presidents. In 1951 she was called upon to testify in a criminal trial against the
IWO, which had been charged by the New York State Insurance Department
of engaging in prohibited political activity. The IWO had been on the US
Attorney General's "subversives" list since 1947. She refused to testify, choosing
instead to take the Fifth Amendment. The IWO was ultimately forced into
dissolution. After that, Louise had various "regular" jobs, like working as a
secretary at a UN associated housing corporation, while she simultaneously
continued to volunteer her time to the progressive movement, serving, for
example, as secretary for the Council on African Affairs and the CRC.

FIGURE 27. Paul Robeson (left), Louise, Mary Lou, and family friends welcome Pat home at Idyllwild Airport (later renamed John F. Kennedy Airport) on his return from Paris, where he had presented the Civil Rights Congress's "We Charge Genocide" petition to the United Nations, 1951. US Immigration agents had just strip-searched Pat and confiscated his passport.

Louise and Pat had also taken in a very consequential houseguest, the actor, writer, and poet Beulah Richardson, whose stage name was Beah Richards, a recent transplant from Los Angeles. One night, in the fall of 1951, Louise and Beulah drafted a call, ultimately signed by fourteen Black women, launching a women's auxiliary of the CRC called The Sojourners for Truth and Justice. The Sojourners attracted most of the leading radical Black women intellectuals and activists, including Charlotta Bass, Dorothy Hunton, Shirley Graham Du Bois, Alice Childress, and Rosalie McGee. Dedicated to fighting racism, sexism, and imperialism, the Sojourners demonstrated

FIGURE 28. Pat speaking at his sixtieth birthday celebration in New York, 1951.

against apartheid at the South African consulate in New York and petitioned the US President, Congress, and Departments of State and Justice to redress the civil rights abuses committed against African Americans, especially those against W. E. B. Du Bois, Pat, Paul Robeson, and Alphaeus Hunton, who were all under indictment. They organized a demonstration in Washington, DC, to protest the imminent jailing of W. E. B. Du Bois, and it attracted 132 Black women from fifteen states. Forming small groups, they went to Congress, attempted to see the president, and entered the Pentagon to protest the war in Korea and the Pentagon's alleged distribution abroad of wind-up dolls with bucked eyes and big red lips that caricaturized Black men.

In 1952, however, within its first year, this extremely creative and courageous Black women's organization was forced to disband, a victim of the Red Scare. Afterward, Louise quietly ceased being an active member of the Communist Party and spent much of the next decade employing her extensive organizing and secretarial skills to help her family make ends meet. She assisted Herbert Aptheker, the eminent Communist historian, in founding the American Institute of Marxist Studies. She was then secretary to one of the officers of the National Health Care Workers' Union and finally ended her working life in her eighties at the Harlem Restoration Project, a thrift shop on 125th Street founded by activist Marie Runyon as a project to assist ex-offenders in reentering the job market.

In 1953 J. Edgar Hoover took a special interest in Nebby and her employment as an administrator at the US Civil Service Commission in San Francisco. She was called in to sign a loyalty oath and was aggressively questioned about Matt's political activities. She was ultimately forced out of her job (and most of her retirement benefits) after having worked for the federal government her entire adult life. Although she did not go to college as a young woman, she always showed a great intellectual curiosity and was an avid reader of fiction, history, and politics. Finally freed from her daily commute across the bay, she went to school and earned an associate degree at Oakland City College. Matt held several positions at the Consumers Cooperative of Berkeley, and he eventually became a manager at the Berkeley Cooperative Federal Credit Union. He stayed active in various local political and civil rights campaigns, although he eventually moved away from the Communist Party. He was a highly sought-after adviser to aspiring community leaders like Ron Dellums and also mentored several young black activists who went on to enter electoral politics in Berkeley, Oakland, Sacramento, and Washington, DC.

Langston entered the 1950s still struggling to make a living from writing—calling himself, at one point, a "literary sharecropper"—and still enduring attacks by McCarthy and his acolytes. In 1950 "Red Channels: The Report of Communist Influence in Radio and Television," published by the American Business Consultants, devoted four pages to him. Meanwhile he worked incessantly just to make ends meet. He finally left his publisher Knopf for Holt, which put out his book-length poem suite *Montage of a Dream Deferred* in 1951, to a lukewarm reception. A year later, Langston followed *Montage* with a collection of short stories, *Laughing to Keep from Crying*. Again, the critics were not impressed, calling the book "uneven." Then, in 1952, Ralph Ellison published *Invisible Man*, which overshadowed *Laughing* and became the first book by a Negro writer to win the National Book Award in 1953.

In March 1953 Langston was subpoenaed by the Senate Permanent Subcommittee on Investigations of the Committee on Government

Operations, popularly known as the McCarthy Committee. Strapped for cash, Langston had to borrow the money to travel to Washington. The appearance turned out to be one of the most humiliating experiences in his life because, for all intents and purposes, he felt pressured to comply with the committee. However, he found subtle ways to be defiant. In 1956 he published his second autobiography, *I Wonder as I Wander,* which put an unapologetic, positive spin on the radical era of the 1930s. He also maintained his friendships with our parents and other Communists, despite the fact that many party members were forced underground and the consequences of having ties with them were real and severe.

Nevertheless, the Red Scare did not keep Langston from writing and publishing books, librettos, poetry, and plays. His speaking engagements fell off some but he was still doing a lot of travelling to Black colleges in the South. By the end of the 1950s and into the 1960s he was traveling and in great demand again, which at this point permanently changed his financial situation. By 1966 he was made an official US delegate to the First World Festival of Negro Arts in Dakar, Senegal. He was constantly being solicited by young African writers for help—which he generously gave, just as he had long been doing with African American writers. He continued to receive numerous honors and awards.

Although Langston, Pat, Louise, Matt, and Nebby all continued to support the Black Freedom Movement in their own ways during the 1960s, mainly as mentors and advisors, it was clear that they were no longer in the eye of the storm. Pat continued to fight quite publicly on behalf of the Communist Party and for the rights of Black people under the law, but the party was a shell of its former self. Besides, the center of political gravity shifted South during the 1950s and early 1960s, and the new leaders were local people, including the veteran Alabama activist Rosa Parks, the former share-cropper Fannie Lou Hamer, the Southern Black students who launched the Greensboro sit ins in North Carolina in 1960, and the dedicated organizers who took on the state of Mississippi with the Freedom Summer campaign of 1960, a massive voter registration drive.

The correspondence between the five friends is infrequent during this decade, but what survives shows the continuation of a much-treasured and deep friendship.

EIGHT

McCarthyism at Home, Independence Movements Abroad

JULY 1950—DECEMBER 1959

In 1950 Nebby Lou was twelve years old and Mary Lou was seven. Our families saw less of Langston during the early 1950s, but he continued to send us books, and we would respond with thank you notes. The surviving correspondence between the five friends is sparse up to the middle of the decade. Some letters were undoubtedly lost, but we suspect the lapse was mostly due to the anti-Communist hysteria of the period.

No correspondence from 1951 has survived, and probably very little was written. Not only were all letters between the five being read by the FBI at that point, but Louise and Pat were under government assault, so it was a busy and tense year for the friends.

In April 1951, Louise was called to testify in the trial of the International Workers Order (IWO) before the Supreme Court of New York State. The IWO had been charged with engaging in political activity, which was illegal for an insurance company. Around the same time, Pat was tried and ultimately found innocent of the contempt of Congress charge that had been leveled against him a year earlier. But the US Justice Department ordered a second trial for June, although an intervention of seventeen African Methodist Episcopal Zion Church ministers fortunately compelled the government to postpone it to 1952. It was a frightening time, and our parents made a great effort to create normalcy for us. That summer, Louise and Mary Lou went to Berkeley to stay with Matt, Nebby, and Nebby Lou. Their house was Louise's safe harbor. She needed to be with those she was closest to, and she also wanted to make sure they would take care of Mary Lou if the need arose.

In September 1956, Noel Sullivan, Langston's benefactor and true friend, died, leaving him $2,000. Although they did not discuss this in their correspondence, the Crawfords and Pattersons knew how this event saddened Langston.

FROM NEBBY, JULY 24, [1950]

[Handwritten]

Dear Lang:

Thank you for sending us "Simple Speaks His Mind." It is nice having an old friend around the house.

I am enclosing two reviews—one from yesterday's [San Francisco] Chronicle the other from May 15, from P.W. [*People's World*]. Needless to say Pele Edices is not colored otherwise she surely couldn't have defended the attitude of Negro men toward women.

Matt is fine—Nebby Lou is away for two weeks at a Girl Scout Camp in the Sierras. It is very lonesome and quiet without her.

Nebby

FROM MARY LOU AND LOUISE, NOVEMBER 3, 1952

[Handwritten]

Nov 3, 1952

Dear Uncle Langston,

How are you? I want to thank you for the book.[1] I am enjoying it very much.

Love,
MaryLou Patterson

Hy Lang:

My daughter is quite terse but each word carries a lot of weight. Thanks so much for including us. Would like to see you—how about calling and coming up[2] to dinner.

Lou

---

1. This was probably Langston's *The First Book of Negroes* (1952), a children's book about Black culture. Incidentally, W. E. B. Du Bois and Paul Robeson were omitted from the book, presumably because it was the height of the Red Scare at the time, and Du Bois and Robeson were publicly accused of associating with the Left progressive movement, which was under fierce attack.

2. The Pattersons were living at 409 Edgecombe Avenue in Harlem at this time. The apartment building was perched on a hill overlooking the Polo Grounds stadium complex. The area was dubbed "Sugar Hill" in reference to the "sweet" life that the middle-class Blacks who lived there had. Working-class and poor Blacks lived mostly in the blighted neighborhoods of central Harlem.

A second trial date was set for Pat in January 1952. In March 1952 he was acquitted. On January 27 three thousand people gathered at Harlem's Rockland Palace to honor Pat for presenting the Genocide Petition to the United Nations. February 1, 1952, was Langston's fiftieth birthday. Later that year, Louise, standing in for Pat, addressed the crowd at the Right to Speak for Peace and Memorial for Willie McGee, a large CRC rally.[3] Langston appeared publicly before the Senate Committee on Permanent Investigations, headed by Senator Joseph McCarthy, on March 23. A few days later he sent the following note and press release to Matt and Nebby.

TO MATT AND NEBBY, [MARCH 26, 1953]

"SIMPLE SPEAKS HIS MIND"[4] BEFORE THE MCCARTHY COMMITTEE

In the open televised hearing of the Senate Committee on Permanent Investigations before Senator McCarthy in Washington on Thursday, March 26, 1953, where Langston Hughes appeared, Mr. Hughes was asked a question concerning the chapter, "When A Man Sees Red" in his book *SIMPLE SPEAKS HIS MIND,* as to the meaning of the chapter, the time when it was written, and if he thought that book should be in the libraries of the State Department's Information Service overseas. Before answering, Mr. Hughes was given an opportunity to reread the chapter while the Committee waited.

Mr. Hughes replied that he felt that since large portions of the book were written in Harlem slang and Negro idioms which foreigners often found difficult to translate or to understand, the book itself might not be understood clearly abroad. But from the standpoint of showing the free exercise in America of one of the basic rights of which we all are proud, namely the right of a citizen or writer to freely criticize any branch of our government or any elected official, he felt the chapter indicated that this basic right was observed in America, and therefore indicated our freedom of press and expression which we have always cherished and in which we all believe.

As to the chapter itself, he stated that it expressed a viewpoint which the character in the book, Simple, shared at the time it was written with a great many other citizens of Harlem who were shocked at an incident that occurred in the House Un-American committee when a member of that committee called a Negro witness a name which cannot be repeated on the air, but which in Harlem is called, "playing the dozens"—that is, talking

3. Black Mississippi prisoner Willie McGee was executed by electric chair in Laurel, Mississippi, on May 8, 1951.
4. This is a play on words. The article refers to Langston by using one of the titles of his Simple stories.

badly about one's mother. This chapter records the shock and horror that such an incident should occur in a committee of our government. But, in this chapter, as throughout the book, the "I" character usually presents an opposite viewpoint from the character, Simple, so varying viewpoints are brought into the volume.

In both the executive closed hearing and in the open hearing of the Committee, Mr. Hughes stated unequivocally under oath that he has never been, and is not now, a member of the Communist Party. The Committee concerned itself almost entirely with certain of Mr. Hughes' early poems of 15 to 20 years ago, most of which are no longer in print and in none of his books, having appeared mostly in magazines or pamphlets of that time. Recent works were offered to show that in recent years Mr. Hughes' writings have expressed no leftist tendencies. Mr. Hughes was thanked by both McCarthy and [John] McClellan for his openness and forthrightness and Senator McClellan suggested that Hughes' earlier works in overseas libraries be replaced by later works.

[Note in margin of mimeographed press release] *Dear Matt and Nebby—In case you all missed this on radio or TV—Only name mentioned in hearing was Paul [Robeson]'s. Movie[5] only once in passing, 90% concerned with my early poems.*

Lang

Despite sharing this news with his friends, Langston was less than candid with them about what had gone on behind the scenes at the hearing. He neglected to tell Matt and Nebby that, prior to the public hearing, he attended an executive session, where he met with subcommittee staff members Roy Cohn and G. David Schine and also with McCarthy himself. He negotiated a deal whereby the committee would allow him to read a prepared statement if he repudiated some of his more radical earlier works and his former Soviet sympathies. He agreed and kept his part of the bargain, only to be betrayed in the public hearing when he was subjected to grueling questioning by McCarthy, John McClellan, and their staff. At the end he was verbally bludgeoned into a final humiliation by being pressed to say that he hadn't been mistreated by the staff or the committee members. After the ordeal, he immediately returned to New York and soon thereafter left the East Coast for a three-month stay at his bucolic retreat at Hollow Hills Farm in the Carmel Valley in California.

5. This is a reference to the unmade film *Black and White,* which Langston, Louise, and Matt traveled to the Soviet Union to be a part of in 1932.

FIGURE 29. Langston faces Senator Joseph McCarthy's US Senate Permanent Subcommittee on Investigations in Washington, DC, 1953. (Copyright Associated Press.)

TO PAT AND LOUISE, JULY 10, 1953

For Pat and Lou—

DEPARTURE

SHE LIVED OUT A DECENT SPAN OF YEARS
AND WENT TO DEATH AS SHOULD A QUEEN,
REGAL IN HER BRAVERY, HIDING FEARS
THAT WERE MORE GENEROUS THAN MEAN—
    YET EVEN THESE,
    FOR FEAR HER LOVED ONES WEEP,
    SHE CARRIED WITH HER
    IN HER HEART TO SLEEP.

Langston

Knowing Thyra [Edwards], ever thoughtful of others, and thinking maybe how she went away, this poem was written.

New York, July 10, 1953.

[Handwritten]

April 24, 1954

Dear Langston,

Just a belated note of thanks for sending me your wonderful book.[6] I can't tell you how much I enjoyed it.

Even though Daddy has had me reading about these people since I was very small, I learned quite a bit.

I was especially interested in Harriet Tubman, whom I knew very little about.

Thanks again,
With Love,
Nebby Lou

For a few years beginning in 1951, Matt was in San Francisco working with the CRC on Wesley Robert Wells's case. Pat was on a tour of the country for the CRC, and he stopped in the Bay Area to meet with Wells for several hours at the San Quentin State Prison, where he was serving his sentence. While he was in town, Pat stayed at the Crawford's home in Berkeley.

The CRC, which had faced persecution since its inception in 1947, continued to be pursued by the government. In the early 1950s the organization was scrutinized by the New York State Legislature's Committee to Investigate Charitable Agencies and Philanthropic Organizations. In April 1954 a grand jury subpoenaed Pat to appear the following month and turn over the CRC's account books. He testified on May 27, 1954, that he was unable to produce the financial records because he did not know their whereabouts. He was found in contempt of Congress and jailed from July 1 to September 30, 1954, at Danbury State Prison in Connecticut. While Pat was incarcerated, a hearing was pending before the federal Subversive Activities Control Board in Washington, DC, to require the CRC to be listed as a Communist front organization. Upon his release, on October 28, Pat was subpoenaed again by a grand jury to give the names of members and supporters of the CRC and its

6. Langston's *Famous American Negroes* (1954).

financial records. He testified in November, and this time he outright refused to produce the CRC books. He was found in contempt of Congress once again and jailed for ninety days.

During the 1950s Pat continued to be involved in the Communist Party, although Louise and Matt quietly eased away from it. Nebby, although sympathetic to the movement, had never been a party member. Although the correspondence between the five friends picked up again in the mid-1950s, when McCarthy is repudiated and the liberation of many African nations begins, it never reached the level it had been at in the 1930s and '40s.

FROM MARY LOU, [FEBRUARY 7, 1955]

Dear Langston,

Thank you very much for the wonderful book about Jazz.[7] I read it + I think it is marvelous. Please send me any other books you might have or written on music. I would be interested in seeing them. My father + mother are both find and they send there love to you, along with me. Please excuse me for not writting sooner, about the book, but the secret is I hate to write letters, and love to receive them. But you can't receive unless you write. Thanks and awful lot.

Sincerely,
Marylouise Patterson

TO MATT AND NEBBY, MARCH 9, 1955

[Letterhead: 20 East 127th Street / New York 35, N. Y.]

March 9, 1955

Dear Matt and Nebby:

Lest you think that I am deceased I send you this line to let you know that it is not true at all. Just a hardworking writer still trying to make a living out of the written word (cullud) and if you realize what that is— without having a best-seller, then you know what I mean. Have also been making records for Folkways lately—JAZZ, RHYTHMS[8] (based on my kids' books) and THE STORY OF NEGRO HISTORY, all LPs just

7. Langston's *The First Book of Jazz* (1955).
8. *The Story of Jazz* (1954) and *Rhythms of the World* (1955), which were both performed by Langston.

recently out. (JAZZ got 5 stars in "Downbeat"—only one so well rated this month). Just about finished a play from "Simple" too. And read about 200 African short stories by writers of color (can't get away from the race) that I've collected from all over English-speaking Africa for an anthology I'm making. (Also got a lot of other things including groundnuts, books, and paintings as gifts from Sierra Leone to Cape Town—and some fascinating letters. If you think we got Jim Crow, you ought to read how they behave in South Africa. Peter Abrahams'[9] TELL FREEDOM gives a good picture, read it, but letters from down there are even better. And some of the short stories are wonderful! I think it will be a FINE book—and the first of its kind in the U.S. of African non-white fiction. They don't use the word Negro so I can't either.) . . . . . Well, anyhow, so it goes. And my place is nothing but a workhouse. And can't make a dime in spite of making time—almost. Have an April 1st deadline on a book I haven't started yet, but expect I'll make it. Only people of the other expression (as the Divinites[10] say for white folks) can spend a year writing a book. Cullud better do 'em in less time—or else. And I refuse to else! . . . . . C-ooo-ld here so I wish I was there. But on the whole it's been a fairly mild winter. New York is as full of culture as ever, but I have been too busy and too broke to partake of much of it. However, I did make Marian Anderson's debut at the Met[11] as a guest of Cornelia Otis Skinner (see picture in current OUR WORLD[12]). The boxes were bursting with cullud guests that night. The Diamond Horseshoe glowed with liberalism and race pride. I'm telling you, it were something. And Marian stirred her witch's pot with vigor, made up like a pretty gypsy, casting spells right and left. (Lord have mercy! Did I say LEFT?). . . . . It's daylight AM. I been working all night so Goodnight! . . . . .

Sincerely
Lang

9. Abrahams was a Kleuring, or "Coloured," South African writer.

10. The Divinites were followers of the African American religious leader Father Divine.

11. Langston is referring to Marian Anderson's historic performance at the New York Metropolitan Opera in January 1955. The concert, in which she sang the part of Ulrica in Giuseppe Verdi's *Un ballo in maschera,* marked the first time an African American singer had performed at the venue. She was fifty-eight years old at the time.

12. *Our World* was a popular magazine about Black life. It was published in New York between 1946 and 1957 by John P. Davis, an attorney who had formerly served as head of the National Negro Congress.

LANGSTON HUGHES
20 EAST 127TH STREET
NEW YORK 35, N. Y.

March 9, 1955

Dear Matt and Nebby: Lest you think that I am deceased
I send you this line to let you know
that it is not true at all. Just a hardworking writer still
trying to make a living out of the written word (cullud) and
if you realize what that is---without having a best-seller,
then you know what I mean. Have also been making records
for Folkways lately---JAZZ, RHYTHMS (based on my kids' books)
and THE STORY OF NEGRO HISTORY, all LPs just recently out.
(JAZZ got 5 stars in "Downbeat"----only one so well rated
this month). Just about finished a play from "Simple" too.
And read about 200 African short stories by writers of color
(can't get away from the race) that I've collected from all
over English-speaking Africa for an anthology I'm making.
(Also got a lot of other things including groundnuts, books,
and paintings as gifts from Sierra Leone to Cape Town---and
some fascinating letters. If you think we got Jim Crow,
you ought to read how they behave in South Africa. Peter
Abrahams' TELL FREEDOM gives a good picture, read it, but
letters from down there are even better. And some of the
short stories are wonderful! I think it will be a FINE
book---and the first of its kind in the U.S. of African
non-white fiction. They don't use the word Negro so I can't
either.)....Well, anyhow, so it goes. And my place is
nothing but a workhouse. And can't make a dime in spite of
making time---almost. Have an April 1st deadline on a book
I haven't started yet, but expect I'll make it. Only people
of the other expression (as the Divinites say for white folks)
can spend a year writing a book. Cullud better do 'em in
less time--or else. And I refuse to else!.....C-o-o-o-ld here
so I wish I was there. But on the whole it's been a fairly
mild winter. New York is as full of culture as ever, but I
have been too busy and too broke to partake of much of it.
However, I did make Marian Anderson's debut at the Met as
a guest of Cornelia Otis Skinner (see picture in current
OUR WORLD). The boxes were bursting with cullud guests that
night. The Diamond Horseshoe glowed with liberalism and
race pride. I'm telling you, it were something. And Marian
stirred her witche's pot with vigor, made up like a pretty
gypsy, casting spells right and left. (Lord have mercy!
Did I say LEFT?).....It's daylight AM. I been working all nigh
so Goodnight!.......Sincerely,   Lang

JAN 30 1955

Take a Blue Note . . .
THE FIRST BOOK OF JAZZ. By
Langston Hughes. Pictures by Cliff
Roberts. Music selected by David
Martin. 66 pp. New York: Frank-
lin Watts. $1.95.

For Ages 12 to 16.

JAZZ, Langston Hughes says
firmly, is fun. Unlike many
of its devotees, he doesn't regard it as a peculiarly esoteric
art; instead he writes with a
refreshing lack of pomposity
and with a clarity which will
delight those who might be,
reasonably enough, confused at
the differences between cool and
hot, swing and bebop. His
analysis of the components and
various styles of jazz is adroitly
threaded into a colorful historical outline. He shows how certain elements from the spirituals, the blues and the weary

From a decoration by Cliff Roberts for "The First Book of Jazz."

field hollers of the slaves were
mingled with merrier elements
of the jubilees, street songs,
minstrel songs and eventually
evolved into distinctively American art. Homage is paid to the
influences and achievements of
the great figures of jazz—especially to Louis Armstrong, whose
career, says Mr. Hughes, "is
almost the whole story of
orchestral jazz in America."
There are two lists of records—
one illustrating the historical
stages of jazz and one containing 100 of the author's own
favorites.   E. L. B.

FIGURE 30. A letter from Langston to Matt and Nebby in which he describes himself as "just a hard working writer trying to make a living out of the written word (cullud)," 1955. (Matt N. and Evelyn Graves Crawford papers, Special Collections & Archives, Robert W. Woodruff Library, Emory University. Copyright © 2015 by The Estate of Langston Hughes, Arnold Rampersad and Ramona Bass Kolobe Co-Administrators. By permission of Harold Ober Associates Incorporated.)

On January 12, 1956, Pat appeared before the US Court of Appeals for the Second Circuit on the second contempt charge. This time he was defended by attorney Milton Friedman. On January 27, 1956, he was acquitted of all charges. The Patterson family moved shortly afterward to a large duplex apartment in Brooklyn, New York. Pat's sister-in-law, Belle Fountain, and family friend Beah Richards also moved into their new home.

FROM NEBBY, JULY 2, 1956

[Handwritten]

July 2, 1956

Dear Lang:

Thank you so much for sending me the Apollo record.[13] I love it and we are getting a big kick out of it. It takes me way—way back into my memories of 1929.

I would have written sooner but there has been the excitement connected with Nebby Lou's graduation from high school. That has passed and the next step is to make a decision about college—never a dull moment.

We are expecting Mary Lou[14] July 4th and possibly Louise later in the summer.

The NAACP just completed their annual convention in S.F. There were lots of important people around. How come you didn't come?

We heard Rev. Martin Luther King speak and he was the highlight of the convention.

Hope you will be coming this way again soon. Love from the three of us.

Nebby

TO MATT AND NEBBY, [JANUARY 6, 1956]

Dear Matt & Nebby:

I've ordered sent you-all directly from the publishers a copy of I WONDER AS I WANDER[15] due out soon—so <u>somebody</u> drop me a line

13. Langston had sent Nebby a recording of some of the performances at the famed Amateur Night at the Apollo, a weekly song contest held at the Apollo Theater in Harlem.

14. Mary Lou and her childhood friend Nora North traveled together to California in the summer of 1956.

15. Published in 1956, *I Wonder as I Wander* is Langston's second autobiography, and it deals with his life in the 1930s. His earlier autobiography, *The Big Sea*, published in 1940, chronicles his experiences up through the 1920s.

and tell me what you think of it—the movie tale and all, PLEASE, before year after next! I'll sign it for you next time I pass your way..... At the moment I'm behind several simultaneous 8-balls—including a book due yesterday that I <u>haven't even</u> started, so on the phone today I told the MAN I'd have it by the 15th—so have to write it in a week. But fortunately, it's a teenager on FAMOUS NEGRO HEROES, so maybe I can do it. That's why this is hastily, but

Sincerely yours,
Lang

Had to cut about 20 chapters out of the WONDER book, down from 780 pages to 400 plus,—and even then it's so big it costs $6,00!! so I can't buy nary one. (<u>But yours.</u>)

FROM NEBBY, DECEMBER 3, 1956

[Handwritten]

Dec. 3, 1956

Dear Lang:

In case you don't have clipping service I thought you might be interested in [the] enclosed review. William Hogan succeeded Joseph Henry Jackson[16] who died some time ago. I like Hogan much better. We had ordered the Pictorial[17] before the review and are looking forward to reading it and also your Wonder book. I'll try to light a fire under Matt to write you his opinion of the Wonder book especially of the experience you shared.

Thanks for remembering us.

Sincerely,
Nebby

---

16. William Hogan and Joseph Henry Jackson were book review columnists for the *San Francisco Chronicle.*

17. Nebby is referring to Langston's book *The Pictorial History of the Negro in America,* published in 1956.

FROM NEBBY, DECEMBER 16, 1956

[Handwritten]

Dec. 16, 1956

Dear Lang:

I like your book.[18] Reading it is like sitting and listening to you tell tales—in fact some of the stories I know I heard word for word between chuckles at our own kitchen table. The message comes through clearly and pleasantly without the use of a sledge hammer. I'm glad there is more to come.

Matt is still reading "I Wonder" and Nebby Lou plans to read it during the Christmas holidays.

I am glad you decided long ago to write for a living but I wonder how you have lived to do it!

Sincerely,
Nebby

FROM MATT, FEBRUARY 24, 1957

Sunday Feb. 24, 1957

Dear Langston:

At long last I am writing to you, after many months of promising myself, "I must write to Lang". I also wanted to wait until I had read "I Wonder as I Wander" before I wrote to you. First, however, I want to thank you for sending the book to us. As usual you are very generous and thoughtful about sending us your books and articles, poems, etc. Although we do not always respond to your generosity we do greatly appreciate receiving your work and prize it highly.

Nebby and I both enjoyed the book very much. Nebby Lou is now reading it and is also getting a great deal of pleasure from it. It is our unanimous opinion that I Wonder as I Wander is one of the smoothest jobs of writing that you have done. Nebby Lou said, "It's beautiful writing". For me the book brought back many memories of incidents of the trip. There was many hardy chuckles as you related the "goings-on" of the "comrades" as they traveled about the USSR. At other times it was hard to believe that so many people could have been so naive about the success of such a venture in the first place. Then I asked myself, "did I or anyone else in the group

---

18. *I Wonder as I Wander.*

give serious thought to whether the whole project was practical or not?"
The answer of course is No. And I agree with your statement of the reasons
why the people in the group undertook the trip. To the extent that I can
reconstruct details of occurrences 25 years ago I was impressed by your
accuracy in describing the development of events in and around the group
during the months of our stay in the Soviet Union. I was also impressed
and in general agreement with your interpretation of the specific factors
relating to the film and the general situation in the USSR at that time.
I think you accomplish anonymity of the members of the group with
finesse, and I am sure that any other treatment presented both practical
and technical problems which could not be resolved at the present time.
I do think that the section dealing with the group and the film misses
some of the vitality and dramatics that the group reflected. Maybe at
another time when consideration of the welfare of others does not demand
such restrictions on the statement of simple facts, you can tell a more
complete story of the many interesting episodes involving individuals in
the group.

Again, I want to say how much we all enjoyed "I Wonder as I Wander"
and will welcome the time when the third volume of your autobiography
appears.

We are all well now. Nebby was in bed with a very severe case of bronchi-
tis a couple of weeks ago, but is completely recovered now. Nebby Lou is
recovering from an operation on her knee. She went skiing during the
winter vacation from college and injured her knee—split a cartilage in the
knee joint. She has been out of school now for about ten days but will
return to school tomorrow, and in a few days will be able to walk without
crutches. She is going to Oakland Junior College and will most likely
enter University of California next semester. She is now 18 years old and
quite a young lady. I am still working at the COOP [Consumers
Cooperative of Berkeley][19] store here. The work is pretty hard but I like
it, and as long as my health holds up I suppose I'll remain there. The
business has grown tremendously in the last few years so that unless there
is a very serious slump in business I'll be able to stay as long as I want
to do so.

The Bay Area continues to expand both in population and in industrial
development. Many new communities have been established on both sides
of the Bay. Thousands of new homes have been built in the Walnut Creek

19. Matt worked for many years at the Berkeley Co-op, and he later took a job in the
Co-op Credit Union, which was originally set up to serve the employees and members of
the store.

area, which is just over the hills east of Berkeley, all down toward San Jose, Milpitas, where Ford Motors built a new plant about three years ago. On the San Francisco side, all down the peninsular San Mateo, Palo Alto, etc. tracts of homes have sprung up. With the growth there has of course been an even greater percentage increase in the Negro population in the general area. And the brothern [bretheren] is making progress here too. We are still a considerable distance from the promised land but we are marching. Some headway has been made in employment in a number of industries where Negroes were barred a few years ago. You would be particularly impressed with the number of Negro toll collectors on the Bay Bridge, at times it looks like whites are discriminated against there. Capwells and some of the other big stores down town now employ a few Negro sales women. At the same time the struggle continues to get FEP [Fair Employment Practices] legislation enacted both in the cities and on [the] state level. The impact of the magnificent developments in the South[20] is present here too. The South is now the yard stick by which is measured the vigor, the determination and the scope of the action taken by Negroes to advance the fight for first class citizenship. The lament and pity for the folks in the South has been replaced by pride, admiration and a kind of looking to the people in the South for leadership in the big struggles ahead.

I suppose you have been interested [in the] international and the national developments of the last year. It is pretty clear that old established ideas, concepts and methods are undergoing change. I am not sure where it all will finally end up, but I am convinced that every day reality will be the starting point for thinking and [an] approach to problems much more than was the case in the past.

I hope you will find some reason to come to California and the Bay Area again soon. It would be very nice to see you and talk with you. So if you can work up a lecture tour in the near future be sure to put Oakland on the schedule.

Received a letter from Louise since I started this letter. She said she saw you at the Negro History Week affair and that she enjoyed it very much.

Nebby and Nebby Lou send love.

Very Sincerely Yours
Matt

20. The yearlong Montgomery Bus Boycott began on December 4, 1955, and it was just one of many new civil rights actions that were occurring throughout the South.

TO NEBBY, [APRIL 23, 1957]

[Postcard]

Worcester

Still flying hither and yon—Spring lectures. But now have only 2 more, after which Ah retires!

Lang

TO LOUISE, MAY 14, 1957

May 14, 1957

Dear Louise:

You know how Aunt Toy [Harper] is about wanting to get to shows well ahead of time! So, since it is an early ["Simply Heavenly"] Opening Night curtain, 8 P.M., I'd suggest that if you are going with Toy and Emerson [Harper], you be at the house about 7. Or else meet her at the theatre. But you can phone her and let her know.

Sincerely,
[Lang]

[Note in top margin] *It will be nice to see you*

TO MATT, MAY 17, 1957

[Postcard from Washington, DC]

Almost everybody was here today for the Prayer Pilgrimage[21]—Mahalia [Jackson], Adam [Clayton Powell Jr.], and Rev. [Martin Luther] King were real fine!

Lang

TO MATT, [AFTER MAY 22, 1957]

[Enclosed: a review by John McClain of Langston's play Simply Heavenly, May 22, 1957.]

[Note in margin] *Well, sir! You never can tell! Lang*

---

21. The Prayer Pilgrimage for Freedom was a demonstration held on May 17, 1957, to commemorate the third anniversary of the landmark *Brown v. Board of Education* school integration Supreme Court decision. An estimated thirty thousand people attended.

FROM LOUISE, JUNE 2, 1957

[Letterhead: Louise Thompson Patterson; handwritten]

6/2/57

Dear Lang—

Your special came this morning as we were in the midst of reading [Brooks] Atkinson in the Times. So it was especially welcome.

Pat, Mary Lou and I will be very happy to accept your invitation for next Tuesday.[22] Thanks and hope we will see you there, too, June 4.

No—I didn't get to Washington but Pat and Beulah [Beah Richards][23] brought back vivid reports.

Since I want to get this right off to you—I'll be signing off.

Love to Toy [Harper],
As ever,
Lou

FROM PAT, JUNE 7, 1957

[Letterhead: WILLIAM L. PATTERSON / Room 810 / 11 Park Place • New York 7 / BArclay 7–5952]

June 7, 1957

Mr. Langston Hughes
20 East 127 Street
New York, New York

Dear Langston:

Louise, Mary-Lou and I saw "Simply Heavenly"[24] Tuesday night. Thanks for the tickets, and may I here and now very belatedly thank you for sending us "I Wonder As I Wander" and several other books. "I Wonder As I Wander" was excellent. Personally, I regard it as the best of the many fine things you have done. It seemed to me that in it you were more appreciative of the impact of social forces upon people than ever before and that the naturalistic approach, that I feel often characterizes your treatment of the reaction of an individual to his or her environment, was absent. The result

---

22. Langston had invited Louise and Pat to a showing of his new play, *Simply Heavenly*.
23. Beah Richards was living with Louise and Pat at this time.
24. Langston's play *Simply Heavenly* originally opened on May 21, 1957, at the 85th Street Playhouse in New York. On August 20 it opened on Broadway at the Playhouse Theatre for a run of sixty-two performances.

was, I saw several individuals in larger dimensions. I saw them in the midst of social conflicts in which they were caught up or which at least were making a marked impact upon their lives.

It is difficult to define my reaction to "Simply Heavenly." I cannot say that I liked it. I am not a theatrical critic. But in a formal sense it did not appeal to me. It seemed loose and not up to your standard of theatrical production. However, I was never a stickler for form if in content a piece of art said something worthwhile. Simply Heavenly does not say what so greatly needs to be said at this moment, Lang, at least not to me. I am not a prude. Some episodes of the animal impulses of a person may be amusing, some valuable educationally, but some may be posed so as to reflect discredit on a people. Then they do not prove that people's affinity to humanity, but rather the opposite. That is the way in which the portrayal of animal appetites which almost dominates Simply Heavenly struck me. It dehumanized the characters. Clearly they did not appear to embody in themselves the qualities of real people.

The characters ate, danced, prepared for the gratification of sexual desires as though these things constituted their range of thought and action. No idea emerges to reveal that the terrible trials of a woman with seventeen kids will force her to find some outlet for "free" expression.

That there are "Simply Heavenly" people no one can deny. But should they not be shown as warped and distorted and some idea be given of the source of their deterioration? Or, are they normal? If they are, what are their counter-parts, abnormal? They neither moved me to sympathy or revulsion. How tremendously complex is the life of a Simple? Your Simple oversimplified it with all the maudlin pathos he sought to inject into it.

Your use of the jazz medium to carry the dialogue along helped it to flow and gave it rhythm. That I feel was fine.

To me, Lang, the play was political. But the politics suited my enemy's— Simple's enemy's—aims and purposes in describing the Negro. The men who derive billions from our misery seek to find a justification for subjecting us to an environment that warps and destroys us to their great profit. Simply Heavenly certainly provides them some justification. This is not the time to aid Simple's enemies, when his friends in Montgomery, Ghana and elsewhere are fighting too desperately to effect fundamental changes. Someone may argue: "Is there no time, no place for laughter?" I heard much laughter there and in the main from Negroes, to whom the subtleties that escaped a white person were clear. The answer is, there is a place for laughter. But the question is, how do you invoke healthy laughter at such an hour as this. I don't think that you do it through an exposure of the frailties of a Simple and his friends.

The social life of the Negro people now runs the gamut of social life in the U.S.A. The people on your stage revealed no real desire for change. They were in the right milieu. But today the emphasis is upon change, fundamental change. The Negro people may make the life Simple endured, but I would today show them reacting differently to what they had been forced to make. Now maybe that would not sell. I don't know; I think perhaps it would.

When Simple tried to show the pressures on him he does it too narrowly and Joyce lacks such human qualities as would have enabled her to help him or he her. So Simple is the product of inner forces, mysterious forces, peculiar to Negroes. He is the eternally recurring primitive Negro, so childishly simple and so simply childish. He is the poor black burden his civilized white brother must carry through life.

The time and place calls, I believe, for something else. Perhaps it ought to approach Dr. W. E. B. Du Bois, who on the same Tuesday night proved something in terms of the role today of the Negro people in America. The Negro can today play a more dominant moral role in American life.

Thanks again. One must do more than dip one's fingers into progressive life. Simple won't help Montgomery. Not everything can be geared to help Montgomery! some say. Perhaps not, but Langston Hughes can help. He has done much to help all of us. His splendid contribution to the National Assembly of Authors and Dramatists was just such a helpful event.[25] Carry on and the best of things for you.

Sincerely,
Pat
William L. Patterson
WLP/b

TO PAT, JUNE 8, 1957

June 8, 1957

Dear Pat,

I'm certainly sorry I wasn't at the theatre the night you-all came, as I would have loved to say hello to you.

Your long letter is greatly appreciated, and your views valid in a number of ways, I am sure. But it's the old story—and the old problem I've been wrestling with for years—how to get everything to suit everybody into one

25. Langston gave a speech to the National Assembly of Authors and Dramatists at the Alvin Theatre in New York on May 7, 1957, entitled "The Writer's Position in America."

piece. When it comes to plays, it is a miracle to end up with anything at all one wishes left in the play—after 20 or 30 other people have had a hand in the creation—from producers and director to actors. The problems with this particular show were legion—so to have left FLYING SAUCERS and MISSISSIPPI is at least something!

Several folks have expressed your viewpoint (with variations) re race, while others as you've no doubt read and heard, take the opposite viewpoint—like Roosevelt Ward. Re sex therein, some feel as you do, others term it a "family show" and come to see it again, bringing the kids. SO? Quien sabe?

If, as you think, it is a lulling show, maybe there is some virtue in lulling with one hand, while lopping with the other.

Semantics!

Hey, now! Anyhow, there's plenty left out of this version of SIMPLE that I wish were in. But in books one has 300 pages to work with, in a play only 80. In publishing, only one editor to contend with (and mine almost never suggest changes). But in the theatre everybody pulls and hauls at a script. So all I can say is, I did the best I could under the circumstances. Next time might be luckier, maybe come out better. Let's hope so!

That it gets your serious consideration, and you write me so helpful a letter, is at least something to be grateful for!

Best ever, and hope to see you and the family soon as work pressures let up—that show threw me back weeks on other deadlines. Besides being the most frustrating, theatre is also about the most time-taking of the arts! Wonder will I ever catch up!

Sincerely,
[Langston]

FROM LOUISE, [AUGUST 19, 1957]

[Postcard from North Truro, Massachusett; handwritten]

Hy Lang—

We're up here till after Labor Day and love it.

You should come up for a good rest after your opening[26] which I hear will be very successful.

Louise

26. Louise is referring to the August 20, 1957, Broadway opening of *Simply Heavenly* at the Playhouse Theatre.

FIGURE 31. Langston and Nebby Lou in Berkeley, 1958.

FROM NEBBY, AUGUST 17, 1958

[Postcard from Mexico D.F.; handwritten]

8/17/58

Hi Lang:

We finally got here and are having a fine time. Such a beautiful land and so many beautiful people! We saw our first bull fight today. My last.

Nebby

FROM NEBBY LOU, AUGUST 19, 1958

[Handwritten]

19 August

Berkeley

Dear Langston–

It's 10:00 PM & I am sitting in a big 'ole gold chair in the living room of the big 'ole Berkeley house reading poetry—your poetry. I bought The Langston Hughes Reader[27] for my mother on her birthday and haven't

27. *The Langston Hughes Reader: The Selected Writings of Langston Hughes* was published in 1958.

been able to keep my hands off of it since. For some strange reason I felt that I must tell you how good I feel just sitting in this big 'ole chair all alone in my big 'ole house, reading what is yours & mine. My parents are in Mexico and I have been spending time digging out old photos etc. from long before I was anything more than a few genes on a few chromosomes. I ran across some snaps from your trip to the USSR and your radiant smile and comical poses made me chuckle with an envious kind of laugh that children have when they see their parents' generation with the same happy, youthful expressions that they (the offspring) sometimes wear.

You must think it strange to hear from me as you only knew me as a child & then not well. Your poetry was always fun to read when I was a youngster, but then I was only amused and not sad or happy when I saw those words.

Now, a 20 yr old woman, your bitter-sweet words make my eyes & mind want to laugh & cry at once! I can't decide which is best, so I end up doing both. I cry because I know that if I live 500 yrs I could never say so much with so few words. But then again it's a comfort to know that someone can say those things that I have trouble verbalizing. I once told my mother, after reading about Emmet Till[28] that I couldn't express to her how I really felt about this murder. All of the intellectualizing on earth about race relations couldn't say it. She said that <u>you'd</u> be able to say it & you did, thank God, in <u>Simple Stakes a Claim</u>. We read the book together, the 3 of us—Mama & Daddy laughing about the past & remembering things that happened before I was born when you were running between N.Y. & Mexico—hungry, young & curious.

The "Reader" is wonderful & I will read it again & again, yes & again until those sweet & sour lines are printed in the deepest fissure of my brain.

I have been in an adventurous mood during this summer so void of adventure & so in between counselling at a day camp and auditing an Anthro course on Africa on campus, I have been reading about adventure—yours & others. I am in the midst of Lincoln Steffen's autobiography—a most edifying tome—and wish so often that I could just take a year or two off from being a college student to run off to any one of 1,000 places to see & learn. My most practical of fathers looks at me often with a sceptic's eye & says "you've got plenty of time for seeing." But there's such an urgency and insatiable energy about being 20 & <u>curious</u>, that I think he has forgotten—or at least says so. My mother just smiles with her sparkling eyes

---

28. Emmett Louis Till (1941–1956) was a fourteen-year-old Chicago youth whose brutal murder by two white men in Money, Mississippi, sparked outrage and an upsurge in the civil rights movement.

& looks at me knowingly for she understands my feelings—the same ones she must have had, and the same that never materialized.

We have spoken of you often of late & wish we'd been able to see you when you were on the West Coast this Spring. Trips East are rare, but there is a <u>slight</u> possibility that I will be in NY for a couple weeks in early Sept. If so, I hope you will be around to share a bit of conversation. The reason for my coming (really an excuse) is to participate in a coordinating meeting for the next World Youth Festival to be held in Vienna next summer. The trip hinges entirely on funds, or the lack of said, but I am going to do my best to get there.

I will bore you no longer & close. Thank you for the "Reader"; I look forward to more & more of your beautiful words being published.

Warmest regards,
Nebby Lou

TO MATT AND NEBBY, DECEMBER 22, 1958

First Draft

Dec. 22, 1958

SAYS WHICH?

Wait!
Oh, just wait!
Wait a little while—
And we'll have our world.

Don't need to spell it out:
The spelling's in the stars.
Don't need to make it plain:
It's a space missile
<u>Way out yonder</u> / In space
Right now,
And it knows where it's going.

What am I talking about?
I hate to tell you,
But if you don't know

Your mammy's in the dozens,
And you yourself
Are nowhere.

Dear Matt and Nebby—

Thanks for that picture which was here when I got back home to New York Harlem last night, and when it fell out of the envelope, *[^late night A.M.]* out came this poem, which really ought to be dedicated to your beautiful child. Where did you-all get so lovely an off-spring? It is only fitting and proper that she should inherit the new world—so just wait a little old long-short while. *(Longer)*
Happy Holidays to you-all!

P.S. I hear tell they done attacked me real good in the January "American Mercury"[29] but I haven't seen it yet. . . . . Just wait a minute!

In 1959 Louise and Langston were working together once again on a project dear to Langston's heart: support for African independence. Langston wanted to show his and other Black artists' solidarity with the continent. Ghana was about to celebrate its second independence anniversary, and a group of Black artists and writers wanted to send the country gifts from the African American diaspora. A founding meeting was held in January 1959 of what was to become the Afro-American Committee for Gifts of Art and Literature to Ghana. In a letter to Louise, Langston reports his progress in convincing fellow writers to donate books and manuscripts to the project.

TO LOUISE, [OCTOBER 14, 1959]

Dear Lou:

All of my Ghana letters went out this weekend. And the first response, complying, has just come in today from William Stanley Braithwaite who offers three books and his manuscript poem about Booker T. Washington written long ago . . . If you see W.E.B. or Shirley [Graham Du Bois], you might prod them along a little bit, or just get the things from them, and save them mailing. This is what I will do with some of the Harlem writers

---

29. *The American Mercury* was a literary magazine started in 1924 by H.L. Mencken and George Jean Nathan. It was initially a platform for serious literary work, but after World War II it turned into a right-wing publication.

I know and see . . . . I am off for lectures in Trinidad the first week in October—if they send the ticket! Best to the family,

Sincerely,

[Langston]

FROM LOUISE, [DECEMBER 1959]

[Note handwritten on an invitation to the holiday cabaret of the Freedom Guild.]

Dear Lang,

This will be awaiting your return from Trinidad—Hope you had a good trip. I enjoyed PuddinHead[30]– Hope you can attend our party.

Love,

Lou

30. *Pudd'nhead Wilson* is a novel by Mark Twain, originally published in 1894. Langston wrote the introduction to a new paperback edition of the book that was published in 1959.

Civil Rights, Black Arts, and the People's Poet

FEBRUARY 1960–AUGUST 1966

By 1960 the worst of the McCarthy period was over, and the Civil Rights Movement was gearing up. Pat was entering his seventies. Louise, Nebby, Matt, and Langston were in their sixties. Nebby had been forced into retirement at that point, but the four others were still working.

Louise was helping Herbert Aptheker establish the American Institute for Marxist Studies in New York City. Matt was working at the Consumers Cooperative of Berkeley and would later take a position at the Berkeley Cooperative Federal Credit Union. Pat was editing the Communist Party newspaper, *The Daily World*. Langston, no longer a pariah in the eyes of the government, was touring for the US Department of State, attending conferences and cultural festivals, writing, and helping young writers. In February 1960 his play *Shakespeare in Harlem* was produced on the Broadway stage.

FROM NEBBY LOU, FEBRUARY 24, 1960

February 24, 1960

Berkeley

Dear Langston,

Glancing over my typewriter I see the pink section of the San Francisco Chronicle, and on page 5 of last Sunday's edition under the heading of Drama is a most literary pose of L.H. I am referring to [Brooks] Atkinson's enthusiastic and most complimentary review of Shakespeare in Harlem. I am sure you have seen it as it is a reprint from the Times. Felt kinda good all over, as some friends of mine might say, but a bit chagrined by the fact that the 41st Street Theatre is 3,000 miles away. I hope that this will make up for your disappointing experience with "Simple Heavenly". Hope it stays around long enough for me to see it, as there is a possibility that I might be establishing myself in New York for a while sometime this year.

'Tis the above possibility which prompted this note. I will elaborate. I have applied to Columbia Graduate School in the School of Social Work for the Fall semester of this year. In thinking of people who might be willing to comment briefly on my "moral character" etc. I was at a loss for some weeks, as what character I have is probably questionable to many important-type folk whose names might be helpful on a list of references. I finally asked 3 professors of mine to fill out the form which Columbia sends out about its applicants' qualifications, but needed one non-academic reference. In an optimistic moment I put your name down. Swear, scream, call me assuming . . . . the deed is done and you will soon receive a short form from the school. Either you're trapped or I am; anyway, I'd appreciate it if you might find a moment in your busy schedule to put down a word or two in my favor.

The whole thing hinges on whether or not the school will give me a fellowship, so I'd like to keep it a secret from my parents until I find out about the financial possibilities, as I don't want to put them in the position of feeling obligated to offer to finance another year of school for me. If I don't receive a grant I will stay out of school for a year and work until I've saved enough to put myself through the Masters program. If you happen to see Louise, please don't mention this to her as she has a tendency to feel obligated to relate such gems of wisdom to my mother at the slightest provocation. All is as usual here with us. . . . fleeting thought: why not bring "Shakespeare" to the Coast. . . . probable reply from L.H.: Ah, you dreamers. Anyhow, one always has a tinge of hope.

Fondest regards,
Nebby Lou

[Note in left margin] *P.S. I have a different address for the semester, as I'm living near campus—in case you want to scold me for my request. (smile) 2532 Regent Street Berkeley*

Nebby Lou did indeed end up going to New York, and she earned a master's degree from Columbia University's School of Social Work in 1962. She stayed with Louise and Pat in Brooklyn at various times but mostly lived in Brooklyn Heights. She befriended Beulah Richardson and Ms. Belle Fountain. She was introduced to W. E. B. Du Bois, James and Esther Jackson, Henry Winston, and other Black Communist radicals.

In the summer of 1960 Mary Lou traveled with her mother to Europe to meet up with Pat, who had departed earlier. Louise didn't know that Pat had been sent to China by the CPSUA and only learned of his whereabouts once she arrived in Paris. After staying in Paris for some time they left for the Soviet Union, but upon their arrival at the airport there they were met by several limousines from the Chinese embassy. After a few days in Moscow they went to China, where they were finally reunited with Pat. By late August, Louise and Mary Lou were back in Moscow. Mary Lou remained in the city to attend the Peoples' Friendship University[1] while Louise and Pat visited other socialist countries on their way home.

FROM LOUISE, JULY 6, 1960

[Postcard from Paris airport; handwritten]

Orly Field—July 6

Hi Lang, Toy and Emerson—

We've had a grand time here thanks to Ollie H. [Oliver Wendell Harrington] and his friends. We went to see Joe [Josephine] Baker's show last nite. As always she is terrific.

Now we are off to Prague and new adventures. Paris has been quite cool—a pleasant relief from muggy N.Y.

Love,
Lou

FROM LOUISE, [SEPTEMBER 7, 1960]

[Postcard from Moscow; handwritten]

Dear Lang—

Here. That back a lot of years—28 in fact—since being here. Had dinner with Lloyd [Patterson]'s family—Vera is a designer + movie artist and vivacious as ever—one son is a poet. Lots of changes here so I recognize very little.

Regards,
Lou

1. Mary Lou graduated from the Peoples' Friendship University in 1968.

FROM LOUISE, [SEPTEMBER 30, 1960]

[Postcard from Tiblisi; handwritten]

Greetings from Georgia!

Interesting to tread paths not seen since 28 years ago. Ran into Harry B. [Blatt] who was here in Tbilisi with his family.

Love to all,
Louise

FROM PAT AND LOUISE, JANUARY 1961

1268 President St.
Brooklyn, New York

January—1961

Dear Friends:

Belated but hearty greetings for the New Year of 1961.

Though tardy, we still wish to greet you by sharing some of the impressions from the trip we were greatly privileged to take to Europe and many socialist countries in 1960. It was an experience that etched deeply into our consciousness the wastefulness and inhumanity of unjust wars and the need to end them forever. It was also a joyful time akin to witnessing springtime when new growth and flowering burst forth from the stubble and bareness of a long hard winter.

Where did we go—to the Soviet Union, Czechoslovakia, Poland, Hungary, Germany, Central Asia. What did we see . . . . . people confidently and at a tempo unknown in the West building a magnificently creative life. The agony, hunger and devastation of war is behind. They have emerged triumphant to make the ideas of peace and plenty a dominant note in world affairs. Building cranes outlined against the sky followed the path of our plane and greeted us where we landed. They symbolize the products of peace—new factories, schools, cultural and sports centers, homes, scientific institutions. A sense of security came to us. Tension was nowhere present. We were among people who do not worry about the present, who are certain of the future. Full employment, education for their children, medical care during sickness and childbirth, provision for their old age are the built-in guarantees of their socialist society.

They are concerned, however, with what the American people are thinking and doing about peace. (We attended the spy trial of the pilot

shot down in an American U-2 plane over Soviet territory.) We accepted
the flowers, warm hospitality and friendship we met everywhere as manifestations of their desire for peace and friendship with the people of our
country. But it takes two sides to make the peace.

The more we saw and heard of the horror that was World War II—the
untold millions of lives lost; the vast devastation; the tremendous setback
to peacetime construction—the more we were able to understand why the
people in all Europe are deeply concerned and seek permanent peace. We
wished that all Americans (who have never had to experience mass bombing, invasion, starvation, concentration camps) could have shared our
experiences. We were in Leningrad where 1,000,000 civilians starved to
death during the 940-day siege of the nazis. In Lidice, the little
Czechoslovakian village which Hitler ordered to be obliterated brick by
brick. We saw Auschwitz, that ghastly concentration camp where
4,000,000 men, women and children from 28 countries died in gas
chambers. In Berlin we stood at the Brandenburg Gate which separates
east and west not only of that famous capital but the very allies who
together defeated Hitler buried deep in the ruins of the Chancellory
nearby.

It is a great temptation to try to tell you more about the people, places
and things we saw during those six months of travel over thousands of
miles. That telling would take a book. (We hope we can relate it later in a
pamphlet, but meanwhile this greeting must get on its way.) All we hope to
convey here is the message the people there and the many visitors we
encountered from Asia, Africa and Latin America might wish all
Americans to hear.

We encountered delegations on goodwill, trade and technical assistance
missions. We saw students from newly independent and still dependent
countries studying to be doctors, engineers, scientists, agronomists that
they may be equipped to help their countries rapidly overcome the backward economic and cultural heritage of colonialism. We watched visiting
sports teams in friendly competition with their hosts and artists widening
cultural understanding. We thrilled to see children of all races being
fortified for the future as they learned to live and play together in the warm
sun and invigorating Black Sea at the international Pioneer camp in Yalta.
We sat with women from 61 countries, many of who had travelled thousands of miles to Warsaw to talk and act for peace and an end to colonial
domination.

All these experiences were object lessons for us in the meaningfulness
and possibilities for peaceful coexistence of all nations and peoples which
many of our government spokesmen attempt to explain away as "soviet

propaganda". But for growing millions in all continents it is a realizable and necessary goal.

So here is our wish for 1961:

Total disarmament to end fears of nuclear world destruction and lay the basis for enduring peace;

Racism and colonialism ended everywhere;

A United Nations with the true representatives of the Congo; the 650,000,000 people of China; all nations of Africa and Asia in their rightful places helping to find peaceful settlements of all differences between nations and peoples.

We have faith that the people of our country can and will come to understand that our future depends on joining this world march to peace and plenty. But all of us, setting aside other differences, have to work together and hard to achieve it.

With all best wishes,
Pat and Louise
William and Louise Patterson*

*Our daughter, who is now among the hundreds of foreign students in Moscow, sends her own cabled greetings to our friends: "This year holds greater promise for peace and freedom. So goodbye 1960, Hello 1961. Happy New Year."

—Mary Lou

[Note at top of first page] *Hi Lang—Saw the children of Lloyd Patterson, who you know I think died in 1942. And now Mary Lou just cabled that one of his 3 sons, Lloyd, Jr. died. Also the 2 daughters of Bob Ross and others. Hope to see you soon. Fondly, Lou*

On January 17, 1961, Patrice Lumumba, the first democratically elected president of the Republic of the Congo, was brutally murdered during a coup that was supported by the United States and Belgium. The murder ignited demonstrations and uprisings all over the world, including in Moscow, where Mary Lou and many others demonstrated in front of the US and Belgian embassies. The students of the Peoples' Friendship University in Moscow were so angered by the murder of Prime Minister Lumumba that they demanded the university be renamed in his honor, which it was.

TO MATT AND NEBBY, [APRIL 13, 1961]

Hy!

LUMUMBA'S GRAVE
  by
  Langston Hughes

Lumumba was black
And he didn't trust
The whores all powdered
With uranium dust.

Lumumba was black
And he didn't believe
The lies they shook
Through their "freedom" sieve.

Lumumba was black.
His heart was red—
They say that's the reason
They killed him dead.

They buried Lumumba
In an unmarked grave,
But he needs no marker:
Air is his grave.
Sun is his grave.
Moon is, stars are,
Space is his grave.
My heart's his grave:
I've marked it there—
    As tomorrow
    Has marked it
    Everywhere.

L.H.

TO LOUISE, JULY 1961

Hy!

   For Louise—Be of good cheer—Langston, July 1961

SIMPLE'S SOLILOQUY FROM "HAMLET"
  by
  Langston Hughes

To be or not to be jim crowed,
That is the question.
Whether 'tis nobles in the flesh to suffer
The bricks and bats of dixiecrats
Or take up arms against a sea of nuisance
And by our sit-ins end them.
In the USA enough! In Mississippi, too!
I say to be or not to be in jail,
That is the question.
Whether 'tis nobler, I ask, to suffer
Jim crow's outrageous fortune,
Or protest against this sea of aggravations
And by protesting end them?
To jail—to sit—no bail:
By picketing to seek an end
To back-aches and unnatural shocks
The south makes Negroes heir to:
To bind them up in knots of civil rights—
'Tis a constipation devoutly to be wished.
To sit—although in jail—Ay, there's the rub!
But locked in jail at night come dreams
When we have thrown off our mortal fear.
Dreams, oh, so great—an end to all
That makes calamity of colored life!
Who would longer bear the whips and scorn
Of our oppressor's wrongs and hatefulness,
Pangs of despised souls, the law's delay,
The impudences of polices and their dogs
Our patience and our meekness had to take?
We can put quietus on it all—yes we can!
Who will jim crow's burden bear these days,
To grunt and sweat under this weary life?

Who would, Like cowards, live a living death—
As if already lost in that dark barn
Where manhood fears to rise and speak its mind?
Who would make us bear those ills we have
Rather than stand up to kluxers who oppose us?
Cane nice white folks make cowards of us Negroes,
And our black hue of resolution whiten
With their pale cast of fear?
Can they our protest water down,
Our sit-ins beg us out of.
To lose the force of action?
Nay! Twice nay! I say:
Dixie, if to be or not to be in jail's
The question—in jail I'll be.
Mississippi will not get the best of me!
To be or not to be—hell!
Hamlet will be free!
And who is Hamlet? Guess who?
Me—Jesse B.—Old Simple <u>Hamlet</u> Me.

From the Chicago Defender

FROM LOUISE, JULY 13, 1961

[Letterhead: Louise Thompson Patterson]

July 13

Dearest Lang:

Thanks a heap for the lovely card and the two very interesting poems. I
know you won't mind that I have sent them to Marylou. She had written
me to send her "Let American be America Again". I am sending her your
and Arna's anthology of Negro poetry [*An Anthology of Negro Poetry for
Young Readers*] which I know she will enjoy and share which includes this
beautiful poem. Lang, you should read her letters. She is doing wonderfully
well at [the Peoples'] Friendship [University] and is very happy. She did very
well the first year, got excellent in all her subjects, and imagine in the
second semester of her first year was already studying science and math in
Russian! She hopes to be in the medical faculty this fall. This summer she is
in Moldavia on a collective farm for July and will spend August in Yalta.

As for me—well, indeed I have been bad luck Lou. On May 27, while
Nebby was here I slipped on a rainy sidewalk on a plastic bag and broke my

ankle in two places. So I am still in a cast and still a prisoner at 1268 [President St. in Brooklyn]. Wish you could come over and if you do have the time, please come.

Read of Harold [Jackman]'s death and the funeral today which of course I couldn't get out to but imagine it was a big one. I've only seen the NY Times so don't know the cause of his death.

How is Toy [Harper]? Better I hope. I tried to reach you while Nebby was here but learned you were in California. Give her and Emerson [Harper] Love from me.

Fondly,
Lou

TO PAT, [SEPTEMBER 28, 1961]

[Birthday card, handwritten]

Hey Pat—

I didn't know you'd had a 70th Birthday until I saw your picture in Political Affairs[2] today. Belated Best Wishes—.

Langston

FROM PAT, SEPTEMBER 28, 1961

September 28, 1961

Langston Hughes
20 East 127 St.
New York, N.Y.

Dear Lang:

Thanks, warm and sincere for your birthday greeting. But everyone can reach 70 if they wait long enough and are extremely careful, more than moderately lucky, had fairly physically sound parents.

These things I have enjoyed. Then there has been a fight to secure respect for human dignity and constitutional rights that has been an exceedingly great incentive to live. I want to see The Day. Hope you'll be present.

Thanks again and the best of the good things available to a good man in this era.

As Ever
Pat
Pat

2. *Political Affairs* was the political issues journal of the CPUSA. It started in 1945.

[Handwritten]

Nov. 16, 1961

Dear Lang:

Thank you so much for sending me The Best of Simple. Simple is always as welcome in our house as you are because he is one of my favorite people. I like the drawings too—especially the cover.

Sorry to have missed seeing you while I was in N.Y. It was a great visit—the first time I stayed long enough to really get the feel of the big city for a long time.

Have you seen the item in the [San Francisco] Chronicle about "Ask Your Mama"?[3] I took a peek at Nebby Lou's copy before forwarding it to her—was pleased to discover I wasn't as square as I had thought.

Matt sends his best. He keeps busy with his present hobby—photography. Has a darkroom and all the trimmings. Would you have ever believed it?

Love,
Nebby

TO MATT AND NEBBY, [NOVEMBER 1961]

LITTLE ROCK[4]
By
Nicolas Guillen

A blues moans its tears of music
In the fine morning,
The white South jerks
Back its whip and strikes. The Negro
Children walk to their school of fear
Between pedagogical rifles.
When Jim Crow arrives
His wings flapping
He will be the teacher,
Lynch's boys their fellow students

3. Langston's epic poem *Ask Your Mama: 12 Moods For Jazz* (1961) had been reviewed in the *San Francisco Chronicle*.

4. Langston translated many of Guillén's works into English, including the poem "Little Rock," which was originally published in 1958.

And in each desk where a nigger sits
They'll have blood for ink and pencils of fire.
Thus the South. Its whip never stops.
In that Faubus world[5]
Under that hard Faubus sky filled with gangrene
Negro children may not walk with the whites to school.
Or even stay softly at home
Or even (no one knows)
Let themselves be beaten into death and into martyrdom.
Or risk themselves in the streets
Or die with a bullet and saliva
Or whistle at a white girl's walk
Or finally, lower the eyes, yes
Bow from the waist, yes
Get down on their knees, yes
In that free world, yes
That Stupid Foster describes
At one airfield and another
While the little white ball
a pleasant little white ball
presidential, for golf, like
a tiny planet rolls across
the lawn, pure, smooth, fine,
green, chaste, tender, soft, yes.
And so now,
Ladies and gentlemen, young ladies
Now children
Now horrible bums and old drunks
Now Indians, mulattos, negroes, half-breeds, now
Think what it would be like, the world
All South.
The world all blood and all whip
The world all white schools for whites
The world all Rock and all Little
The world all yanqui, all Faubus. . . .
Think for a moment

Imagine it for a single instant.

5. Orval Eugene Faubus (1910–1994) served six consecutive terms as governor of Arkansas. He was a staunch segregationist, and in 1957 he defied the US Supreme Court's school desegregation ruling and ordered the Arkansas National Guard to stop nine African American students from entering Little Rock Central High School.

[Note in margin] *Hey, you-all: Sure enjoyed having your letter. Talked to your daughter on the phone not long ago. She seemed O.K. and interested in her studies. I'm going to Africa again—Lagos Arts Festival in December.*[6] *Africa even got me in the White House lately!*[7] *(Like Jews have Israel, at this stage, seems good to have a "nation" even if by proxy!) I didn't see the GUARDIAN*[8] *mention of [ASK YOUR] MAMA. What date? Thanks for the clipping.*

Langston

FROM LOUISE, NOVEMBER 28, [1961]

11/28

Dear Lang:

On 11/18 we mailed you an announcement of our Marylou's marriage to a Cuban engineering student at [the Peoples'] Friendship [University].[9] The entire box of 300 we were sending out at the time was stolen from a post office box but a few were mailed later by someone a checkup shows. We sent one to Toy and Emerson [Harper], too, and you can imagine my dismay in not knowing who got it and who didn't. Would you let me know on the attached card. How are you—sorry could not get to 11/12 affair but had my whole family to dinner—heard it was a crowded-out success.

Love,
Lou

6. The Lagos Arts Festival was a cultural event designed to highlight connections between African and African American artistic expressions in literature, music, and dance. The festival was sponsored by the American Society for African Culture, which was later revealed to have been a CIA front organization.

7. On November 3, 1961, Langston attended a White House luncheon in honor of President Leopold Sedar Senghor of Senegal, who had personally requested that he be invited. Senghor, who was a famous poet in his own right, and Martinique's Aimé Césaire had cofounded the Négritude literary and cultural movement in France.

8. The *National Guardian,* founded in New York City in 1948 by supporters of the Henry Wallace presidential campaign, was an independent leftist paper often identified with the Socialist Party.

9. MaryLouise married Roberto Camacho Caballero in Moscow on October 12, 1961. The marriage was dissolved in 1970.

TO LOUISE, [DECEMBER 1, 1961?]

[Editors' note: This letter was probably dated November 1 by mistake, as it was in response to Louise's letter to Langston on November 28. He probably wrote it on December 1.]

November 1, 1961

Dear Lou:

No, the wedding announcement never did come. But our cards must have crossed, as I'd written you for her address so I could send her a book. And Nebby Lou had already told me the news on the phone..... They tell me a Harlem little theatre group revived our LIMITATIONS OF LIFE[10] recently and it's as funny as ever. I'm going to bring DYWTBF [*Don't You Want to Be Free?*] up to date.... Come see my BLACK NATIVITY[11] opening at the 41st St. Theatre on Monday, Dec. 11, for the Christmas season. Gospel-song-play. Rehearsals look good.....

Best ever,

Lang

TO LOUISE, [LATE 1961]

[Postcard]

Dear Lou:

You said you was gonna send me Lloyd Patterson's son's name and address—the one who wants to be a poet—so I could send him a book. And you didn't do no such a thing.... Also, your daughter's, so I could send her one, too..... Come see my BLACK NATIVITY gospel song-play opening at the 41st Street Theatre Monday, December 11, a day before I go to Africa again.

Sincerely yours truly,

Lang

Dr. Hughes

10. Langston wrote the one-act play *Limitations of Life* for the Harlem Suitcase Theatre in 1938. The name was a twist on the title of Fannie Hurst's 1933 novel, *Imitation of Life*.

11. Langston wrote *Black Nativity* in 1961. It is a traditional Christmas play with gospel singing, dancing, and poetry.

FROM LOUISE, DECEMBER 4, [1961]

[Handwritten]

12/4

Dear Lang—Yes our cards did cross and I re-read yours to try to figure out if you were answering & concluded as above. I'm sending along another announcement just to make it official. The addresses are:

Marylou Patterson (still uses maiden name)
% John Pittman
9 Gorky St.—Apartment 8
Moscow, U.S.S.R.

However I would suggest in both cases you send to John and inside indicate who they are for as a newspaper man he has certain special privileges—doesn't have to pay duty, etc. But here's Jimmy's address

James Patterson
Katuzova Ul. Dom. 2 Kb. 18—Moscow

I certainly shall try to get down to the show Black Nativity. Tell me how you like "Purlie".[12]

Fondly,
Lou

[Note above salutation] *Where you going in a fuss this time?*

TO LOUISE, DECEMBER 6, 1961

December 6, 1961

Dear Lou:

The announcement is BEAUTIFUL. Thanks a lot for remembering us..... And for the addresses. I've sent several of my books: the new ASK YOUR MAMA, Best of SIMPLE, etc., so you might tell John [Pittman] or Marylou if you write to be on the lookout for them..... Show rehearsals go

12. The Broadway play *Purlie Victorious* (1961) was written by Ossie Davis. It was made into a Hollywood film called *Gone Are the Days!* in 1963 and then a musical, *Purlie,* in 1970.

well. Actors singing up a breeze. Only the management is not speaking to each other! A gospel Nativity will at least be different! . . . . . PURLIE I loved! . . . . . Hope it's still on when I come back from Nigeria so I can see it again. Lionel Hampton, Randy Weston, Nina Simone, whole lots of folks are going. I had to buy a white tux to MC the shows in. My old black one wilted when I was there last year. So HOT! . . . . . Happy Holidays to you-all! Eat well—for me!

Lang

TO MATT AND NEBBY, [1962]

[Card with a drawing of a girl]

Doesn't this look a bit like Nebby Lou?

Lang

FROM MARY LOU, AUGUST 2, 1962

[Picture postcard from Moscow; handwritten]

8/2/62

Dear Langston,

Thank you very much for your new book—I read it over our vacations that just ended yesterday and I guess I never laughed more, or felt so close to home again as I did when I was reading your book. I've been away for a long time, and seen many things and shall yet see many more, and I'm growing taller, wider and deeper I guess like the Mississippi—and once in a while I get to thinking about home—and when I feel like that I take out my Anthology of Negro Poetry or my new book about jazz and just curl up and read for hours.

Thanks again Lang very much. I would also appreciate your collection of African poetry if you could send it.

Stay well—keep writing.

MaryLou

In the summer of 1962 Pat went to California for a vacation. He stayed with Matt and Nebby. They visited Yosemite and other Northern California tourist sites, and Pat and Matt had many personal and political discussions.

FROM PAT TO MATT AND NEBBY, [AUGUST 18, 1962]

The Crawfords
1399 Delaware St
Berkeley, Calif.

Dear friends—

Even where the friendship is as warm and close as is ours there is need for an expression of thanks after such an experience as was my vacation—a special expression of thanks of appreciation and if I may say so of love. And so I make it again. You made my vacation an event. Thanks a million.

Of course the trip to Yosemite is included when I say that, as is the American–Dorset track meet and the ball games. These incidents colored the event but our discussions, the meeting with Harriet [Eddy] in Palo Alto and San Mateo gave spiritual and ideological uplift to it. Don't think I am forgetting the affair at 1399.[13] That too helped. It was good to meet with old and new friends and acquaintances.

How will I repay you? Being a working man I can only say I shall try to work better. That I promise which is naturally no guarantee. Well no guarantees can be given. I can work more but that does not mean better. The Russians have a saying: "Better less but better". So I guess it's a qualitative rather than a quantitative matter.

Got home to find the Pittmans[14] here. They left the next morning before I got up so I only called out hello. Probably you have seen them. They all look well and wouldn't listen to any talk about East. Found mail from Mary Lou and Lola [Patterson] and found plenty of work.

Incidently I wonder if you can ask the Sun Reporter to send me a few copies of the July 28th issue. I am pushing the editorial and the peace page spread. And do something for me—this to Nebby—read over my letter to [Carlton] Goodlett that appeared Aug 1st and tell me if it had too many big words and don't spare my feelings as such criticism is necessary.

Incidently I did not say so-long to Walter B. or to Revels [Cayton] if this is done for me I shall request whatever gods there be to have mercy on the soul of the kind one.

I will not complain that I was not permitted to do my share while there. Some other way will have to be found to make that up. This is aside from the comment made on the first page.

Tell Matt he had better do something about the [San Francisco] Giants. Their tendency to fold in the stretch is well known. Maybe Nebby better

13. 1399 Delaware St. was the address of the Crawford home in Berkeley.
14. John Pittman and his family had been visiting.

speak to _her_ Willie [Mays] and tell him to get well and get going. Of course I shall be satisfied either way. I like the Giants but I think the [Los Angeles] Dodgers best and I want to see the [New York] Yankees beaten. It don't much matter who does the job.

If Nebby Lou sees Carl or Francis give my greetings and the same goes for Buddy [Green] and his family in fact it goes for all friends of yesterday and today.

Matt dear friend it's "tough nuggies" but we hold the winning hand. Don't draw too many new cards play those you have the other guy is bluffing now and the world knows it. The new world's values are obvious. True there are no "paper tigers" here but we beat any kind.

My love rides with this mail.

Louise traveled to the USSR again in 1962 to see Mary Lou and her husband, Roberto Camacho Caballero. The three visited the city of Sochi on the Black Sea coast and stayed at a lovely resort not ordinarily available to students.

FROM LOUISE, AUGUST 20, 1962

[Postcard from Sochi, USSR; handwritten]

8/20 Sochi

Greetings from Marylou, Roberto and I from the charming resort— remember it? We are here for August and having a relaxed time in the sun and sea. Was July in Moscow and will be home in Sept. Heard very fine reports on Spoletti—congratulations.

Lou

FROM PAT TO MATT AND NEBBY, [OCTOBER 28, 1962]

Matt Crawford
1399 Delaware
Berkeley Calif.

Dear Matt and dearer Nebby:

I added the latter not because this letter will interest Nebby to the extent that I hope it will activize you Matt but rather to let Nebby [know] if reassurance is needed, that she is not out of my mind and her opinion is respected.

Matt, I have come to the conclusion that from the myths of superiority and inferiority is brewed the most intoxicating dreams posed by man. Pass over for a moment the economics of Nazism which as a motivating factor was dominant and you come to the task of mobilizing the people. That was done on the basis of intoxicating them with the myths of Aryan—the blue eyed Germanic blonds—right to rule. Little would the people enjoy from any economic supremacy of the Junker[15]-Monopolists-Racists. But the idea of superiority made them drunk, doped and duped them, made them as sheep. Trace our own country's development. Every step has been based on national superiority and the core of that was here at home white supremacy dominated national chauvinism and national chauvinism bred arrogance, cynicism and myths of eternal grandeur.

The black man can't afford any such unscientific approach to basic social problems or any other problems.

But although this is Sunday I did not intend this letter to be a sermon— just a warning that hell looms for the unwary and that myths distort and prevent serious thought.

I want to write about Jack Levine's exposure of the role of the American secret police.[16]

It must I believe be used in the fight for a government which will protect the rights of all impartially.

Levine links the police who should curb subversion to the racists, anti-Semites, political black-mailers, sadists, murderers to the subversives, the war provocateurs the most dangerous men in the country (See *Nation* article)[.]

I believe that in the exposure of the role of government in our exploitation these tasks assigned or assumed by the FBI must be shown in their great magnitude, and relentlessly condemned. A police that will arrest those who violate the constitutional rights of anybody is needed. The violation of the rights Negroes must enjoy if they are to become merged with the nation of which they are a part although aparts upsets the normal development of our society in all respects.

Black youth, ministers all others should study the role of the police. Delegations on a state and city level must seek to end that governmental action. But the fight against the FBI, the state within a state is most important.

15. Junkers were members of the landed nobility of Prussia and Eastern Germany.

16. Jack Levine was a former FBI agent who revealed the agency's massive infiltration of the CPUSA in his article "Hoover and the Red Scare," which was published in the October 20, 1962, issue of *The Nation* magazine.

I wrote Carlton [Goodlett] about editorializing on the matter.

Incidently I spoke with him as he passed through and raised several questions.

Hope you will get a chance to speak with our youth about this struggle. It is a logical phase of the broader fight and is a strategically important point of conflict.

John Pittman would be a splendid person with whom to talk. Revels [Cayton] would have an angle and entry to a vital force. Here the refusal to unload ships that were scheduled to touch in Cuba was the act of gangster controlled union.[17] Of course the FBI and other government agencies treat with gangsters. They need these worthies for such contingencies.

Hope you saw about the demonstration of Spelman-Morehouse students for peace.[18] Magnificent linking of Negro fight with broadest human need[.] Real thinking, smart action, courage, understanding.

Nebby Lou—Louise send love.

Pat

In 1961 W. E. B. Du Bois left the United States to live in Ghana, at the invitation of the then Ghanian president Dr. Kwame Nkrumah, to work on an Encyclopedia Africana. At his departure he wrote a letter to Gus Hall, head of the U.S. Communist Party, requesting membership in the party. His request was granted. He died in Ghana on August 27, 1963.

FROM PAT, OCTOBER 23, 1963

October 23, 1963

Mr. Langston Hughes
20 East 127th St.
New York, N.Y.

Dear Langston:

In a letter over my signature which appears in the current issue of the Afro-American I am made to say that the adherence of Dr. Du Bois to Marxist philosophy was "consciously" left out of your very splendid

17. In October 1962, after the Cuban Missile Crisis, the United States imposed an embargo against Cuba which involved making it illegal for any foreign ship that had been to Cuba, and all other ships from that shipping company, to dock in a US port.

18. Students from Spelman and Morehouse colleges in Georgia had been demonstrating in downtown Atlanta for the desegregation of movie theaters.

comments on the Dr. which appeared in the Afro's magazine section—October 12th.

Please believe me when I say I hold no such belief. I consider the omission quite accidental for I have noted that on other occasions you have noted the historic fact.

Sincerely Yours
Pat
William L. Patterson

FROM NEBBY, DECEMBER 5, 1963

[Handwritten]

Dec. 5, 1963

Dear Lang,

I didn't phone you the Sunday after the opening of Tambourines to Glory[19] because I knew you would be sleeping later than usual and didn't want to disturb you. I left for home early the following Monday.

We enjoyed Tambourines. It was quite exciting to be your guest on the opening night.[20] My mission in New York was a difficult one[21] but there were some pleasant moments and the evening at the theatre was certainly among them.

Matt is fine—busy as usual trying to make these white folks treat us right.

Berkeley has an ambitious program going on education, employment and housing and Matt is very active in it.

Nebby Lou is fine. I know you are always busy but if you have a chance call her some time.

I hope Tambourines has a long and successful run. You looked great. Evidently the rigors of getting a play on Broadway agree with you.

Fondly,
Nebby

19. Langston had written *Tambourines to Glory,* a black gospel musical play, in 1956. It was mounted at New York's Little Theatre on Forty-Fourth Street in November 1963.

20. Nebby was visiting New York in the late fall of 1963 and had been Langston's guest to the opening of *Tambourines to Glory.* Louise had probably also attended the show with them.

21. Nebby had gone to New York to take care of Nebby Lou, who had been ill.

FROM PAT, [AUGUST 1964]

[Handwritten]

Langston Hughes
20 East 127th St. New York City

Dear Lang,

I liked your column of July 17th. It contained however, or rather failed to contain, factual material which I for one regarded as universally known.

Three petitions formulated by Negroes or initiated by them have reached the Secretariat and Human Rights Commission of the United Nations. You mentioned two.

As General Secretary of the Civil Rights Congress I presented the third which was very largely my document, a petition entitled "We Charge Genocide: The Crime of Government Against the Negro People"[22] to the General Assembly at the Palais Chaillot in Paris in 1951. On the same day that petition was present[ed] to the UN here in New York by Paul Robeson.

Any petition which follows will be the 4th.

I am satisfied that you could not have heard of Genocide am therefore enclosing copy.

Best of health to you

Sincerely
(Pat) William L. Patterson.
Please excuse paper and handwriting but secty on vacation.
WLP

TO PAT, AUGUST 10, 1964

[Letterhead: 20 East 127th Street / New York 35, N. Y.]

August 10, 1964

Dear Pat:

Thanks immensely for sending me now WE CHARGE GENOCIDE. My copy somehow got lost, strayed or stolen over the years, and when I was writing my POST column (in a hurry as usual to make a deadline) I couldn't find any trace of it, or date (or if) it was presented officially to the U.N., but I felt almost certain that it had. The others were mentioned in

---

22. *We Charge Genocide: The Historic Petition to the United Nations for Relief from a Crime of the United States Government Against the Negro People* was edited by Pat and published in 1951.

THE NEGRO YEARBOOK on my shelves. I am very glad to have your book again and will surely be able to make use of it in the future.

I am glad to see Joe North at the masthead of a magazine[23] again, and have just sent him a poem that grew out of the riots,[24] so it should be timely.

In September I am invited to the Berlin Festival of the Arts, whose accent this year poetry-wise is on African and Afro-American cultures. I haven't been to Berlin since 1932, en route to the USSR, although a number of my books have been translated in both East and West Germany in recent years, and I get lots of fan letters from both sides. Speaking of fan letters, I got a PILE, result of my riots columns in the POST, 2/3 pro, 1/3 anti "Go back to Africa with the rest of the apes" type, mostly unsigned. So many, I haven't read half of them yet.

I hear tell Lou is in California. Give her and the young ones my best when they return. Right now I am working against time to get off to Europe. . . . . Cordial regards,

Sincerely,
Lang

Mary Lou and Roberto had their first child, Sandra, in Moscow in March 1964. Louise, Mary Lou, and Sandra visited the Crawfords in California that summer.

Nebby Lou moved to Ghana in 1965 to teach English to young French-speaking Africans who were studying radio and television production in Accra.

FROM NEBBY LOU, OCTOBER 12, 1965

[Postcard from Accra, Ghana; handwritten]

12 October 1965

Accra

Dear Langston—

This is truly a bustling capital. It is good to be in Africa. Hope you are well.

Love,
Nebby Lou

23. Joseph North founded and ran *American Dialog* magazine from 1964 to 1972.

24. On July 18, 1964, rioting broke out in Harlem after police fatally shot a fifteen-year-old black youth. The rioting spread to Rochester, New York, on June 24 and to Philadelphia, Pennsylvania, on August 24.

TO MATT, [NOVEMBER 1965]

[Handwritten on program notes for the cantata Let Us Remember.[25]*]*

Dear Matt—

Maybe you-all could hear this. I can't make it because of [Harry] Belafonte TV film[26] starting rehearsals next week.

Lang

P.S. Had a nice card from your daughter in Ghana.

FROM NEBBY, NOVEMBER 17, 1965

[Handwritten]

Wed. Nov. 17, 1965

Dear Lang,

I am sorry the flu bug made it impossible for either of us to hear your cantata. I had been watching the paper for publicity but saw nothing until Sunday, Nov. 15th. There may have been some special publicity for the Jewish community that I wouldn't know about being culud.

I am enclosing Dean Wallace's review from today's [San Francisco] Chronicle. I hope the program will be repeated so we can hear it.

Thanks for <u>Simple's Uncle Sam</u>. He furnished us with some good laughs during our siege with the flu. I get a big kick out of Cousin Minnie. She is exactly like a cousin of mine who was the black sheep of the family. The extra amusing thing about my cousin was that her name was Lily.

We spent our vacation at Big Sur this year and made a couple of trips to Carmel which stirred up pleasant memories of years ago when we visited you there.

Take care & don't get the flu—it is miserable.

Nebby

25. The cantata *Let Us Remember,* which Langston wrote with composer David Amram, was commissioned for the biennial convention of Reformed Judaism.

26. Harry Belafonte and Sidney Poitier coproduced the TV special *The Strollin' Twenties,* written by Langston. It was broadcast on CBS in February 1966 and showcased many of the top black artists of the day.

In late 1965 Langston toured Europe for almost two months, sponsored by the US State Department. He took young African American writers Paule Marshall and William Melvin with him. After the tour he went to Africa for several months.

FROM LOUISE, JANUARY 3, 1966

[Handwritten]

1/3/66

Dear Lang—

You'll probably be in Paris when this reaches your house—got your card and am glad to know the flu didn't keep you from taking off. Hope the show will be a huge success.

Thanks for sending us the book [*Simple's Uncle Sam*]. I spent several evenings (between coughs and sneezes) enjoying Simple's observations.

I'm all right now and would be back to work if I could get there.

Pat and Marylou join me in greetings for a 1966 of greater peace and plenty for all of us.

Fondly,
Lou

Mary Lou returned to New York in 1965 to give birth to her second child, who was born in March of 1966. She named the baby Evelyn Louise, after Nebby Lou.

After working for some time as an instructor at the Ghana Institute of Languages, Nebby Lou had moved to Paris to start a job as an editorial assistant and translator at the International Union Against Tuberculosis, a public health agency affiliated with the World Health Organization.

FROM NEBBY LOU, AUGUST 8, 1966

[Postcard from Paris with image of Ethiopian Emperor Menelik II, handwritten]

8 August 1966

Paris

Langston—

You are a dear and thoughtful soul for sending me the clippings. Saw Sandy [Bethune] the other day and he too mentioned receiving same. Matt and Nebby are in London. I will join them this week. Fondest regards from me and your admirer Menelik II!!

Love,
Nebby Lou

In July 1966, on his way back to the United States from Senegal, Langston passed through Paris, where Nebby Lou was living. Her parents, Matt and Nebby, were visiting her at the time, and the four of them went out to dinner at a little restaurant in the Latin Quarter. Langston teased Nebby Lou, telling her that she had no business speaking French better than him. It was a joyous reunion. After saying their goodbyes on a street corner facing Notre Dame Cathedral, Matt, Nebby, and Nebby Lou watched their dear friend Langston walk up the Boulevard Saint-Michel. It was the last time they would see him; the following year he was gone.

GLOSSARY PERSONAE

ALBERGA, LAURENCE O. Jamaican agricultural worker. Alberga was one of the twenty-two young Black people who traveled to the USSR in 1932 to film *Black and White*. He disagreed with the Soviet explanation for the postponement of the film.

ALSTON, CHARLES. 1907–1977. Painter, sculptor, illustrator, muralist, and teacher. Alston was an important visual artist during the Harlem Renaissance, and he figured prominently in the Black art scene of 1930s.

AMRAM, DAVID. Born 1930. Composer, conductor, multi-instrumentalist, and author. Amram incorporated jazz and folkloric and world music into his repertoire and worked with many famous musicians. He wrote the cantata *Let Us Remember* with Langston.

ANDERSON, MARIAN. 1897–1993. Opera and concert singer. Anderson had a beautiful contralto voice and was one of the most celebrated singers of the twentieth century. In 1939 the organization Daughters of the American Revolution refused to allow her to sing for an integrated audience at Constitution Hall in Washington, DC, unwittingly creating an international furor. First Lady Eleanor Roosevelt and President Franklin D. Roosevelt intervened, and Anderson sang on Easter Sunday in front of an integrated crowd of seventy-five thousand at the Lincoln Memorial. The concert was broadcast live over the radio to an audience of millions.

ANISSIMOV, JULIAN. 1889–1940. Russian. Lyric poet, writer, and critic. Anissmov translated Langton's poems into Russian and then befriended him during his stay in the Soviet Union in 1932–1933

AOSTA, AMEDEO UMBERTO ISABELLA LUIGI FILIPPO MARIA GIUSEPPE GIOVANNI DI SAVOIA-AOSTA. Also known as Prince Amedeo, Duke of Aosta, or simply Duke of Aosta. 1898–1942. Third Duke of Aosta, Italy, and cousin of King Victor Emmanuel III of Italy. Prince Amedeo served as the Italian Viceroy of Ethiopia during World War II and fought in the Italian armed forces in North and East Africa. He surrendered to the British in Ethiopia in July 1941 and was sent to a prisoner-of-war camp, where he died.

APTHEKER, HERBERT. 1915–2003. Scholar, historian, and professor. Aptheker's many seriously researched books on African American history and the history of slave rebellions helped form the academic basis for the discipline of African American studies at universities in the United States and around the world. He was a member of the CPUSA.

ATKINSON, BROOKS. 1894–1984. Journalist. Atkinson was the *New York Times'* drama critic from 1925 to 1960, with a break in the 1940s when he went abroad as a foreign correspondence for the *Times.*

BAKER, JOSEPHINE. Born Freda Josephine McDonald. 1906–1975. Dancer, singer, actress, and political activist. Baker expatriated to France in the 1920s and later became a French citizen. Her participation in the French Resistance during World War II earned her the *Croix de Guerre,* a French military honor. She was famous for her "banana dance" cabaret number. She was called the "Black Pearl" and the "Bronze Venus."

BARNETT, ETTA MOTEN. 1901–2004. Film and stage actress, contralto singer, community and civic activist, and philanthropist. Barnett's signature role was "Bess" in the opera *Porgy and Bess,* which opened on Broadway in 1942. Ira Gershwin had written the part with her in mind. In 1933 she performed for the incoming president, Franklin Delano Roosevelt, at the White House, becoming the first African American to do so.

BARNETT-LEWIS, ELIZABETH. Barnett-Lewis owned the Hotel Vincennes in Chicago. She was married to "Pop" Lewis, who ran the Platinum Lounge in the hotel's basement.

BASS, CHARLOTTA. Circa 1889–1969. Publisher, editor, journalist, and civil rights activist. Bass published a Los Angeles African-American newspaper, the *California Eagle,* from 1912 to 1951. She was the vice-presidential candidate in 1952 on the Progressive Party ticket with Vincent Hallinan, who was running for president. She was one of the original signers to the Sojourners for Truth and Justice call in 1951, and she made J. Edgar Hoover's list of Communist subversives.

BATES, RALPH. 1899–2000. British writer and journalist. Bates helped organize the International Brigade, which fought on the side of the elected Spanish Loyalist government in Spain's civil war against General Franco's forces, and founded the brigade's newspaper, *The Volunteer for Liberty.* He became disillusioned with the Soviet Union after it invaded Finland in 1939, and he wrote an article about the event entitled "Disaster in Finland" for *The New Republic* magazine, in which he announced his abandonment of the Communist cause. Langston met him in Spain.

BEARDEN, ROMARE. Circa 1911–1988. Painter, collage artist, and muralist. Bearden was one of the great American painters of the twentieth century.

BELAFONTE, HARRY. Born Harold George Bellanfanti Jr. Born 1927. Singer, songwriter, stage and screen actor, social activist, orator, and author. Belafonte was close friends with Dr. Martin Luther King and Paul Robeson. He won many performance awards.

BENNETT, GWENDOLYN "GWENNIE." 1902–1981. Writer, poet, and artist. Bennett was a vital figure in the Harlem Renaissance. She was one of the cofounders of the African-American literary magazine *Fire!!,* which she also contributed to. She was the head of the Harlem Community Art Center from 1938 to 1941, but she was fired for suspected Communist associations. She was friends with Langston and Louise.

BETHUNE, LEBERT "SANDY." Jamaican writer and academic. Bethune met Langston in 1931, and the two became friends. At the time he was living in Paris. He subsequently became a professor of Africana Studies at the State University of New York, Stoney Brook.

BETHUNE, MARY JANE MCLEOD. 1875–1955. Educator and civil rights leader. Bethune was an advisor to President Franklin D. Roosevelt and a friend of First Lady Eleanor Roosevelt. In 1943 Martin Dies, a US congressional representative from Texas, who was chair of the House Un-American Activities Committee, publicly accused her of being a Communist. She founded a school in Florida that is today known as Bethune-Cookman University.

BILBO, THEODORE GILMORE. 1877–1947. Politician. Bilbo was a staunch segregationist and racist and an open member of the Ku Klux Klan. He was twice elected governor of Mississippi, serving from 1916 to 1920 and again from 1928 to 1932. He later served in the US Senate from 1935 to 1947. He was prevented from taking his Senate seat in 1947 because of racist comments he made during his reelection campaign.

BONTEMPS, ARNAUD "ARNA" WENDELL. 1902–1973. Writer, poet, playwright, librarian, educator, and professor. Bontemps was an important member of the Harlem Renaissance and Langston's close friend. He headed Fisk University's library for over twenty years. He also served as curator of the James Weldon Johnson Collection at the Beinecke Library of Yale University. He collaborated and corresponded with Langston for over three decades.

BRADFORD, ROARK WHITNEY WICKLIFF. 1896–1948. Journalist, writer, and playwright. Bradford wrote the novel *John Henry* in 1931. It was later made into a Broadway musical starring Paul Robeson and Ruby Elzy.

BRAITHWAITE, WILLIAM STANLEY. 1878–1962. Writer, poet, literary critic, and academic. Braithwaite was a professor of Creative Literature at Atlanta University.

BREEN, BOBBY. Born 1927. Canadian singer and Hollywood screen actor. Breen was RKO Pictures' leading child star from the 1930s to the early 1940s. He acted in the 1939 film *Way Down South,* cowritten by Langston and Clarence Muse.

BRIDGES, HARRY ALFRED RENTON. 1901–1990. Australian-born labor leader. Bridges led the International Longshore and Warehouse Union for forty years, from 1937 to 1977. He helped organize the "Big Strike" of 1934, a four-day general strike in San Francisco, which was the first general strike on US soil. He was unsuccessfully prosecuted during the 1930s and 1940s for Communist affiliations but was finally found guilty in 1950, although the conviction was overturned by the Supreme Court in 1953.

BRIGHT, JOHN MILTON. 1908–1989. Screen writer, journalist, director, and political activist. Bright was blacklisted during the McCarthy Communist witch-hunt of the 1950s.

BROOKS, CHARLES WAYLAND "CURLY." 1897–1957. Politician. Brooks was a Republican Illinois senator from 1940 to 1949. He was a supporter of the Chicago-based International Harvester Company.

BROWDER, EARL RUSSELL. 1891–1973. Political activist and writer. Browder led the CPUSA from 1930 to 1945. He dissolved the party in 1945, stating that capitalism and socialism could peacefully coexist, and renamed it the Communist Political Association, restructuring it as an educational Marxist group. The CPUSA was reconstituted in 1945, and Browder was expelled from the party in 1946.

BROWN, LAWRENCE "LARRY" BENJAMIN. 1893–1973. Pianist, composer, arranger, scholar, and music historian. Brown worked as tenor Roland Hayes's piano accompanist from 1918 to 1923, and he then accompanied Paul Robeson for over three decades. He helped Robeson bring Negro spirituals to concert audiences worldwide.

BROWN, LULA MAE. See Thompson, Lula Mae

BROWNING, IVAN HAROLD. 1891–1971. Singer, actor, and entertainer. Browning sang opera to show music. In the 1920s he appeared in Eubie Blake's musical review Shuffle Along on Broadway.

BURNS, BEN. Born Benjamin Bernstein. 1913–2000. Journalist. Burns wrote for several Communist papers, including People's World (the CPUSA's West Coast newspaper) and the Midwest Daily Record, where he worked for Pat. In 1941 he joined the Chicago Defender, a black weekly newspaper. He went on to found Ebony magazine in 1945, and he worked there until 1954. In January 1941 he wrote a scathing review in People's World of the statement Langston gave defending "Good-Bye Christ."

BURROUGHS, MARGARET TAYLOR GOSS. 1917–2010. Educator, social and civil rights activist, community organizer, writer, and artist. Burroughs was an important part of the Chicago arts community during the WPA era. She and her husband, Charles Burroughs, founded the Southside Community Art Center, the DuSable Museum, and the National Conference of Artists. She was friends with Langston and the Pattersons.

CALDWELL, ERSKINE PRESTON. 1903–1987. Novelist, short story writer, and playwright. Caldwell wrote prolifically about poverty, racism, and social problems in the South. His works include the novel God's Little Acre and the play Tobacco Road.

CALLOWAY, CABELL "CAB." 1907–1994. Bandleader, arranger, singer, and performer.

CALVIN, FLOYD JOSEPH. 1902–1994. Journalist, radio broadcaster, and writer.

CAMACHO CABALLERO, ROBERTO JUSTINIANO. Born 1940. Cuban. Camacho Caballero was a member of the first group of students sent abroad by the new revolutionary Cuban government to study at Peoples' Friendship University in Moscow. He married MaryLouise in 1962. They had two children: Sandra Elizabeth, deceased, and Evelyn Louise.

CAMPBELL, DICK. 1903–1994. Actor, director, producer, and publicist. Campbell was a key theater figure during the Harlem Renaissance. He cofounded the Negro People's Theatre in 1935 and the Rose McClendon Players in 1937. He was a staunch advocate for Black actors.

CAMPBELL, ELMER SIMMS. 1906–1971. Illustrator and cartoonist. Campbell worked for *Esquire* magazine.

CARMON, WALT. 1894–1968. Writer and editor. Carmon edited *New Masses* magazine. He was a member of the CPUSA and lived in the Soviet Union for many years.

CARTIER-BRESSON, HENRI. 1908–2004. French photographer. Cartier-Bresson is considered the father of photojournalism. He shared an apartment with Langston in Mexico in 1938. The two men remained friends until Langston's death.

CAYTON, HORACE ROSCOE. 1903–1970. Sociologist, educator, researcher, government official, and columnist. Cayton was the director of the Good Shepherd Community Center (later renamed the Parkway Community Center), which supported the literary and arts movement in Chicago in the 1930s and 1940s known as the Chicago Black Renaissance. In 1945 he coauthored, with African American sociologist and anthropologist St. Clair Drake, a landmark study of Black migration, race, and urban life in Chicago called *Black Metropolis: A Study of Negro Life in a Northern City*. His maternal grandfather was Hiram Rhodes Revels. His brother was Revels Cayton. He was married to Irma Jackson Cayton (later Irma Cayton Wertz); they divorced in 1942. He was friends with Langston and the Pattersons.

CAYTON, IRMA JACKSON. *See* Wertz, Irma Cayton

CAYTON, REVELS. 1907–1995. Labor leader. Cayton was a member of the Communist Party and its League of Struggle for Negro Rights in Seattle. He moved to the San Francisco Bay Area in the 1930s, where he worked as an activist and a union organizer. He was the grandson of Senator Hiram Rhodes Revels. He was close friends with Matt and Nebby.

CHAPIN, CORNELIA VAN AUKEN. 1893–1972. Sculptor. Chapin was employed to assist the socialite and philanthropist Charlotte Osgood Mason.

CHEN, EUGENE. 1878–1944. Chinese Trinidadian lawyer and politician. Chen was a friend of Sun Yat-Sen's. He became the foreign minister of the Republic of China in 1925.

CHEN, JACK. 1908–1995. Chinese Trinidadian journalist, cartoonist, and writer. Chen wrote *A Year in Upper Felicity*. He was the son of Eugene Chen and the brother of Sylvia Chen Leyda.

CHEN LEYDA, SYLVIA. Born Si-Lan Chen. 1909–1996. Chinese Trinidadian writer and dancer. Chen Leyda practiced ballet, and she also developed a new genre, anti-colonial dance. She wrote an autobiography, *Footnote to History*. She studied ballet at the famous Bolshoi Ballet in Moscow, where she met and fell in love with Langston. She later married Jay Leyda, an avant-garde filmmaker. She was the daughter of Eugene Chen and the sister of Jack Chen.

CHILDRESS, ALICE. 1912–1994. Playwright, actor, social activist, and author of books for children and adults. She was a close friend of Louise and Beah Richards and joined them in Sojourners for Truth and Justice.

CLARK, GWYN SHANNON "KIT." 1913–? Langston's stepbrother. Clark's father married Langston's mother when Kit was two years old and Langston was an adolescent.

COOK, MERCER. Born Will Mercer Cook. 1902–1987. Professor and diplomat. Cook was head of the Department of Romance Languages at Howard University and the US ambassador to Nigeria, Senegal, and the Gambia in the 1960s. He was a friend of Langston's and collaborated with him on the translation into English of Jacques Roumain's book *Gouverneurs de la Rosée* (*Masters of the Dew*).

COOPER, HUGH. 1865–1937. US Army colonel and self-educated civil engineer. Cooper was the chief consulting engineer during the building of the Dnieprostroi Hydroelectric Power Plant and Dam in Soviet Russia (which, at the time of its completion, was the largest dam in Europe). The construction coincided with Louise, Langston, and Matt's trip to Moscow in 1932. He conspired against the making of the film *Black and White*.

CULLEN, COUNTEE. 1903–1946. Poet, writer, and editor. Cullen was an important figure in the Harlem Renaissance. He collaborated with Langston on several books of poetry. In 1928 he married Nina Yolande Du Bois, the daughter of W. E. B. Du Bois, in a hugely celebrated Harlem wedding, but they divorced in 1930. Their divorce was rumored to have been based on his alleged homosexual relationship with his friend Harold Jackman.

CUNEY, WILLIAM WARING. 1906–1976. Poet. Cuney participated in the Harlem Renaissance and was a member of the Harlem Suitcase Theatre. He encouraged Langston, who was a friend of his, to attend Lincoln College. The two later worked together in the 1950s on a poetry anthology, *Lincoln University Poets: Centennial Anthology 1854–1954*.

DAVIS, JOHN PRESTON. 1905 –1973. Lawyer, activist, and intellectual. Davis was one of the founders of the literary magazine *Fire!!,* along with Langston and others, in 1926. He was a member of the Communist Party, and he cofounded the National Negro Congress in 1935.

DELANY, HUBERT THOMAS. 1901–1990. Lawyer, judge, and early civil rights activist. In 1955 the mayor of New York, Robert F. Wagner, refused to reappoint Delany to the bench, reportedly because of his left-wing views. He was the brother of the famous Delany sisters, Sadie and Bessie, who were civil rights pioneers.

DE PAUR, LEONARD ETIENNE. 1914–1998. Composer, choral director, and arts administrator.

DIES JR., MARTIN. 1900 –1972. Politician. Dies served as a Democratic Texas US congressman for seven terms. He was the first chair of the House Un-American Activities Committee, which was initially called the Dies Committee. It was initially set up to investigate the Ku Klux Klan and German espionage activity, but it quickly devoted itself to leading an anti-Communist crusade, accusing many of having Communist sympathies, including Shirley Temple and Mary McLeod Bethune.

DIVINE, REVEREND MAJOR JEALOUS. Born George Baker. Popularly known as Father Divine. Circa 1876–1965. Spiritual leader. Divine founded an interracial nonsectarian church called the Peace Mission Movement. He supported the Communist Party in the 1930s.

DIXON, CHARLES DEAN. 1915–1976. Conductor, composer, and musician. Dixon was the first African American to conduct the New York Philharmonic Orchestra. He also conducted numerous orchestras in Israel and Europe.

DODSON, OWEN. 1914–1983. Poet, novelist, and playwright. Dodson was part of the generation that followed the Harlem Renaissance.

DOMINGO, WILFRED ADOLPHUS. 1889–1968. Jamaican journalist, writer, editor, businessman, and social activist. Domingo participated in the Garveyite, socialist, and Communist movements in Harlem.

DORAN, DAVID. 1910–1939. Labor organizer. Doran was a member of the CPUSA. He joined the Abraham Lincoln Brigade, the American contingent of the International Brigade, which fought in the Spanish Civil War against General Franco's forces.

DOUGLAS, AARON "DOUG." 1898–1979. Painter, muralist, sculptor, illustrator, and educator. Douglas illustrated many books in his distinctive modernist style, including Langston's *Fine Clothes to the Jew* (1927). He and his wife, Alta, were close friends of both Langston and Louise. They were neighbors of the Pattersons at 409 Edgecombe Avenue, a famous Harlem apartment building that has been home to many African American professionals, artists, and political leaders. Louise, Pat, and Mary Lou lived in the building during the 1950s.

DOUGLAS, ALTA MAE. Née Sawyer. 1904–1958. Married to modernist painter Aaron Douglas.

DOUGLAS, MELVYN. Born Melvyn Edouard Hesselberg. 1901–1981. Stage and screen actor. Douglas won two Oscars, one Tony Award, and one Emmy. He was a known liberal and was active in the Anti-Nazi Popular Front in Hollywood in the 1930s. He was married to actress and Democratic Party politician Helen Gahagan Douglas.

DOUGLASS, FREDERICK. Born Frederick Augustus Washington Bailey. 1818–1895. Statesman, orator, debater, social activist, abolitionist, and writer. Douglass penned three autobiographies: *Narrative of the Life of Frederick Douglass, an American Slave* (1845); *My Bondage and My Freedom* (1855); and *The Life and Times of Frederick Douglass* (1881).

DREISER, THEODORE HERMAN ALBERT. 1871–1945. Writer, journalist, poet, and social activist. Dreiser is best known for his novels *Sister Carrie* (1900) and *American Tragedy* (1925). He led the National Committee for the Defense of Political Prisoners. He joined the CPUSA right before his death.

DU BOIS, SHIRLEY GRAHAM. Born Lola Shirley Graham. 1896–1977. Author, playwright, composer, musicologist, and social activist. Du Bois wrote wonderful children's books. She was a member of the Sojourners for Truth and Justice and the CPUSA. She married W. E. B. Du Bois when she was fifty-four and he was eighty-three, and the two stayed together until his death.

DU BOIS, WILLIAM EDWARD BURGHARDT "W. E. B." 1868–1963. sociologist, writer, scholar, educator, historian, and editor. Du Bois was one of the greatest American intellectuals, visionaries, and minds of the twentieth century. He was the founder of the NAACP and served as its director from 1910 to 1934. He also founded the Pan-African Association. He established *The Crisis,* one of the most influential African-American journals, and was its editor until 1934. He was the author of twenty-one books, including *The Souls of Black Folk* (1903), and the editor of fifteen others. He ran afoul of the US government in the 1950s because of his progressive political stance, and he, along with Paul Robeson, Pat, and others, had his passport revoked. In 1961 he left the United States for Ghana, at the invitation of the then Ghanaian President Kwame Nkrumah, to work on the *Encyclopedia Africana,* an encyclopedia of Africa and the African diaspora. He publicly joined the CPUSA immediately after his departure. He died in Ghana and is buried there. At the time of his death he had been married to Shirley Graham Du Bois for twelve years. They were both friends of Louise and Pat and Langston.

DUNHAM, KATHERINE. 1909–2006. Anthropologist, dancer, choreographer, author, educator, and social activist. Dunham founded and led the Katherine Dunham Dance Company. She was known for her incorporation of African and Caribbean styles of movement into modern dance technique.

DYETT, THOMAS BENJAMIN. 1889–1985. Lawyer and civil rights activist. Together with Pat and George Hall, Dyett formed the first Black law firm in New York City, Dyett, Hall and Patterson. He served as deputy commissioner of New York City Department of Corrections and later as a member of the New York State Commission of Corrections. In 1957 he formed another law firm, Dyett,

Alexander and Dinkins. One of his partners in this firm, David Dinkins, became New York City's first Black mayor in 1990.

EDDY, HARRIET. 1879–1966. Librarian. Eddy helped develop the system of county libraries in California. She went to the Soviet Union in the late 1920s to assist in organizing public libraries there and maintained close ties with Russian colleagues and friends throughout her life. She was a friend of the Crawford's

EDICES, PELE. Born Phyllis DeLappe. 1916–2009. Writer, artist, political cartoonist, journalist, and social activist. Edices edited the Women's Page of *People's World,* the CPUSA's West Coast newspaper.

EDWARDS, THYRA. 1897–1953. Social worker, teacher, and social activist. Edwards lived in Chicago during the 1930s and 1940s and edited *The People's Voice* newspaper and *The Negro Digest* magazine. She was friends with Langston and Louise.

EHRENBERG, ILYA GRIGORYEVICH. 1891–1967. Russian writer, journalist, translator, and cultural figure. Ehrenberg had more than one hundred titles to his name. He was a leading member of the Jewish Anti-Fascist Committee.

EL CAMPESINO. *See* González, Valentín González

ELLINGTON, EDWARD KENNEDY "DUKE." 1899–1974. Composer, arranger, pianist, and bandleader. Ellington led famous orchestras from 1923 to 1974. He played at Carnegie Hall on January 21, 1943, before an integrated audience, a first for the venue.

ELZY, ROBERT J. 1884–1972. Educator and social worker. Elzy served as the executive director of the National Urban League's New York branch in the 1930s.

ELZY, RUBY. 1908–1943. Soprano. In 1935 Elzy played the role of "Serena" in the Broadway premier of the opera *Porgy and Bess.* In 1940 she played opposite Paul Robeson in *John Henry* on Broadway. The play was a flop.

FAUSET, JESSIE REDMON. 1882–1961. Poet, essayist, literary critic, teacher, and novelist. Fauset was an important poet of the Harlem Renaissance. She was the literary editor of NAACP's *The Crisis* magazine. She was the author of *The Chinaberry Tree* (1931).

FILATOVA, LYDIA. Russian translator. Filatova was a friend of Julian Anissimov and also worked as his assistant. She assisted Langston during his stay in Moscow in 1932–1933.

FISHER-SPENCER, DOROTHY "DOT." Fisher-Spencer was close friends with Louise and Nebby from adolescence. As young women, they were dubbed "the three mosquitoes." She was briefly married to concert singer and actor Kenneth Spencer.

FORD, JAMES W. 1893–1957. Politician. Ford was a leader of the CPUSA. He ran for vice president on the Communist Party's national ticket in 1930, 1932, and 1936. He also served in several high positions in the international Communist movement.

FORT-WHITEMAN, LOVETT. 1894–1939. Politician and activist. Fort-Whiteman was the first African American Communist. He was dubbed "the Reddest of the Blacks." He lived many years in the Soviet Union, where he collaborated in writing an early draft of the screenplay of *Black and White* in 1932. He died in a Siberian labor camp.

GARNER, GEORGE ROBERT. 1892–1971. Singer, actor, and musical director. Garner was the first African American to solo at the Chicago Symphony Orchestra and the first to lead in a production at the Pasadena Playhouse in California.

GARNER, SYLVIA. Singer and actress. Garner was one of the twenty-two to travel to the USSR in 1932 to produce the ultimately canceled film *Black and White*.

GARVEY, MARCUS MOSIAH. 1887–1940. Jamaican publisher, journalist, entrepreneur, orator, and activist. Garvey founded the Universal Negro Improvement Association and African Communities League (UNIA-ACL). He was a staunch proponent of Black nationalism and Pan-Africanism. He founded the Black Star Line, a shipping company dedicated to taking Blacks back to Africa. At its height, the UNIA organized more Black people of the African diaspora into a single organization than any time before or since.

GAVIN, EUGENE VICTOR. 1910–? Gavin was a member of the Young Communist League. He was an early volunteer for the Spanish Civil War and fought with the Abraham Lincoln Brigade. He was severely wounded during the war and lost an eye.

GELLERT, LAWRENCE "LOU." Born Laslow Grünbaum. 1898–? Writer and music historian. Gellert immigrated to the United States from Hungary when he was seven years old, and he grew up in New York City. He amassed a large collection of field-recorded African American blues and spirituals while living and traveling in the South in the 1930s. He was accused of having fabricated the material. He disappeared in 1979.

GLESCOE, MARGARET. Mother of Lloyd Patterson, who went on the 1932 *Black and White* film trip to Moscow and stayed in the USSR, marrying a Russian woman, Vera Aralova, and starting a family. Glescoe went to the USSR to help take care of her grandson and remained in the country. She became a correspondent, writing about her impressions of Soviet life and labor. Her articles were printed in the *Chicago Defender* newspaper.

GOLD, MICHAEL "MIKE." Born Itzok Isaac Granich. 1894–1967. Journalist, novelist, literary critic, and editor. Gold was at one time considered to be "the dean" of US proletarian literature. He was the founding editor of *New Masses* literary magazine, which published progressive articles by both Black and white writers.

GONZÁLEZ, VALENTÍN GONZÁLEZ. Known as El Campesino (the Peasant). 1904–1983. Spanish military commander. González was a brigade commander in the Republican Ejército Popular (People's Army) of the Second Spanish Republic, which was fighting against the army of General Franco. Langston and Louise both met him when they visited Spain during the war.

GOODLETT, CARLTON. 1914–1997. Doctor, social-political activist, leftist, and publisher. Goodlet founded the *San Francisco Sun Reporter,* a Black weekly newspaper, and built it from a small weekly tabloid to an influential newspaper chain. He used his influence to champion civil and labor rights. He was a member of the World Peace Council and was a close friend of Pat's.

GORDON, WALTER ARTHUR. 1894–1976. Political figure. Gordon was the second African American to be named a college All-American football player, after Paul Robeson. He played for the University of California, Berkeley. In 1955 he was appointed governor of the US Virgin Islands, where he later became a Federal District Judge. He married Elizabeth Fisher, the sister of Dorothy Fisher, one of Louise and Nebby's dearest friends.

GORKY, MAXIM. Born Alexei Maximovich Peshkov. 1868–1936. Russian writer, playwright, and political activist. Gorky was the founder of the socialist realism literary style.

GOSS, MARGARET. *See* Burroughs, Margaret Taylor Goss

GRAFFIS, HERBERT BUTLER. 1893–1989. Columnist and golf sports writer for the *Chicago Sun-Times.*

GRANICH, GRACE. 1895–1971. Political activist. Granich and her husband, Max, established Higley Hill Camp in Wilmington, Vermont, in 1946. Mary Lou was one of their young summer campers in the early 1950s. They were members of the CPUSA.

GRANICH, MAX "MANNY." 1896–1987. Political activist. Granich, along with his wife, Grace, founded the Higley Hill Camp. He was the brother of communist journalist Mike Gold.

GREEN, WALTER "BUDDY." Reporter. Green worked for *People's World* newspaper in San Francisco. He was friends with Matt, Pat, and Nebby.

GRIMKÉ, ANGELINA WELD. 1880–1958. Writer and poet. Grimké's writings revealed great racial violence but were neither well received nor well publicized. She was an open lesbian. She was named after her white great aunt, Angelina Grimké Weld, a famous abolitionist and advocate for women's rights.

GROSSMAN, AUBREY. 1911–1999. Civil rights lawyer. Grossman, whose practice was based in San Francisco, represented Harry Bridges (head of the Congress of Industrial Organizations) in the 1930s, Vietnam War draft evaders in the 1960s, and Native Americans in the 1970s. As a member of the Civil Rights Congress, headed by Pat, he participated in the lengthy defense of Willie McGee, a Black man accused of raping a white woman. In 1950, during the course of the trial, he opened the door to his room at the Heidelberg Hotel in Jackson, Mississippi, for what he thought was a representative of Western Union only to be viciously attacked and beaten by a white mob swinging blackjacks. He was friends with the Crawfords and the Pattersons.

GUILLÉN, NICOLÁS. Born Nicolás Cristóbal Guillén Batista. 1902–1989. Cuban journalist, political activist, Communist, and writer. Guillén was the national poet of Cuba. He and Langston both covered the Spanish Civil War. Langston was the first to translate his work into English. Langston encouraged him to write about the Afro-Cuban experience, which ended up bringing him to national prominence.

HAMID, SUFI ABDUL. Born Eugene Brown. 1903–1938. Religious and labor leader. Hamid was dubbed the "Black Hitler of Harlem" and considered by some to be a dubious character. He was arrested for giving openly anti-Semitic speeches in the late 1930s. He had a religious temple and "mosque" in Harlem that he called the Universal Holy Temple of Tranquility.

HAMMOND, JOHN "JOHNNY." Born John Henry Hammond II. 1910–1987. Record producer, musician, talent scout, music critic, and artistic promoter. Hammond was born into a wealthy New York family and made his career in the music industry. He encouraged integration in the jazz music scene. He was a friend of Louise's in the 1930s.

HAMPTON, LIONEL. 1908–2002. Jazz vibraphonist, pianist, percussionist, composer, arranger, bandleader, and actor. Hampton is one of the great names in jazz.

HANDY, WILLIAM CHRISTOPHER "W.C." 1873–1958. Composer, songwriter, music teacher, band leader, tenor, choral director, cornetist, and trumpeter. Handy was a renowned and influential blues artist who became known as the "Father of the Blues." He composed the famous song "Saint Louis Blues."

HANSEN, HENRY. 1884–1977. Journalist, editor, literary critic and historian. Hansen was the literary editor for *New York World* and many other New York newspapers.

HARMON, WILLIAM E. 1862–1928. Real estate developer and philanthropist. Harmon was a patron of the Harlem Renaissance. In 1926 he started a foundation in his name that gave awards "for distinguished achievement among Negroes." Recipients included Langston, Countee Cullen, and Claude McKay.

HARPER, ETHEL DUDLEY BROWN ("AUNT TOY"). Seamstress and clothing designer. Harper was a childhood friend of Langston's mother. She and her musician husband, Emerson, shared various homes with Langston in New York.

HARRINGTON, OLIVER WENDELL "OLLIE." 1922–1995. Cartoonist and social satirist. Harrington was the creator of Bootsie, a cartoon social commentator in the *Pittsburgh Courier* newspaper. He immigrated to Paris in 1951 to escape US government persecution. A decade later he received political asylum in East Berlin, where he lived until his death.

HASTIE, WILLIAM HENRY. 1904–1976. Lawyer, judge, professor, government official, and advocate for civil rights. Hastie was the first African American federal judge, appointed by President Roosevelt in 1937. In 1943 he resigned his position as civilian aide to Secretary of War Henry L. Stimson in protest of racially segregated training facilities in the US Air Force.

HAYWOOD, HARRY. Born Haywood Hall Jr. 1898–1985. Communist leader, organizer, and writer. Haywood was a member of the African Black Brotherhood and later became a leading figure in the CPUSA. He lived in the Soviet Union from 1925 to 1930. Louise mentions him being in the USSR in a letter to her mother written on July 14, 1932. His 1975 autobiography is *Black Bolshevik*.

HERNDON, ANGELO BRAXTON. 1913–1997. Labor organizer. Herndon was arrested and convicted of insurrection under an arcane Georgia law for organizing Black and white workers in Atlanta in 1932. He served two years and was then released, thanks to the efforts of the International Labor Defense Committee, which was headed by Pat at the time. However, he was convicted again by the Georgia Supreme Court, but in 1937 the US Supreme Court overturned the ruling and threw out the law that it was based on as well.

HERRING, HUBERT. Circa 1889–1967. Herring served as the executive director of the American Interracial Seminar, a group of people interested in improving race relations in the United States in the 1930s.

HILL, LEONARD. Social worker. Hill was a student at Howard University when he went on the trip to the USSR to make the ultimately canceled film *Black and White* in 1932.

HOLT, NORA. 1890–1974. Nightclub performer. Holt was the first Black woman to receive a master of music degree from the Chicago Music College. She was known as one of the most glamorous individuals of the Harlem Renaissance.

HOOVER, JOHN EDGAR. 1895–1972. Hoover was the first director of the Federal Bureau of Investigations, which he led for almost fifty years. He was a rabid anti-Communist, racist, and homophobe (he was rumored to have been a closeted homosexual). He waged relentless war on millions of Americans who had any kind of leftist association and kept extensive dossiers on them.

HOPKINS, IRMA IRENE. Hopkins was a schoolmate of Louise's when the two were children in Northern California. She later moved to Los Angeles.

HOPKINS, NORMAN WILLIAM. Circa 1899 –? Hopkins was married to Irma Hopkins.

HORNE, LENA MARY CALHOUN. 1917–2010. Singer, dancer, stage and screen actress, and civil rights activist.

HUISWOUD, HERMINA DUMONT "HERMIE." 1893–1961. Translator, social activist, and socialist. Huiswoud, along with her husband, Otto, was active in the Surinamese independence movement in Europe. The couple was friends with Langston and the Pattersons.

HUISWOUD, OTTO EDUARD GERADUS MAJELIA. 1893–1961. Surinamese political activist. Huiswoud was the leader of the Surinamese independence movement and a member of the African Black Brotherhood. He was a charter member of the CPUSA and the first Black to join the party. He was the CPUSA's representative to the Executive Committee of the Comintern in 1922, and that year, along with Claude McKay, he addressed the 4th World Congress in Moscow on the "Negro Question." In the fall of 1932 he accompanied the *Black and White* film group on their tour of Soviet Central Asia.

HUNTON, WILLIAM ALPHAEUS. 1903–1970. Intellectual, author, and social activist. He was the executive director of the Council on African Affairs in which capacity he was imprisoned for six months in 1951 for contempt of court under the McCarran Internal Security Act of 1950.

HURSTON, ZORA NEALE. 1891–1960. Folklorist, playwright, actor, essayist, and fiction writer. Hurston was a protégé of the philanthropist Charlotte Osgood Mason and probably introduced Langston to her. Langston and Hurston traveled and worked together until their dispute over the rights to the play *Mule Bone.* The dispute cost Langston Mason's patronage and his friendship with Hurston. Hurston was known to be difficult by her friends and literary associates. She became politically conservative later in life and died in relative obscurity and poverty.

HYNES, WILLIAM F. Police captain. Hynes was head of the Los Angeles Police Department's notorious intelligence division, which was known as the Red Squad in the 1930s.

ICKES, HAROLD LECLAIR. 1874–1952. US administrator and politician. Ickes was Secretary of the Interior for thirteen years under President Roosevelt and also served as a member of his cabinet. In 1939 he introduced Marian Anderson to seventy-five thousand people who were gathered to hear her sing at the Lincoln Memorial after she was denied the use of Constitution Hall by the Daughters of the American Revolution. He ordered the desegregation of the national parks, including those in the South, in the 1930s.

INGRAM, REX. 1895–1969. Stage, film, and TV actor. In 1962 Ingram became the first African American to be hired for a contract role in a TV soap opera. He was one of the most talented and renowned actors of his time.

INGRAM, ZELL. 1910–? American artist, sculptor, and art teacher. Ingram met Langston through the Jelliffes while Langston was in Cleveland finishing his play *Mulatto* and recovering from the nasty breakup with his patron, Charlotte Mason, and the loss of his friendship with Zora Neale Hurston. In 1931 Ingram borrowed his mother's car, and he and Langston drove from Cleveland to Florida, where they boarded a boat and set off on an extensive trip of the Caribbean.

JACKMAN, HAROLD. 1901–1961. Teacher, editor, and patron of the arts. Jackman assisted Carl Van Vechten in establishing the James Weldon Johnson Collection at Yale University's Beinecke Library. He was friends with Langston and Countee Cullen (he is alleged to have been Cullen's lover). He corresponded with Langston up to the time of his death.

JACKSON, ESTHER COOPER. Born 1917. Social worker and civil rights activist. Jackson cofounded the Southern Negro Youth Congress and was later the cofounder and editor of the magazine *Freedomways,* a left-wing theoretical, political and literary journal that was in publication from 1961 to 1985.

JACKSON, JAMES EDWARD. 1914–2007. Civil rights activist. Jackson was a chemist and pharmacist by training, but he became interested in the civil rights movement while studying at Howard University. He was one of the cofounders of the Southern Negro Youth Congress and became a leader within the CPUSA, where he held various leadership positions. In 1951 he was indicted by the US government under the Smith Act.

JACKSON, MAHALIA. 1911–1972. Gospel and Negro spiritual singer and actress. Jackson had a powerful contralto voice that many, including Dr. Martin Luther King, considered to be the greatest female gospel voice ever.

JELLIFFE, ROWENA WOODHAM. 1892–1992. Social worker, civil rights and political activist, and theatrical promoter. Jelliffe and her husband, Russell, pioneered an interracial theater in Cleveland that became known as the Karamu House. It produced its first play with an interracial cast in 1917. By the 1960s the theater had over four thousand members. It had a resident acting group known as the Gilpin Players, named after the African American actor Charles Gilpin. Jelliffe helped integrate Wade Park Manor dining room and worked with Dr. Martin Luther King in the 1960s.

JELLIFFE, RUSSELL W. 1891–1980. Social worker, civil rights and political activist, and theatrical promoter. Jelliffe and his wife, Rowena, cofounded the Karamu House theater in Cleveland. The couple received numerous awards for their theater work. Jelliffe belonged to the NAACP and other interracial civic groups.

JENKINS, KATHERINE. Social worker. Jenkins roomed with Louise and Mother Thompson. She and her fiancé, George Sample, were part of the *Black and White* film delegation to Moscow in 1932.

JOHNSON, DOROTHY "DOT." Johnson was prominent in Los Angeles's African American women's social circles. She was friends with Langston, the Pattersons, and the Crawfords.

JOHNSON, JAMES P. 1894–1955. Pianist and composer. Johnson's music was considered a pivotal connection between ragtime and jazz piano styles. He helped popularize the stride style of playing.

JOHNSON, JAMES WELDON. 1871–1938. Lyricist, editor, educator, writer, social activist, and historian. Johnson was the executive secretary of the NAACP from 1920 to 1930. In 1900 he wrote the lyrics to "Lift Every Voice and Sing," which his brother, John Rosamond Johnson, had written the music to. The song became known as the Negro national anthem.

JONES, EDITH. Jones worked at the IWO and was part of the staff of the Harlem Suitcase Theatre.

JONES, MILDRED. Jones was an art student at the Hampton Institute when she went on the *Black and White* film trip to the USSR in 1932. She stayed on for a year afterward, working for the English-language newspaper *The Moscow News*.

JONES, ROBERT EARL. 1910–2006. Stage and screen actor. Jones got his start acting in Langston's Harlem Suitcase Theatre. He was the father of actor James Earl Jones.

JOSEPHSON, BARNEY. 1902–1988. Nightclub and restaurant owner. Josephson opened the club Café Society in Greenwich Village in 1938 with John Hammond. It was the first racially integrated nightclub in New York City. Billie Holiday first sang "Strange Fruit" there.

JUNGHANS, KARL. 1897–1984. German film director, cinematographer, actor, and dramaturge. Junghans was to be the director of the film *Black and White*. He dated Sonia Slonim, author Vladimir Nabokov's sister.

KOESTLER, ARTHUR. Born Kösztler Artúr. 1905–1983. Hungarian-British author and journalist. Koestler joined the Communist Party in Germany in 1931, although he resigned from it seven years later. His novel *Darkness at Noon* (1940) brought him international notice. He met Langston in the southern USSR while Langston was there in 1932–1933.

LANGSTON, JOHN MERCER. 1829–1897. Abolitionist, attorney, professor, US congressman, and activist. Langston and his brothers were born free in Virginia. His father was Ralph Quarles, his mother's white slave owner, originally from England. His older brother Charles was Langston Hughes's maternal grandfather. Langston is believed to have been the first Black ever elected to public office in the United States when he was elected as town clerk in 1855 in Ohio. He helped found Howard University's law school and served as the school's first dean, from 1868 to 1875. In 1888 he was elected as a member of the US House of Representatives from Virginia and served one term, from 1890 to 1891.

LANHAM, HENDERSON LOVELACE. 1888–1957. Lawyer, politician, and US congressman. Lanham served as a member from Georgia of the US House of Representatives from 1947 to 1957. He was acting chair of the House Select Committee on Lobbying Activities, which subpoenaed Pat in 1950.

LEARY, LEWIS SHERIDAN. 1835–1859. Harnessmaker. Leary was the first husband of Langston's maternal grandmother, Mary Sampson Patterson Leary Langston. They both served as conductors on the Underground Railroad. Leary was one of the twenty-one men with John Brown in the attack on the federal arsenal at Harper's Ferry, Virginia. He was fatally shot during the raid.

LENIN. Born Vladimir Ilyich Ulyanov. 1870–1924. Russian revolutionary, intellectual, author, lawyer, philosopher, and economic theorist. Lenin funded the Soviet Communist Party. He was the leader of the 1917 Russian Revolution and the founder of the Union of Soviet Socialist Republics. He established the Communist International.

LEONARD, CHARLES. Writer and producer. Leonard worked at Columbia Pictures. He produced Wallace Thurman's play *Harlem* on Broadway. He was blacklisted for his alleged leftist views.

LEWIS, JUANITA. Singer. Lewis was one of two singers who went to the USSR in 1932 to film *Black and White*.

LEWIS, MOLLIE VIRGIL. *See* Moon, Mollie Virgil Lewis

LEWIS, THURSTON MCNAIRY. Lewis went on the 1932 trip to Moscow to film *Black and White*. He sided with Ted Poston, Laurence Alberga, and Henry Lee Moon against the official Soviet explanation for the cancellation of the film. He was allegedly once a member of the CPUSA.

LIEBER, MAXIM. 1897–1993. Polish literary agent and alleged spy. Lieber was a prominent New York literary agent in the 1930s and 1940s. He fled to Poland in 1950 after Whittaker Chambers implicated him as a Soviet spy.

LINDSAY, POWELL. 1905–1987. Actor, director, playwright, and producer. Lindsay wrote the play *Young Man of Harlem* in the late 1930s for the Harlem Suitcase Theatre, although the theater closed before producing it.

LOCKE, ALAIN LEROY. 1886–1954. Writer, philosopher, educator, professor, and patron of the arts. Locke was the first African American Rhodes Scholar. He headed the philosophy department at Howard University for almost forty years. He is heralded as having been the father of the Harlem Renaissance. He conceived of and edited *The New Negro: An Interpretation* (1925), an anthology of Harlem Renaissance writings. He was a protégé and friend of the philanthropist Charlotte Osgood Mason. When Louise came to New York in 1928, she obtained a fellowship, through Locke, with the New York Urban League to study social work. Locke may have introduced Louise to Mason.

LOUIS, JOE. Born Joseph Louis Barrow. Also known as the "Brown Bomber." 1914–1981. Professional boxer. He held the title of World Heavyweight Champion from 1937 to 1949. His second match against Max Schmeling (whom Nazi leaders were extolling as a representative of Germanic Aryan race superiority) in June 1938 was considered one of the most famous boxing matches of all time and one of the major sports events of the twentieth century.

LOVE, VAUGHN. 1907–1990. Love went to Spain with the Abraham Lincoln Brigade to fight against a fascist takeover of the country by General Franco. The Abraham Lincoln Brigade's forces were integrated at time when the US Army was segregated. Both Louise and Langston met him in Spain.

LUCAS, RADCLIFFE "RADDY." Lucas was Langston's companion, secretary, and chauffeur on his first trip through the South.

LUMUMBA, PATRICE EMERY. 1925–1961. Congolese independence leader and politician. Lumumba helped the Republic of the Congo win independence from Belgium in June 1961. He then served as the first prime minister of the country. He was murdered in 1961 during a coup that was supported by the CIA and Belgium. Mobutu Sese Seko, a puppet tyrant, was placed in power and brutally reigned the Congo until 1997.

MARBURY, ELIZABETH "BESSY." 1856–1933. Literary and theatrical agent and producer. Marbury represented Zora Neale Hurston, George Bernard Shaw, Oscar Wilde, and other notables.

MASON, CHARLOTTE OSGOOD. Born Charlotte Louise Van Der Veer Quick. 1854–1946. Socialite and philanthropist. Mason was a wealthy and influential patron of the Harlem Renaissance, which she became attracted to through her interest in African "primitivism." She believed it was important that Negroes remain in their natural state of "primitiveness." Her protégés included Alain Locke, the Mexican painter Miguel Covarrubias, Zora Neale Hurston, and Langston. Paul Robeson is reported to have refused her largesse. She insisted on being called "Godmother." It was said that she received her protégés while seated on an elevated, throne-like chair. She briefly employed Louise as secretary to Langston and Hurston. In her unpublished memoir, Louise described that she found out that she was considered one of Mason's "godchildren" and was expected to regularly send her thank you cards, which Louise acquiesced to. When Louise became part of a dispute between Langston and Hurston over the play *Mule Bone,* Mason fired her.

MAYNOR, DOROTHY LEIGH. 1910–1975. Soprano, concert singer, music educator, and actress. Maynor toured the world in the 1930s and '40s with her composer husband, Will Cook, although the two never performed in the United States, where venue doors were closed to her because of racism. She founded the Harlem School of the Arts in 1964 and took enrollment from twenty students to one thousand by the time she retired, in 1979. She was friends with Louise, Pat, and Langston.

MAYS JR., WILLIE HOWARD. Born 1931. Professional baseball player. Mays played for the New York Giants, and he followed the team when it moved to San Francisco in 1957. He ended his career back in New York City with the Mets. He was elected to the Baseball Hall of Fame in 1979. He was nicknamed the "Say Hey Kid."

MCCARTHY, JOSEPH. 1908–1957. Politician. McCarthy, a Republican, served as a US senator from Wisconsin from 1947 to 1957. He was chair of the Senate Committee on Government Operations, which contained the Senate Permanent Subcommittee on Investigations. He became the most visible face of the Cold War and the anti-Communist witch-hunts of the 1950s when he held up a list of supposedly known Communists working in the State Department during a speech in Virginia in 1950. His fanatical reign of terror ended when he was officially censored by the US Senate in December 1954 for unethical investigative methods after he turned his "Red Scare" tactics on the US Army. The US Army hearings that he instigated in 1953 were the first government hearings ever televised. The term "McCarthyism" is based on his demagogic and discriminatory tactics.

MCCLELLAN, JOHN LITTLE. 1896–1977. Politician. McClellan was a Democratic senator from Arkansas from 1943 to 1977. He was chair of the Senate Permanent Subcommittee on Investigations.

MCCLENDON, ROSE. Born Rosalie Virginia Scott. 1884–1936. Stage actress, theater administrator, and director. McClendon was the leading African American actress of her time, and she was called the "Negro First Lady of the Dramatic Stage" and the "Sepia Barrymore." She appeared or starred in eleven Broadway plays and cofounded the Negro People's Theatre in Harlem with Dick Campbell.

MCCONNELL, FANNIE MAE. 1911–2005. Editor. McConnell's first marriage was to Ligon Buford, who worked with her at the Negro People's Theatre in Chicago, where she was director. The marriage ended in divorce. She later married author Ralph Ellison and was essential to the development and completion of his book *The Invisible Man* (1952).

MCCORMICK, ROBERT RUTHERFORD "COLONEL." 1880–1955. Newspaper publisher. McCormick was the owner and publisher of the *Chicago Tribune* newspaper. He was a conservative Republican and an anti-unionist. His family owned the International Harvester Company.

MCDANIEL, HATTIE. 1895–1952. Film actress and singer. McDaniel won the Academy Award for Best Supporting Actress in 1940 for the role of Mammy in *Gone with the Wind* (1939), becoming the first African American to win an Academy Award.

MCGEE, MARCELLA WALKER. 1904–1997. Librarian and social and community activist. Together with her second husband, Lewis Allen McGee, a Unitarian minister and her brother, George Walker, Jr., they formed the Interracial Free Religious Fellowship of the Unitarian Church in Chicago's Black community. Initially they met at the Abraham Lincoln School Center that had been established by Pat.

MCGEE, WILLIE. 1916?–1951. Laborer. McGee was sentenced to death by an all-white jury in Mississippi in 1945 for the rape of a white woman. However, the "evidence" against him was highly questionable. The CRC defended him, but they ultimately lost the exhausting eight-year legal fight, and McGee was electrocuted by the State of Mississippi in 1951. Civil rights fighters considered his execution a legal lynching. His case was a cause célèbre, and he was supported by notables such as Albert Einstein, Josephine Baker, William Faulkner, and Jessica Mitford. Bella Abzug was on his final legal team.

MCKAY, FESTUS CLAUDE. 1889–1948. Jamaican-American writer, poet, journalist, and political activist. McKay was a founding member of the African Blood Brotherhood, which was active from 1919 to 1922. His membership in the CPUSA is disputed, but he did travel to the USSR several times during his life. At the 4th World Communist Congress, he urged the Comintern to take up the "Negro Question" and support the formation of a "Black Belt" in the southern United States. He responded to the twenty-five major race riots of the violent "Red Summer" of 1919, which occurred when returning Black World War I veterans demanded their civil and human rights, by writing his most famous poem, *If We Must Die,* which became known as the 1919 anthem of the Negro. He repudiated his earlier Marxist ideas before he died and joined the Catholic Church.

MCKENZIE, ALAN. Salesman. McKenzie was part of the *Black and White* film delegation to Moscow in 1932. He was the only member of the CPUSA on the trip.

MCPHERSON, AIMEE ELIZABETH KENNEDY SEMPLE. 1890–1944. Canadian religious leader. McPherson was a self-anointed religious fundamentalist and a pioneer radio evangelist. She founded the International Church of the Foursquare Gospel, known as the Foursquare Church. She was a rabid anti-Communist and verbally attacked Langston in November 1940 when he made a speaking appearance in Pasadena, California, denouncing his poem "Goodbye, Christ."

MELLA, JULIO ANTONIO. 1903–1929. Cuban student organizer. Mella founded the Cuban Communist Party. He was president of Cuba's first National Congress. He started the University of Havana's Jose Marti Club. He was expelled from the university in 1925 and arrested. After his release he fled to Central America. He was assassinated in 1929 on a street in Mexico while walking with photographer Tina Modotti.

MENELIK II, ABETO. Baptized Sahle Maryam. 1844–1913. Ethiopian emperor and king. Menelik claimed to be a descendant of the Queen of Sheba and King Solomon. He defeated Italian invaders at the famous battle of Adwa in 1896. Ethiopia is the only African country never to be colonized by Europeans. He consolidated and modernized Ethiopia.

MILLER, DORIS "DORIE." 1919–1943. Cook in the US Navy. Miller was serving on the USS *West Virginia* during the Japanese attack on Pearl Harbor on December 7, 1941. He bravely took over a machine gun, which he had not been trained to fire, and shot down four of the seven attacking Japanese aircraft, becoming one of the first heroes of World War II and the first African American to be awarded the Navy Cross. He died during war, when the escort ship he was on was torpedoed by the Japanese. Langston mentions him in his poem "Jim Crow's Last Stand" (1943).

MILLER, JUANITA ELLSWORTH. 1903–1961. Social worker. Miller cofounded the League of Allied Arts in 1939 in Los Angeles. She and her husband, Loren Miller, worked for racial equality and civil rights and against housing discrimination. They participated in philanthropy and the arts. The couple had two sons, Loren Jr. and Edward.

MILLER, LOREN. 1903–1967. Lawyer, judge, and social activist. Miller was the publisher and owner of the *California Eagle,* a Los Angeles African American newspaper, and also one of the paper's journalists. He went on the *Black and White* film trip to USSR in 1932. He was a California Supreme Court Justice from 1964 to 1967.

MILLS, FLORENCE. Born Florence Winfrey. 1896–1927. Singer, dancer, and comedian. Mills was known as the "Queen of Happiness."

MITCHELL, ABRIEA "ABBIE." 1884–1960. Soprano opera singer. Mitchell sang the part of Clara in the 1935 premiere of *Porgy and Bess.* She married composer Will Marion Cook, and together they performed all over Europe. Their son was Will Mercer Cook, known as Cook Mercer, a friend of Langston's.

MONTERO, FRANK CURLE. Montero was a student at Howard University when he went on the *Black and White* film trip to the USSR in 1932.

MOON, HENRY LEE. 1901–1985. Journalist, editor, and civil rights advocate. Moon went on the *Black and White* film trip to the USSR in 1932. He became director of public relations for the NAACP in 1948.

MOON, MOLLIE VIRGIL LEWIS. 1908–1990. Pharmacist, social worker, and public relations executive. Moon was a graduate student at Columbia University's Teachers College when she went on the *Black and White* film trip to the USSR in 1932. She later married Henry Lee Moon.

MOONEY, THOMAS "TOM." 1882–1942. Political activist, socialist, and labor leader. Mooney was framed and wrongly convicted of the San Francisco Preparedness Day bombing in 1916 and jailed at San Quentin State Prison in California. He was finally pardoned in 1933.

MOORE, RICHARD BENJAMIN. 1893–1978. Barbadian writer, civil rights activist, and Communist. Moore advocated the use of the term African Americans instead of Negro for Blacks. He joined the African Blood Brotherhood in 1919. In 1928 he ran for US Congress on the Communist Party ticket. In 1935 he became an International Labor Defense organizer in New England and advocated justice for the Scottsboro Boys. He owned the Frederick Douglass Book Center in Harlem.

MORA, CONSTANCIA DE LA. 1906–1950. Spanish feminist and writer. Mora was born into an aristocratic family. She fought in the Spanish Civil War against General Franco. Her autobiography, *In Place of Splendor,* was published in 1939. She was a member of Spain's Communist Party

MOSS, CARLTON. 1909–1997. Screenwriter, actor, filmmaker, cultural scholar, and social critic. Moss made a number of documentaries about African Americans. He left the set of Elia Kazan's film *Pinky* (1949) because he felt the film demeaned African Americans.

MOTEN, ETTA. 1901–2004. Actress, contralto singer, and community activist. Moten's signature role was Bess in the 1942 Broadway production of *Porgy and Bess.*

MULZAC, HUGH NATHANIEL. 1886–1971. St. Vincent-Grenadines. Ship captain. Mulzac commanded the SS *Booker T. Washington* in World War II, making him the first African American shipmaster of a US Merchant Marine ship. The ship was christened by Marian Anderson and had an integrated crew.

MUNI, PAUL. Born Meschelem Meier Weisenfreund. 1895–1967. Polish-American stage and film actor. Muni was active during the 1930s and '40s. He read Langston's poem *Freedom Plow* over the Blue Network radio station on Monday, March 15, 1943, the day Mary Lou was born.

MUSE, CLARENCE EDOUARD. 1889–1974. Actor, screenwriter, director, composer. Muse was the first African American to star in a Hollywood film (*Broken Earth,* in 1936). He and Langston cowrote the screenplay for *Way Down South* (1939).

NORTH, JOSEPH. Born Jacob Soifer. 1904–1976. Ukranian-American writer, poet, editor, and journalist. North edited *New Masses* magazine in the 1930s and then worked as a writer and foreign correspondent for the *Daily Worker,* the newspaper of the CPUSA.

NUGENT, RICHARD BRUCE. 1906–1987. Writer and painter. Nugent was part of the Harlem Renaissance. He was an open homosexual at that time. He was friends with Langston and Louise.

PADMORE, GEORGE. Born Malcolm Ivan Meredith Nurse. 1902–1959. Trinidadian journalist and author. Padmore was an early member of the CPUSA, and he became a leading Pan-Africanist. Once a friend and ally of Pat's, their friendship ended after Padmore left the communist movement and embraced a more Black nationalist political orientation. He served as an advisor to Ghanaian president Kwame Nkrumah in post-independence Ghana.

PATEL, RAJNI. 1915?–1980. Indian lawyer, judge, and independence activist. Patel was president of the Congress Pradish Committee of Bombay. He had been a member of the leftist Indian Students Federation in his youth. He met Paul and Eslanda Robeson when he was studying law in London in the late 1930s, at which time he was a member of the India League. After his studies he traveled to the United States and was deeply angered by the racism he saw. He met Langston at a party at Noel Sullivan's estate in Carmel. Upon his return to India, he was arrested, accused of anti-British and anti-war propaganda activities.

PATIÑO, FELA, CUCA, AND DOLORES. The three Patiño sisters were friends of Langston's father, and they cared for him until he died in 1919 in Mexico City. He left everything to them in his will. They took care of Langston when he traveled to Mexico after his father's death. Louise visited the sisters in 1933.

PATTERSON, LLOYD. Patterson was on the 1932 *Black and White* film delegation to Moscow. He stayed in USSR and married a Russian woman, Vera, who was a clothing and theater designer. They had three sons together, one of whom was James Patterson.

PATTERSON, LOLA. Born 1935. Russian engineer. Patterson is Pat's oldest daughter, from his second marriage, to Vera Gorohovskaya, during his stay in Moscow in the 1930s. She currently lives in New York.

PERCY, WILLIAM ALEXANDER. 1885–1942. Poet and writer. Percy wrote *Lanterns on the Levee: Recollections of a Planter's Son* (1941). He was from the Mississippi delta.

PETERSON, DOROTHY RANDOLPH. 1897–1978. Teacher, aspiring actress, and patron of the arts. Peterson used her father's Brooklyn home for literary salons. She was a member of the Negro Experimental Theatre from 1929 to 1931. She taught Spanish most of her life.

PHARR, EULAH. Circa 1897–1989. Cook and housekeeper. Pharr worked for the wealthy San Franciscan Noel Sullivan, who was one of Langston's patrons. She and Langston became good friends.

PHILLIPS, HILARY. Phillips was a founding member of the Harlem Suitcase Theatre. He was the theater's codirector and an executive committee member.

PITTMAN, JOHN. 1906–1993. Writer, journalist, and social political activist. Pittman was the *Daily Worker*'s correspondent to Moscow in the early 1960s, the same time that Mary Lou was studying at the Peoples' Friendship University. She visited him and his family often while she was living in Moscow. He knew Matt from his early days in Berkeley.

PORTIER, SIDNEY. Born 1927. Bahamian actor, film director, author, and diplomat. Portier became the first Black man to win an Oscar for Best Actor in 1964 for his role as Homer Smith in *Lilies of the Field*. Since 1997 he has been the ambassador of the Bahamas to Japan.

POSTON, THEODORE "TED" ROOSEVELT MAJOR. 1906–1974. Journalist, short story writer, and union organizer. Poston was known as the dean of Black journalists, as he was the first African American staff reporter at a major daily newspaper—the *New York Post*. He was active in the formation of the Newspaper Guild. He was a member of Roosevelt's "Black Cabinet," an informal group of African Americans who advised and served the administration. Poston went on the *Black and White* film trip to the Moscow in 1932 with Louise, Matt, and Langston, but he disagreed with what they believed to be the reason for the postponement of the film.

POWELL JR., ADAM CLAYTON. 1908–1972. Politician, pastor, and civil rights activist. He followed in his father's footsteps and became an Abyssinian Baptist Church pastor. He was the first African American elected to the US Congress from New York. He served from 1945 to 1971. In 1944 Langston wrote the lyrics for the theme song of Clayton's first campaign, "Let My People Go," despite the fact that Langston's name was on the Department of Justice's subversives list. In 1961 Clayton became chair of the Committee on Education and Labor, and he used his position to support important social legislation. In 1967 he was accused of corruption and excluded from his seat, although he won it back with a Supreme Court decision in 1969.

PRIMUS, PEARL EILEEN. 1919–1994. Trinidadian-American modern dancer, choreographer, anthropologist, and teacher. Primus has been called "the grandmother of African-American dance." She saw the need to promote African dance as an art form worthy of study and performance. She choreographed a dance piece to Langston's poem, "The Negro Speaks of Rivers" (1920). She was friends with Louise, Langston, and Pat.

RAM, JAGJIVAN. Also called Babuji. 1908–1986. Indian independence freedom fighter, social reformer, and politician. Singh believed in nonviolent disobedience and resistance. He was imprisoned twice in India for publicly denouncing India's participation in World War II. He rose from the "untouchable" caste to be appointed to various ministerial positions in the Indian government, including deputy prime minister and minister of defense. He was the youngest minister in Nehru's government.

RANDOLPH, ASA PHILIP. 1889–1979. Civil rights activist and labor leader. Randolph organized and led the Brotherhood of Sleeping Car Porters, the first predominantly Black labor union. He later organized the 1963 March on Washington. He was member of the Socialist Party.

REISSIG, HERMAN F. Protestant minister and activist. Reissig was an official of the American League for Peace and Democracy. He supported the Loyalists during the Spanish Civil War.

RICHARDS, BEAH. Born Beulah Elizabeth Richardson. 1926–2000. Stage, film, and TV actress, poet, playwright, writer, and social activist. Richards met the Pattersons at the Los Angeles home of actress Frances Williams and they became good friends.

RICHARDSON, THOMAS. Richardson was the executive director of the Harlem Suitcase Theatre.

RICKS MCGEE, MARCELLA WALKER. *See* McGee, Marcella Walker

RIVERA, DIEGO. 1886–1957. Mexican painter, muralist, and social activist. Rivera was a member of Mexican Communist Party. He was married to the famous Mexican painter Frida Kahlo.

ROBERSON, MASON. Circa 1907–1977. Journalist. Roberson founded the Bay Area's first African American newspaper, *The Spokesman,* and worked as a journalist for the paper. He also wrote for *People's World,* the West Coast Communist Party newspaper. He was friends with Matt, Nebby, and Langston.

ROBESON, ESLANDA CARDOZA GOODE. 1896–1976. Writer, actor, anthropologist, and activist. Robeson married Paul Robeson in 1921 and in 1925 became his business manager. She received a degree in anthropology in 1973 from the London School of Economics while they were living in London. In the mid to late 1930s their son, Paul Jr., was schooled in the Soviet Union, where her two brothers were living. By 1938 they had all returned to the United States. Like Paul, she was called to testify before Congress during the 1950s. At her hearing, when asked if she was a member of the Communist Party, she took the Fifth Amendment. Her passport was revoked until the ruling was overturned by the US Supreme Court in 1958.

ROBESON, PAUL LEROY. 1898–1976. Stage and screen actor, concert singer, All-American college athlete, lawyer, scholar, newspaper publisher, polyglot, and political activist. Robeson had a rich and distinctive baritone voice and was famous both nationally and internationally as one of the greatest American singers of his age. He was politically progressive and a champion of oppressed peoples everywhere. Throughout his life, he led, participated in, and lent his name to many civil rights struggles and progressive causes. He traveled to the Soviet Union for the first time in 1934. In 1938 he went to Spain to support the Loyalists, who were fighting General Franco's fascist regime. He and Pat met in 1920 in Harlem. They ended up getting married to two best friends, Minnie

Sumner and Eslanda Cardoza Goode. Pat's marriage to Sumner ended in an early divorce, but Paul stayed married to Goode until his death.

ROMILLY, RITA. 1900–1984. Dancer, dance instructor, and actress. Romilly was known for the integrated parties she threw with Harlem Renaissance notables.

ROSE, BILLY. Born William Samuel Rosenberg. 1899–1966. Broadway impresario, producer, showman, writer, lyricist, composer, director, and theater owner. Rose was known as the "Little Napoleon of showmanship." In 1943 he produced the play *Carmen Jones* on Broadway with an all-Black cast.

ROSENWALD, JULIUS. 1862–1932. Businessman, clothier, manufacturer, and philanthropist. Rosenwald was one of the owners of the department store chain Sears, Roebuck and Company. He created the Julius Rosenwald Fund, which donated millions of dollars to the development of rural schools for Black children in the South and gave grants to emerging Black artists and others. Langston received two Rosenwald grants.

ROSS, ROBERT "BOB." Ross went to the Soviet Union in the 1920s and stayed, finding work acting in films and lecturing. He married there and had two daughters, Ella and Ina.

ROUMAIN, JACQUES. 1907–1944. Haitian writer, poet, ethnologist, and militant political activist. Roumain is best known for his posthumously published novel, *Masters of the Dew* (1944), which was translated from French by Langston. In his youth Roumain was a leader of a student movement against the US occupation of Haiti. He was arrested for his militant opposition to the Haitian government in 1928 and released in 1929. In 1934 he founded the Haitian Communist Party (Pati Kominis Ayisyen). He lived in exile for several years in New York. In 1944, when he was back in Haiti, he died under mysterious circumstances. He was thirty-seven years old.

RUDD, WAYLAND. ?–1952. Actor. Rudd was the first African American actor to portray Othello in a white professional company on an American stage. He also performed in Eugene O'Neill's *Emperor Jones*. He went on the *Black and White* film trip in 1932 and stayed in the Soviet Union.

RUNYON, MARIE. Born 1915. Social and housing activist. Runyon ran an organization called the Harlem Restoration Project, which restored abandoned and neglected apartment buildings in Harlem, often employing ex-convicts and people assigned by the New York City Department of Probation.

SACCO, FERDINANDO NICOLA. 1891–1927. Italian-born anarchist. Sacco was an associate of the Italian anarchist Luigi Galleani. He and Bartolomeo Vanzetti were accused of murdering two men during an armed robbery in Braintree, Massachusetts, in 1920. Many thought they were framed, including Pat, who went to Boston to join the mass protests against their impending execution. In 1925 a man named Celestino Madeiros confessed to the crime. The Sacco and Vanzetti case became a national and international cause célèbre. Despite the public outcry, the two were executed in 1927. Pat described in his autobiography, *The*

Man Who Cried Genocide, that the case was a political awakening for him, as he realized that Blacks were not the only objects of racist subjugation and lynching.

SAMPLE, GEORGE. Sample went on the *Black and White* film trip to Moscow in 1932, along with his fiancé, Katherine Jenkins.

SANGIGIAN, MARY. 1912–2007. Armenian-American artist. Sangigian married Theodore Ward in June 1940. She was a member of the Harlem Suitcase Theatre at one point.

SAVAGE, AUGUSTA. 1892–1962. Sculptor, teacher, and activist. Savage was associated with the Harlem Renaissance and was a close friend of Louise's. They had a political salon in the early 1930s called Vanguard.

SAVAGE, MARY. Savage was Louise's maternal cousin. She moved to New York from Cincinnati to live with Louise and Mother Thompson. She took care of Mother Thompson while Louise was in Russia. She was a member of the Harlem Suitcase Theatre and was friends with Langston and Pat.

SCHMELING, MAX. 1906–2005. German boxer. Schmeling was considered a potent symbol of Nazi Aryan dominance and power. He was heavyweight champion of the world in 1930 and 1932. He knocked out Joe Louis in their first match in 1936. Their rematch in 1938 was considered the sports event of the century. Louis knocked Schmeling out in the first round.

SEGURE, ROSE. Social worker. Segure was allegedly operating as an undercover FBI agent for many years while working as a Communist Party functionary in California. She coordinated a course on community services at the California Labor School and helped organize the Science for Victory Committee at the University of California.

SELASSIE, HAILE. Born Lij Ras Tafari Makonnen. 1892–1975. Ethiopian regent and politician. Selassie's 1930 coronation as Emperor of Ethiopia is seen as the birth of the Rastafarian movement. He was known by many names, such as the Emperor of Ethiopia, the Lion of Judah, the King of Kings.

SENGHOR, LÉOPOLD SÉDAR. 1906–2001. Senegalese poet, writer, cultural theorist, and politician. Senghor was the first president of Senegal. He founded the *négritude* philosophical movement.

SHAW, GEORGE BERNARD. 1856–1950. Irish playwright, writer, journalist, and socialist. Shaw cofounded the London School of Economics. He won a Nobel Prize for Literature in 1925 and an Oscar in 1938 for the screenplay of *Pygmalion.*

SIMONE, NINA. Born Eunice Kathleen Waymon. 1933–2003. Singer, pianist, songwriter, arranger, and social activist. Simone was known as the "High Priestess of Soul." She sang jazz, blues, pop, and folk music and was very popular.

SKINNER, CORNELIA OTIS. 1897–1993. Author and stage and screen actress. Skinner lived in New York and was friends with Langston.

SMITH, NEIL HOMER. Journalist and postal clerk. Smith went on the *Black and White* film trip to the USSR and stayed on in the country, helping to modernize the Soviet postal system.

SOLOMON, SAM B. Also known as the Moses of Miami. ?–1966. Editor, undertaker, voter, and civil rights organizer and activist. Solomon was active in the 1930s and '40s in Miami. He edited *The Miami Whip,* a Black weekly newspaper in Florida. In 1939 he led a march of over two thousand African Americans to the polling booth. He demanded African American voting rights and capital improvements in the living conditions in "Black Town" Miami through the Negro Citizen Service League, of which he was the president. The demonstration was successful, and in 1941 over fifty thousand African Americans registered to vote. The Ku Klux Klan marched and hung a black man in effigy, but Solomon was quoted as saying the Blacks would still vote, which they did. Langston penned a poem to him, "Ballad of Sam Solomon," which was published in 1941.

SPENCER, KENNETH LEE "KEN." 1913–1964. Opera and bass baritone concert singer and stage and film actor. Spencer was prominent in the 1930s and '40s. He married Dorothy Fisher, Louise and Nebby's closest friend. In 1950 he moved to Germany, where he continued to have a successful artistic career.

SPINGARN, ARTHUR BARNETTE. 1878–1971. Lawyer. Spingarn was Langston's lawyer and a patron of the Harlem Renaissance. He was head of the legal committee of NAACP. Howard University's library, Moreland-Spingarn, was named after him after he donated a large collection of African American works to the institution.

STEFFENS, LINCOLN. 1866–1936. Influential journalist, writer, lecturer, and political philosopher. Political leftist. Steffens was one of the original muckrakers. He was a member of the Carmel, California, chapter of the John Reed Club. He was friends with Langston and Noel Sullivan. He was married to Australian-British journalist and activist Ella Winter. His autobiography, *The Autobiography of Lincoln Steffens,* was published in 1931.

STILL, WILLIAM GRANT. 1895–1978. Conductor, composer, jazz arranger, and oboist. Still wrote over 150 compositions. He was considered the dean of African American composers. He composed the music for Langston's musical, *Troubled Island,* which premiered in 1949.

STOKOWSKI, LEOPOLD. 1882–1977. British composer, organist, choirmaster, and conductor. Stokowski was a political liberal.

STOWE, LELAND. 1899–1994. War correspondent. Stowe won a Pulitzer Prize in 1930. He lived in France.

SULLIVAN, MAXINE. 1911–1987. Singer, musician, and stage and screen actress. Sullivan was considered one of the best jazz vocalists of the 1930s, before the emergence of singers like Ella Fitzgerald, Sarah Vaughn, and Billie Holiday.

SULLIVAN, NOEL. 1890–1956. Patron of the arts. Sullivan was a wealthy man from San Francisco and a patron of the Harlem Renaissance. He became one of Langston's most faithful supporters, offering him lodging in his homes in San Francisco, Carmel, and the Carmel Valley in California so that he could write in peace. He included Langston, when he was in town, in most of his social gatherings. He was the nephew and heir of US Senator James D. Phelan.

TALMADGE, EUGENE. 1884–1946. Politician. Talmadge was a staunch segregationist and white supremacist. He was twice elected governor of Georgia, serving from 1933 to 1937 and from 1941 to 1943.

THOMPSON, LULA MAE BROWN TOLES. Circa 1875–1933. Domestic and pastry cook. Thompson was Louise's mother. Her first husband was William J. Toles, Louise's father. Shortly after she gave birth to Louise in Chicago, she divorced Toles and moved to the Northwest. There she met and married Hadwick Thompson, whose last name Louise adopted. Thompson often passed for white, which enabled her to get work all over the Northwest, although this meant she was often forced to board Louise with strangers. Later she and Louise lived together on and off until her untimely death from metastatic ovarian cancer in New York.

THURMAN, HOWARD. 1900–1981. Theologian, minister, writer, philosopher, educator, and civil rights leader. Thurman was Dean of Chapel at Howard and Boston Universities. He married Sue Bailey, one of Louise's close friends.

THURMAN, SUE BAILEY. 1904–1996. Author, lecturer, and historian. Thurman was an advisor to Mahatma Gandhi. She founded and edited *AfroAmerican Women's Journal* (1940–1944), the organ of the National Council of Negro Women. She lived with Louise and her mother in Harlem until she married Howard Thurman.

THURMAN, WALLACE "WALLY." 1902–1934. Writer, playwright, Hollywood screenwriter, editor, literary critic, and publisher. Thurman was one of the original figures of the Harlem Renaissance and the New Negro Movement. He lived in a rooming house he and Zora Neale Hurston dubbed the Niggerati Manor with Langston and other young Black writers. In 1929 his play *Harlem* became the first play written by an African American to be produced on Broadway. It had ninety-three performances. He was briefly married to Louise. Langston described him as brilliant, cynical, and bitter. His books include *The Blacker the Berry* (1929) and *Infants of the Spring* (1932). He was editor for the provocative and politically progressive literary magazine *Fire!!* It folded after the first issue, although it created a huge controversy and left a legacy.

TILL, EMMETT LOUIS. 1941–1955. Till was a fourteen-year-old Chicago youth who was savagely mutilated and murdered by two white men from Money, Mississippi. His murder sparked national outrage and triggered an upsurge in the 1950s Civil Rights Movement.

TOLSON, MELVIN BEAUNORUS. 1898–1966. Poet, educator, columnist, politician, debater, and activist. Tolson worked to organize farm laborers and tenant farmers. He was portrayed by Denzel Washington in the 2007 film *The Great Debaters*.

TOOMER, JEAN. Born Nathan Eugene Toomer. 1894–1967. Poet and novelist. Toomer was part of the Harlem Renaissance. His first book, *Cane* (1923), is considered his finest.

VAN VECHTEN, CARL. 1880–1964. Writer, journalist, and photographer. Van Vechten was a patron of Harlem Renaissance artists. He was a close friend and promoter of Langston's. He also promoted Nella Larsen, Rudolph Fisher, Countee Cullen, Wallace Thurman, James Weldon Johnson, Paul Robeson, and many others. He was very close to Zora Neale Hurston. He brought Langston to Alfred and Blanche Knopf, the founders and owners of the Alfred A. Knopf publishing house, who published Langston's first book and many of his others. He established the James Weldon Johnson Collection at the Beinecke Library of Rare Books at Yale University, where Langston's papers are now archived.

WALKER, CHARLES RUMFORD. 1893–1974. Editor, journalist, and author. Walker wrote several books, most notably *American City* (1937).

WALLACE, DEAN. Critic. Wallace was a cultural critic for the *San Francisco Chronicle*.

WALLACE, HENRY AGARD. 1888–1965. Politician. Wallace was the thirty-third vice president of the United States, serving from 1941 to 1945 under President Franklin D. Roosevelt. He had been a liberal Republican, but he became a Democrat because of his support of the New Deal. He spoke out during the 1943 race riots in Detroit, saying, "we cannot fight to crush Nazi brutality abroad and condone race riots at home." In the 1948 presidential campaign he ran unsuccessfully for president on the Progressive Party ticket. Among other issues, he advocated ending the nascent Cold War and segregation.

WALROND, ERIC DERWENT. 1898–1966. Guyanese writer and journalist. Walrond edited Universal Negro Improvement Association's official organ, *Negro World* magazine, and later worked for *Opportunity,* the journal of the Urban League.

WARD JR., ROOSEVELT. Also known as Douglas Turner Ward. Born 1930. Stage and screen actor, director, writer, and playwright. Ward wrote a column entitled "The Pitch" for the CPUSA's New York newspaper, the *Daily Worker.* He cofounded the Negro Ensemble Company. He won many awards for acting and playwriting.

WARD, THEODORE "TED." 1902–1983. Playwright, actor, and journalist. Ward was known as the "Dean of Black Playwrights." He cofounded the Negro Playwrights Company in Chicago with Langston, Paul Robeson, and Richard Wright. He wrote for the *Daily Worker,* the New York newspaper of the CPUSA.

WATERS, ETHEL. 1896–1977. Blues, jazz and gospel singer and stage and film actress. Waters was the first African American woman to have a leading role on Broadway.

WELLS, WESLEY ROBERT. 1909–1975. Wells was only nineteen when he was first sent to prison. He was originally accused of possession of stolen property, a suit, and sentenced to five years in San Quentin State Prison in California. He was later convicted of assaulting a prison guard at the prison and sentenced to death. Wells's case was taken up by the National Lawyers' Guild and the CRC, and after a nation-wide grassroots organizing and publicity campaign, his sentence was commuted to life without the possibility of parole. He was incarcerated from 1928 to 1974, except for brief periods when he was paroled but soon arrested again.

WERTZ, IRMA JACKSON CAYTON. 1911–2007. Social worker. Wertz joined the first Women's Auxiliary Army Corps during World War II. She was married to Horace Cayton. They divorced in 1942.

WESTON, RANDY. Born 1926. Jazz pianist, composer, and arranger. Langston requested that Weston play at his funeral, which he did.

WHEELER, MYRA. Wheeler was an Ohio friend of Langston's and Louise's.

WHIPPER, LEIGH. 1876–1975. Stage and screen actor. Whipper had a sixty-five-year career.

WHITE, CONSTANCE. Social worker. White was a member of the 1932 *Black and White* film group.

WHITE, JOSH. Born Joshua Daniel White. 1914–1969. Folk, blues, and political protest singer, guitarist, songwriter, actor, and civil rights activist. White was a friend of President Franklin D. Roosevelt's, and in 1941 he became the first African American singer to give a White House Command Performance. The outspoken progressive political stance he expressed in his speeches and songs brought him to the attention of right-wing McCarthyites, who attacked him from the late 1940s to the 1960s. Although this persecution ended his musical career, his playing style influenced many white and Black guitarists and folk singers for years afterward.

WHITE, WALTER FRANCIS. 1893–1955. Civil rights activist. White became executive secretary of the NAACP in 1931 and led the organization for almost twenty-five years.

WILLIAMS, BERT. 1874–1922. Bahamian comedian, singer, actor, and dancer. Williams was one of the outstanding entertainers of the Vaudeville era. He was the first Black to appear on a Broadway stage.

WILLS THORPE, FRANCES ELIZA. Social worker and naval officer. Wills Thorpe worked as Langston's secretary and booking assistant from 1938 to 1939 while finishing her social work degree. She then joined the Navy, and in 1944 she became one of the two first Black women to graduate from the US Naval Academy. She wrote a book about her experiences entitled *Navy Blue and Other Colors: A Memoir of Adventure and Happiness,* which was published posthumously in 2007.

WINCHELL, WALTER. 1897–1972. Newspaper and radio gossip columnist. Winchell was a powerful conservative commentator known for his ranting style and his racist and anti-Communist views.

WINSTON, HENRY M. 1911–1986. Political leader, civil rights activist, and writer. Winston served as the chairman of the CPUSA from 1966 to 1986. He was indicted by the US government under the Smith Act and sentenced to jail. While in prison, he developed a brain tumor, which was diagnosed and treated too late to spare his eyesight. Upon his release he said, "I may have lost my sight but I haven't lost my vision."

WINTER, ELLA. Born Leonore Sophie Winter. 1888–1980. Australian journalist and political activist. Winter met Langston at the Carmel, California, chapter of the John Reed Club in the 1930s. At the time, she was living with her ex-husband, Lincoln Steffens.

WOLFE, JACQUES. 1896–1973. Romanian-born composer. Wolfe researched African American music and was known for his particular interest in Negro spirituals.

WOMACK, MORTELIA. Womack was W. E. B. Du Bois's secretary in 1933. She was friends with Aaron and Alta Douglas and Louise.

WRIGHT, RICHARD "DICK" NATHANIEL. 1908–1960. Novelist, short story writer, poet, and journalist. Wright was a member of CPUSA for short while in the 1940s. He wrote for Pat's Chicago newspaper, the *Midwest Daily Record*. He was most widely lauded for his seminal 1940 novel, *Native Son,* and was the first African American writer to be published by the Book-of-the-Month Club.

YERGAN, MAX. 1892–1975. Activist. Yergan went to South Africa as a Baptist missionary for the YMCA in the 1920s. He became a Communist in the 1930s. He was the first African American to teach in the New York City public colleges. He taught Negro history and culture at City College but was fired after one year for his progressive leanings. He was elected the second president of the National Negro Congress. He cofounded the International Committee on African Affairs (later to become The Council on African Affairs) with Paul Robeson in 1937. He ended up as a staunch anti-Communist.

ZINBERG, LEONARD "LEN." 1911–1968. Screen and magazine writer and novelist. Zinberg wrote crime and detective novels under the pseudonyms Ed Lacy and Steve April. He was a member of the CPUSA.

INDEX

Page numbers in italics indicate photographs.

Anissimov, Julian, 98–99, 102–3, 345
anti-Communism, xx, xxn, 2–3, 26–27, 57,
    177, 263, 285–301, 296n1, 304; and
    contempt charges against Pat, xxvi, 288,
    295, 297, 300–301, 304; and "Goodbye
    Christ" attacks on Langston, 180–81,
    187, 200–203, 201nn13–14, 206–7,
    206n; and Ku Klux Klan, 123n25; and
    loyalty oaths, 183, 293; and red-baiting,
    126, 126n29, 187; and Red Scare, xi, xx,
    xxn, xxvi, 9, 180–81, 181n7, 280n7,
    286–87, 292, 294, 296n1. See also
    HUAC; McCarthy, Joseph/McCarthy
    Committee
Anti-Imperialist League, 111, 111n3
Anti-Nazi League, 156
anti-Semitism, 132, 337
Aosta, Duke of, 216, 345
Apollo Theater (Harlem), 145, 145n7;
    recording of Amateur Night, 304,
    304n13
Aptheker, Herbert, 293, 319, 346
Aristophanes: *Lysistrata,* 52
Armstrong, Henry, 119, 119n17
Armstrong, Louis, 198n6
Arrowsmith (1931 film), 39, 39n22
Ashwood, Michael, 151n16
Associated Negro Press, 27, 102
Association for the Study of Negro Life and
    History, 6
Astor, William Waldorf, 7
At Home Abroad (play), 121, 121n19
Atkinson, Brooks, 310, 346
Atlanta University, 187, 263, 273–76
Auschwitz concentration camp, 323
Austin, M.C., 15
Austin State Hospital (Tex.), 217

Bailey, Sue, 80, 86, 120
Baker, Josephine, 321, 346
Balanchine, George, 197n
Baldwin, James, 287
Ballet Caravan, 167
Baltimore Afro-American newspaper, 27,
    102, 102n, 133, 136, 140–41; *The Big Sea*
    serialization in, 196; "Jim Crow's Last
    Stand," 227n; Langston as war corre-
    spondent for, 27, 133, 136, 140–41

Banks, Paul, 41
Barnett, Claude, 102
Barnett, Etta Moten, 346
Barnett-Lewis, Elizabeth, 223, 346
Basie, Count, 238
Bass, Charlotta, 200, 291, 346
Bates, Ralph, 171, 174, 190, 190n2, 346
Bay Area Council Against Discrimination,
    233, 233n
Bearden, Bessye, 48
Bearden, Romare, 48, 346
Beavers, Louise, 119
Beimler, Hans, *134*
Belafonte, Harry, 342, 342n26, 346–47
Bennett, Gwendolyn "Gwennie," 214, 347
Bergman, Ingmar, xxiv
Berkeley Cooperative Federal Credit
    Union, 293, 307n, 319
Berlin Festival of the Arts, 341
Berry, Faith, xiv
Beth Eden Baptist Church, 30
Bethune, Mary McLeod, 29, 29n18, 32n5,
    45, 170, 347
Bethune, Sandy, 343, 347
Big White Fog (play), 197, 197n, 198–99
Bilbo, Theodore Gilmore, 271, 271n4, 347
"Black and Tan Fantasy" (song), 239
Black and White (1932 film project), 4, 4n,
    15–16, 44n39, 48–108, 203; African
    scenes for, 75; benefits to raise money
    for, 58; and collective farms, 77; and
    Constitutional Day (Soviet Union), 77;
    contracts for, 74, 84, 89; costumes/
    properties for, 67; delay of, 75–77, 80;
    and Dnieprostroi Dam, 90–91, 97, 99,
    101; and food, 73–74, 77–78, 85, 89, 93,
    97, 100; funding for, 49–50, 49n1, 53,
    58–65, 67, 71, 74, 84, 89, 94, 99–100;
    and Grand Hotel (Moscow), 73–74, 77,
    80, 85, 88–89, 94; and illness/injuries,
    74, 79, 99; in *I Wonder As I Wander,*
    207, 210–11, 306–7; and Kalinin home,
    76–77; and language difficulties,
    77–78, 98; and laundry, 80; and Lenin-
    grad reception, 72; and luggage, 72; and
    majority faction/report, 81–85, 89–90;
    and McCarthy Committee, 298, 298n;
    and Meschrabpom Film Company, 50,

Chen, Eugene, 349
Chen, Jack, 115, 350
Chen Leyda, Sylvia, 99, 115, 350
Chicago American, 241n
Chicago Daily Times, 240
Chicago Defender, 3, 3n3, 182, 187, 196; "The Duke Plays for Russia" (column), 238–240; "Here to Yonder" column, 226, 237–240, 271, 274–75, 283; and Simple (everyman character), 3, 3n, 226, 326–27
Chicago Examiner, 241n
Chicago Sun, 250
Chicago Times, 252
Child, Julia, xxiii
Childress, Alice, 291, 350
The Christian Century, 38–39, 38n20
Churchill, Winston, 257n; "Iron Curtain" speech, 180
CIA (Central Intelligence Agency), 183, 331n6
CIO (Congress of Industrial Organizations), 27, 233, 236; CIO-Robeson broadcast, 247; Council Minorities Committee (Calif.), 181–82, 255–56; and Matt, 181–82, 255–56
Citizens for Victory Committee, 233n
Civil Rights Congress (CRC), xvii, xviin6, 16n17, 186–87, 288–89, 288n7; and IRS, 289; and Louise, 290, 297; and Matt, 300; and Pat, xviin6, xxvi, 186–87, 277, 283, 288–89, *291,* 297, 300–301, 340, 340n; Right to Speak for Peace and Memorial for Willie McGee rally, 297; and Robeson, Paul, 288–89, *291,* 340; The Sojourners for Truth and Justice women's auxiliary, 291–92; "We Charge Genocide: The Crime of Government Against the Negro People," 288–89, 289n, *291,* 297, 340, 340n
Civil Rights Movement, 179–180, 183, 185–86, 286–87, 289, 294, 308, 308n, 315n, 319, 338, 338n18
Civil Service Commission, US, xx, 293
Civil War, US, 174
Clark, Carolyn, 1, 118, 128–29, 132, 137–38; death of, 142–43. *See also* Hughes, Carrie (mother)
Clark, Gwyn "Kit," 137, 137n45, 164, 350

Cohn, Roy, 298
Cold War, 177, 183–86, 285–87, 288n6
College of Chiropractic and Drugless Physicians (San Francisco), 15
Columbia Broadcasting Company, 151, 154
Columbia University, 5, 12, 25; Brander Matthews Theatre, 284; Columbia Theatre Associates, 284; School of Social Work, 320
Comintern, 19, 22–24, 54, 181n7; and Anti-Imperialist League, 111; and *Black and White* (1932 film project), 82–83, 82n, 85, 91, 94; and International Labor Defense (ILD), 45n42; Negro Commission, 23; and Profintern, 82, 82n
Communist Party, xvii, xxi, xxiv, 1, 22–26, 28, 52; and *Black and White* (1932 film project), 48, 76, 76n22, 85; and Cold War, 177, 183–84; and Du Bois, W. E. B., 338; FBI infiltration of, 337n16; and International Labor Defense (ILD), 16, 16n17; and International Worker's Order (IWO), 115; and Langston, 4, 9, 187, 294, 298; and League of Struggle for Negro Rights, 8; and Louise, 35, 126, 135, 181, 292, 301; and Matt, 16–17, 293, 301; and McKay, Claude, 22–23; and National Negro Labor Council, 16–17; Negro Commission, 23, 28; and Pat, 13–14, 135, 140, 140n1, 181–82, 184, 294, 301; and propaganda, 76, 81, 106; and red diaper babies, xxviii, xxviiin; and Scottsboro Nine of Alabama, 4–5, 8; and United Front, 132, 132n36; and World War II, 179–180
Communist Political Associations, 184
Compass, 283, 283n
Congregational Church, 29, 29nn, 38n20, 109. *See also* American Interracial Seminars Project
Congress, US, xxvi, 5, 90, 180, 183, 213–14, 213n, 241n, 271, 271n4; and contempt charges against Pat, 288, 295, 297, 300–301, 304; House Select Committee on Lobbying activities, 288; Senate Committee on Permanent Investigations, 297–98, *299;* and Sojourners' demonstrations, 292. *See also* HUAC;

King, Martin Luther Jr., 304, 309
Knopf, 160n24, 171, 191, 195, 197, 200, 204,
    206, 284, 293
Koestler, Arthur, 97, 217–18, 360
Komsomol, 97, 97n34
Korean War, 183, 292
Ku Klux Klan, 16n17, 21, 123, 123n25; and
    "Kleagle," 123, 123n25
Kurosawa, Akira, xxiv

La Follette, Robert M., 33n9
La Follette, Suzanne, 33n9
Lagos Arts Festival, 331, 331n6
LaGuma, James, 24
Langston, John Mercer, 5, 360
Langston Hughes: The Dream Keeper (docu-
    mentary), 31, 31n1
Lanham, Henderson Lovelace, 288, 360
Lawson, Edward, 150
Lawson, John Howard, 146n10
Leadbelly, xxiv
League of American Writers, 144, 144n4,
    195, 219
League of Nations, 43n34
League of Struggle for Negro Rights, 8, 24
League of Women Voters, 268
Leary, Lewis Sheridan, 5, 360
Lee, Robert E., 5n
Left Theatre (Tokyo), 111–12
Lend-Lease Act (1941), 208
Lenin, Vladimir, x, 2, 19, 22, 76n22, 86n26,
    132n37, 360; Leninism, 14, 28; tomb of,
    88
Lennox Players, 154
Leonard, Charles, 202, 360
Levin, Nathan W., 146
Levine, Jack, 337, 337n16; "Hoover and the
    Red Scare," 337n16
Lewis, Abraham, 133–34
Lewis, Juanita C., *70*, 84, 89–90, 99, 360
Lewis, Mollie Virgil. *See* Moon, Mollie
    Virgil Lewis
Lewis, Sinclair: *Arrowsmith,* 39n22
Lewis, Thurston McNairy, *70*, 74, 79,
    81–89, 93, 93n31, 101, 101n38, 361
Liberal Forum, 52
Liberator, 22
Lieber, Maxim, 111, 111n2, 130, 138, 361

Lincoln, Abraham, 141
Lindsay, Powell, 151n17, 167–69, 361
Lindsay, Vachel, 6
Locke, Alain Leroy, 7–8, 11, 42, 44, 361;
    The New Negro, 7–8
Los Angeles Dodgers, 336
Louis, Joe, 199–200, 199n11, 361
Love, Vaughn, 148, 150, 361
Lucas, Radcliffe "Raddy," 29, 51, 361
Lumumba, Patrice, 324–25, 361

Mabley, "Moms," 198n6
Mais, Roger, 252–54; *And Most of All Man,*
    252
Mamba's Daughters (play), 153, 153n20
Mao Zedong, xxvii, xxvii*n*
Marbury, Elizabeth "Bessy," 41, 361
Marshall, Paule, 343
Martin, Lawrence, 252
Martinsville Seven, 288n7
Marx, Karl, x, 2, 72n
Marxism, 21–22; and Bates, Ralph, 174; and
    death penalty in Tennessee, 183; and Du
    Bois, W. E. B., 338–39; Louise's study of,
    35–37, 43, 45, 107; Pat's study of, 13–14,
    28
Mason, Charlotte Osgood, 6, 11–12, 11n13,
    25, 29, 31–32, 32n3, 40, 42, 42n29, 44,
    361
Massie, Thalia, 36
Massie criminal trials (1931), 36, 36n14, 43,
    43n32
Mayakovsky, Vladimir: "Black and White,"
    101–2, 101n40
May Day, 110, 110n
Maynor, Dorothy, 209–10, 362
Mays, Willie, 336, 362
McCarthy, Joseph/McCarthy Committee,
    xi, 3, 180, 184, 287, 301, 319, 362; Lang-
    ston's appearance before, xx, 3, 293–94,
    297–98, *299*
McClain, John, 309
McClellan, John, 298, 362
McClendon, Rose, 39, 44, 48–49, 60, 63,
    121, 168, 168n26, 362–63
McCleod, Norman, 55
McConnell, Fannie Mae, 157, 363
McCormick family, 240–41, 241n, 363

106, 115n; and Matt, 30, 123, 233;
NAACP juniors, 129; and red-baiting,
126, 126n29; and UN petition, 289n;
and White, Walter, 287; and World
War II, 178
Nagasaki bombing, 285
Nathan, George Jean, 317n
The Nation, 6, 337n16
National Assembly of Authors and Drama-
tists, 312, 312n
National Book Award, 293
National Committee for the Defense of
Political Prisoners, 109
National Council of the League of Struggle
for Negro Rights, 110
National Federation for Constitutional
Liberties, 16n17, 186
National Guardian, 278, 278n6, 331, 331n8
National Health Care Workers' Union, 293
National Negro Congress (NNC), 110, 122,
122n23, 135, 137, 137n46, 186, 302n12;
"the Call," xviin3; and Langston, xviin3,
152, 267–68, 271; and Louise, 122, 135,
137; and Matt, xvii, xix, 126–27, 155–56,
233, 263, 267–68, 271, 271n4; and "Oust
Bilbo" petition campaign, 271, 271n4;
and Pat, 263; and Robeson, Paul, 263,
267, 271; and UN petition, 289n; and
World War II, 179
National Negro Labor Council, 16–17
National Student Federation of America,
58, 58n6
National Urban League, 24, 24n11
National War Labor Board, 179
Nazis/Nazism, 177, 184, 216, 228n, 230, 239,
323, 337
Nazi-Soviet Non-Aggression Pact, 171, 180
Nearing, Scott, 54
Negro Digest, 242, 242n
Negro History Week, 207, 308
Negro People's Front, 141
Negro People's Theatre (Chicago), 215
Negro Playwrights Company, 197n
Negro Question, 24, 256
The Negro Yearbook, 340–41
Never No More (play), 39, 39n25, 44, 44n38
New Deal, 26, 26n, 27n15, 120n, 122n23
The New Freeman, 33, 33n9

New Masses, 35, 35n10, 47n49, 61, 118, 130,
187, 228, 251, 251n
New Negroes, 7–8, 21, 55
New Negro Movement, 7, 22. *See also*
Harlem Renaissance
New Negro Theatre (Los Angeles), 156,
156n, 157, 202, 202n15
The New Republic, 36, 48, 171
New York Amsterdam News, 45n41, 54, 101,
142
New York City Opera, 280–81, 280n8
New Yorker, 118, 118n12
New York Herald Tribune, 44, 44n37, 46,
80, 83, 90
New York Metropolitan Opera, 302, 302n11
New York Post, 164
New York State Insurance Department,
290
New York State Legislature's Committee to
Investigate Charitable Agencies and
Philanthropic Organizations, 300
New York Times, 224, 310, 319, 328; Book
Review, 218
New York Workers School, 180
New York Yankees, 336
Niebuhr, Reinhold, 29n18
1931 (play), 39, 39n24
Nkrumah, Kwame, 338
Non-Aligned Movement, 285–87, 285n
Norford, George, 155
Normandie (ship), 144–45
North, Joseph "Joe," 118, 148, 341, 341n23,
366
North, Nora, 304n14
North German Lloyd, 70, 70n
NSA (National Security Agency), 183
NSC-68, 286
nuclear weapons, 285–86
Nugent, Bruce, 33, 366

Oakland City College, 293
Oakland General Strike (1946), *269*
Oakland Junior College, 307
Odets, Clifford, 39n24
Office of War Information, US, 239
Of Thee I Sing (play), 39, 39n26
OGPU (Joint State Political Directorate,
Soviet Union), 207, 207n

Okies, 25, 25n13
Omega Psi Phi, 41, 41n
O'Neill, Eugene, 39n26, 111
Opportunity, 102, 150
Orchestra Hall (Chicago), 214
Ossipoff, Comrade, 79
Ottley, Roi, 177, 287
Our World, 302, 302n12
Owen, Chandler, 21

Padmore, George, 283, 366
Page, Myra, 101
Parks, Rosa, 294
Patel, Rajni, 192, 366
Patiño, Fela, Cuca, and Dolores, 32n4,
    116–17, 116n11, 215, 366
Patterson, Anya, 80n
Patterson, Frederick, 137
Patterson, James, 324, 332–33
Patterson, James Edward, 12
Patterson, Lloyd, *70,* 84, 89–90, 114–15,
    114n5, 321, 324, 332, 366
Patterson, Lola, 80n, 335, 366
Patterson, Louise Thompson, ix–xiv, xx–
    xxix, 1–4, 9–12, 15–18, 29, 277; and 409
    Edgecombe Avenue (Harlem), 168, 171,
    174–75, 190, 190n1, 191, 193, 199, 277,
    296n1; and Abraham Lincoln School
    (Chicago), 263; and American Institute
    of Marxist Studies, 293, 319; and Ameri-
    can Interracial Seminars Project, 29,
    29n18, 32–33, 32n4, 38, 38n20, 40,
    46–47, 109; arrest of, 115, 115n; assisting
    Langston with typing/correspondence,
    63, 63n; biography of, 9–12, 11n12, 29;
    birthday of, 162; birth of MaryLou, xiv,
    xx–xxi, 182, 226, 229, 232, 242–45, *244,*
    245; and *Black and White* (1932 film
    project), 4, 4n, 15–16, 44n39, 48–51,
    58–65, 67–91, *69, 70,* 95, *95,* 99, *100,* 103,
    106–8; as breadwinner of family, 290;
    and broken ankle, 327; in Chicago, xx–
    xxi, 9–10, 122, 136, 138, 156–57, 167, 181,
    186, 198–200, 203, 205, 221–24, 226,
    229, 263–64, 268, *272;* and Civil Rights
    Congress (CRC), 290, 297, 340, 340n;
    and Communist Party, 35, 126, 135, 181,
    292, 301; and comrade shoes, 130–31;

and Council on African Affairs (CAA),
    280, 280n7, 288, 290; and Du Sable
    Center (Chicago), 263, 270–73; and
    Fifth Amendment, 290; greeting Pat at
    Idyllwild Airport, *291;* at Hampton
    Institute, xxii, 6, 10–11; and Harlem
    race riot, 110; and Harlem Restoration
    Project, 293; and Harlem Suitcase
    Theatre, 142, 145, 148–154, 157–58,
    161–68, 189, 202; and International
    Worker's Order (IWO), 110, 115, 128–
    131, 138, 142, 148n14, 229, 270, 290, 295;
    invitation to *Simply Heavenly,* 309–10,
    310n22; and leg injury, 263–65, 270;
    light complexion of, 10, 78; living in
    Brooklyn, 304, 320, 328; marriage to
    Pat, 181; and Mason, Charlotte Osgood,
    11–12, 11n13, 29, 31–32, 32n3; mentioned
    in Nebby Lou's letters, 320; and
    National Negro Congress (NNC), 122,
    135, 137, 137n46; and Negro History
    Week, 308; possibility of imprisonment,
    289, 295; pregnancy of, 229, 232; and
    public speaking, 33, 33n8, *34,* 62, 109,
    121–22, 126, 135–39, 297; return from
    Soviet Union, 86, *92, 93–94,* 103, 106,
    109; return to Harlem, 186–87, 263, 277,
    280; and Right to Speak for Peace and
    Memorial for Willie McGee rally, 297;
    rumors about, 118; and Scottsboro Nine
    of Alabama, 26, 60, 62–63, 63n9, 109,
    135; and Second World Congress
    Against Racism and Anti-Semitism,
    134–35, 134n41; as secretary at UN
    associated housing corporation, 290;
    Shakespeare in Harlem dedicated to, 181,
    197–98, 200, 200n, 211–12, 221–22, *231;*
    and Sojourners for Truth and Justice,
    291–92; and Spanish Civil War, 27,
    27n16, 133–39, *135,* 138n48, 148nn13–14,
    230; testifying in trial of IWO, 290,
    295; and Toledo earrings, 138–39,
    138n48; tour of Soviet Asia, 84, 86–88,
    91, *92,* 94–95, *95,* 109; travel to Europe/
    socialist countries (1960), 321–24; trips
    to Mexico, 29, 32n4, 116; trips to South,
    US, 29; trip to New England, 33; vaca-
    tion in California, 157–58; vacation in

Patterson, William L. *(continued)*
140n2, 237, 240–42, 246–47, 249–254,
259–261, 273–74, 275–76, 277, 283,
310–12, 322–24, 328, 338–39, 340; to
Matt, 335–36, 336–38; to Nebby, 335–36,
336–38
Patterson, William L. "Pat," works: *The
Man Who Cried Genocide,* xxiii, xxiii*n,*
13–14; "We Charge Genocide: The
Historic Petition to the United Nations
for Relief from a Crime of the United
States Government Against the Negro
People," 340–41, 340n
Peace Congress, 144, 144n5
Peck, Luther S., 273
Pentagon, US, 292
Peoples' Friendship University (Moscow),
321, 321n, 324, 327, 331
The People's Voice, 250, 250n
People's World, 140n1, 205–6, 206n, 296
Percy, William Alexander, 366; *Lanterns on
the Levee,* 209–10
Peterson, Dorothy Randolph, 145, 156, 161,
215, 366
Pharr, Eulah C., 122, 125–26, 159, 161, 197,
204, 208, 219–221, 234, 366; boyfriend
of, 224; car accident of, 190, 192; and
illness, 189, 201–2, 211; visiting Lang-
ston in Harlem, 266, 269–270
Phillips, Hilary, 145–46, 151, 158, 163, 167,
367
Phyllis Wheatley Club, 15
Pickens, Willie, 57
Pittman, John, 37n16, 333, 335, 335n, 338, 367
Plant in the Sun (play), 162, 164–65
Poitier, Sidney, 342n26
Policy Kings (1939 play), 151, 151n16
Political Affairs, 328, 328n
Popular Front, 26, 132, 132n36, 181n8, 184.
See also United Front
Portier, Sidney, 367
"Portrait of Bert Williams" (song), 239
"Portrait of Florence Mills" (song), 239
Poston, Theodore R. "Ted," *70,* 81–85,
87–90, 93, 93n31, 101, 101n38, 106, 121,
170, 367
Powell, Adam Clayton Jr., 182, 250n, 287,
309, 367

Powell, Alma Graves, 17, 29, 232, 278
Powell, Helene, 29
Powell, Joy, 29
Powell, Lloyd, 29, 232
Powell, Ozie, 122–25, 122n24
Prayer Pilgrimage for Freedom (Washing-
ton, DC, 1957), 309–10, 309n
President's Committee on Civil Rights
(1947), 185; *To Secure These Rights*
report, 185
President's Committee on Fair Employ-
ment Practice (1943), 179
Primus, Pearl, 268, 367
Profintern, 82, 82n
Progressive Party, US, 184–85, 279
Prosser, Gabriel, 125n17
Purlie (play), 333n

Rahn, Muriel, 284
Ram, Jagjivan, 214–15, 367
Rampersad, Arnold, xiv
Randolph, A. Philip, 21, 178–79, 250, 368
Ray, Satyajit, xxiv
Reconstruction, 286
Red Army, 233, 239
red-baiting, 126, 126n29, 187
"Red Channels: The Report on Commu-
nist Influence in Radio and Television"
(American Business Consultants), 293
Redfield cartoon, 174
Red Scare, xi, xx, xx*n,* xxvi, 180–81, 280n7,
286–87, 292, 294, 296n1; and "Lavender
Scare," 9; "Little Red Scare," 181
Red Shirts, 118, 118n14
Red Squads, xvii, xvii*n2,* xx, 26, 52, 57, 59
Red Square (Moscow), 110, 110n
Red Summer (1919), 13n14, 21
Reed, John, 47, 47n49
Reese, Ruth, xxiv
Reformed Judaism convention, 342, 342n25
Reissig, Herman F., 145, 368
Rhodes, Clarence C., 15
Rice, Elmer, 271n3
Richards, Beah, xxiv, 291, 304, 310, 310n23,
320, 368
Richardson, Beulah. *See* Richards, Beah
Richardson, Thomas "Tommy," 157,
161–64, 166–67, 368

Richardson, Willis: *The Chip Woman's Fortune*, 145, 145n9

Ricks McGee, Marcella Walker. *See* McGee, Marcella Walker

Ringe, Helen, 46, 46n45, 75, 80, 87

Rivera, Diego, 46–47, 47n49, 368

Road to Life (1932 Russian film), 73, 73n18, 77

Roberson, Mason, 129, 155–56, 207, 368

Robeson, Eslanda, x, 288, 368; *Paul Robeson, Negro*, 46, 46n47

Robeson, Paul, x, xix, xx, xxiv, 12–13, 233, 250, 368–69; article on Jamaica, 278; biography of, 46, 46n47; CIO-Robeson broadcast, 247; and Civil Rights Congress (CRC), 288–89, 340; and Council on African Affairs (CAA), 280n7, 288; and Du Sable Center (Chicago), 270, 270n; and Harlem Suitcase Theatre, 163–64; and *John Henry* (play), 164, 164n, 166, 168, 191; and Langston, xx, 140n2, 141, 180, 207, 298; and National Negro Congress (NNC), 263, 267, 271; and Negro Playwrights Company, 197n; omitted from *The First Book of Negroes*, 296n1; passport revoked, 289; and Pat, xix–xx, 12, 140n2, 196, 247, 273–75, *291;* and Patel, Rajni, 192; and Ram, Jagjivan, 214; and Salute to Paul Robeson (Chicago), 273–75

Rockefeller, John D., 28n

Romilly, Rita, 162, 369

Roosevelt, Eleanor, 160–61, 219

Roosevelt, Franklin Delano, 26–27, 26n, 137, 141, 174, 178–79, 185, 246, 246n8, 257n

Root, Lynn, 197n

Rose, Billy, 271, 369

Rosenberg, Ethel and Julius, 286–87

Rosenwald, Julius, 214, 369

Rosenwald Foundation, 29, 214, 217

Ross, Robert "Bob," 324, 369

Roumain, Jacques, 191, 215, 369

Rudd, Wayland, 44, 44n39, 68, *70,* 89–90, 369

Runyon, Marie, 293, 369

Russian Revolution (1917), 2, 19, 21, 76, 109, 126, 132n37; anniversary of, 86, 86n26, 94, 98, 98n35, 100; and "Octoberize," 133, 133n

Russian War Relief, 238–240

Sacco, Nicola, 2, 13–14, 13n15, 16n17, 369–370

Salk, Jonas, 286

Sample, George, 39, 46, *70,* 73, 75, 83–84, 99, 162–63, 370

San Francisco Chronicle, 296, 305n16, 319, 329, 329n3, 342

San Francisco Giants, 335–36

Sangigian, Mary, 163–64, 370

San Quentin State Prison (Calif.), 300

Santa Fe Trail (film), 211

Saturday Evening Post, 200–203, 206

Savage, Augusta, 107, 109, 370

Savage, Mary, 32, 87, 107, 137–38, 156–58, 161, 163, 193, 198, 204–5, 210, 215, 219, 221, 225, 230, 232, 245, 370

Savoy Ballroom (Harlem), 238

Schine, G. David, 298

Schmeling, Max, 199–200, 370

School for Democracy (Chicago), 250

Schwartz, Arthur, 121n20

Scottsboro Nine of Alabama, xvii, xviin6, 4–5, 8, 16, 16n17, 26, 45–46, 45n42, 58, 109; and "Ballad of Ozie Powell," 122–25, 122n24; and *Black and White* (1932 film project), 73, 77, 98, 122; and "Christ in Alabama," 45, 45n44; and Langston, 26, 59–60, 62–63, 110; and Louise, 26, 60, 62–63, 63n9, 107, 135; march from New York to Washington, DC for, 109; and Matt, 16, 26, 45n42, 110; and Pat, xvii, xviin5, 16, 26, 135, 137; and *Scottsboro Limited,* 52, 145

Second World Congress Against Racism and Anti-Semitism, 134–35, 134n41

Seeger, Pete, xxiv, xxvii

Segure, Rose, 266–67, 370

Selassie, Haile, 141, 370

Semple, Jesse B.. *See* Simple (everyman character)

Senghor, Léopold Sédar, 370

Sentinels (play), 44, 44n39

Shakespeare, William: *A Midsummer Night's Dream,* 165–66, 198n6

Thurman, Howard, 38, 38n19, 107, 372
Thurman, Sue Bailey, 36–39, 45, 372
Thurman, Wallace "Wally," 18, 24, 35,
    38n19, 114, 114n4, 202, 202n16, 372;
    death of, 110, 114n4, 116, 116n10; *Infants
    of the Spring*, 55, 55n
Thurmond, Strom, 185
Till, Emmett Louis, 315, 315n, 372
Toles, William, 9
Tolson, Melvin, 201, 372
Toomer, Jean, 24, 116, 116n9, 372
Touré, Sekou, 286
Town Hall program. See *America's Town
    Meeting of the Air* (NBC Radio)
Trenton Six, 288n7
The Tropics after Dark (musical revue), 195
Trotsky, Leon, 132n37; Trotskyites/Trot-
    skyism, 132, 132n37, 170, 184
Trud (workers' newspaper), 101, 101n97
Truman, Harry, 185–86, 285–86
Tubman, Harriet, 300
Tuskegee, 137, 208–9
Twain, Mark: *Pudd'nhead Wilson*, 318, 318n

Unemployed Councils, 26
Unis, Muriel, 162–63
United Front, 132, 132n36, 141. *See also*
    Popular Front
United Nations, xxvi, 324; and CRC "We
    Charge Genocide" petition, 288–89,
    289n, *291*, 297, 340, 340n; Human
    Rights Commission, 289, 289n, 340;
    Secretariat, 289, 340
United Steel Workers, 233
Universal Holy Temple of Tranquility
    (Harlem), 145, 145n8, 154
Universal Negro Improvement Association,
    21
University of California, Berkeley, 10, 38,
    307
University of California, Hastings College
    of the Law, 12, 250
University of Chicago Laboratory School,
    187, 280
University of North Carolina, Chapel Hill,
    45, 45n40, 45n44
University of the Toiling People of the East
    (Moscow), 14, 28

Urban League, 120–21
USO (United Service Organizations), 253

Vaderland (Berlin, Germany), 70–71
Vanderbilt, Muriel, 210, 210n
Vanguard Club, 109
Van Vechten, Carl, 1, 25, 373
Vanzetti, Bartolomeo, 2, 13–14, 13n15, 16n17
Venice International Film Festival (1932),
    73n18
Veterans Bureau, US, 29
Vidali, Vittorio, 118n13
Vollmer, Lula, 44n39

Waldrond, Eric, 46
Walker, Charles Rumford, 48–50, 373
Walker, C.J., Madame, 7
Wallace, Dean, 342, 373
Wallace, Henry A., xvi–xviii, xvi*n*1, 184–
    85, 246, 246n8, 263, 279, 331n8, 373
Walrond, Eric, 24, 373
Ward, Roosevelt, 313, 373
Ward, Theodore "Ted," 158, 163–64, 197n,
    373
War Poems of the United Nations (David-
    man), 228n
Washington, Booker T., 137, 317
Washington, Jesse, 20
Waters, Ethel, 121, 153, 209, 218–19, 232n,
    373
Way Down South (1939 film), 152, 152n, 161,
    164–65, 168
Weill, Kurt, 271n3
Wells, Wesley Robert, 300, 373–74
Wertz, Irma Jackson Cayton, 199, 222, 374
West, Dorothy, 24, 68, *70*, 84, 89–90, 99,
    110
West Coast Waterfront Strike (1934), 16,
    16n18, 27, 126, 126n30, 127; Joint Strike
    Committee, 126–27
Western Writers Congress, 127, 127n31
Weston, Randy, 334, 374
Wheaton, Elizabeth Lee: *Mr. George's
    Joint*, 222, 224, 224n
Wheeler, Myra, 167, 374
Whipper, Leigh, 145, 374
White, Constance W., *70*, 89–90, 374
White, Josh, 268, 374

White, Walter, 283, 287, 374
white philanthropy, 10–12, 28n, 29, 37, 44
Wilberforce University, 241
William E. Harmon Foundation Award,
    42, 42n30
Williams, Bert, 374
Williams, Mig, 267
Willkie, Wendell, 246, 246n8
Wills, Frances, 166–67, 169, 374
Wilson, Woodrow, 22
Winchell, Walter, 289, 374
Winston, Henry, 320, 374–75
Winter, Ella, 161, 375
Wolfe, Jacques, 191, 375
Womack, Mortelia, 46, 217, 375
Woman's City Club (Cleveland, Ohio), 121
Woodson, Carter G., 5–6
Workers International Relief organization,
    50n
Workers Publishers, 138
Works Progress Administration (WPA),
    27, 27n15, 170, 196
World Health Organization, 343
World's Fair (NY), 157, 163
World's Fair (San Francisco), 153, 153n19,
    166
World Tourist, 65, 67
World War I, 19–22
World War II, 27, 27n16, 160–61, 163,
    177–78, 182–84, 229–230, 232–33;
    African campaign, 233; British retreat

from Dunkirk, 216–17; and defense
    work, 230, 232–33, 233n, 279; and demo-
    bilization, 285; end of, 182–83, 285,
    322–23; German invasion of Russia, 180;
    Langston's support of war effort, 182;
    and Lend-Lease Act (1941), 208; Lou-
    ise's views on, 174; Pearl Harbor, 178;
    and returning veterans, 182–83; and
    Russian War Relief, 237–240; Soviet
    invasion of Finland, 171, 174; US entry
    into, 178, 216
World Youth Festival (Vienna), 316
Wright, Albert "Chalky," 119, 119n17
Wright, Richard "Dick," 170, 174, 224, 375;
    and Book-of-the-Month, 170; *Million
    Voices,* 224; *Native Son,* 170, 170n29;
    and Negro Playwrights Company,
    197n

Yaddo writers' colony (Saratoga Springs),
    226, 228–29, 247–252
Yergan, Max, 209, 214, 233, 375
YMCA (Berkeley), 267
YMCA (Harlem), 154
Yosemite, 334–35
A Young Man of Harlem (play), 151, 151n17,
    167, 169
YWCA (Harlem), 150, 153

Zero Hour (play), 200
Zinberg, Leonard "Len," 153, 155, 375